FOLK PHYSICS FOR APES

The chimpanzee's theory of how the world works

DANIEL J. POVINELLI

University of Louisiana at Lafayette

in collaboration with

JAMES E. REAUX, LAURA A. THEALL
AND STEVE GIAMBRONE

OXFORD
UNIVERSITY PRESS

OXFORD

UNIVERSITY PRESS

Great Clarendon Street, Oxford OX2 6DP

Oxford University Press is a department of the University of Oxford. It furthers the University's objective of excellence in research, scholarship, and education by publishing worldwide in

Oxford New York

Auckland Bangkok Buenos Aires Cape Town Kolkata Chennai
Dar es Salaam Delhi Hong Kong Istanbul Karachi Kuala Lumpur
Madrid Melbourne Mexico City Mumbai Nairobi São Paulo
Shanghai Taipei Tokyo Toronto

Oxford is a registered trade mark of Oxford University Press in the UK and in certain other countries

Published in the United States by Oxford University Press Inc., New York

First published 2000
Reprinted (with corrections) 2003

British Library Cataloging in Publication Data available

Library of Congress Cataloging in Publication Data

1 3 5 7 9 10 8 6 4 2

ISBN 0 19 857219 0
Typeset by EXPO Holdings, Malaysia
Typeset in Minion by 10/13 pt
Printed in Great Britain

To Ted and Joan

'Honored Members of the Academy!

You have done me the honor of inviting me to give your Academy an account of the life I formerly led as an ape.

I regret that I cannot comply with your request to the extent you desire. It is now nearly five years since I was an ape, a short space of time, perhaps, according to the calendar, but an infinitely long time to gallop through at full speed as I have done, more or less accompanied by excellent mentors, good advice, applause and orchestral music, and yet essentially alone…

In revenge, however, my memory of the past has closed the door against me more and more. I could have returned at first, had human beings allowed it, through an archway as wide as the span of heaven over the earth, but as I spurred myself on in my forced career, the opening narrowed and shrank behind me; I felt more comfortable in the world of men…'

from Franz Kafka, *A Report to an Academy*

FOREWORD

In his parable *Penguin Island,* Anatole France relates how the old, blind monk, Saint Maël, inadvertently baptized a group of penguins, mistaking them for human beings. When the news reached heaven, it caused, so we are told, neither joy nor sorrow but extreme surprise. The Lord himself was embarrassed. He gathered an assembly of clerics and doctors, and asked them for an opinion on the delicate question of whether the birds must now be given souls. It was a matter of more than theoretical importance. 'The Christian state,' Saint Cornelius observed, 'is not without serious inconveniences for a penguin…. The habits of birds are, in many points, contrary to the commandments of the Church.' Penguins, once burdened with a soul, would surely get into unforseen—and undeserved—moral difficulties. Saint Augustine concurred: 'If, Lord, in your wisdom you pour an immortal soul into them, they will burn eternally in hell in virtue of your adorable decrees.'

The learned assembly, being unable to resolve the matter satisfactorily among themselves, decided to consult Saint Catherine. 'This is what was usually done in such cases,' France notes, 'Saint Catherine while on earth had confounded fifty very learned doctors. She knew Plato's philosophy in addition to the Holy Scriptures, and she also possessed a knowledge of rhetoric.' And, indeed, when it came to it, her solution was certainly a neat one: she recommended that the baptized penguins should be granted an immortal soul–'*but one of small size*'. So it was decided. And the rest of France's book tells the tragicomic history of how these small-souled beings made out over the next millenium.

Daniel Povinelli, too, knows philosophy in addition to the scriptures of comparative psychology. Anyone who has heard him lecture will recognise his mastery of rhetoric. And he has, besides, a capacity that, so far as I know, even Saint Catherine never aspired to: he is a first rate observer and experimenter, empirically careful almost to the point of obsession, while methodologically ingenious to the point of poetry. Had the assembly gone to Povinelli, instead of Catherine, for advice about what to do about those awkward penguins, I would trust him to have come forward with a rather different and better solution. Having put the birds to the experimental test, he would have proposed that the answer lay not in *quantity* of soul but *quality*. Let the penguins be given souls, not of a smaller size but, as befits their nature, souls of *a different type and shape.*

Folk Physics for Apes is a plea to the scientific community to think again—on the basis of the new evidence that Povinelli and his colleagues have accumulated in the last decade—about one of the most cherished assumptions of contemporary psychology: namely, that ape minds and human minds are in fact basically of the same type and shape, that there is no great qualitative gulf between human ways of construing the world and apes' ways, that apes are in effect just like us, only less so. Through a series of cleverly linked experiments, Povinelli and his team have slowly but surely undermined this conventional wisdom. And here, in a thrilling exposition of both the evidence and the theoretical speculations it has prompted, they set out their stall.

When this book was first published in 2000, predictably its arguments were met by certain critics with a mixture of anxiety and outrage. This was not—and still is not—what many people wanted to hear. As Saint Gal complained of the man originally responsible for baptizing the penguins, 'Maël has created great theological difficulties and introduced disorder into the economy of mysteries.' No less a charge was and is levelled in certain quarters against Povinelli.

Yet, as this book enters a new edition, here's a chance to celebrate not just its courage and originality but its scientific integrity. No one, including Povinelli, can think that this is the last word. Nonetheless there can be no question that he has recast the terms of the debate. From now on, *these* are the arguments that must be addressed on their own evidential and theoretical terms by those who still want to insist that apes see the world the way that human beings do (or, since this in the end is the more important lesson, that human beings see the world the way that apes do). It has taken a large soul to pursue these lines of research to where they have led—and a large soul to write this book. Every reader, soul for soul, will want to match it.

Nicholas Humphrey
February 2003

Anatole France (1904/1925) *Penguin Island*. Trans. A.W. Evans. pp. 30–32. Bodley Head London.

AN INITIAL WORD ABOUT 'FOLK PHYSICS'

> **phys·ics** (fiz'iks) *n* **1.** *(used with a sing. v.)* The science of matter and energy and of interactions between the two, grouped in traditional fields such as acoustics, optics, mechanics, and thermodynamics, as well as modern extensions including atomic and nuclear physics, cryogenics, and particle physics.[1]
>
> **Physics** is the most basic of the sciences, concerning itself with the interactions of energy, matter, space, and time, and especially with questions of what underlies every phenomenon.[2]

Surely chimpanzees and other apes do not possess scientific theories about matter and energy, let alone group them into academic sub-disciplines. Indeed, the idea that they have any kind of science at all seems a bit preposterous. So, why have we invoked the term 'physics' in the title of this book?

The reason is simple: chimpanzees, like us, must confront the world of matter and energy every moment of their waking lives. And so, like us, they must possess some kind of understanding or knowledge about the movements and interactions of the objects that surround them. This knowledge may not constitute a science, of course, but it may well be a body of knowledge that is, to some extent or another, organized and coherent. To make the point clearly, think for a moment about our own infants and children. Modern psychological research has revealed that they know a surprising amount about how and why the physical world works the way it does. Indeed, from a very early age infants and children are already constructing quite sophisticated ideas about concepts such as gravity, force, mass, and shape. And yet we would not want to say that these infants and children have developed a science of physics. Of course, there may be striking parallels between how children come to discover the regularities of the world and the methods that scientists use (observation, experimentation, revising one's ideas in the light of new evidence, etc.), but to describe this as a formal science of physics may be too far a stretch for most readers.

On the other hand, we might be perfectly comfortable talking about infant's and children's 'folk physics', that is, their common-sense understanding of how the world works, as well as why it works in the way that it does. Likewise, chimpanzees and other nonhuman species may possess a kind of folk physics as well. However, short of simply guessing, there is no principled way of knowing ahead of time how similar or different the ape's folk physics is to our own.

---

1   *The American Heritage College Dictionary*, (3rd edn, 1993), p. 103 1. Houghton Mifflin, Boston.

2   Paul Peter Urone (1998), *College physics*. Brooks/Cole, Pacific Grove.

Of course, it is possible simply to suppose from the outset that because chimpanzees are so closely related to us, and because they must confront more or less the same physical universe as we do, they understand the world in a very similar manner. We adopt a different approach. The purpose of the research reported in this book is to break down this general supposition of similarity into a series of specific, testable hypotheses concerning chimpanzees' understanding of concepts such as gravity, force, mass, shape, and physical connection (to name just a few), and then to subject these hypotheses to serious experimental scrutiny.

PREFACE

My earliest impressions of chimpanzees were, to put it mildly, rather absurd. I was only an adolescent at the time, and, for whatever reason, I was particularly susceptible to romantic interpretations of the underlying psychology of these remarkable animals. In my own defense, let me note that there was no shortage of such images in the popular culture in which I grew up. There were the spellbinding television programs of Jane Goodall's chimpanzees looking lovingly into each other's eyes (and hers), and then embracing, kissing, and even making and using simple tools. There was the virtual icon of Wolfgang Köhler's chimpanzee, Grande, standing atop a tower of boxes that she had constructed in order to seize some otherwise out-of-reach bananas, with Sultan, Köhler's star pupil, looking on with a 'sympathetic left hand' (see Köhler 1927, Plate IV; reproduced as Fig. 3.1 in this volume). And, of course, there was the language-trained Washoe, wielding over 160 signs from American Sign Language, who kept alive Franz Kafka's dream[3] that an ape would, perhaps any day now, methodically begin to divulge what it was like to be a member of another species. There was Tarzan's Cheetah and Lancelot Link, there was the veteran chimpanzee actor named J. Fred Muggs, and there was the constantly changing band of juvenile chimpanzees at Lil's Performing Chimps (an organization that seemed to have cornered the market on the supply of photographic images for ape greeting cards). There were the chimpanzees named Ham and Enos that had been launched into space, and the chimpanzees who had taken over the Earth in the futuristic settings of the five successive *Planet of the Apes* films. And finally, of course, there were the chimpanzees who were secretly plotting their escapes from zoological gardens all around the world.

None of this should have mattered in the least. But it did matter. Of course, I now know that most of these images had been carefully cropped, edited, and/or rehearsed to produce the animal intended: the innocent ape (living free in nature), the buffoon ape (both smart and absurd enough to be like us after all), or the ambassador ape (methodically tapping out a message in some arcane code intelligible only to the laboratory scientist). But to the uninitiated, the combined effect of it all was to create a modern legend—a myth about an animal who, behind a thicker coat of hair, a more prognathic face, and an eerie silence, carefully guarded a mind nearly identical to our own. To be

---

3 Franz Kafka's (1936/1952) short story, *A Report to an Academy*, details the angst of a chimpanzee who has been educated by humans in order to provide an account of what it is like to be an ape. The prescient insight of Kafka is that the human-educated chimpanzee no longer knows what it was like to be a member of his birthright species.

sure, the myth admitted that there were appropriate and subtle psychological differences between humans and chimpanzees. But at the end of day these were portrayed as
differences which would interfere with, not assist in, our quest to understand who these
animals really were. In certain variations of the legend, these differences were woven
into a much broader mythology—one in which chimpanzees were endowed with every
human trait that was good and noble, but were excused from any of our faults. You see,
by the time I was growing up, the human hand had already seized the ape; it had
dressed, photographed, filmed, and then simply forgotten it—largely because it was
widely believed that we had already correctly sized-up the ape. Most people were convinced that the human mind had penetrated the ape's transparent attempt to look different from us, had perceived it as biological kin, and then, firmly and irrevocably,
concluded that it was not an 'it' after all. The ape was the unspoiled human; the human
was the fallen ape.

These early impressions of chimpanzees were still at work when I met my first chimpanzee, up close and personal, just over a decade ago. Of course, like any serious young
scientist, I designed and conducted my experiments, and diligently recorded and
reported the hundreds of trials it took the chimpanzees to learn what, in truth, seemed
like a rather basic problem—a problem that should have been well within the abilities of
the chimpanzee geniuses that I had learned about in my youth. But rather than confronting these findings directly, I found excuses for them. That was easy. After all, in the
sometimes cult-like atmosphere surrounding studies of chimpanzees, apologies came
ready-made. For example: the chimpanzees were simply distracted or playing around,
less motivated, and maybe even bored. And when these explanations seemed implausible, it was always possible to imagine that they were simply too intelligent for our tests:
they were intentionally trying to foil our efforts to understand them. They were not,
after all, above such trickery.

It was only later, after I began studying human infants and children, that, like a
drunken man slowly sobering, I began to understand that many of my most cherished
beliefs about chimpanzees were based on faith, not evidence. And, as I began to confront the differences between how chimpanzees and young children responded to our
non-verbal inquiries into the nature of their mental processes, I began to see how inad-
equate my earlier research had been. In time, I realized how far we were from even
approximating the level of rigor and attention to detail that would be necessary to make
reliable progress in so difficult a scientific field. In short, I realized that we needed to
start over and create an environment in which rigorous scientific research on chimpanzee cognition could be conducted without losing sight of either the very special
nature of these animals, or the profound questions that had motivated me (and so many
others) to compare the minds of humans and apes in the first place.

This conversion occurred slowly, but it gathered momentum in 1991, when I
launched a long-term project at the University of Louisiana designed to follow the intellectual development of a group of seven chimpanzees from their infancy into their

adulthood. I selected seven 2- to 3-year-old chimpanzees to participate in the project: Megan, Jadine, Brandy, Candy, Apollo, Kara, and Mindy. Half of this project was dedicated to investigating their understanding of the mental world; their theory, as it were, of the psychological causes and consequences of behavior. But rather than providing clear and compelling evidence that chimpanzees harbor an understanding of internal mental states (such as perceptions, intentions, desires, and beliefs), our results consistently suggested that, despite their aptitude for reasoning about behavior, they might know very little (if anything) about the minds that orchestrate that behavior. Even in simple cases, such as knowing whether others have the experience of seeing things, our tests consistently suggested sharp differences between chimpanzees and human children (see Chapter 2). I found these results difficult to accept—and to some extent still do. But after almost a decade, and dozens of experiments in which our chimpanzees have insisted (with a more or less unanimous voice) that they have a profoundly different view of the social world than us, I have slowly come to see the similarities between their species and our own in a very different light (see Chapters 2 and 12 of this volume).

Faced with a complex mosaic of similarity and difference in how humans and chimpanzees understand the social world, questions about their understanding of the physical world naturally began to assert themselves. Initially, one of my Master's students, James Reaux, became interested in a simple tool-using problem that Elisabetta Visalberghi and her colleagues had used with capuchin monkeys, and decided to test our chimpanzees using the same paradigm (see Chapter 4). Of course, there was strong historical precedent for exploring the ability of chimpanzees to make and use tools (dating at least to Wolfgang Köhler's efforts during the early years of the First World War). But only rarely had investigators asked what exactly chimpanzees (and other nonhuman primates) understood about the causal principles underlying their use of tools. And, as the results of our initial studies began to suggest that our chimpanzees failed to appreciate some fairly basic causal principles, we decided to launch a systematic research program (in parallel to our project on social understanding) to explore the nature of our chimpanzees' understanding of folk physics in the context of their use of tools. This book reports the results of nearly 30 experiments we conducted with this aim in mind.

Obviously, this work would not have been possible without the effort of many people. Perhaps no one deserves more special mention than Anthony Rideaux of Jeanerete, Louisiana. Anthony and I began working together in October of 1991, and in the ensuing years he has shown extraordinary calm in the face of the impatient and often unruly behavior of what began as a group of mischievous, and sometimes downright cantankerous, apes. The seven chimpanzees that Anthony has trained and assisted in testing over the past eight years began as a band of stubborn, uncooperative animals who wanted just two things: to be chased and tickled, and to be fed bananas and vanilla wafers. But through an admirable mixture of understanding, respect, and curiosity, Anthony has molded them into a well-behaved experimental group of subjects who look forward to the multiple sessions of testing in which they participate five days a week. Clearly, this project owes Anthony a debt that is not only difficult to repay, but probably impossible.

A second special debt of gratitude is owed to my three collaborators on this work. First, I need to sincerely thank James Reaux, who, after receiving his Master's degree in psychology (for which he was awarded the 1997 Conference on Southern Graduate Schools' award for the year's outstanding thesis), became the Study Director for the chimpanzee component of our laboratory. Not only did Jim's initial interest in chimpanzee folk physics serve as a spark in this research project, but his professionalism and attention to detail in running our laboratory has allowed us to achieve a level of rigor and productivity that we would never have achieved otherwise.

The second collaborator on this project, Laura Theall, became involved in our research program as an undergraduate research assistant. Later, after graduating, she became the laboratory's first full-time Study Review Coordinator. She has added a dimension of care and concern not just for the quality of the studies reported here, but for all of our comparative research projects over the past several years. In addition, she has tirelessly labored to coordinate the seemingly endless hours of independent coding of the video records that are necessary to analyze our experiments.

To the third collaborator on this project, Steve Giambrone, I owe both a professional and a personal debt; professionally, for his philosophical input to the underlying conceptual aspects of the project over the past several years, and personally, for his unwavering support of (and efforts on behalf of) our ongoing effort to create a center for advanced study in comparative cognition.

Finally, the three of us also owe a sincere debt of gratitude to Conni Castille, who, toward the end of these experiments, joined our group as Study Director for the Center for Child Studies, and actively participated in the seemingly endless meetings and discussions which served as the springboard for this work.

Finally, on behalf of myself and my collaborators, I wish to thank the following students who, over the past five years, assisted in the testing of the chimpanzees on the experiments reported here: Bridgett Simon, Jason Valdetero, Gerald Falchook, Britten Clark, Ido Toxopeus, Sarah Little, Roxanne Walsh, Jodie Dupre, Angela Brummett, Leah Patin, Cindy Minneart, Lori Babineaux, Walter Welch, Donna Bierschwale, Danielle Bacqué, Ben Olivier, Corey Porché, Ryan Brasseaux, Cathy Davidson, Julie Landry, Kyle Hebert, and Jean Torres.

The original artwork in this volume was drawn by Donna Bierschwale and my father, Theodore J. Povinelli. I thank them both for the many hours they spent producing the first-rate illustrations throughout the book. The photographs were taken by Donna Bierschwale, Danielle Bacqué, and Corey Porché.

My colleague, Todd Preuss, joined me here in New Iberia in 1996, and since then he has been a constant source of knowledge and inspiration. He generously devoted many hours of reading in order to help me beat several of the chapters in this volume into submission. Furthermore, he was instrumental in obtaining long-term financial support from the McDonnell Foundation, which will allow our research to continue.

Support from the administration of the University of Louisiana was critical to this project. Without explaining the numerous and vital roles they played in ensuring that this costly research was able to continue, I wish to thank Bill Greer, Jeff Rowell, Wayne Denton, Steve Landry, Duane Blumberg, and the President of the University of Louisiana, Ray Authement. Financial support for the research was provided by the State of Louisiana, the National Science Foundation, and the National Institutes of Health, and, most recently, a Centennial Fellowship from the James S. McDonnell Foundation.

The studies that we report in this volume were conducted over a period of five years. They began when Megan and her peers were on the cusp of adolescence and concluded (at least so far as this volume is concerned) when they were full adults. Of course, like any legitimate scientific enterprise, our own research is really part of a much larger work-in-progress—one that began at the start of this century, and one that will continue long in the future. Indeed, even here in New Iberia, research concerning the 'folk physics' of apes continues unabated, branching out in numerous directions. Nonetheless, we believe that this project provides at least an initial glimpse into what appears to be an understanding of the physical world that is both similar to and yet profoundly different from our own.

New Iberia, Louisiana   Daniel J. Povinelli
August 2000

CONTENTS

In landmark research, Povinelli goes beyond observations of the tool-using capacities of chimpanzees to investigate the cognitive sources of those capacities. His book reads like a great detective story, in which each finding provides the clues that guide the next step of the inquiry. The result is a rich and fascinating portrait of the mind of a species that is so like our own and yet so different.

Elizabeth S. Spelke, MIT

This is one of the most important books to appear in cognitive science in the last decade. In this rich, engaging and very important book, Povinelli describes his latest research program exploring chimpanzees' understanding of the physical world... Everyone who is interested in cognition should read it — not just comparative psychologists but philosophers, anthropologists, developmentalists and cognitive scientists of all kinds, and curious laymen, too.

Alison Gopnik, University of California at Berkeley

Povinelli and his colleagues have already led the way in revising scientists' ideas about apes' social knowledge. The clever and insightful research described in their important new book will likewise revolutionize ideas about how apes understand the physical world. It signals a fundamental change in the way we view the minds of our closest relatives and should be read by anyone interested in the development and evolution of intelligence.

Sara J. Shettleworth, *University of Toronto*

Rumours of Povinelli's revolutionary discoveries about the differences between how apes and humans think about the world have been circulating among academic colleagues — often misrepresented, sometimes only half-believed. Here now is the authorized version, and the conclusions are as compelling as they are shocking... Povinelli's research calls us back to biological reality and demonstrates how greatly human mental capacities have in fact diverged from those of our nearest relatives. The book he has written is gripping, brilliant and brave.

Nicholas Humphrey, author of A History of the Mind and Leaps of Faith

Without doubt, Povinelli is the international leader of the field of non-human primate cognition, and his original and ground-breaking experimental studies have led to new understandings of the minds of monkeys and apes. His previous studies illuminated the limits of social understanding or 'folk psychology' in these animals. In this new book, Povinelli attacks a different domain, that of 'folk physics', to probe how much of how little our primate cousins understand about the important topic of physical causality. In putting their minds tinder his microscope, Povinelli simultaneously uncovers clues about the evolution of human cognition.

Simon Baron-Cohen, Co-Director, Autism Research Centre, Cambridge University

CHAPTER 1

FOLK PHYSICS CANNOT BE ASSUMED

DANIEL J. POVINELLI

This book is the result of a five-year project designed to explore how chimpanzees conceive of the physics that underlies their use and construction of simple tools. The project was designed to use experimental techniques to explore what chimpanzees understand about why tools produce the specific effects that they do. In doing so, the project begins with a clear recognition that chimpanzees naturally make and use simple tools in the wild, and that in captivity these activities may be even further elaborated and refined (see Chapter 3). However, our project seeks not so much to document tool use and manufacture by chimpanzees, but to elucidate the nature of the mental representations that guide this behaviour. In short, we want to explore their 'folk physics' of tool use and manufacture.

Although it may seem like an odd way of introducing our work, we are quite fond of reflecting on what our most dogged skeptic might say about this project, and in particular, whether it is even necessary in the first place: '*Look,*' the skeptic might begin, '*isn't it obvious that chimpanzees and other great apes understand the physical principles governing simple tool use in just about the same manner that we do? Haven't we all seen enough* National Geographic *specials to know that chimpanzees make and use tools spontaneously and naturally? They crack nuts open using hammer stones and they construct simple fishing-wands to extract termites from their mounds. So why do we need to bring them into the laboratory and test them on their ability to use tools? Anyhow, didn't some famous German psychologist—Köhler, maybe?—demonstrate almost a century ago that captive chimpanzees can use tools in remarkable ways, such as stacking boxes on top of one another to gain access to bananas suspended out of reach?*' As we mentioned, starting with this skeptical voice may seem odd to some readers, suggesting that we have accepted a defensive posture from the outset. Nothing could be further from the truth. After all, on our very best days as scientists, this skeptical voice repeats over and over in our minds, reminding us of the fact that our project is a difficult one indeed.

But where does this skeptical voice come from? We believe it derives from an assumption about animals that is very difficult to escape. It is an assumption that the eighteenth-century philosopher, David Hume, found to be unassailable; it is an assumption that was present over a century ago when the field of comparative psychology was being founded by Charles Darwin; and it is an assumption that was even explicitly stated when the field was formally codified by Darwin's champion, George John Romanes. Even today, the invisible tentacles of this assumption run deep and tangled through our efforts to understand the minds of other species. The assumption, quite simply, is that when it comes to trying to compare the mental lives of humans and other species, analogous behaviors imply analogous minds. For over three centuries, philosophers and scientists alike have, to greater and lesser degrees, assumed that when we see animals behave in ways that look very similar to us, they must be thinking in ways that are very similar to us. As we shall see, this idea has come to be known as *the argument by analogy*—so-named because the argument relies on an analogy of sorts between what we believe to be the causal connection between our own thoughts and behaviors (namely, that our thoughts *cause* our behaviors) on the one hand, and the behavior and (inferred) thoughts of nonhuman species, on the other. Simply put, since we know that some particular thought (let us call it 'thought X') caused some particular behavior ('behavior Y') in us, then if we see behavior Y in an animal, it must have been caused by something very much like thought X.

As should be obvious by now, it is precisely the argument by analogy that gives rhetorical force to the skeptical outlook we introduced earlier. Recall that, in the case of tool use and tool making, the skeptic's position is that when we see chimpanzees cracking nuts using hammer stones and anvils in the same manner that humans do, it is a safe bet to assume that they understand the physical principles in the same manner we do.

Thus, the intuitively persuasive appeal of the argument by analogy forces us to ask whether we really need to proceed with carefully controlled, laboratory-based tests of chimpanzees' understanding of tool use. We have come to believe that the answer is a resounding 'yes.' And, as we shall see, the reason for this answer is that there is an alternative to the skeptic's position—an alternative to the conclusion dictated by the argument by analogy. As we shall explain more fully and clearly in Chapter 2, *it is possible that similar behavior—even among closely related species—does not guarantee a comparable degree of psychological similarity.* Indeed, escaping the argument by analogy allows us to take a fresh look at the mental lives of other species, a look which may one day allow us to see them without the fog of our own way of thinking about the world shrouding their true natures.

Folk physics versus scientific physics

The experimental and theoretical work that we present in this book is not about whether chimpanzees can use and/or make tools. The skeptic is quite correct in asserting that we already know that chimpanzees and other animals do this (see Chapter 3). Rather, our project is an attempt to probe chimpanzees' understanding of the physics that allow such acts of tool using and making in the first place—their folk physics of tools. By 'folk physics' we simply mean the kind of understanding of the physical world that develops naturally and spontaneously during the development of human infants and children (see Chapter 3), and later permeates our adult, common-sense conception of why the world works the way it does. Indeed, it is sobering to note that, with all but rare exceptions, the wealth of research on tool use and tool construction by chimpanzees and other nonhuman primates has not addressed the fundamental distinction between understanding *that* tools work versus understanding *why* they work (see Chapter 3). And it is only the latter question that directly addresses the issue of folk physics.

The notion of folk (or naive) physics can be explicitly contrasted with more scientific descriptions of why the world works the way it does. For one thing, our common-sense, folk physics is best suited to cope with the kinds of objects and events that we encounter on a day-to-day basis. Indeed, there is a sense in which our folk physics is not really designed to provide accurate descriptions or explanations of the universe, but first and foremost is designed to produce accurate predictions about how the universe will behave in those situations that we are likely to encounter. In saying this, we mean that our folk physics is less concerned with unusual or exotic events, or with anticipating differences that are so small that they rarely make a difference, than it is with providing a useful (albeit sometimes inaccurate) causal framework for guiding our interactions with the physical world. In contrast, scientists working in the various sub-disciplines that comprise the field of physics are constantly struggling to produce ever more accurate descriptions and predictions. In doing so, they regularly move beyond asking *how* the world works, and wind up asking *why* it works the way that it does—a process that frequently leaves them appealing to phenomena which are not visible to the naked eye (or the other similarly unaided senses). In practice, this directly leads physicists to the unusual case, precisely because it is the unusual case which frequently allows them to carve up nature at the joints (so to speak), thus allowing them to construct more accurate theories about how things are really put together.

One consequence of this difference between folk and scientific physics is that they sometimes yield answers that are at odds with one another. Consider, for example, Galileo's experiments in which he attempted to determine whether cannon balls (weighing as much as 200 pounds) would strike the ground sooner than musket balls (weighing only $1/2$ pound) when they were simultaneously released from a height of about 300 feet. The common-sense, intuitive belief about the fate of these two falling objects (a belief still held by the majority of the world's population) is that the cannon ball will hit the lawn long before the musket ball. Galileo's scientific considerations, however, led him to predict that they would arrive together—a fact almost perfectly borne out by the experimental research he conducted at the University of Padua in the late 1500s. Indeed, in his landmark treatise, *Dialogues Concerning Two New Sciences* (1638/1914), Galileo illustrated the contrast between our intuitive beliefs about such falling objects versus the results of his experiments in an imaginary exchange between Salviati (the educator) and Simplicio (the student-skeptic). After being presented with the experimental evidence, Simplicio resists the obvious experimental contradiction of his intuitions: 'Your discussion is really admirable,' he concedes to his opponent, Salviati, 'yet I do not find it easy to believe that a bird-shot falls as swiftly as a cannon ball' (p. 64).

Seemingly well armed with our modern knowledge of Newtonian mechanics, many of us may smile a bit at Simplicio's resistance to the overwhelming experimental evidence. However, for better or worse, we all retain a fair amount of Simplicio within us. An impressive body of scientific research has demonstrated that as adults we retain beliefs about the motions of objects that are scientifically inaccurate. Michael McCloskey and his colleagues, for example, showed that even educated high school and college students continually display systematic errors in their reasoning about moving objects (e.g. Caramazza *et al.* 1981; McCloskey and Kohl 1983; McCloskey *et al.* 1980). For example, people typically believe that, if someone is running, and they release an object, the object will fall in a straight line to the ground from its initial point of release—oblivious to the empirical fact that the forward motion of the object combines with a steadily accelerating downward motion, resulting in the object following a parabolic trajectory to the earth. McCloskey (1983) has concluded that the reason why people make such errors in judgements about moving objects (both in hypothetical situations and in situations in which they are actually asked to produce a given effect) is not because they have no theory of physics, but rather because they have a different, intuitive theory[1] of moving objects:

> [The errors] arise from a general, coherent theory of motion that adequately guides action in many circumstances but is nonetheless at variance with Newtonian mechanics. It is therefore the misconceptions embodied in an intuitive physical theory that occasionally give rise to errors in judgements about motion. The intuitive theory bears a striking resemblance to the pre-Newtonian theory of impetus. (p. 123)

McCloskey and his colleagues have even shown that this intuitive theory of impetus (one shared by philosophers three centuries before Newton) is quite resistant to change. In one study, they demonstrated that even after being educated to the contrary, many misconceptions about the physics of moving objects remain unaffected. In particular, people tend to believe that objects remain in motion once they are released because they acquire an internal force (called impetus), which gradually diminishes over time. Newtonian physics explicitly denies such a thing as impetus. However, McCloskey and his colleagues discovered that even after passing a course in Newtonian physics, students still tended to appeal to the (mistaken) idea of impetus in explaining common physical events. One interpretation of such findings is that humans are born into the world prepared to construct certain ideas about the physical world—theories that may be at odds with the underlying reality of the world.

---

1   There is considerable debate over whether our knowledge about such matters is best described as 'theories' or as collections of relatively unintegrated beliefs. However, for our purposes, this distinction is of relatively minor significance. (For a thorough discussion of the role of theory in cognitive development, see Gopnik and Meltzoff 1997.)

The discrepancies between our intuitive or naive beliefs about the physical world on the one hand, and our scientific beliefs on the other, may lead some to conclude that our folk physics do not really constitute a 'physics' at all. But we disagree. After all, the *accuracy* of a given set of beliefs about the underlying causal structure of the world is not what delineates 'physics' from other systems of belief. For example, pre-Newtonian notions about mechanics are woefully incomplete compared with our more modern models of the physical world, and yet we would not want to conclude that there was no such thing as physics prior to Newton. Clearly, the accuracy of our physics (as measured against some unachievably perfect knowledge of the universe) does not, strictly speaking, demarcate what is and is not 'physics'. As we shall see in Chapter 3, even young infants and children are sensitive to, and later explicitly reason about more than just the contingencies among the events that their senses detect unfolding around them. In some cases, they seem to appeal to unobservable processes and variables in much the way that adults or even scientists do. Although these infants and children do not use the terminology that we do, and their understandings differ from our own in certain ways, from infancy forward they seem to process (and increasingly reason about) physical interactions in terms of ideas very much like gravity, force, space, mass, intrinsic connection, shape, cause-and-effect, etc. Our general point is that, regardless of how well or poorly our folk physics actually maps onto the underlying, real physics of the universe, this system of beliefs shares several key features with scientific physics. One feature in which we shall be particularly interested is the attempt to understand the observable macroscopic world of objects in terms of unobservable states and processes.

At this point, one might wonder why evolution has allowed any discrepancy at all to exist between our folk physics on the one hand, and our scientific physics on the other. Why would the process of evolution have produced organisms who possess knowledge about the physical world that is inaccurate? A moment's reflection, of course, leads to the obvious answer that evolution is solely concerned with what works. If our naive, somewhat inaccurate folk physics makes the right predictions in the range of circumstances that humans typically face, then so much the better for organisms who possess such a belief system. Humans are born into the world either knowing, or prepared to quickly learn to know, about those aspects of folk physics that are relevant to our everyday encounters with the physical world. Presumably, what mattered most during the course of human psychological evolution was not the *accuracy* of our beliefs about the physical world, but how well those beliefs allowed our ancestors to predict and manipulate the world in ways that were important to their survival and reproduction. In this sense, the reason why our folk physics does not include notions such as special relativity, for example, is just a particular instance of the broader reason why discrepancies exist between folk and scientific physics—our ancestors rarely encountered situations in which understanding the relativity of time was important to their reproduction and survival.

Probing chimpanzees' folk physics through their use and manufacture of tools

The distinctions that we have just drawn between folk physics on the one hand, and scientific physics on the other, raise another, frequently-raised question about our investigations of chimpanzees' understanding of tool construction and use. Again, let us listen to the voice of our skeptic: '*Well, if you're not interested in whether chimpanzees understand the more difficult, scientific aspects of physics, but instead, all you want to know is whether they share our common-sense understanding of the world, doesn't this render your project trivial? After all, chimpanzees and other nonhuman primates—indeed, a diverse array of species!—confront essentially the same physical world that we do, and in many cases, they react the same way we do. So why doesn't the similarity between the ways in which our two species make and use tools virtually guarantee that we share a roughly similar folk physics?*' We admit, of course, that to resist this assumption would be tantamount to claiming that even though chimpanzees and humans perceive the same physical world, even though we witness the same interactions among objects in that world, and even though we engage in structurally similar (in some cases, nearly identical) actions upon those objects to achieve similar ends, for some reason our two species understand what we are doing in different ways.

Admittedly, to people who have not had the opportunity to give this matter very much thought, such a claim would seem to fly in the face of common sense. However, unfortunately for the field of comparative psychology, it is not just the average person who has succumbed to the alluring appeal of this particular brand of common sense. As we have already seen, in philosophical circles, this idea has come to be known as the argument by analogy—an argument, which as we shall see in the next chapter, is as old as our species' systematic thinking on the matter, and yet deeply flawed.

However, there is an alternative approach that does not suffer from the flaws of the argument by analogy. We can design and carry out carefully planned, but nonetheless simple experiments which have the ability to reveal what these animals know about why tools produce the specific effects that they do. In short, although their spontaneous, naturally-occurring use of tools cannot be used to make strong inferences about their folk physics, carefully controlled experimental procedures can. In this sense, although the chimpanzees' ability to use and make tools cannot by itself reveal the nature of their folk physics, it does provide an almost ideal context in which to carefully explore it.

Plan of the book

The plan of this book is as follows. In Chapter 2, we illustrate the inherent flaws in assuming that similarity in spontaneous behavior across even closely related species can safely be used to infer similar psychological processes. In short, we indict the argument by analogy. To gain some perspective on the general problem, we examine a domain of knowledge other than folk physics. In particular, we compare human and chimpanzee folk psychology. Like folk physics, folk psychology refers to our naive, common-sense understanding of a particular class of objects—in this case, other living organisms. In particular, we examine whether chimpanzees, like humans, appreciate that other organisms have internal psychological experiences such as desires, emotions, beliefs, and plans. When chimpanzees look at, and interact with each other, do they realize that they are dealing with both an observable, physical body and an unobservable, subjective mind?

Chimpanzees' understanding of other minds constitutes a rather dramatic test case for the argument by analogy. After all, given the sobering degree of similarity in the social behavior of humans and chimpanzees, one might naturally assume that the two species understand the social world in a similar manner. We review our previous empirical research on this question and propose that humans and apes appear to interpret the exact same behaviors in radically different ways—an outcome that places the argument by analogy in serious jeopardy. However, far more important than the fate of the argument by analogy is the fate of our ability to explain how such remarkable behavioral similarities could exist between the two species if one of them lacks such a seemingly foundational aspect of social understanding. To this end, we offer an evolutionary model of why similarity in spontaneous social behavior across species does not guarantee similarity in psychological processes—an idea which is, it its most general form, so counter-intuitive that David Hume once proclaimed that it could only appeal to 'the most stupid and ignorant' of scholars. Finally, we offer a detailed critique of the argument by analogy, and in the process provide theoretical support for our evolutionary model.

In Chapter 3, we return to the question of folk physics and, in particular, we explore the very limited existing evidence on the question of whether chimpanzees and other nonhuman primates appreciate the abstract causal relations that underpin their use and construction of tools. In contrast, we examine the wealth of evidence which suggests that human infants and children develop an explicitly causal understanding of the world around them. Of course, there is considerable overlap in how and for what purposes humans and chimpanzees make and use simple tools, a similarity which, on the surface, suggests a similar kind of understanding of the basic causal principles involved. We show, however, that the presence of similar behavior in this context cannot be used to presume the presence of a comparably similar folk physics.

In Chapters 4–11 we present the results of more than two dozen experiments that we conducted between 1994 and 1999 to investigate whether chimpanzees' knowledge about the physical interactions of objects (in the context of tool use and construction) is comparable to our own. These experiments are divided into conceptual groups that attempt to explore their understanding of gravity, transfer of force, size–shape interactions, physical connection, and object transformation. Collectively, the results suggest that, although chimpanzees and humans receive largely the same perceptual information about how objects interact in the world, the chimpanzees' manner of conceiving of why these interactions occur is quite different from our own.

Finally, in Chapter 12, we spell out the case for believing that, just as complex social behavior may have evolved long before there were organisms that could understand the psychological states that underpin such behavior, so too may tool using and tool making have evolved long before anything like the kind of folk physics found in our species was present. In both cases, cognitive specializations that arose within the human lineage during the past four million years or so—sometime *after* humans and chimpanzees began their separate evolutionary journeys—may have forever transformed our understanding of both the social and physical worlds.

CHAPTER 2

ESCAPING THE ARGUMENT BY ANALOGY

DANIEL J. POVINELLI AND STEVE GIAMBRONE

In this chapter, we expose the logical weakness in assuming that the similarity in the natural behavior of humans and chimpanzees implies a comparable degree of similarity in the mental states which attend and generate that behavior. In short, we formally challenge the argument by analogy. We need to emphasize right away that we are not indicting arguments by analogy in general. Rather, we indict what has come to be known as 'the argument by analogy' for the existence of other minds—an argument which has been frequently offered as a priori support for the claim that other species possess particular mental states that are nearly identical to our own (see below). Thus, we show how this particular argument by analogy is deeply flawed.

We begin by focusing on the case of social understanding, and in particular the question of whether commonalities in social behavior can be used to infer that chimpanzees, like us, reason about unobservable mental states (e.g. beliefs, desires, perceptions) as causes of behavior—or, to use other terminology, whether they possess a 'theory of mind' (a concept we shall explain in more detail shortly). We focus on a comparison between humans and chimpanzees, not because other species are uninteresting, but rather because chimpanzees present the most dramatic test case for the argument by analogy. After all, if the argument by analogy cannot be sustained when it comes to behaviors that we share in common with our nearest living relatives, it can hardly be expected to survive more general scrutiny.

At first glance, chimpanzees' knowledge about mental states and physical causality may seem quite unrelated. After all, in the first case we are dealing with the world of animate, breathing, and seemingly volitional things; in the second case we are dealing with things which, by definition, do not carry these signatures of life. Despite these differences, however, both questions share at least one obvious common concern: do humans and chimpanzees share the ability to conceive of abstract, unobservable variables as explanations of the social and physical events that cascade around them? In the case of social behavior, these variables take the form of mental states such as desires and beliefs; in the case of tool use and manufacture, they take the form of phenomena such as gravity, force, mass, and the like.

Briefly put, our aim in this chapter is to expose the inherent weaknesses in the argument by analogy and, simultaneously, to show how the nature of psychological evolution may virtually guarantee that many of the behaviors that we share in common with other species are associated with radically different mental representations. In doing this, we set the stage for a complementary account (see Chapter 12) of how both chimpanzees and humans may use and make tools in similar ways, and yet develop very different understandings of why they produce the effects that they do.

The argument by analogy: a primer

The modern origins of the idea that similarity between the natural behavior of humans and animals can be used to infer similar mental states can be traced to the eighteenth-century philosopher, David Hume. In Book I of his *Treatise* (1739–40), Hume laid out a simple doctrine, which later became known as the argument by analogy. Hume argued that whenever humans and animals are seen to exhibit similar behaviors, similar underlying psychological causes must be at work. 'This doctrine', he noted, 'is as useful as it is obvious... 'Tis from the resemblance of the external actions of animals to those we ourselves perform that we judge their internal [actions] likewise to resemble ours...' (p. 176). He continued:

> When...we see other creatures, in millions of instances, perform like actions, and direct them to like ends, all our principles of reason and probability carry us with an invincible force to believe the existence of a like cause. 'Tis needless in my opinion to illustrate this argument by the enumeration of particulars. The smallest attention will supply us with more than are requisite. The resemblance betwixt the actions of animals and those of men is so entire in this respect, the very first action of the first animal we shall please to pitch on, will afford us an incontestable argument for the present doctrine. (p. 176.)

Hume was at least right in concluding that his argument was obvious, as is evident from the fact that a similar line of reasoning persuaded other theorists as well. Not the least of these was Darwin, who was convinced from their behavior that there 'was no fundamental difference between man and the higher mammals in their mental faculties' (1871/1982, p. 446).

The underlying reasons for Darwin's conviction were not, however, completely scientific. As it turns out, Darwin had a problem—or at least he thought he had a problem. He knew that the harshest reaction to his theory of evolution would not concern his claims about the evolution of animals. Although the devoutly religious would find any claim for evolution objectionable, the most severe resistance would center around what his theory suggested about the non-divine origins of humans. Indeed, Darwin's meticulous documentation of the similarities and differences among living and extinct species might easily have been brushed aside as merely interesting, if the implications for human origins were not so apparent. After all, by the time *The Origin of Species* was published in 1859, Europeans had already been forced to accept the remarkable morphological and behavioral similarities between monkeys, apes, and humans. Thus, the average Victorian had already reached the conclusion that what really separated humans from other animals was not their bodies, but their minds.

Here, then, was Darwin's problem. On the one hand, he knew that if he dwelled on the case of human beings, he might merely inflame general anti-evolutionist sentiments. On the other hand, if he let the mind escape evolutionary scrutiny by allowing for its divine origin (as did the co-discoverer of the principle of natural selection, Alfred Russell Wallace), this might raise a cloud of suspicion around the entire theory. As he later put it: 'If no organic being excepting man had possessed any mental power, or if his powers had been of a wholly different nature from those of lower animals, then we should never have been able to convince ourselves that our high faculties had been gradually developed' (1871, p. 445). Although Darwin perceived this problem early on, in *The Origin* he attempted to sidestep it by offering only a few, guarded comments about humans: 'Much light', he vaguely promised, 'will be thrown on the origin of man and his history' (1859, p. 373). However, Darwin was already privately preparing the evidence that humans, too, were a species descended. As he later confessed in *The Descent of Man*: 'During many years I collected notes on the origin or descent of man, without any intention of publishing on the subject...as I thought that I should thus only add to the prejudices against my views' (1871, p. 389).

By the late 1860s, Darwin felt that the time had come to outline the evidence that every aspect of humans, including the most seemingly divine aspects of our minds, had been produced through the action of natural selection. In Chapters 3 and 4 of *The Descent*, Darwin laid out the case for believing that the difference between the minds of humans and other animals was 'certainly one of degree and not kind' (p. 494). 'My object...' Darwin wrote, 'is to shew [sic] that there is no fundamental difference between man and the higher mammals in their mental faculties... With respect to animals very low on the scale, we shall give some additional facts...shewing [sic] that their mental powers are much higher than might have been expected' (p. 446). In the ensuing pages, he offered an impressive (and often amusing) array of anecdotes to illustrate the remarkable intellectual abilities of animals. Monkeys 'revenged themselves' (p. 449), dogs played 'practical jokes' (p. 450), and in general animals were 'constantly seen to pause, deliberate, and resolve' p. 453).[1]

Darwin's method for comparing the mental abilities was admittedly loose: 'As no classification of the mental powers has been universally accepted...we will select those

---

1   Indeed, less than halfway through Chapter 3, Darwin felt confident that his essential task was complete: 'It has', he remarked, 'I think, now been shewn [sic] that man and the higher animals, especially the Primates...[a]ll have the same senses, intuitions, and sensations,— similar passions, affections, and emotions, even the more complex ones, such as jealousy, suspicion, emulation, gratitude, and magnanimity; they practice deceit and are revengeful; they are sometimes susceptible to ridicule, and even have a sense of humour; they feel wonder and curiosity; they possess the same faculties of imitation, attention, deliberation, choice, memory, imagination, the association of ideas, and reason, though in very different degrees. The individuals of the same species graduate in intellect from absolute imbecility to high excellence. They are also liable to insanity, though far less often than in the case of man.' (1871, pp. 456–7.)

facts which have struck me most, with the hope that they may produce some effect on the reader' (Darwin 1871, p. 446). But underlying his approach was the unquestioned assumption that where humans and other animals exhibited similar behaviors, so too they shared similar mental faculties. And, naturally, these were the very same mental faculties that were known (presumably through introspection) to accompany the human behaviors. Darwin's approach was soon taken up by John George Romanes. Romanes' goal was to formalize Darwin's proposal that mental evolution followed the same general principles as organic evolution, and he did so in two major treatises, published in 1882 (*Animal Intelligence*) and 1883 (*Mental Evolution in Animals*).

Romanes' ambition was no less than to establish a new scientific discipline—comparative psychology. Drawing an analogy to comparative anatomy, he argued that 'just as anatomists aim at a scientific comparison of the bodily structures of organisms, so [comparative psychology] aims at a similar comparison of their mental states' (Romanes 1883, p. 5). But anatomists had access to dead bodies that could be pinned and dissected; what comparable substance would comparative psychologists dissect? Understandably, Romanes turned to the only source of material that was available— anecdotal reports of the behavior of animals. Although he apologized for having no other alternative, Romanes relied on these accounts to launch his new science of comparative psychology. But unlike Darwin, Romanes clearly articulated the method for using the spontaneous behavior of animals to infer their mental states—a method with definitively Humean overtones: 'Starting from what we know of the operations of my own individual mind, and the activities which in my own organism they prompt, we proceed by analogy to infer from the observable activities of other organisms what are the mental operations that underlie them' (Romanes 1882, pp. 1–2). Comparative psychology was thus born with the argument by analogy.

The conviction of Darwin, and the method of Romanes, were both just restatements of Hume's doctrine from a century earlier: where humans and animals share similar behavior, so too must they share similar minds. Indeed, Hume may have had more faith in the method than Romanes, given his belief that there could not be 'the least suspicion of mistake' (1739–40 p. 176) when using his doctrine. His concluding remark was that he had provided 'rather invincible proof' of the doctrine's validity (p. 179).

In the twentieth century, the argument by analogy has come to be better associated with Bertrand Russell's (1948) use of it to counter solipsistic arguments against the existence of other human minds (as opposed to its original formulation for establishing the presence of animal minds). In one sense, this is justified, because Russell's version of the argument is extended and carefully stated:

> From subjective observation [i.e. introspection], I know that A, which is a thought or feeling, causes B, which is a bodily act... I know also that, whenever B is an act of my own body, A is its cause. I now observe an act of the kind B in a body not my own, and I am having no thought or feeling of the kind A. But I still believe on the basis of self-observation, that only A can cause B; I therefore infer that there was an A which caused B,

though it was not an A that I could observe. On this ground I infer that other people's bodies are associated with minds, which resemble mine in proportion as their bodily behavior resembles my own. (p. 486.)

A moment's reflection on Russell's solution to the problem of other human minds reveals that it is merely a special case of the broader solution offered by Hume, Darwin, and Romanes. Russell was dealing with the psychological gulf between our own personal experiences and those of other humans, whereas Hume, Darwin, and Romanes were coping with the gulf between the human mind and the minds of other species. In both cases, however, the problem is the same—given the inherently personal nature of our psychological states, how can we know for certain whether any other organism has the same internal states that we do? The argument by analogy provides a broad solution to this problem.

Indeed, we are now in a position to provide a formal statement of the argument by analogy as it applies to the question of whether other species are capable of a particular kind of cognitive process: the ability to explicitly reason about the mental states of the self and others. Many terms have been coined to refer to this ability, such as 'mental state attribution', 'folk psychology', and 'theory of mind'. For our purposes in laying out the formal structure of the argument we use the term sometimes preferred by philosophers: 'second-order mental states'. Such psychological states are termed 'second-order' because they are not simply mental states, they are mental states *about* mental states. In any event, a suitably modified version of Russell's argument can be stated as an inductive argument with three premises and a conclusion:

P1 I (and other humans) exhibit bodily behaviors of type B (i.e. those normally thought to be caused by second-order mental states).

P2 Chimpanzees (and other species) exhibit bodily behaviors of type B.

P3 My own bodily behaviors (and those of other humans) of type B are usually caused by my (and other humans') second-order mental states of type A.

C Therefore, bodily behaviors of type B exhibited by chimpanzees are caused by their second-order mental states of type A; and so, *a fortiori*, chimpanzees have second-order mental states of type A.

This, then, is what *we take to be the most common argument* for inferring, from comparisons of the naturally-occurring behavior of humans and chimpanzees, that chimpanzees possess a theory of mind—that is, that they explicitly reason about such things as intentions, desires, plans, emotions, and beliefs (or, in the philosophical jargon used above, that they possess second-order mental states). At the end of this chapter, we expose the logical weakness in this argument.

Having provided a rough sketch of the origins and formal structure of the argument by analogy, we now ask whether this solution to the problem of other minds offers a useful way for thinking about higher-order cognitive states in species other than our own.

Comparing social understanding

There can be little doubt that our species, at least, reasons about internal psychological states. Although the form of such knowledge varies from culture to culture, in societies around the world humans exhibit a stubborn penchant for explaining behavior in terms of underlying mental states (for examples, see Avis and Harris 1991; Vinden 1996; Vinden and Astington 2000; reviews by Lillard (1998) and by Povinelli and Godfrey (1993)). Even in our own culture, where a peculiar brand of psychologists (radical behaviorists) admonished us for doing so for the better part of a century, we move through our daily lives effortlessly pausing to reflect on our own thoughts, wants, desires, and beliefs, as well as similar states in others. In short, our species seems to possess a natural disposition for constructing an understanding of the self and other in explicitly mental (or psychological) terms.

But do other species similarly conceive of this inherently private dimension of the self and other, and, like us, suppose that behavior is a product of such internal mental states? Over twenty years ago now, David Premack and Guy Woodruff (1978) framed this question succinctly by asking whether chimpanzees have a *theory of mind*. 'A system of inferences of this kind', they observed, 'may properly be regarded as a theory because such [mental] states are not directly observable, and the system can be used to make predictions about the behavior of others' (p. 515). Premack and Woodruff suggested an affirmative answer to the question of whether chimpanzees possess such a theory of mind, offering some limited experimental evidence that chimpanzees might be able to reason about the intentions of others. However, it is now clear that this issue is far too complex to be resolved by the results of any single experiment. Over the past eight years, we and others have developed a diverse set of experimental procedures for investigating various facets of theory of mind, and these results point to a very different conclusion than the one reached by Premack and Woodruff. Indeed, our own research highlights the possibility that humans may have evolved a cognitive specialization for reasoning about mental states—an ability not found in other species; not even chimpanzees.

An exploration of the similarities and differences in how humans and chimpanzees understand the social world represents an excellent test case for the argument by analogy. After all, perhaps no where else is the argument more persuasive. First, in their general anatomical structure, chimpanzees look very much like us. Second, the range of facial and bodily expressions that they exhibit are remarkably similar to our own. And finally, they engage in a wide range of complex behaviors that in our species seem to be intimately tied up with an appreciation of the psychological dimension of self and other. Deception is an excellent example. Indeed, perhaps nothing has convinced more people that chimpanzees (and other nonhuman primates) possess some kind of theory of mind than their spontaneous acts of social deception (see, for example, de Waal 1982, 1986; Whiten and Byrne 1988). How, the skeptic demands to know, could chimpanzees possibly effectuate an act of deception without reasoning about the mental state of the other individual? We shall return to this question toward the end of this chapter.

Seven minds *Pan*: a systematic approach to studying social understanding in apes

A number of years ago, however, it became apparent to us that a new approach to comparing social understanding in humans and chimpanzees (*Pan troglodytes*) was needed. But exactly what kind of approach was best? On the one hand, the spontaneous, uncontrolled behavior of these animals suggests that they possess a theory of mind very similar to our own. Indeed, in one frequently encountered version of the debate over how best to study the cognitive abilities of chimpanzees, a kind of 'hyper-naturalism' has been invoked in an effort to carry the day. On this view, only the 'natural' behavior of wild chimpanzees can inform us as to their true cognitive abilities, because only chimpanzees in the wild are ensconced in just the right setting to draw out their evolved psychological abilities (see McGrew 1992). No matter, of course, that chimpanzees raised appropriately in any setting grow up to display the very same set of social behaviors highlighted as particularly revealing by field researchers. No matter, also, that questions about the internal architecture of chimpanzee psychology are virtually impossible to address in the rain forest. And certainly no matter that the dichotomy between chimpanzees raised in the wild and in captivity is a false and misleading one to begin with (see Köhler 1927; Yerkes 1943).

And so, in considering the best approach to systematically studying the similarities and differences between human and chimpanzees, we turned to a laboratory-based approach. After all, uncovering how the human mind works requires examining humans in controlled, laboratory settings; surely the same requirements will apply in the case of chimpanzees. Indeed, any project that seeks to move beyond romantic ideas about the cognitive abilities of apes needs to examine animals who can be tested under controlled circumstances. This does not, however, imply that these animals should be raised in stark isolation or in small cages. Quite to the contrary. If it is to be valid, any such project requires normal, healthy animals, who display a full suite of chimpanzee behaviors (from the relaxed bouts of social grooming, to the deafening, late-afternoon pant-hoots). In short, a valid project requires chimpanzees who have been raised in a comfortable, spacious setting that has drawn out their normal social and cognitive abilities. Ironically, one incidental consequence of raising captive chimpanzees in this kind of captive setting is that they typically wind up far more healthy than their distant cousins in the wild—animals who are frequently racked by infections, unhealed wounds, and parasitic infestations.

Thus, as we considered how to design a long-term project to compare human and chimpanzee cognitive development, the question was not *whether* a laboratory-based approach would be appropriate, but rather, what kind of laboratory-based approach would be best. Within the parameters just outlined, several options were available, each with its own strengths and weaknesses. For example, it was possible to take a single chimpanzee, raise it in the company and culture of humans, and present the animal with a battery of psychological tests as it developed. Indeed, this had been one of the traditional approaches to studying the intelligence of apes (Gardner and Gardner 1971; Hayes 1951; Kellogg and Kellogg 1933; Kohts 1935; Premack 1976; Rumbaugh 1977). But several aspects of this kind of approach were worrisome. First, would it be possible to maintain the necessary degree of scientific objectivity during the course of such a project? And even if it were, would anyone else be convinced of its objectivity? Finally, could such a project meet one of the central requirements of any scientific undertaking—with only a single subject, could it be meaningfully replicated? Another approach was to test large numbers of captive chimpanzees living in social groups. But there were serious problems here as well. For example, without sufficient exposure to humans, how could we be confident that the animals were comfortable enough with our testing procedures that they would perform at the upper limits of their abilities?

After considering a wide range of options, we settled on the following course. We selected seven 2- to 3-year-old chimpanzees (one male and six females) who had been reared together in a nursery with human caretakers (see Fig. 2.1). Five of these apes (Mindy, Jadine, Brandy, Kara, and Candy) had been raised from birth in the nursery. They had worn diapers as they played together for their first year of life; they had been bottle fed and rocked by human caretakers; they had slept in cribs together at night. Two others (Megan and Apollo) were raised by their mothers in a social group for about a year until they joined the others in the nursery. During the early years of our project, these seven animals spent most of each day in their outdoor compound playing and interacting with each other. Once or twice a day, however, they were divided up into pairs and led to a room where they participated in a variety of simple cognitive tests.

As part of this long-term project, when these seven apes were about four years of age, we moved them to a new indoor–outdoor compound that was connected to a specially designed testing facility (see Fig. 2.2(a)–(b)). This facility allowed us to test each ape in turn for about 10–20 minutes at a time. Thus, while the others played, one of them could be transferred into an outside waiting area, which was connected by a shuttle door to an indoor testing room (see Fig. 2.2(b)). Typically, this animal waited outside as a trial was set up indoors. When the shuttle door opened, the animal was free to enter the lab and respond to the task. A plexiglas panel separated the apes from the humans. We used this panel even when the apes were young enough that it was unnecessary. We did so for two reasons. First, we wanted to develop some very unambiguous procedures for measuring their responses. But more important, we wanted to establish a predictable setting and routine that could be maintained throughout their youth, and on into their adolescence and adulthood as they reached their full size and strength. That this approach has paid off is clear from the fact that as young adults our animals still participate in testing two or three times a day. Indeed, as the final studies reported in this book were being conducted, babies had been born to four of our females (Kara, Jadine, Megan, and Mindy). The experimental research on their understanding of tool use that we report in Chapters 4–11 was conducted over a four-year period during which time our apes passed from juveniles to adolescents to full adults. A timetable of these experiments is provided in Appendix I.

Figure 2.1 Seven chimpanzees (Group Megan) who have formed the basis for our long-term project exploring the nature of chimpanzees' reasoning about the social and physical world. These chimpanzees began this project when they were $2^1/2$–$3^1/2$ years old. They were between the ages of four and five years when these photographs were taken.

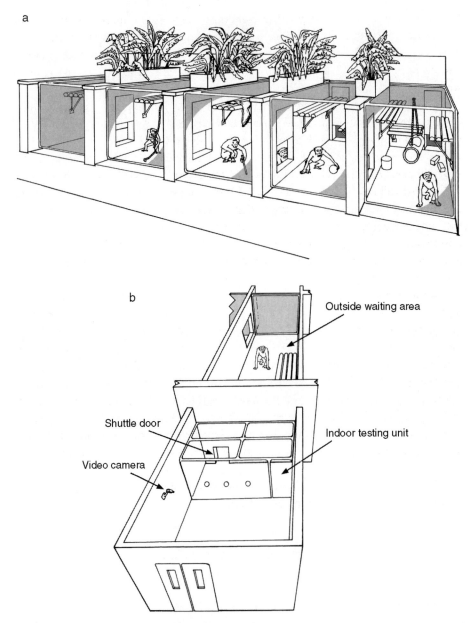

Figure 2.2 (a) The living area for Megan and her peers, showing their indoor–outdoor living areas. (b) Close-up diagram of outdoor waiting area and indoor test unit showing the shuttle door connection, plexiglas partition, and experimental working space.

This, then, was our approach: rear a cohort of chimpanzees together, while simultaneously exposing them to human culture; follow them through their juvenile years into adulthood, and compare their understanding of the social and physical world to that which develops in human children. Because such work required as fair a set of comparisons with young children as possible, we also established a center where we could conduct similar experiments with young children. To be sure, our project has had its limitations, but as will become clear, it has had its unique set of strengths as well.

For the past eight years, these seven apes—Megan, Kara, Candy, Jadine, Brandy, Mindy, Apollo—have participated in dozens of experiments investigating their understanding of mental states such as attention, intention, desire, knowledge, and belief, as well as their understanding of self (for example: Povinelli and Eddy 1996*a,b,c*, 1997; Povinelli and O'Neill 2000; Povinelli *et al.* 1993; Povinelli *et al.* 1994; Povinelli *et al.* 1997*b*; Povinelli *et al.* 1998; Povinelli *et al.* 1999; Reaux *et al.* 1999; Theall and Povinelli, 1999). In addition, they have participated in dozens of experiments which have probed their understanding of folk physics (some of which are reported in this book). Much of this research was designed so that in addition to assessing their understanding at any given moment in time, we could also conduct longitudinal assessments of their cognitive abilities as they grew up.

In what follows, we describe one particular aspect of their social understanding that we have addressed in considerable detail, and one that we consider to be foundational for the entire construct of theory of mind: whether they appreciate that others have internal, visual experiences. In short, whether they know that others 'see'. On the one hand, this would seem to be a fairly simple question. On the other hand, pursuing this question has offered some of the most intriguing and unexpected results of our entire research program—results that have exposed glaring weaknesses in the argument by analogy. On the bright side, however, these results have led us to develop a new framework for thinking about the evolution of social understanding—a framework which offers a principled alternative to the argument by analogy, and a very different way of thinking about how to compare the minds of humans and other animals. Indeed, this new framework holds out the promise of significantly advancing our understanding of the mental lives of both chimpanzees *and* humans.

Do chimpanzees understand that others see? A test case for the argument by analogy

The eyes: from meaningful stimuli to signals of seeing

During the first several years of our project, we devoted a considerable amount of time to trying to determine whether apes (like us) interpret the eyes as windows into the mind—and in particular, whether they have a concept of 'seeing'. Humans, of course, understand seeing as far more than just a geometric relation between eyes and objects and events in the world. We conceive of it as a subjective or psychological part of an experience that the other person is having: 'She *sees* me'. This level of understanding seeing may emerge quite early in human development—possibly by as young as two years of age (see Gopnik *et al.* 1995; Lempers *et al.* 1977; Povinelli and Eddy 1996*b*, experiment 15).[2]

Appreciating the idea that others 'see' is, in some sense, foundational to the entire question of theory of mind—at least with respect to our human understanding of the mind. After all, most of our social interactions begin with a determination of the attentional state of our communicative partners, and from that point forward we constantly monitor their attentional focus throughout the interaction. Nothing can disrupt a social interaction more quickly than realizing that someone is no longer looking at you. Furthermore, the appreciation that we *see* (and hence experience) each other is the glue that seems (to us, at least) to bind us to our communicative partners. True, we can arrive at this feeling of connection in other ways (for example, talking over the telephone does not make it impossible to establish a sense of psychological connection to the other person). Nonetheless, the notion that the other person 'sees' is a basic, foundational assumption which, from our subjective point of view, seems to hold together most person-to-person interactions.

Before we can describe our research efforts to determine if chimpanzees, like us, possess an appreciation that others 'see', we need to draw several crucial distinctions— distinctions that must be kept firmly in mind if we hope to make progress on what is already a very difficult problem. We begin by pointing out that many organisms—certainly not just primates—are highly sensitive to the presence of eyes, eye-like stimuli, and the faces of other individuals (e.g. Blest 1957; Burger *et al.* 1991; Burghardt and Greene 1988; Gallup *et al.* 1971; Perrett *et al.* 1990; Ristau 1991; see review by Argyle and Cook 1976). The evolutionary origins of this sensitivity may derive from at least two sources. The first source may have been the evolutionary emergence of predation. Clearly, the ability to detect a set of eyes looming in the visual field must have been strongly favored very early on by natural selection. After all, those organisms who could rapidly detect and react to such stimuli undoubtedly lived to produce more offspring than those who could not.

The second evolutionary source of an interest in the face and eyes of others may have emerged in the context of group living. For highly social animals, the visual gaze of

---

2   John Flavell and his colleagues have identified two developmental transitions (or levels) in how children understand 'seeing' (see Flavell *et al.* 1978; Flavell *et al.* 1980; Flavell *et al.* 1981; Lempers *et al.* 1977; Masangkay *et al.* 1974). By two to three years of age, children appear to realize that visual perception connects people to objects or events in the external world. At this first level, they appreciate whether someone can or cannot see something. By four years of age, however, children come to understand seeing on another, deeper level. They understand that seeing is associated with a particular internal vantage point on the world. Related research has confirmed these findings by demonstrating that 4- to 5-year-olds, but not younger children, appear to understand that visual perception causes internal knowledge states in both the self and others (Gopnik and Graf 1988; O'Neill and Gopnik 1991; O'Neill *et al.* 1992; Perner and Ogden 1988; Povinelli and deBlois 1992*a*; Ruffman and Olson 1989; Wimmer *et al.* 1988). It is only the first level of understanding visual perception which concerns us here.

others provides important clues about impending or ongoing social interactions. For example, Chance (1967) argued that primate dominance hierarchies can be accurately assessed by noting who is paying attention to whom, implying that there is much useful information for a social primate to gather by attending to the gaze-direction of others. Also, unlike solitary animals, social organisms can obtain some protection from predators by paying attention to movements of the eyes and heads of their group mates. Indeed, a major theory of the evolution of sociality is that group living has evolved in direct response to predation pressure (Alexander 1974). One proposal in this regard argues that living in groups allows animals to detect predators sooner than would be possible otherwise, and hence confers a better chance of escaping (van Schaik *et al.* 1983). Thus, the sudden shift (or unusual orientation) of the head and/or eyes of a nearby group mate could be exploited as a means of detecting a nearby predator. Clearly, organisms who use such information to discover the exact location of the attacking predator would have a better-than-average chance of escaping unscathed.

An interest in the eyes and gaze-direction of others also emerges early in human infancy. For example, in a landmark report, Michael Scaife and Jerome Bruner (1975) demonstrated that very young infants will turn and look in the direction in which they see someone else looking. Since then, a number of carefully controlled studies have explored the emergence of gaze-following (or, as Scaife and Bruner called it, 'joint visual attention'). Although there is disagreement about the exact timing of its development, certainly some capacities related to gaze-following emerge as early as six months (Butterworth and Cochran 1980; Butterworth and Jarrett 1991; Corkum and Moore 1994, 1998; Moore *et al.* 1997). By 18 months, however, the ability is well consolidated, as infants of this age will: (1) follow an adult's gaze into space outside their own visual field; (2) precisely locate the target of that gaze; and (3) reliably follow gaze in response to eye movements alone (without accompanying movements of the head).

Even before infants display a robust form of gaze-following, they are already displaying a sensitivity to the faces and eyes of others. Making eye contact, for example, is a highly significant emotional experience for infants long before they appreciate the attentional aspect of seeing. And, as we noted above, it is not just human infants who display such sensitivity. In primates, at least, mutual gaze serves to mediate complex social interactions. In many species of anthropoid monkeys, for example, direct eye contact is part of a relatively stereotyped threat display (Perret *et al.* 1990; Redican 1975). Thus, direct eye contact is avoided, even in the context of friendly social interactions (e.g. de Waal 1989). In contrast, mutual gaze plays a more flexible role in humans and other great apes. Here, mutual gaze is an important factor in mediating both agonistic and affiliative social interactions (Bard 1990; Gómez 1990; Goodall 1986; Köhler 1927; Schaller 1963; de Waal 1989). In chimpanzees, for example, establishing mutual gaze seems to be especially important during 'reconciliatory' social interactions that immediately follow conflicts (de Waal 1989). In more experimental settings, Gómez (1990, 1991) has reported the apparent use of mutual gaze by a young gorilla as a means to enlist the assistance of human caretakers, and Povinelli and Eddy

(1996*c*, experiment 1) have provided evidence that chimpanzees are drawn to interact more with individuals who are making direct eye contact with them than others who are not.

Of course, having said all of this, we must now address the truly thorny issue of whether the evolved sensitivity to the presence, direction, and movement of the eyes indicates an understanding of their connection to internal mental states—even simple ones such as attention. For example, does the bird who averts from striking a butterfly after having been flashed a set of eye spots (e.g. Blest 1957) entertain the notion of having been 'seen'? In this case, our intuition may reply, 'no', but perhaps only because birds are involved. Worse still, what about gaze-following and mutual gaze in human infants, or possibly other species? Clearly, many of these behaviors inhabit a contentious, middle ground where intuitions clash.

For example, some researchers interpret the mutual gaze that occurs between human infants and adults, as well as among great apes during complex social interactions, as prima facie evidence of an understanding of the attentional aspect of seeing (e.g. Bates *et al.* 1975; Gómez 1996*b*). And, admittedly, there is a certain allure to the idea that, because mutual gaze in adult humans is often attended by representations of the mental states of others, comparable behavior in human infants (or other species) is probably attended by similar representations. But is mutual gaze in apes (for example) really attended by the same psychological representations as in adult humans, or is this just a projection of our own way of thinking onto other species?

Based on his work with an infant gorilla, Gómez (1990, 1991, 1996*a,b*) has argued that great apes use mutual gaze to enlist a human's assistance, and that this is evidence of 'a strategy to control the visual attention of the human addressee'—a strategy said to be 'comparable to that of human infants at the beginning of preverbal communication' (Gómez 1996*a*, 1996*b*, p. 138). Similarly, spontaneous acts involving tugging on the caregiver's clothing before establishing mutual gaze and making requests are described by Gómez as 'ostensive', which he defines as 'a way to express and assess communicative intent' (p. 131). Does this mean that the ape simply understands the behavioral configurations that lead to successful social interactions, or does it also mean that the animal represents the caregiver as possessing (unobserved) internal attentional states? Gómez (1996) seems to favor the latter interpretation: 'To engage in ostension', he argues 'one has to be capable of some degree of mindreading, including the attribution of mindreading abilities to the receiver. Thus, if great apes are capable of some form of ostension, this would mean that they are reaching into one of the most complex aspects of human communication' (p. 145).

A similar clash over intuitions exists with respect to the phenomenon of gaze-following in human infants. Thus, although gaze-following is a behavior with obvious practical utility, its psychological causes remain less clear. Some developmental psychologists, such as Simon Baron-Cohen, interpret gaze-following as prima facie evidence that infants are explicitly aware of a psychological connection between self and other (Baron-Cohen, 1994, 1995; see also Franco, in press). On this interpretation, infants turn to follow their mother's gaze because they know that she is looking *at* something, that she *sees* something, or that something has engaged her *attention*. This account grants infants their first (albeit limited) glimpse into the visual psychology of other people. Other researchers are more cautious, maintaining that gaze-following (especially in very young infants) may have little to do with an appreciation of internal psychological states (Butterworth and Jarrett 1991; Moore 1994; Povinelli and Eddy 1994, 1996*a,b*; Tomasello 1995). Processes such as hard-wired reflex systems, learned behavioral contingencies, and attentional cueing have all been offered as possible explanations for the early forms of gaze-following. Finally, there is a middle ground that interprets the behavior as a causal precursor to a later-emerging, more explicit representation of attention in toddlers. On this view, early gaze-following can be seen as a fairly automatic response, which later provides a context for developing an understanding that attention is something distinct from action itself.

Clearly, we need to move beyond intuition, and instead ask whether we can experimentally disentangle alternative psychological accounts of mutual gaze and gaze-following. After all, if we could do so, we might be able to begin making real progress toward understanding whether other species (especially those most closely related to us) reason about visual perception in the mentalistic manner that we do.

Chimpanzees: gaze-following

To begin to sort out these issues, let us focus on the issue of gaze-following, and ask whether chimpanzees possess abilities similar to those found in human infants—and if so, the extent of similarity between the two. Ultimately, such investigations ought to allow us to determine whether humans and great apes share a common developmental program controlling the expression of these behaviors. Having sorted out the behaviors related to gaze-following that humans and chimpanzees share in common, we can then move on to ask about the underlying causes of the behaviors.

Following numerous suggestive accounts from field researchers, between 1993 and 1995 we conducted the first experimental studies of gaze-following in nonhuman primates (Povinelli and Eddy 1996*a,b*, 1997; Povinelli *et al.* 1999). Initially, we simply sought to determine whether our chimpanzees would reliably follow the gaze of others (see Povinelli and Eddy 1996*b*). Our procedure involved having each subject enter the test lab and use their natural begging gesture to request an apple or banana from a familiar experimenter who sat facing them. On most trials, the experimenter immediately handed the subjects the food. On probe trials, however, each subject was randomly administered three conditions that had been carefully choreographed ahead of time. On *control* trials, the experimenter looked at the subject for exactly five seconds, and then handed him or her a reward as usual. These trials allowed us to determine the subjects' baseline levels of glancing to specific locations in the room. On *eyes+head* trials, the experimenter turned his or her head and looked at a target above and behind the chimpanzee for five seconds (see Fig. 2.3(a)). On *eyes-only* trials, the experimenter diverted only his or her eyes to the same target, keeping the rest of the head motionless. The results depicted in Fig. 2.3(b) reveal several things. First, the chimpanzees virtually never looked above and behind themselves on the control trials. In clear contrast, not only did they follow our gaze on the trials involving whole head motion, they even did so in response to eye movements alone. We have now replicated and extended this effect on a number of occasions and have demonstrated that chimpanzees follow gaze with at least the sophistication of 18-month-old human children (see Table 2.1).

These findings were important because they experimentally established that chimpanzees, like humans, are extremely interested in where others are looking. More recently, researchers in David Perrett's laboratory and Michael Tomasello's laboratory confirmed our speculation that gaze-following might be widespread among primates (Emery *et al.* 1997; Tomasello *et al.* 1998). Indeed, this research tends to confirm our earlier speculation that gaze-following evolved through the combined effects of dominance hierarchies (needing to keep track of who is doing what to whom) and predation (exploiting the reactions of others to discover the location of potential predators), and hence ought to be widespread in social animals (see Povinelli and Eddy 1996*a*).

Having established that chimpanzees and humans share a common behavioral system related to gaze-following, we now turn to the more central question of how this similarity might help us to understand whether or not chimpanzees appreciate that others 'see'.

Knowing that you cannot see through walls

If you have ever witnessed a chimpanzee following your gaze, you will know that it is almost impossible not to assume that he or she is trying to figure out what you are looking at. But what excludes the possibility that they are strictly reasoning about your behavior—turning and looking in the same direction as you, and thus winding up looking where you are looking, having never once entertained any idea about your

Table 2.1 Behavioral evidence that humans and chimpanzees possess a homologous psychological system controlling gaze following

Behavior	18-month-old human infants	Juvenile/adult chimpanzees
Respond to whole head movement?	yes	yes
Respond to eye movement alone?	yes	yes
Left/right specificity?	yes	yes
Follow gaze outside immediate visual field?	yes	yes
Scan past distractor targets?	yes	yes
Account for opaque barriers?	?	yes

Sources: Butterworth Cochran 1980; Butterworth and Jarrett 1991; Povinelli and Eddy 1996*a,b*, 1997; Povinelli *et al.* 1999; Tomasello *et al.* 1998; (Call *et al.* in press).

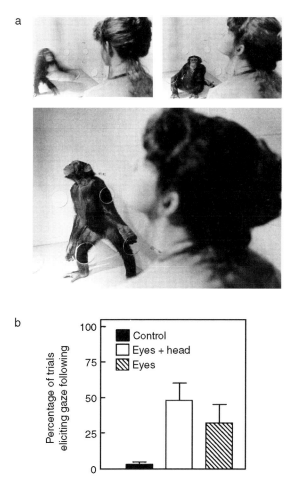

Figure 2.3 (a) Like 18-month-old human infants, chimpanzees follow the gaze of others into areas that are outside their immediate visual field: Mindy enters test unit, Danielle moves her head and eyes to a predetermined target above and behind the chimpanzee, and Mindy responds by rapidly orienting her head and body to the same location. (b) Results of a typical gaze-following experiment with chimpanzees. Chimpanzees follow the gaze of an experimenter in response to both eyes+head movement and eye movement alone. They do not look to comparable locations on control trials, where the experimenter simply stares at the ape.

internal attentional state? In order to make an intelligent choice between these different accounts of gaze-following, we need to flesh them out a bit more clearly, and determine if they generate different predictions about how apes (and human infants) might respond in more revealing circumstances.

On one account, chimpanzees and other nonhuman primate species (and even human infants) might understand 'gaze' not as a projection of an internal psychological state of attention, but as a directional cue (i.e. a vector leading away from the eyes and face). Thus, perhaps the ancestors of the modern primates merely evolved an ability to use the head/eye orientation of others to direct their own visual systems along a particular trajectory. If so, once the visual system of the observing animal encountered something novel, the operation of the mammalian orienting reflex (Pavlov 1927; Sokolov 1963) would guarantee that *both* the target animal and the observing animal would end up attending to the same object or event, without either of them having represented the other's internal attentional state (Fig. 2.4(a)). In contrast to this psychologically sparse interpretation, we also considered a second account: apes might follow gaze because they appreciate its connection to internal attentional states. In short, they are motivated to turn and look where you are looking because they want to know what you *see*. It is necessary to have a shorthand label for these alternative kinds of accounts, and so we hereafter refer to them as the 'low-level' and 'high-level' accounts, respectively. Thus, the so-called high-level model stipulates that chimpanzees form concepts about internal mental states (in this case, attention) and use these concepts to help interpret the behavior of others. In contrast, the low-level model supposes that chimpanzees cogitate about behavioral propensities, not internal mental states.

In considering how to distinguish between these explanations of gaze-following, it occurred to us that if nonhuman primates reason about the attentional aspect of gaze, this might be revealed in situations in which they witness another animal's gaze being obstructed by an opaque barrier such as a tree (or in the case of captivity, a wall). If the high-level account of their gaze-following abilities were correct, and if an observing animal were to witness another animal in the situation depicted in Fig. 2.4(b), the observing animal should be capable of understanding that the other ape cannot see through the obstruction. If so, the observing ape should look around the barrier to determine what the other ape was actually looking at. In contrast, the low-level account predicts that the observing chimpanzee would project a vector away from the other ape's face and scan along this path until something novel triggers an orienting reflex, and, if nothing novel is present, eventually stop scanning altogether.

We tested these possibilities in our laboratory (see Fig. 2.5(a); Povinelli and Eddy 1996*b*, experiment 2). To begin, we covered half of the plexiglas panel with an opaque partition from ceiling to floor. Thus, the chimpanzees could still enter the test lab, approach an experimenter, and request some fruit by begging through a hole in the plexiglas. However, the partition blocked the apes' view into a small area of the room behind the partition—an area into which only the human could see. On most trials, the subjects simply entered the lab, gestured to the human, and were handed the food. However, several experimental conditions allowed us to test the accounts described above. In one condition, as soon as the chimpanzee reached through the plexiglas, the experimenter looked at the subject while executing a choreographed series of irrelevant movements for precisely five seconds. This condition (along with some others) allowed us to measure the subject's ambient levels of glancing to various locations in the room (Fig. 2.5(a)). In contrast, on the crucial test trials the experimenter leaned and glanced at a predetermined target on the front of the partition (see Fig. 2.5(a)). Would the apes

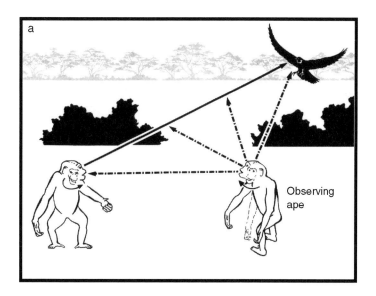

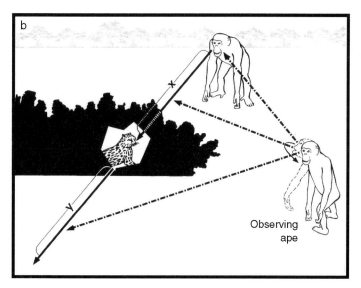

Figure 2.4 (a) A target animal looks at a descending predator, and an observing animal, after witnessing the head movement of the target animal, turns and looks in the same direction. The observing animal's behavior may be mediated by an understanding that the other ape has 'seen' something, or by fairly low-level psychological mechanism (see text for details). (b) The target animal looks along a particular trajectory, but his or her gaze is obstructed by an opaque barrier. If the observing animal appreciates the idea of seeing, he or she may realize that the other's gaze is obstructed by the barrier; if low-level mechanisms are at work, the observing animals may simply scan an the line represented by x+y (see text for details).

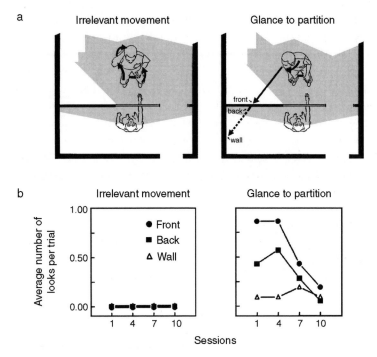

Figure 2.5 The opaque barrier test. (a) An experimental recreation of the naturalistic event depicted in Fig. 2.4(b). The question concerns whether the chimpanzee will attempt to look around the partition to the human's side when the experimenter looks at a target on the front of the opaque partition, but not when the experimenter engages in irrelevant movements. (b) Results from the opaque barrier test. Note that in the glance-to-partition condition, the apes look around to the human side of the partition and not to the back of the test unit, whereas they do not do so in the irrelevant movement condition. See text for details.

attempt to look around the partition to the experimenter's side, or would they follow a vector away from the experimenter's face until they wound up looking behind themselves at the back wall of the test lab? In short, would they appreciate that the experimenter's vision was blocked by the partition? The accounts described above generated very different predictions about the answer our apes would provide.

As can be seen in Fig. 2.5(b), the chimpanzees' reactions were unambiguous—they behaved in exactly the manner predicted by the high-level explanation. Instead of automatically turning their heads toward the back of the test unit, the apes leaned forward and looked around to the back of the partition (Fig. 2.5(b)), exactly as if they understood that the experimenter could not see through it. Thus, despite the fact that the experimenter was never *really* glancing at anything, the apes looked around the partition on both the first and second occasions that they experienced this condition, until gradually stopping altogether. In contrast, they almost never looked around the partition when the experimenter merely engaged in irrelevant movements (Fig. 2.5(b)). This general finding has now been independently replicated and extended by Michael Tomasello and his colleagues (Tomasello, personal communication, 1999).

These results troubled us, but not because we were particularly committed to low-level models of chimpanzee cognition. Rather, our disconcerted feeling emanated from the results of over a dozen other experiments (using quite different methods) that we had conducted prior to the opaque barrier test—experiments which suggested a very different answer from the one implicated by the opaque barrier test. In what follows, we summarize these other experiments, and explore whether they are truly incongruent with the results of our gaze-following studies, and indeed, whether we need the high-level model to explain our apes' abilities to 'understand' that gaze cannot pass through opaque barriers.

Knowing that others see you

Our first approach to asking our apes about 'seeing' had been to determine if they understood the psychological distinction between someone who could see them and someone who could not. We initially addressed this question by focusing on the natural begging gesture of chimpanzees (see Fig. 2.6). Chimpanzees use this gesture in several communicative contexts, including situations in which one ape is attempting to seek reassurance from another, or in cases where one ape is attempting to acquire food from

Figure 2.6 The chimpanzee's natural begging gesture. Megan gestures to Angela in response to seeing an out-of-reach apple. These gestures are frequently accompanied by the animal alternating her gaze back and forth between the food item and the human.

another. Every day, our apes spontaneously use this gesture to request treats such as bananas, apples, sweet potatoes, onions, carrots, or even candy from their caretakers and trainers. For example, our chimpanzees frequently see us walk past their compound with some food, and immediately reach out, with their palms up (to 'request' the item, as it were) and then look into our eyes. Thus, this seemed like an ideal natural context in which to explore whether they appreciated that their gestures needed to be seen in order to be effective. (For a detailed description of the methods and results of these studies, see Povinelli 1996; Povinelli and Eddy 1996a; Reaux et al.1999).

We began by training the apes to enter the lab and gesture through a hole directly in front of a single, familiar experimenter who was either standing or sitting to their left or right. On every trial that they gestured through the hole directly in front of the experimenter, this person praised them and handed them a food reward. In short order, the apes were all reliably gesturing through the correct hole toward the experimenter (Fig. 2.7(a)–(c)).

Of course, we already knew that chimpanzees were inclined to direct their begging gesture toward us. What we really wanted to know was how the chimpanzees would react when they entered the test lab and encountered not one experimenter, but two— one who could see them (and therefore respond to their gestures), and one who could not. With this in mind, we created several clear cases (at least from our human point of view) of *seeing* versus *not seeing*. Although it is true that it was humans who carefully designed and rehearsed these scenarios, we should be quick to point out that we did not simply pluck them out of thin air. Rather, we studied our animals' spontaneous play, and then modeled our scenarios after several of the behaviors we had frequently seen them exhibit spontaneously. At the time, one of their favorite pastimes was to use objects in their enclosure to obstruct their vision. For example, they would place large plastic buckets over their heads, and then carefully move around their compound until they bumped into something. Occasionally, they would stop, lift the bucket (to peek, as it were), and then continue along on their blind strolls. Although the buckets were their favored means of obstructing their vision, they also used plastic bowls, burlap sacks, pieces of cardboard, and even their hands to produce the same effect. From a common-sense point of view, it seemed hard to deny that they knew exactly what they were doing—preventing themselves from seeing. In the end, these natural behaviors inspired the conditions depicted in Fig. 2.8(a)–(d). In order to keep the animals alert and motivated, we tested them in sessions consisting of ten trials. In each of these sessions, eight of these trials were of the easy variety (with only a single experimenter present), whereas the other two involved the seeing/not seeing conditions shown in Fig. 2.8(a)–(d).

So how did the animals react when they encountered two familiar experimenters, one who could see them, the other who could not? They entered the lab, but then (measurably) paused. And yet, having apparently noted the novelty of the circumstance, they

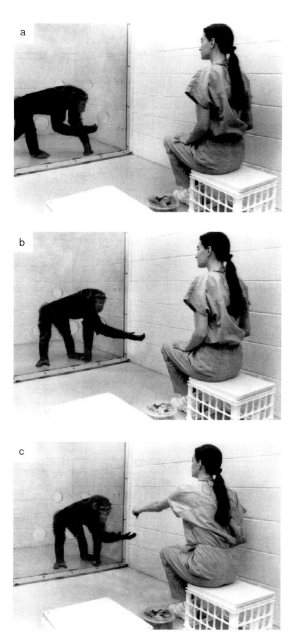

Figure 2.7 A 'standard trial' sequence for the seeing/not-seeing tests with Mindy. (a) Mindy enters the test unit and orients to Roxanne (who is either seated on the left or right). (b) Mindy gestures to Roxanne. (c) Roxanne responds by reaching down, taking a piece of food, and handing it to her.

were then just as likely to gesture to the person who could *not* see them, as to the person who could. This was true in three of the four conditions: buckets, blindfolds, and hands-over-the-eyes. In each of these conditions, the chimpanzees displayed no preference for gesturing toward the experimenter who could see them. In contrast, on the easy surrounding trials, the apes gestured through the correct hole (in front of the only experimenter present) 98 per cent of the time. Thus, despite their general interest and motivation, when it came to the seeing/not seeing conditions, the animals appeared oblivious to the psychological distinction between the two experimenters.

There was, however, one exception. Unlike the blindfolds, buckets, and hands-over-the-eyes trials, on back-versus-front trials (in which one person faced toward the ape and the other faced away; see Fig. 2.8(d)) the animals gestured to the person facing forward from their very first trial forward. Here, then, the animals seemed to have the right idea: 'Gesture to the person who can see.' But why the discrepancy? Why should the apes perform well on a condition in which one of the experimenters was facing them and the other facing away, but then not on any of the other conditions? In defense of the high-level account, it could be argued that the back/front condition was simply the easiest situation in which to recognize the difference between seeing and not seeing. And, despite the fact that the animals had measurably paused before making their choices in the other conditions as well, and despite the fact that we had observed them adopt these other postures in their play, the idea that back/front was simply a more natural distinction felt appealing.

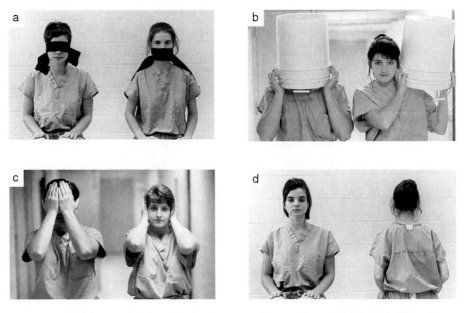

Figure 2.8 Conditions used in the original seeing/not-seeing experiment. (a) blindfolds (b) buckets (c) hands-over-the-eyes (d) back/front.

However, despite the seeming clarity of our intuitions, there was another, more mundane potential explanation of these results. Compare Fig. 2.8(a)–(c) to Fig. 2.8(d). It was possible that on the back/front trials the apes were merely doing what we had, in effect, trained them to do—enter the test lab, look for someone who happened to be facing forward, and then gesture in front of him or her. Rather than reasoning about who could see them, perhaps the apes were simply executing a procedural rule that we had inadvertently taught them. Worse yet, perhaps evolution had simply sculpted them to gesture to the front of others, without any concomitant appreciation that others 'see'.[3]

At this point, several ways of distinguishing between these possibilities occurred to us. If the high-level account were correct (that is, if the back/front condition was simply the most natural case of seeing/not seeing), then the apes ought to perform well on other, equally natural conditions. Here, for example, is another situation that our apes experience on a daily basis. One of our females approaches a group of others who are facing away from her. As she gets closer, one of the other apes turns around and looks over her shoulder toward the approaching animal. Now, although the approaching female notices this behavior, does she understand that the other ape is *psychologically* connected to her in a way that the others are not? The new condition that this consideration inspired ('looking-over-the-shoulder', Fig. 2.9(a)) was of interest in its own right, but we had an even stronger motivation for testing the apes on such a condition. Recall that the low-level account could explain our apes' excellent performance on the back/front condition by positing that they were simply being drawn to the frontal posture of a person. But in this new, looking-over-the-shoulder condition, there was no general frontal posture—just the face of one experimenter and the back of the other one's head. Thus, the low-level account generated the seemingly implausible prediction that the apes would perform well on the back/front condition, but randomly on the looking-over-the-shoulder trials. In contrast, the high-level model predicted the seemingly more plausible outcome in which the apes would gesture to the person who could see them.

---

3   Tomasello *et al.* (1994) have reported that, in spontaneous interactions with each other, captive chimpanzees use different communicative signals depending on the behavioral posture of the recipient. For example, they use visually-based gestures only when the recipient is facing them. Although this may seem like prima-facie evidence that chimpanzees appreciate that others 'see', a moment's reflection reveals the ambiguity of such evidence. From an evolutionary perspective, in order for visually-based gestures to have evolved in the first place, they must have been linked to a disposition to execute them when the recipients were in a posture to receive them (i.e. facing the senders). Clearly, however, this system could have evolved without the sender appreciating that the recipient needed to *see* the gesture. Rather, the disposition to gesture toward the front of another may be controlled by the sender's recognition of the postural state of the recipient. For a more detailed discussion of this distinction, see Theall and Povinelli (1999).

To our surprise, however, and in full support of the low-level model, on the looking-over-the-shoulder trials the apes did not prefer to gesture to the person who could see them. In direct contrast, they continued to perform without difficulty on the back/front trials. This result made a deep impression on us. No longer was it possible to dismiss our original results by supposing that the animals thought that we were peeking from under the buckets or blindfolds, or between our fingers. No, here we had made 'peeking' clear and explicit, and yet the apes still performed according to the predictions of the low-level model. The experimental dissection of the fronts of the experimenter from their faces (using a posture that our apes must witness every day), sobered us to the possibility that perhaps our animals genuinely might not understand that the experimenters had to *see* their gesture in order to respond to it. More disturbing still, the results seemed to imply that even for the back/front condition our apes might have no idea that the experimenter facing away was 'incorrect'— rather, this was simply a posture with a lower valence. After all, the animals were perfectly willing to choose the person in this posture on fully half of the looking-over-the-shoulder trials.

We had difficulty accepting the implications of these results. We had witnessed our apes using their begging gesture in both testing and non-testing situations on hundreds of occasions, and had always been comfortable in assuming that they conceptualized what they were doing in the same manner that we did. In fact, it was almost impossible not to do so. They would approach us, stick out their hands, and then look up into our eyes. Was it really possible that a behavioral form so instantly recognizable to us could be understood so differently by them?

Thus, despite the fact that the high-level model had done a very poor job at predicting how our apes would react to our tests, we nonetheless remained deeply skeptical of the alternative, low-level model. And so, after further reflection, we decided to examine our animals' reactions to several other conditions, such as one involving screens (Fig. 2.9(b)). In order to go the extra mile, before we began testing them in this condition, we familiarized the apes with the screens by holding the screens in front of our faces and playing 'peek-a-boo' with the animals. We even let the apes play with the screens themselves. And yet despite all of this, when it came to testing, the apes responded in the same manner as they had before; they were just as likely to choose the person who could not see them as the person who could.

It would be an error to conclude from these data that our chimpanzees were incapable of learning the distinctions in question. Chimpanzees are alert, cognizing organisms, extremely attuned to the behaviors that unfold around them. So it would be truly surprising if they failed to learn anything after repeated experience on our tests. And to be fair to our apes, we had intentionally kept the number of test trials in each experiment to a minimum (typically four) and, furthermore, we had interspersed these (difficult) trials at a relatively low frequency among easy trials involving only a single experimenter. Our reason for doing so was twofold. First, we wanted to keep the important trials (the ones involving a choice between someone who could see them and someone

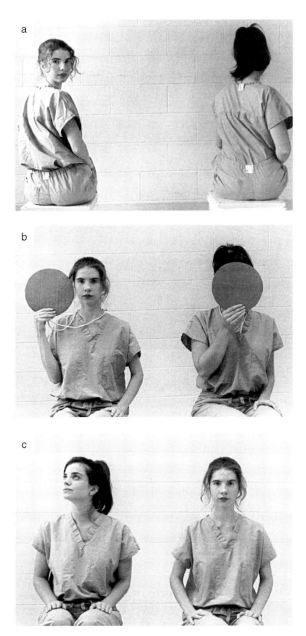

Figure 2.9 (a) The looking-over-the-shoulder condition. (b) The screen-versus-no-screen condition. (c) The attending-versus-distracted condition.

else who could not) as novel as possible. Second, we wanted to minimize their rate of learning—after all, we were interested in what they understood ahead of time, not what they could learn through trial-and-error.

Nonetheless, after enough experience of gesturing to the experimenter with the screen covering his or her face and not being handed a reward (experience they received across several experiments), their performances began to improve, until finally they were reliably gesturing to the person who could see them. Indeed, follow-up studies revealed the interesting (although not completely unexpected) fact that our apes' correct responding had generalized from the screens condition to the looking-over-the-shoulder condition as well.

At this point, it was possible to walk away from these studies concluding that the apes had simply learned another procedural rule—'Gesture in front of the person whose face is visible'. However, nothing seemed to eliminate the possibility that although they did not do so immediately, they might have finally figured out what we were asking them—'Oh! It's about *seeing*!' We devised several additional procedures for distinguishing between these possibilities. First, we administered the original set of conditions to the apes (blindfolds, buckets, etc.). The high-level account predicted that, because they had finally learned the task was about seeing, the apes would perform excellently on all of them. The low-level account also predicted excellent performance—except in the blind-folds condition (where blindfolds covered the eyes of one person and the mouth of the other). Why did the models differ in their predictions about the outcome of blindfolds condition? Because in this condition, an equal amount of the face of each person was visible (see Fig. 2.8(d)). Although it is perfectly obvious to us that only one of the exper-imenters in this condition can see, if our apes had merely acquired a set of arbitrary pro-cedural rules about the presence or absence of the face, then on the blindfolds test they would be forced to guess who was correct—choosing the person whose eyes were covered as often as the person whose mouth was covered. And, to our amazement, that is precisely what our animals did.

With more experience, however, our apes were even able to pass the blindfolds condi-tion, raising the same kind of difficult question. Had they finally figured out the seeing/not seeing contrast, or had they merely added a final part of a rule structure of the following type: frontal posture > face > eyes. After puzzling over how to distinguish between whether they were reasoning about the eyes as the locus of 'seeing' or whether they were using just another stimulus in their rule structure, we arrived at a new condi-tion: attending-versus-distracted (see Fig. 2.9(c)). In this test, we confronted the chim-panzees with two experimenters, both of whose eyes and faces were both clearly visible. However, only one of them had his or her head directed toward the ape. The other appeared (to us) distracted, with her head directed above and behind the chimpanzee. The high-level model predicted that the apes would gesture to the experimenter who was visually attending, whereas the low-level model, because the eyes and faces were present in both cases, predicted that they would gesture to each of them equally. The results were striking. The apes entered, looked, and then followed the distracted exper-imenter's gaze up and into the rear corner of the ceiling. Nevertheless, the subjects were

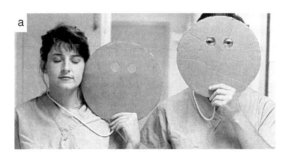

Figure 2.10 Two conditions used to distinguish the relative importance of the eyes versus the face (and whether they appreciate 'seeing'): (a) face vs. eyes; (b) eyes vs. no eyes. (c) Mindy gesturing to the correct experimenter.

then just as likely to gesture to the distracted person as toward the person who was looking in their direction! It was exactly as if they responded to the information about the distracted experimenter's direction of gaze without interpreting its attentional significance.

Finally, we tested the apes on the most subtle version of this task we could imagine: eyes-open-versus-closed. Although they initially had no preference for the person whose eyes were open, after a number of trials their performance improved. However, even here, additional control tests revealed that when the eyes and face were pitted against one another (see Fig. 2.10), the face rule was more important! In short, through trial-and-error learning (probably aided by an innate sensitivity to the face, eyes, and overall posture of others) our apes appeared to have learned a hierarchically organized set of procedural rules: (1) gesture to the person whose front is facing forward; (2) if both fronts are present (or absent), gesture to the person whose face is visible; and (3) if both faces are visible (or occluded), gesture to the person whose eyes are visible. *Seeing*, then, did not appear to be a concept recruited by the chimpanzees to help them decide to whom they should gesture.

All of this may seem confusing, especially given our earlier account of how our chimpanzees seemed to enjoy obstructing their own vision during their spontaneous bouts of play. Were there crucial methodological limitations in our seeing/not seeing tests that somehow prevented our apes from displaying an (existing) understanding of seeing? Although possible, there are other alternatives. To illustrate one of these, let us reflect on the following example. An ape feels an irritation on its arm and scratches it. The explanation of this action seems simple—the animal produces a behavior (scratching) that is associated with a reinforcing experience (the cessation of itching). And, as much as our folk psychology resists the idea, the 'peek-a-boo' games we observed our apes playing may be explained in a similar manner: they place a bucket over their heads because it produces an interesting, pleasurable experience. In other words, we are suggesting that the *experience* of visual occlusion need not be represented any more explicitly than any other sensation (e.g. the soothing that results from scratching). Such an account could reconcile the seemingly incongruous aspects of our data: our animals' natural ability to produce visual deprivation in their play behavior, right alongside their bemusement when asked to explicitly reason about such visual deprivation in others.[4]

Validating the task

In reflecting on the results just described, we considered the possibility that we had underestimated the difficulty of our task. It was possible that our chimpanzees might understand the attentional aspect of seeing, but that our particular task simply required

---

4   Of course, it is also possible that chimpanzees have a better understanding of their own mental states than the mental states of others, a possibility addressed by Povinelli and Prince (1998). However, the relation between understanding one's own mental states and those of others is a difficult philosophical and psychological problem (see Gopnik 1993).

a more sophisticated understanding of visual perception than we had thought (for example, such as the connection between seeing and knowing). Worse yet, our task might be tapping into capacities unrelated to the question of seeing. In order to gain a better perspective on this problem, we turned to what is known about the development of young children's understanding of seeing. Findings from several laboratories had converged to suggest that an understanding of seeing as attention is beginning to be consolidated in young children by about 2^1/$_2$ years of age (Gopnik *et al.* 1995; Lempers *et al.* 1977; see discussion in Povinelli and Eddy 1996*a*, Chapter 5). Thus, we reasoned that if our tests were measuring an understanding of the attentional aspect of seeing, then 2^1/$_2$- to 3-year-old children ought to perform quite well on them. On the other hand, if the tasks required an understanding of the connection between seeing and knowing, which develops at around four years in human children (see Footnote 2), then younger children should perform poorly. We investigated this by training 2-, 3-, and 4-year-old children, over a three- to five-week period, to gesture to familiar adult experimenters to request brightly colored stickers. We then tested them on several of the conditions we had used with the apes (screens, hands-over-the-eyes, and back-versus-front). Unlike the apes, the children were correct in most or all of the conditions from their very first trial forward—even the majority of the youngest ones we tested.[5]

Genuine vs. 'as-if' understanding

By the end of the initial set of over a dozen experiments that we conducted with our apes, they were able to learn new conditions within just three or four trials. As we have seen, several of the final experiments provided confirmation for our idea that the apes were relying on a hierarchical rule structure concerning the front, face, and eyes of the experimenters. Nonetheless, by the end of these studies, our apes were behaving exactly *as if* they understood something about seeing as a mental event. They would approach two familiar caretakers, look at each one, and then gesture in front of the person who could see them. Indeed, as we have seen, after over a dozen experiments our apes were

---

5   Comparing the cognitive abilities of chimpanzees and young children is a strategy that has been advocated for quite some time (e.g. Köhler 1927; Povinelli and deBlois 1992*a*,*b*; Premack and Premack 1983; Witmer 1909). However, comparisons of this sort frequently tend to portray chimpanzees as developmentally arrested children (e.g. Parker and Russon 1996) and tend to envision cognitive evolution as having occurred exclusively through a process of terminal addition (a process whereby descendant species acquire new 'stages' of cognitive development by simply tacking on new abilities to the terminal stages of their ancestral species (e.g. Parker and Gibson 1979)). Although these ideas are not completely inaccurate, they miss the complexity of evolutionary processes, and in particular both overlook or downplay the fact that new abilities may, more often than not, be woven in alongside ancestral developmental pathways early in development, interacting with the ancestral abilities to greater or lesser degrees (for a full discussion of these issues, see Povinelli and Eddy 1996*a*; Povinelli and Giambrone, in press; Povinelli *et al.* 1996*b*).

performing in much the same manner as 2-, 3- and 4-year-old children performed on their very *first* trials.

We have now arrived at the heart of the problem that we promised to address at the beginning of this chapter: does the fact that humans and chimpanzees engage in similar behavior imply that similar mental states accompany the behaviors? Furthermore, does the answer to this question depend on how the behavior in question arises? For example, is there a psychological distinction between a 2- to 3-year-old child who arrives at our center and performs perfectly from her very first trial forward on our seeing/not seeing tests, and our chimpanzees, who, after months of differential feedback, finally learn to do likewise? In considering this question, it is important not to trivialize what our chimpanzees had learned. Although at each critical juncture in the experiments, their understanding of seeing was best predicted by the low-level model, by the end of these tests the apes were using the direction of the face and the presence or absence of the eyes as the bases for their choices. Although the low-level model explained their use of these features in terms of a psychological system which reasons about physical postures, in some sense the low- and high-level models share common properties. After all, even though the high-level model envisions that the apes possess a psychological system that interprets these postures in terms of underlying mental states, it must nonetheless use information about the physical postures of the experimenters. Perhaps the most striking way of thinking about this is to realize that *whatever the underlying differences in interpretation, chimpanzees and 2- to 3-year-old children are attending to the exact same physical stimuli as they make their decisions.*

The problem might be best stated from the point of view of the children. Prior to visiting our center, these children have had numerous semi-structured experiences of 'seeing' and 'not seeing' (in the context of playing with their parents and peers). Thus, long before participating in our tests, the children have been confronted with games, and even 'real' social experiences in which they have had to cope with the distinction between seeing and not seeing. Although their reactions to these situations were not yoked to receiving or not receiving a sticker, surely the range of their responses were linked to a range of differential responses from their parents and peers. Of course, our chimpanzees had many such experiences as well. Thus, the question we wish to raise is simple. How do the kinds of experiences received by children compare with the kinds of experiences received by our chimpanzees? And even more directly, what can such comparisons tell us about the psychological structures that cause and/or accompany the final behavioral outcomes?

At this point, two separate arguments present themselves. On the one hand, it is possible to question whether the 2- to 3-year-old child's performance on our task really reflects an understanding of seeing/attention in the first place. After all, our tests with the children were not nearly as extensive as those with the apes, primarily because even most of the youngest children performed correctly from their very first trial. However, those initial tests consisted of conditions which could be solved by the face rule. Perhaps a low-level model of the 2-year-olds' behavior would better predict their reactions on more complicated tests. Although possible, there is independent evidence that 2- to 3-year-olds understand the concept of seeing/attention (see Baldwin 1991, 1993; Gopnik *et al.* 1995; Lempers *et al.* 1977). So we move to the second argument, which is of more central importance to this chapter. Given the amount of experience that children have with explicitly created instances of 'seeing' and 'not seeing' by their parents and siblings, how do we know that it is not precisely this experience that allows the child to create the idea of visual attention in the first place? If so, then perhaps the apes' *final* trials in our experiments are more comparable to the children's very first trials. In other words, perhaps chimpanzees simply need sufficient experience to allow them to construct a concept of seeing-as-attention. Thus, although the low-level model best predicted our apes' behavior at each critical experimental fork in the road, as it were, this might only have been the case because our tests were chasing the apes' concurrent construction of the idea of attention.

Cognitive scientists who view the mind as being composed of many separate, informationally encapsulated systems (or 'modules') will immediately object to this idea, claiming that the insularized nature of social understanding excludes this possibility. Yes, they admit, children have such seeing/not seeing experiences in play, but these experiences are largely incidental to the development of their understanding of mental states in others. On this view, their knowledge of the mental state of attention matures biologically—it is not constructed through experience (Fodor 1983). Perhaps some of these experiences are critical to triggering biologically pre-prepared modules, but the structures are essentially there, simply waiting to be turned on. On this view, only the apes' initial trials would be diagnostic; what they learn through trial and error is simply not relevant to the question of cognitive development. Apes either naturally and spontaneously develop an understanding of seeing, or they do not; changes in task performance that occur as the result of feedback should be assigned to an 'as-if' category of understanding.

But such objections derive most of their force through empirically underdetermined theoretical positions. Although there are good reasons for considering stronger and weaker versions of modularity theory in the development of cognitive structures, there is nothing about our knowledge of cognitive development that forces us to accept this view. Indeed, several theorists have argued that specific kinds of experiences may play a crucial role in cognitive development in chimpanzees. For example, David Premack (1988) argued that training his chimpanzees to use a symbol for same/different judgements about objects altered the natural state of their cognitive structures allowing them to engage in abstract analogical reasoning. More recently, Michael Tomasello (1995) has resurrected the argument that exposure to human culture dramatically affects the cognitive development of apes—in this case, the apes' understanding of joint attention. If opinions matter, we favor accounts of cognitive development that emphasize the role of complex epigenetic interactions that occur during development. But in the final analysis, the similarity between the construction of bodily structures (including the brain) on the one hand, and the construction of concepts related to mental states, on the other hand, remains unclear. In fact, the ambiguity of this comparison manifests itself quite clearly in the context of interpreting the results of our seeing/not seeing experiments. For example, some researchers have interpreted our results as evidence that chimpanzees do not understand seeing, whereas others have focused on our apes' final performances and have concluded that they do. With respect to the latter claim, our apes' ability to learn to gesture to the person who could see them could be taken as evidence that they came to understand the attentional aspect of seeing in one of two ways: (1) they finally figured out what we were (awkwardly) asking them; or (2) they finally *constructed* an explicit concept of seeing (which they typically do not need to function in their society). In either case, our results could be interpreted as showing that reasoning about the mental dimension of seeing is not beyond the capacity of chimpanzees.

In summary, then, there are at least three distinct ways in which to characterize the nature of the social understanding connected with our chimpanzees' final, successful performances on the seeing/not seeing tests that we gave them:

1. A first possibility is that before participating in our tests, our apes did not possess a concept of attention. However, through the differential feedback they received, and our refinement of the tests, they came to construct such a concept, and, indeed, learned one of its sensory bases (i.e. seeing).

2. A second possibility is that our apes entered the tests with a general, amodal conception of attention (perhaps interpreting attention as being governed by proximity, as opposed to sensory channels such as seeing, hearing, touching, etc.). However, again through the feedback that our tests provided, they finally constructed the notion of *visual* attention.

3. A final possibility is that our apes neither entered nor exited our tests with an understanding of the mental state of attention. Rather, they constructed an 'as-if' understanding of seeing-as-attention. On this view, our feedback procedures simply sculpted their behaviors into a form which matched our own.

Although there may be certain theoretical reasons for favoring one of these accounts over the others, in assessing our empirical results we found little reason to exclude any of them (Povinelli and Eddy 1996*a*, p. 134).

Longitudinal reflections

The above considerations left us in a difficult quandary: how were we to distinguish between radically different, but nonetheless viable accounts of what our apes had learned in our tests?

Fortunately, at least one way of distinguishing among these possibilities presented itself about a year after we had completed the studies just described. At this point our apes were seven years old. In the context of preparing them for a different set of experiments concerning their understanding of joint attention, we returned to our seeing/not seeing protocols, and tested them on the eyes open/closed procedure. To our surprise, rather than finding this easy, the animals were just as likely to gesture to the person who had their eyes open as to the person who had their eyes closed. Indeed, even after four dozen trials of this condition, the subjects were still not responding above chance. At first, we assumed that this was because eyes open/closed was the most subtle condition of all of those we had previously used, and therefore the animals may have never developed a robust understanding of it. Intrigued, we decided to test the apes on the screens condition—the condition with which they had the most previous experience. However, again to our surprise, it was only after four dozen trials of this condition that the animals' performances began to creep up to levels significantly above chance. We were thus forced to consider the possibility that despite the fact that our apes had been almost 90 per cent correct on their final series of the screens condition a year earlier, they had apparently not consolidated this understanding into a form that would endure throughout a year of participating in other tests.

Although a retention of performance would not have been particularly informative, this failure of retention was. Consider again the children who had participated in our tests a year earlier. Imagine these same children returning to our lab a year later. The contrast between the enduring understanding that they had apparently constructed during their second year of life and the failure of our apes to retain what they had learned a year earlier, suggests in a rather dramatic manner that, despite superficial similarities in the performances of the chimpanzees and children, the two species might nonetheless have parted company conceptually very early on.

Let us emphasize the significance of our apes' absence of retention on this test by pointing out that these animals were not simply lounging around, playing idly in the sun during the year which intervened between these two longitudinal time-points. On the contrary, they had participated in at least a dozen other experiments, all of which were designed to probe their potential understanding of attention (or other mental states; see Moses *et al.*, unpublished data; Povinelli and Eddy 1996*b,c*, 1997; Povinelli and O'Neill 2000; Povinelli *et al.* 1998; Povinelli *et al.* 1999; Theall and Povinelli 1999). Indeed, in many of these studies, visual attention played a prominent role. Although these tests provided no better evidence that our apes possessed a genuine understanding of attention (or any other mental state), our fortuitous findings on the longitudinal seeing/not seeing task raised a much broader, and much more interesting question: how did the experiences on these various tests interact with each other?

One might naturally assume that such experiences would build cumulatively, mutually reinforcing each other in a manner that would assist our apes in homing in on, and better understanding, the questions we were posing to them. Indeed, we carefully planned the nature and sequence of our tests with this assumption in mind. To some extent, of course, this would almost have to be true. But our animals' failure to rapidly understand even the easiest of the seeing/not seeing conditions at the second longitudinal time-point caused us to realize that we needed to think more clearly about the exact manner in which their testing experiences were interacting with each other.

Certainly skills accumulate. Indeed, we have ample evidence that abilities that our apes learned at one time-point were retained years later. For example, once they learn how to use a tool, they typically remember how to do so for a very long period of time. But then why did they exhibit such poor retention on the seeing/not seeing tests? There are several possible explanations. One is that, despite a full year of experiences on tests that should have helped to clarify the central construct that we were asking them about (i.e. the mental state of attention), our apes failed to integrate these new experiences with their older ones. More intriguing still, these new experiences might actually have interfered with what they had learned a year earlier. Indeed, if our apes had never deeply understood why they were rewarded after gesturing to the person with, for example, the bucket on the shoulder (as opposed to the person with the bucket over the head), then such rules might never have been well-consolidated—especially given that we did not over-train them on any of the conditions. Given a rather weak understanding to begin with, rules or relations learned during intervening tests may have displaced or interfered with these older structures. In more stark terms, if our apes had no concept of attention, then from their perspective all of our tests might have just seemed like a mere collection of arbitrary social stimuli with nothing more concrete than our reinforcement procedures uniting them.

We were so struck by the apes' weak retention at this second time-point that when they turned eight to nine years of age, we conducted a final series of experiments using these same procedures. Now our apes were on the cusp of adulthood. Indeed, within just a few months the group's first baby would be born to Kara, the oldest female in our group. It seemed reasonable to suppose that if our chimpanzees were going to develop a notion of seeing it ought to have emerged by this point. Our strategy for these final longitudinal tests was twofold. First, we exposed the animals to the main conditions we had administered two years previously (screens, buckets, blindfolds, eyes open/closed, distracted/attending, and back/front). We did this to determine whether they would understand these conditions immediately (perhaps indicating a qualitative change in their understanding), or whether they would be forced to relearn them. Second, we intended to design some new conditions that would allow us to make some stronger inferences about whether they had finally developed an appreciation of the attentional aspect of seeing.

Despite their physical maturity, however, the apes initially responded to our tests in the same manner they had in the previous years. In the majority of the conditions, the apes displayed little evidence that they preferred to request food from the person who could see them. However, they did perform at levels exceeding chance in the buckets condition, and as usual, they were perfect on the back/front trials. There was no easy way to characterize these results. The outcome of the buckets condition might suggest that the apes were able to use the face rule, but their poor performance on the screens condition (in which the face rule could work just as well) did not support this idea.

Next, we administered eight more trials of each of these conditions, and with this additional experience, the animals' performances improved to levels exceeding chance in five of the six conditions. The sole exception was the eyes open/closed condition. (Why the animals had greater difficulty on eyes open/closed is unclear. Perhaps it was simply a more subtle discrimination. On the other hand, it is possible that the apes thought the eyes might pop open at any moment.) At any rate, on the whole, these results seemed to fit the hierarchical rule model that had predicted the apes' performances during the previous two years. In that model, the eyes rule was the least important, and indeed, at this point there was only limited evidence that they were even using it. They *did* perform well on the blindfolds condition (which could be solved by the eyes, but not the face rule). Nonetheless, with the exception of Megan, the animals did not appear to understand the eyes open/closed condition yet. Furthermore, the subjects had relearned the distracted/attending condition, which could not be satisfied by any of these rules (because in this condition both of the experimenters' eyes and faces were visible).

Collectively, these results suggested that the apes were in the process of learning not just a set of hierarchical rules, but also, because these rules could not work all of the time (e.g. in the distracted/attending condition), they were constructing *condition-specific* rules which relied on more strict discriminations between two specific postures. After reflecting on this possibility, we decided to mix together the correct (seeing) and incorrect (not seeing) options from each of several of the different conditions (see Fig. 2.11). We reasoned that if the apes had learned a set of condition-specific rules, then their performance would decline if we mixed a *correct* option from one condition with an *incorrect* option from another. On the other hand, if the apes had extracted a context-independent understanding that certain configurations were correct (e.g. 'Gesture to the person holding a screen over the shoulder'), they could be expected to perform well on these mixed conditions. Finally, we considered the eyes open/closed condition that the majority of the subjects did not yet understand. We reasoned that by mixing the *incorrect* option from the eyes condition (eyes closed) with the *correct* option from one of the conditions on which they were performing well (blindfolds), we might uncover whether the apes understood these correct options as abstractly 'correct', or whether they were understood as correct only within the context of other options known to be 'incorrect'.

The mixture of correct and incorrect options from conditions on which the apes were already performing well posed no problem for the animals—in these cases they performed at levels exceeding chance. In direct contrast, when we mixed the *correct* option from a condition on which they were performing well, with the *incorrect* option from the one on which they were not, they gestured equally to both options. Together, these results provided further evidence that the apes were learning a rule about gesturing to a person whose face was visible, and that this rule could be flexibly deployed when we mixed the different options from such conditions together. However, their inability to move beyond this rule on the mixed conditions that involved the incorrect, eyes-closed option, suggested that the apes were treating the conditions as problems to be solved by comparing physical postures, not by reasoning about who could see them. Megan, however, did not fit this pattern. She performed well on both the final series of eyes open/closed trials (6/8 correct) and the mixed conditions involving eyes closed (6/8 correct), performing significantly above chance.

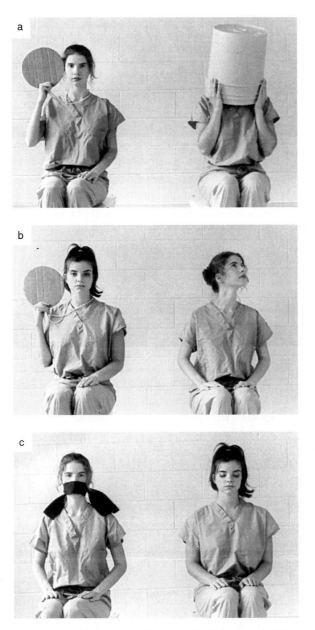

Figure 2.11 The mixed conditions used in the longitudinal study of our chimpanzees' understanding of the distinction between seeing and not-seeing. (a) +screens/-buckets (b) +screens/-distracted (c) +blindfolds/-eyes.

Megan's performance intrigued us because she, unlike the others, had also learned the eyes open/closed condition during the first time-point in this longitudinal project (see Povinelli and Eddy 1996a, experiment 13, p. 100)—although she did not appear to remember it at the second time-point, and showed a learning curve during the final time-point. Nonetheless, such a subtle discrimination was impressive, and we knew that some other researchers might interpret this as evidence that she, at least, had finally learned something about seeing *per se*. Her performance thus provided a focal point for our final experimental attempt to pit the predictive power of the low- and high-level models.

Recall that the low-level model stipulated that the apes were learning a set of procedural rules in which the front, face, and eyes (in descending order of importance) served as the bases for their choices. If this were true, then even for Megan the frontal aspect of a person would be more important than whether the other person's eyes were open. To this end, we constructed the new condition shown in Fig. 2.12, in which the *correct* option from looking-over-the-shoulder was combined with the *incorrect* option from eyes open/closed. This presented the animals with a choice between someone facing forward with eyes shut, versus someone facing away from them, but looking over the shoulder with eyes wide open. We also tested the apes on three other conditions: back/front, eyes open/closed, and looking-over-the-shoulder (a condition that our apes had not experienced in $2^1/_2$ years). The low-level model predicted that the subjects would succeed on the looking-over-the-shoulder condition because they could use the face rule. However, it also predicted that on the new mixed condition the subjects would

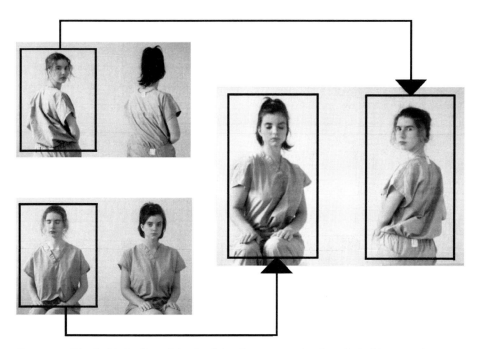

Figure 2.12 The final 'mixed' condition involving the *correct* option from the looking-over-the-shoulder condition vs. the *incorrect* option (eyes closed) from the eyes-open-vs-eyes-closed condition. See text for the theoretical significance of this condition.

prefer the *incorrect* option! The reason for this counter-intuitive prediction is because of the postulated dominance of the front rule: when the subjects applied the front rule it could be immediately satisfied, thus leading them to gesture straight-away to the person facing forward—even though his or her eyes were closed.

The results of this final test provided striking confirmation for the low-level model. First, as expected, the subjects tended to prefer the correct person on the looking-over-the-shoulder trials. Second, and most important, the subjects performed significantly *below* chance in the mixed condition, meaning that they preferred to gesture to the person who was facing forward but who could not see them—exactly as the low-level model had predicted. Although this was striking enough, there were additional aspects of the data set that were even more revealing. Three of the apes (Megan, Brandy, and Kara) were almost perfect on the looking-over-the-shoulder and eyes open/closed conditions (8/8, 8/8, and 7/8, respectively, for the two conditions combined). Thus, these three animals exhibited a strong understanding of the conditions from which the novel, mixed condition had been composed. Yet when they were confronted with these conditions mixed together, Megan, Brandy, and Kara exhibited an overwhelming preference for the *incorrect* option—selecting the person with eyes closed on 4/4, 4/4, and 3/4 trials, respectively! However one chooses to interpret these results, they certainly do not support the idea that Megan, or any of the other animals, selected the eyes-open option because they understood that this person could 'see' them.

Gaze-following and 'seeing': toward a reconciliation

Although it was hard not to be impressed by the utility of the low-level model in predicting our apes' behavior on the seeing/not seeing tests just described, we pondered the model's apparent underestimation of their abilities on the opaque barrier test described earlier. One possible reconciliation between these data sets was to question the generality of the results of seeing/not seeing tests. For example, perhaps the apes just had trouble simultaneously reasoning about the visual perspectives of two persons, or perhaps they had difficulty understanding themselves as objects of visual attention.

With these ideas in mind, we explored whether our apes would show better evidence of understanding the attentional aspect of visual perception in situations that more directly involved their gaze-following abilities (see Povinelli *et al.* 1999). First, we taught our chimpanzees, as well as 3-year-old children, to search under two opaque cups for a hidden treat. Next, we occasionally kept them ignorant as to the treat's location, but instead let them witness an experimenter turn and look either at the correct cup (*at-target*) or above the correct cup (*above-target*) (see Fig. 2.13(a)–(b)). We reasoned that if the subjects understood the referential significance of the gaze of the experimenter, they ought to select the correct cup on the at-target trials, but should choose *randomly* between the two cups on the above-target trials. The latter prediction is the key one, because organisms with a theory of attention (for example, human children) should interpret the distracted experimenter as being psychologically (attentionally) disconnected from the cups—conveying no information about the location of the reward.

And, as predicted, the 3-year-old children selected the cup at which the experimenter was looking on the at-target trials but chose *randomly* between the two cups on the above-target trials. This result provided crucial evidence that our theory of what the task was measuring was correct. In direct contrast, however, the chimpanzees responded equally well on the at-target and above-target trials. They entered the test unit, moved to the side of the apparatus in front of the experimenter's face, and then chose the nearest cup. Did the apes simply not notice the direction of the experimenter's gaze on the above-target trials, thereby confusing them with the at-target trials? Hardly. They followed the experimenter's gaze by looking above and behind themselves on over 71 per cent of the above-target trials (as compared to only 16 per cent of the at-target trials). Thus, unlike 3-year-old children, our apes behaved according to the predictions of the low-level model—a model which assumed that, despite their excellent gaze-following abilities, they do not understand how gaze is related to subjective states of attention.

Figure 2.13 Conditions used to assess whether our chimpanzees appreciated the referential aspect of gaze: (a) at target (b) above target.

These results suggest a way of reconciling the apparent ability of our apes to reason about whether someone's gaze is blocked by opaque barriers, with the extensive data suggesting that they do not appreciate that others 'see'. Such a reconciliation can begin by abandoning the argument by analogy, and then proceed by exploring the possibility that identical behaviors may be generated and/or attended by different psychological representations. For example, consider the following explanation of the results of the opaque-barrier test—one which does not invoke an understanding of attention. Given that chimpanzees possess a strong propensity to follow gaze, it seems quite plausible to suppose that this system is modulated by general learning mechanisms. Thus, with sufficient experience following the gaze of others in the real world, these animals may quickly learn how 'gaze' interacts with objects and obstructions. In particular, they may simply learn that when they follow someone else's gaze to an opaque barrier, the space behind the barrier is no longer relevant. We have not yet tested this model against its alternatives. Instead, we offer it to illustrate that our apes' seemingly deep understanding of gaze on the opaque barrier test deserves as much critical scrutiny as was brought to bear on their initial performances on the seeing/not seeing tests. Furthermore, it highlights the broader (and often overlooked) point that so-called 'positive' results in studies of chimpanzee cognition are rarely held to the same level of scrutiny as are so-called 'negative' results.

Beyond seeing: a broader look at social understanding in chimpanzees

It would be misleading to leave matters at this. After all, if this were the sum total of our knowledge of chimpanzees' understanding of mental states, it might only suggest that their species conceives of visual perception in a very different manner from our own (for a range of possibilities, see Povinelli and Eddy 1996a, Chapter 6). Although this would be interesting in its own right, other aspects of our research, as well as research from other laboratories, reveals a far more intriguing picture. Below, we briefly summarize a few other projects concerning chimpanzees' understanding of pointing, attention-getting behaviors, intentional versus accidental actions, the intentions of partners during acts of cooperation, and knowledge and belief. It is our judgement that, in those cases where they have been allowed to choose from an appropriate range of alternatives, chimpanzees have elected not to have their social understanding be subsumed under the rubric of 'theory of mind'.

Comprehending pointing

It did not escape our notice that the ability of chimpanzees to use their gestures to 'choose' among people or objects might, by itself, suggest that they understand something about the mental lives of others. Let us begin by asking a seemingly simple question: do chimpanzees gesture in ways that convince us that they are attending to the psychological states of others? Consider the case of pointing. If we ignore for the moment the question of whether chimpanzees display the same topographic form of the pointing gesture as humans (index finger extension), several general statements can be made. First, none of the long-term field studies of chimpanzee social behavior have reported evidence that this species exhibits pointing as part of their natural gestural repertoire (e.g. Goodall 1986; Nishida 1970), nor have more focused investigations of chimpanzee development reported the emergence of such gestures (Plooij 1978; Tomasello *et al.* 1994). However, chimpanzees do possess one gesture (*holding out a hand*; Bygott 1979) that structurally resembles pointing—although it does not appear to be used as a generalized indicating or referencing device, but rather appears to be used for the purpose of food-begging, solicitations for bodily contact, or as a means of recruiting allies during conflicts (Goodall 1986; de Waal 1982).

On the other hand, there is agreement that captive chimpanzees exhibit the kinds of gestures depicted in Figs 2.6 and 2.7, which are often accompanied by gaze-alternation between the desired object and the communicative partner (Call and Tomasello 1994; Gómez 1991; Krause and Fouts 1997; Leavens *et al.* 1996; Povinelli and Eddy 1996*a*; Povinelli *et al.* 1992; Savage-Rumbaugh 1986; Woodruff and Premack 1979). However, there is considerable disagreement about the nature of the psychological processes that shape and attend these behaviors. Some researchers have leaned heavily on the argument by analogy and have concluded that the degree of similarity between human and chimpanzee communicative gestures is so great that the psychological processes underwriting and attending them must also be similar. (For a particularly straightforward statement of this position as applied to the question of whether chimpanzees 'point', see Leavens *et al.* 1996). In contrast, other researchers have remained more skeptical (see below).

We believe that the best available evidence supports the conclusion that chimpanzees do not interpret the pointing-like gestures of themselves or others in the manner that we do. Despite previous claims that chimpanzees comprehend the referential aspect of pointing (e.g. Call and Tomasello 1994; Menzel 1974; Povinelli *et al.* 1992), more recent studies, which have controlled for the distance between the pointing hand and the potential hiding locations have revealed that, unlike 2-year-old human children, chimpanzees use simple distance-based cues to guide their searches. For example, we experimentally explored what our chimpanzees understood about pointing by teaching our seven apes (across dozens of trials) to pick a box to which their caregiver pointed (for a complete description of these experiments, see Povinelli *et al.* 1997*b*). Initially, they learned that if they opened the box to which the experimenter pointed (see Fig. 2.14(a)), they would discover a food reward inside. There was no reward inside the other box.

After training the apes to exploit our pointing gestures in this manner, we considered several alternative ways in which they might understand what they were doing. One set of possibilities (the 'referential comprehension' model) was that the apes understood the idea of reference all along, but either just needed some experience in order to apply it in this particular context, or were just distracted by certain procedural aspects of the

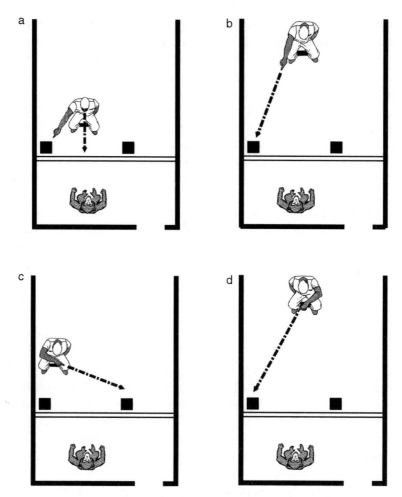

Figure 2.14 (a) training and (b)–(d) testing configurations used to assess whether chimpanzees appreciate pointing as a referential gesture, or whether they interpret the gesture as a local physical cue to locate a hidden reward.

test. However, an alternative set of possibilities (the 'physical cue' model) was that the apes learned either a distance-based rule such as, 'Open the box closest to the caregiver's hand' or a local-cue rule such as, 'Open the box+finger/hand configuration'. The referential comprehension and physical cue model implied very different things about what our apes understood about the pointing gesture. The referential model implied that they understood at least the proto-declarative aspects of the gesture (i.e. that the experimenter was 'commenting' on the location gesturally). In contrast, the physical cue model (both the distance- and local-cue model variants) implied that the apes were simply exploiting the gesture as a physical cue to locate the box that contained the reward.

We pitted these general models against each other by confronting our apes, as well as 2- to 3-year-old children, with numerous configurations of an experimenter pointing to one of two boxes. In the first study, we simply moved the experimenter's hand away from the correct box to a position 120 cm from the correct box and 150 cm from the incorrect box (see Fig. 2.14(b)). If the local-cue model were correct, the subjects' performances ought to fall apart. On the other hand, both the referential understanding and cue-distance model predicted continued success. The chimpanzees' reactions were telling. First, on the easy trials, where the experimenter's hand was just 5 cm from the correct box, the apes had no difficulty whatsoever in selecting the correct location. In contrast, when the experimenter's hand was 120 cm away from the correct box, five of the seven animals selected the boxes at random—despite the fact that on every trial they looked directly at the experimenter before making a choice. In other words, simply moving the experimenter's hand further away from the box crippled the ability of most of our apes to locate the food.

Interestingly, however, two of our apes (Kara and Apollo) continued to perform well. But did they do so because they were using a rule about choosing the box closest to the experimenter's hand (the explanation offered by the cue-distance model), or because they understood the gesture as a declarative act communicating the location of the food (the explanation offered by the referential comprehension model)?

In order to tentatively choose between the cue-distance and referential understanding models, we constructed a number of new configurations for both the apes and a group of 26-month-old children. Two of the most relevant cases are depicted in Fig. 2.14(c)–(d). In one case, the experimenter's pointing gesture was clearly directed at one of the boxes, but the tip of his index finger was positioned equidistant between the two boxes (Fig. 2.14(d)). In the other case, the finger/hand of the experimenter was actually closer to the *incorrect* box, even though he was clearly referencing the correct box (Fig. 2.14(c)). The results provided unambiguous support for the cue-distance model. Despite the fact that they glanced at the experimenter before responding on virtually every trial, the apes (including Kara and Apollo) consistently chose the box that was closest to the experimenter's hand—regardless of what box was being referenced. Furthermore, when the pointing gesture was equidistant from the two boxes, but nonetheless clearly referenced only one of the boxes, all of our apes chose randomly. In contrast, 26-month-old children performed excellently even in the most difficult conditions. It is important to note that previous studies (including some of our own) which had suggested that nonhuman primates might understand the referential aspect of pointing did not employ the kind of controls that could rule out either the local-cue or cue-distance models that were implicated in the experiments just described (examples of such previous claims can be found in the following sources: Call and Tomasello 1994; Menzel 1974; Povinelli *et al.* 1992).

How, then, can we account for the incontrovertible evidence of pointing-like gestures in captive chimpanzees? We propose that chimpanzees construct pointing-like gestures from their existing behavioral repertoire (such as 'holding out a hand') precisely because humans consistently respond to these behaviors in a manner that the chimpanzees themselves neither understand nor intend (see Povinelli and O'Neill 2000; Povinelli *et al.*, in press). Indeed, it is easy to imagine how through their interactions with humans, apes might come to develop a gesture that looks similar to pointing. But this is really simply skirting the more central point, which is far more sobering: because chimpanzees possess several natural gestures that involve arm extensions (e.g. goal-directed reaching, food begging, ally recruitment), and because humans automatically interpret such gestures mentalistically, it is hard to imagine the circumstances under which captive chimpanzees would *not* develop a gesture that structurally resembles pointing—regardless of how they understood it. Indeed, a similar process may be at work in the development of pointing early in human infancy (e.g. Desrochers *et al.* 1995; Kaye 1982; Leung and Rheinghold 1981; Povinelli *et al.*, in press *a*; Vygotsky 1962). However, by 18–24 months human infants may 'redescribe' these gestures in light of their developing theory of mind (e.g. Karmiloff-Smith 1992). Indeed, if these developments in social understanding are unique to humans, then even the gestures of chimpanzees which strongly resemble pointing may never be understood in a similar manner.[6] The fact that captive chimpanzees do not produce these gestures for their chimpanzee peers, but rather restrict them to their interactions with humans, would seem to be additional evidence to support this view.

Attention-getting behavior

Anyone who has spent a significant amount of time around chimpanzees (or dogs or cats, for that matter) will be familiar with the fact that animals know how to get your attention. For example, if you are passing out juice to our apes, and are focused on one of them in particular, the ones who are waiting have no compunctions against pulling on your shirt, tapping on the fence meshing, slapping the floor, or even making distinctive (and loud!) vocalizations—all in what are apparent attempts to get you to hurry up and give them some juice. Indeed, chimpanzees display such 'attention-getting' behaviors in much the same way as young children do, encouraging the inference that they must be reasoning about your internal attentional state. At any rate, it certainly *feels* exactly as if they are trying to redirect your attention (your mental state of attention) toward them.

---

6   Not all researchers appreciate this distinction. For example, Leavens *et al.* (1996) argue that if the final form of the gesture in chimpanzees looks identical to that found in human infants and children, then the same psychological interpretation should be applied to both species. But this view would apply to chimpanzee actors as well. For example, in the 1987 film *Project X*, Matthew Broderick plays a young air force pilot who is assigned to a top secret military escapade designed to teach apes to operate flight simulators. The star pupil, a juvenile chimpanzee named Virgil, exhibits many pointing gestures (replete with index finger extension) throughout the film—including pointing to the sky to express his life-long desire to escape 'the surly bonds of earth'.

But, here again, the ugly problem arises as to whether these behaviors indicate that the apes are reasoning strictly about your behavior ('Hey, hurry up and give me some juice!') or about both your behavior and your internal visual/attentional state ('Hey, look at me! Now, hurry up and give me some juice!'). Although this distinction may seem minor, it is exactly the difference between an organism who understands others as physical bodies and an organism who appreciates that there are minds within those bodies.

We realized we could begin to investigate this problem by confronting our chimpanzees with a single experimenter who was sometimes attentive to them and sometimes not (see Theall and Povinelli 1999). On most trials, each chimpanzee simply entered the test unit, gestured to the experimenter, and was immediately handed a food reward. On the crucial trials, however, as soon as the chimpanzee gestured, the experimenter activated a 20-second timer. During this 20-second period, the experimenter engaged in one of four behaviors. The experimenter either (1) stared directly at the subject and attempted to maintain direct eye contact; (2) made direct eye contact with the subject while engaging in slight back-and-forth movements of the head (a signal of 'attention' in chimpanzees); (3) closed their eyes and waited; or (4) looked above and behind the subject. The first two conditions can be thought of as 'attentive' cases (after all, in these cases the experimenter maintained a state of visual attention with the ape throughout the 20-second waiting period). The latter two conditions, in contrast, can be thought of as 'inattentive' cases (the experimenter was visually inattentive to the ape during the waiting period). We predicted that if the subjects appreciated the psychological differences between the experimenter's attentional states in these different conditions, they ought to display more non-visual based attention-getting behaviors (i.e. touching/slapping the experimenter, banging on the plexiglas, or vocalizing), and display them sooner, in the inattentive cases than in the attentive cases. In contrast, if the apes were simply reasoning about the relevant behavioral states and outcomes (e.g. 'She hasn't handed me any food yet'), then there ought to be no difference in the overall level or temporal patterning of gestures across the 20-second waiting periods in the two cases. And indeed, although our apes readily engaged in the relevant attention-getting behaviors (they displayed at least one such behavior on over 70 per cent of the trials), they did not exhibit more of them, longer durations of them, or display them sooner in the inattentive cases as compared to the attentive ones.

Because it has been cited by others as evidence against our view (see Whiten 1998), and because it illustrates how careful one must be in conducting this kind of research, we need to consider a similar study that was conducted by Juan-Carlos Gómez with several juvenile chimpanzees. Although a detailed report of his experiment and its results has never been published, Gómez (1994, 1996a,b) has described the study in summary format on several occasions. He constructed a situation in which his juvenile chimpanzees needed an experimenter's assistance in order to obtain a food reward. And, as in our study, Gómez varied the attentional state of the experimenter from trial to trial (e.g. eyes open versus closed). He reported that his chimpanzees engaged attention-getting behaviors on about 50 per cent of those trials when the experimenter adopted an *inattentive* posture (Gómez 1996*b*). And in seeming contrast to our findings, he reported that the proportion of *attentive* trials in which his chimpanzees used attention-getting behaviors was only 3 per cent (Gómez, personal communication, 1998). Thus, in his study, the chimpanzees appeared to display more attention-getting behavior on the inattentive trials than on the attentive ones—exactly what one would expect if they understood the differing mental state of the experimenter on the attentive and inattentive trials.

How can we account for the apparent discrepancy between our findings and those reported by Gómez? We believe that the key difference lies in a crucial methodological flaw in Gómez's study. On *inattentive* trials, the experimenter did not respond to the chimpanzee's initial request for food (after all, they did not know that request had been made), and thus the apes frequently went on to engage in additional behaviors. In contrast, according to Gómez (1996*b*), on *attentive* trials 'the human was looking at the chimpanzee and would immediately answer any request' (p. 142). Thus, on the attentive trials, *the chimpanzees were immediately handed a food reward*, thus eliminating the need for displaying any further gestures—attention-getting or otherwise! In short, the experimental design employed by Gomez was simply incapable of distinguishing between whether the higher levels of attention-getting behaviors on the inattentive trials occurred because the apes appreciated that the experimenter was visually disconnected from them, or simply because they were not being handed a food reward! Our study, in contrast, equated the amount of time the chimpanzees were waiting in the inattentive and attentive trials. And, when this control was employed, the chimpanzees indicated once again that although they are quite sensitive to the behavior of others, they do not seem to interpret this behavior in mentalistic terms.

Distinguishing intended from unintended actions

Like our understanding of attention, the distinction between intended and unintended (accidental or inadvertent) behavior is a core aspect of our human folk psychology. Indeed, it appears to be a distinction that is appealed to even in cultures very different from our own (see Povinelli and Godfrey 1993). Do chimpanzees similarly interpret actions as being based upon underlying intentions, and hence distinguish between intended and unintended behavior? We investigated this by having our apes request juice or food from two strangers. After several successful interactions with each person, we staged one of two events, each associated with one of the strangers. One of the strangers accidentally spilled the juice intended for the ape, whereas the other slowly and deliberately poured the juice onto the floor (or, in another experiment, ate the food themselves). We wanted to know if, despite the fact that they failed to receive food from both of the strangers, the animals would distinguish between the two categories of action. After all, one had poured out the juice intentionally, the other had done so accidentally. When it came to the critical trials in which they had to select one of the two strangers to give them more juice, the chimpanzees did not avoid the one who had previously poured out the juice intentionally. Young children, in contrast, begin to make such distinctions by about three years of age (e.g. Shultz *et al.* 1980; Yuill 1984). Using quite different procedures, other researchers have also obtained evidence which suggests that chimpanzees may not draw on underlying intentions in judgements of accidental versus deliberate outcomes (Call and Tomasello 1998).

Cooperating with others

Partially as a result of Meredith Crawford's (1937, 1941) early work in Robert Yerkes' laboratory, chimpanzees have gained a reputation as being able to intentionally cooperate with each other. And, indeed, there can be little doubt that many primates can and do cooperate with each other in both natural and captive settings (e.g. Boesch 1994). However, although he did not state so explicitly, of interest to Crawford was whether the cooperating animals appreciated each other as psychological agents. In Crawford's (1937) first project, pairs of chimpanzees were trained to pull separate ropes to retrieve a box that was too heavy to manage alone. Although it is often overlooked, just to achieve this result required an extensive amount of training. Slowly, however, the animals began to attend to each other, and after about 50 sessions or so, they began watching each other, eventually even exhibiting limited instances of touching each other when one of them wandered 'off task'. But was this evidence that they understood the intentional state of the partner, or was it another instance of chimpanzees reasoning about each other's behavior?

Recently, we explored these possibilities in a study with our apes (see Povinelli and O'Neill 2000). After training two 'expert' apes to cooperate on the rope-pulling task, we then paired them (on several occasions), one by one, with familiar peers who were ignorant about the nature of the task. The results of this study, perhaps more so than any others we have obtained, were extraordinary. There was not a single instance in which one of the expert apes attempted to direct the attention of the ignorant animals to the relevant features of the task. It is not that the expert apes were oblivious to the fact that the other animal needed to be near the ropes; they looked at their naive partners at levels far exceeding the frequency with which their naive partners looked at them. Indeed, there were a number of noteworthy occasions on which the naive partner approached and inspected the ropes, causing the expert partner to rush forward and pull the rope that she typically used, while at the same time completely ignoring the other apes' actions! The expert partners appeared to realize that another animal needed to be near the ropes, but not that the other ape possessed his or her own subjective understanding of the situation. Young children appear to develop an appreciation of such states in their cooperative partners by about two or three years of age (e.g. Brownell and Carriger 1990).

Knowledge and belief

Given that an appreciation of the simple aspects of attention and intention appears to be among the earlier-emerging aspects of the 'human' theory of mind, it would seem unlikely (based on the evidence examined thus far) that chimpanzees develop an under-standing of even more advanced mental states, such as knowledge and belief. Consistent with this idea, several reassessments of early studies of chimpanzees' understanding of knowledge and ignorance (e.g. Povinelli *et al.* 1990; Premack 1988) have indicated that these results may have been the result of the animals' reasoning about observable con-tingencies, as opposed to the mental states of knowledge or belief (see Povinelli 1994; Povinelli and Eddy 1996*a*; Sober 1998). Indeed, in a recent (and particularly well-con-trolled) investigation, Call and Tomasello (1999) tested chimpanzees and orangutans for their understanding of false belief. This investigation offered compelling evidence that, despite their ability to understand the procedural aspects of the task, these animals were not able to represent other individuals as agents who possess mistaken beliefs—the so-called acid test for a theory of mind (e.g. Bennett 1978; Dennett 1978; Harman 1978; Wimmer and Perner 1983).

The reinterpretation hypothesis: an alternative to the argument by analogy

Having just explained why we believe that humans and chimpanzees possess very dif-ferent ways of conceiving of the social world, we now offer our account of how this seemingly counter-intuitive situation may have evolved.

To begin, we need to emphasize the fact that, although there are profound psycholog-ical differences between humans and chimpanzees, there can be absolutely no doubt that chimpanzees are alert, thinking organisms, who are finely attuned to the complex-ities of the social and physical universe that unfolds around them. Simply because their minds differ from ours in some rather profound ways, does not imply that chimpanzees are 'black boxes' (as the behaviorists would have it), devoid of internal mental represen-tations. Quite the contrary. Chimpanzees, like most animals, should be regarded as cognitive creatures—organisms whose senses receive information about the world and whose brains translate that information into a neural code that reduces and 'represents' the external world in a way that can later be used to support their behavior. Thus, any discussion of the 'psychology' of chimpanzees must begin with an unwavering affirmation that they are cognitive creatures.

Of course, we recognize that our general reader may be somewhat puzzled at this point. On the one hand, we argue that chimpanzees are thinking organisms who share similar behaviors with us. On the other hand, we seem to be making the unsettling claim that the spontaneous behavioral similarities between humans and chimpanzees do not, by themselves, provide evidence for similar psychological states. We shall now offer a theoretical defense for both of these claims.

Reinterpreting existing behaviors

The reinterpretation hypothesis begins by arguing that complex social behavior does not have its origins in psychological skills related to reasoning about mental states.

Indeed, our position concerning the relation between complex social behavior and theory of mind can be summed up in the form of two general claims. First, only a small amount of social cognition involves reasoning about mental states, and second, the ability to reason about mental states evolved long *after* most of the complex mammalian (and specifically primate) social behaviors had already emerged.

In effect, we are proposing that complex social behaviors evolved independently of the ability to reason about mental states. We envision two broad phases of primate social evolution. First, we imagine that much of primate social evolution was driven by fairly ancient psychological processes, coupled with selection for certain physiological, attentional, behavioral, and morphological structures subserving these social behaviors. Thus, in our model, the behavioral forms that primatologists are fond of calling deception, empathy, grudging, and even reconciliation, all evolved and were in full operation long before there were any organisms that could interpret these behaviors in mentalistic terms. In short, these behaviors did not evolve because our earliest mammalian and primate ancestors possessed the means of representing the minds of their fellow group mates. Rather, these behaviors evolved because they became inevitable as selection honed psychological–behavioral systems to maximize each group member's inclusive fitness. Unlike proponents of the so-called social intelligence hypothesis (see below), we do not suppose that the psychological demands of living in a social group required an understanding of the psychology of other group members. On the contrary, we suspect that, in the thick of social interactions, reasoning about the *behavior* of other group members would work quite well (and probably better) than reasoning about their behavior *and* their mental states.

The second phase of psychological evolution relevant to social behavior may have been restricted to the human lineage. For any number of reasons (some of which we discuss below), it is possible that, as our lineage was evolving an ability to represent the mental states of others, we did not shed our ancestral psychological systems that were designed for reasoning about the behavioral propensities of others. Rather, we believe that our new psychological systems for representing and explaining already-existing behaviors in terms of mental states were woven in alongside these ancestral systems. Thus, the reinterpretation model posits that most of the basic behavioral patterns present in our ancestors (as well as the psychological mechanisms for producing them) remained undisturbed by the evolution of theory of mind. What really changed was that for the first time these behaviors were explicitly interpreted in light of an explanatory system we now call 'theory of mind.'

The evolution of social cognition revisited
In order to fully appreciate how the reinterpretation model stands in contrast to the argument by analogy, it is necessary to consider more traditional ideas about the connection between the evolution of complex social behavior, on the one hand, and social understanding (theory of mind) on the other. Indeed, the reinterpretation model stands in contrast to much previous formal and informal thinking about the connection

between social complexity and theory of mind. The traditional *informal* reasoning has gone something like this: '*How could chimpanzees—especially chimpanzees!—exhibit the remarkably sophisticated social behaviors so eloquently described by Jane Goodall (1971, 1986), Frans de Waal (1982, 1989, 1996) and others, without possessing a fairly firm understanding of others as psychological agents?*' Such reasoning is understandable. After all, the social world of primates is one in which dominance status, recent positive or negative interactions, and complicated and shifting alliances all play major roles in determining what should be done next. Witness, for example, the persuasive appeal of the well-documented evidence of deception in nonhuman primates (e.g. Byrne and Whiten 1991; de Waal 1982, 1986, 1992; Whiten 1996; Whiten and Byrne 1988). In particular, Richard Byrne and Andrew Whiten have championed using unplanned observations of spontaneous, naturally-occurring instances of deception as evidence of 'mindreading' (theory of mind) in chimpanzees and other nonhuman primates. In order to deceive others, they have argued, you need to create a mistaken belief in their heads—something that is only possible if you can conceive of such things as 'beliefs' in the first place. Although these researchers admit that some anecdotes can be explained in terms familiar to classical learning theorists, they maintain that many of these anecdotes are best explained by assuming that the animals are reasoning about the mental states of each other (Byrne and Whiten 1991).

This kind of informal thinking has encouraged the more formal proposal that theory of mind skills evolved hand-in-hand with increasing social complexity—what has come to be known as the 'social intelligence hypothesis'. The earliest statements of the social intelligence hypothesis were offered by Alison Jolly (1966) and Nicholas Humphrey (1976), who attempted to link the evolution of primate intelligence with the need to reason about inherently social problems. Nicholas Humphrey (1976, 1980), in particular, argued that the need to reason about the social maneuverings of other group mates might have honed an ability in primates to reason about each other's mental states (their beliefs, intentions, and desires)—leading them to become what he termed 'natural psychologists'. More recently, a number of authors have made this claim more explicit in the context of arguing that abilities related to theory of mind evolved specifically to cope with problems created by living in large groups (see, for example, Baron-Cohen 1995; Byrne 1995). The idea goes something like this:

> Given that humans use their understanding of mental states to predict the behavior of others, and given that many other highly social mammals (especially nonhuman primates) also need to predict each other's behavior, theory of mind would be an extremely useful ability for them to have. It would thus seem to follow that those species with the most complex forms of social behavior would also have the most well-developed theory of mind.

To a greater or lesser degree, much previous thinking about the evolution of theory of mind has hovered around the idea that it evolved as a means to allow for novel and more sophisticated social behaviors. Indeed, some researchers and theorists believe that once social living became widespread among primates, evolution had no real alternative but to construct a psychological system for making inferences about other minds. Some, such as Jerry Fodor (1983), argue that our theory of mind skills evolved precisely because they provide us with a powerful, easy-to-use theory for understanding and predicting the behavior of others—'…exactly what we need when we are in the thick of a social situation' (p. 24), asserts Simon Baron-Cohen. Indeed, Baron-Cohen (1995) goes on to suggest that:

> Mindreading [theory of mind] is good for a number of important things, including social understanding, behavioral prediction, social interaction, and communication. The lack of competitive alternatives to mindreading that could produce equal or better success…makes it clearer why natural selection might have latched onto mindreading as an adaptive solution to the problem of predicting behavior and sharing information. I mean, what other real choice did Nature have? (p. 30.)

The idea, then, is simple. Rather than reasoning about the behavior of others (a process frequently caricatured as unparsimonious, cumbersome, or unwieldy), evolution selected for a 'simpler' ability to reason about the mental states of others. But, of course, such reasoning would seem to imply that theory of mind skills ought to be widespread among the social primates. The fact that the best available evidence suggests that not even chimpanzees possess an appreciation of mental states would seem to raise some serious problems for this idea.

Social intelligence without theory of mind

As we have seen, many theorists find it implausible to suppose that the complex social dynamics of chimpanzees and other nonhuman primates could be successfully carried out by psychological systems which reason strictly about behavioral propensities. We now offer some evidence that such systems (whether parsimonious or not) can be quite feasibly implemented, and can reproduce the detailed social dynamics characteristic of primate social groups. To do so, we turn our attention to a particular computer simulation of chimpanzee social dynamics called *ChimpWorld*, designed and built by Lucian Hughes (1993). We do so in order to explore how realistic simulations of chimpanzee societies may emerge from autonomous agents which make sophisticated decisions, but which possess no theory of mind. These agents can be thought of as having minds (after all, they harbor 'internal' representations of the external world), but not theories of mind.[7]

ChimpWorld simulates chimpanzee society by modeling individual chimpanzees as independent artificial intelligence programs and then allowing social behavior to emerge from their unprogrammed interactions. To an observer, *ChimpWorld* appears on the computer monitor as if one were watching a group of chimpanzees from about 10 feet up, through a window. These artificial chimpanzees are observed in three-dimensional

---

7 The following description of *ChimpWorld* is derived from an unpublished manuscript by Povinelli and Hughes (1993). Much of the discussion is provided in far greater detail in Hughes (1993).

animation (derived from film footage of real chimpanzees) as they engage in the signature activities of real chimpanzees—mating, foraging, resting, making friends, grooming, threatening, etc. *ChimpWorld* offers a number of interface tools which allows the user to record what happens, to create experimental situations, and to view the on-line internal state of each of the chimpanzees' 'minds' (the current values of a number of parameters of the autonomous programs). It is possible to place as many chimpanzees of different ages and sexes as one wishes into a scene, as well as to place food resources in various locations in various quantities.

The chimpanzees are generated by cloning them from an ideal chimpanzee, with standard forms for males, females, and particular personality types. One of the most important points about *ChimpWorld* is that each chimpanzee operates autonomously in a turn-taking fashion. First, a given agent scans the *ChimpWorld* universe and categorizes the world into increasingly complex terms (e.g. a female chimpanzee named Megan perceives instances of the concepts 'male', 'ally', 'ally-nearby', 'male-soliciting-female', 'ally-near-male-soliciting-female', etc.). Next, it arrives at a set of plans that it could in principle execute given the agents, situations, and objects that it has just registered. The actual list of objects and events that each agent might encounter is extensive, and each agent has at its disposal over 70 plans available for use. When implemented in combination, the actual number of possible unique chains of behaviors increases in a factorial fashion. From this, the agent then decides what to do.

But faced with so many possibilities, how do these chimpanzees actually decide what to do? Each agent is equipped with a motivation system which boils down to an evaluative criteria by which it can judge the value or worth of a particular plan, goal, or event in a given context. To explore a simple example, the physical energy cost of actually moving around (reflected motivationally in *ChimpWorld* by 'fatigue') acts as a criterion by which a chimpanzee can select among different routes to a food source. The shorter route is valued more highly because it will cost less in terms of 'fatigue'. Thus, motivational assessment influences the selection of various plans. Similarly, two contemplated food site goals (e.g. 'banana stand' or 'fig tree') will be ranked in worth relative to their respective abilities to reduce 'hunger' (ultimately determined by the energy content of the food source). By the same token, the chimpanzee agents will attend to the activity of other agents according to the fear or aggression they elicit (which are determined by the value systems of 'prestige', 'political fear', and 'aggression'). For example, the alpha male's activity is almost always of interest to nearby subordinates. Thus, *ChimpWorld* agents express their values through a complex set of motivations, which determine interesting events for attention, help to determine their goals, and ultimately select appropriate plans. These proximate motivations thus shape the fundamental behavior of the agent.

The value systems of the artificial chimpanzee agents were constructed in such a fashion as to capture as much of natural chimpanzee motivation as possible. They include the value of physical energy (with motivations of 'hunger' and 'fatigue'), reproductive fitness (with motivation of 'libido'), political struggles for material resources such as food and mates (with motivations of 'material fear', 'material aggression'), political struggles for dominance itself (with motivations of 'political aggression' or 'ambition', 'political fear'), and finally, alliance politics (with motivations of 'collective prestige', 'bonding', 'political fear', and 'aggression'). The hierarchical structure of a *ChimpWorld* agent begins at the level of its broad value systems, and descends through its proximate motivations, down to the level of its plans and goals.

It is important to realize that each agent has independent and dynamic goals. That is, the agents do not possess a fixed and unchanging ranking of goals (e.g. a 'goal tree'). Instead, the relative ranking of each potential goal at any given moment depends on dynamic variables such as current motivational state (i.e. food is valued to the extent that the chimpanzee is actually hungry) and the current range of available resources (i.e. what foods are actually within travel distance). In this sense, *ChimpWorld* is in no way analogous to a production of a play. Instead, it is more like an improvisation company in the sense that although many of the same lines and gestures will be reused from one performance to the next, each performance will be unique because there is no script to follow. Each actor will respond to the behavior of others depending upon the exact mood or thought that is elicited at that particular moment in time.

Naturally, a given act by *ChimpWorld* agents is not a simple expression of a single motivation. Chimpanzees in the real world do not go to food sources simply because they are hungry. Likewise, *ChimpWorld* agents are constantly faced with tradeoffs and interactions among their various motivations. An agent deciding which of two distant food sources should be visited may opt for the less rich one because it is closer, or perhaps because a political rival of greater dominance is near the richer site. Alternatively, if that rival is present, but allies of the agent are also within recruiting distance, then the interactions of the motivations may lead to the adoption of the plan to travel to the richer site after all. In a different example, a normally fearful subordinate may resist a superior's attempt to take its food because the added value of the food makes resistance worthwhile, or perhaps because allies are nearby and the potential success of resistance may increase the prestige of the agent.

It should be obvious from the above description that *ChimpWorld* agents are sophisticated artificial intelligence programs which simulate many aspects of chimpanzee behavior and interact with each other to produce realistic simulations of chimpanzee societies. Like real chimpanzees, these programs contain a number of motivations which, after several cost-benefit calculations, prompt a wide range of realistic chimpanzee behaviors. Through a number of experiments which manipulated variables such as food resource distribution, number of males, number of estrous females, personality types, etc., Hughes (1993) was able to demonstrate that chimpanzee-like social structures emerge from the artificial agents' deployment of their low-level plans.

For our purposes, the most instructive point about *ChimpWorld* is that its agents can be thought of as creatures with minds—that is, they possess simulated goals, motivations, plans, and knowledge, and they continually update and modify these desires and beliefs on the basis of their previous actions (as well as new information obtained by their simulated perceptual senses), but they do not have access to (or representations of) the plans and knowledge possessed by the other agents. In short, each individual artificial chimpanzee can be thought of as having a mind, but no 'theory of mind'. This point is especially poignant in light of the fact that Hughes' (1993) original plans for *ChimpWorld* called for designing chimpanzee agents with the capacity to reason about each other's mental states. However, this procedure never became necessary. Agents which did not explicitly represent the beliefs of others were able to generate the social complexity necessary to provide a realistic approximation of chimpanzee political struggles (see Hughes 1993).[8]

It is worth noting that more recent efforts are underway to model dynamic primate social interactions which are more informed by what is known about primate brain architecture, and in particular, the interaction among specific brain regions. For example, Alan Bond, of the California Institute of Technology, has recently described and implemented a new class of information-processing models for primate social agents (Bond 1996, in press *a*, in press *b*). In his models, the primate brain is represented as a set of specialized areas, each with its own spatial localization and clustered inter-connectivities. These brain regions are envisioned and implemented as two hierarchies: a perception hierarchy and a planning and action hierarchy—with interconnections between the two. The perception hierarchy can be thought of as data representing external situations (ascending from the particular to the increasingly general). Likewise, the planning and action hierarchy is constructed so as to represent increasingly general situations, plans, and controls. Together, this perception–action hierarchy (designed as a system model of the primate brain and implemented through predicate logic expressions and inference rules) can be shown to successfully reproduce coherent behavioral states which change dynamically on time-scales of the order of just a few hundred milliseconds. Again, the significant point for our purposes is that complex, social behavioral patterns, which involve dynamic interactions among particular agents, can be simulated in a system which represents the behavior, but not the minds of other group members.

Although computer simulations cannot provide a principled answer to the question of whether real, flesh-and-blood chimpanzees reason about each others' mental states, they do shed some light on one of the central claims of the reinterpretation model; namely, that living in social groups may have selected for increasingly sophisticated abilities to reason about the past, present, and future behavior of other group members, without necessarily selecting for an ability to reason about the mental states of other group members. In short, these simulations offer clues as to how social complexity might be generated by psychological systems which do not reason about mental states.

---

8   The programming procedures necessary for such systems have already been outlined and implemented (e.g. Maida *et al.* 1991). Indeed, it is of direct interest to us that simulations of a class of problems involving one agent recovering from a mistaken belief about an object to which another has referred, have shown that there is no need for the agents to represent each other's beliefs in order to recover from the error (Maida 1992; Maida and Tang 1996).

These simulations expose the weakness of Baron-Cohen's (1995) assumption that Nature had no alternative but to select for theory of mind. Nature most certainly did have an alternative—to continue to hone the ability to reason about behavior. And, more broadly, one of the central claims of the reinterpretation hypothesis is that the notion that theory of mind is the only useful way of coping with social problems may simply be an illusion created by psychological abilities unique to our species—the very same illusion which makes the argument by analogy seem so compelling.

Implications for the causal role of second-order mental states

The reinterpretation proposal has deep, and somewhat disturbing implications for understanding both human and chimpanzee behavior. In the case of humans, for example, it suggests that we may have a far less accurate view of the relation between our mental states and our behavior than we are inclined to think. After all, because the ancestral systems were not discarded as we evolved theory of mind abilities, humans may have been left in the philosophically awkward position of having multiple psychological causes for the same behaviors—only some of which penetrate into the highest levels of our conscious experience. Indeed, we suspect that most of the ancient psychological mechanisms which drive our moment-to-moment behaviors do not intrude into our reflective conscious experience, and therefore we are frequently left to misdiagnose the psychological causes of our behaviors.

Thus one of the central implications of the reinterpretation hypothesis is that introspection is poorly suited to reveal the exact causal structure between our conscious psychological states and our overt behaviors. In the case of gaze-following, for example, introspection may lead us to conclude that our representation of the other person's mental state of attention plays at least a necessary role in causing us to turn and follow his or her gaze. Although we would not deny that this may be true in some cases, we would forcefully challenge the claim that such representations *always* play this kind of 'but for' role in the generation of the gaze-following response. Indeed, in this particular case, we would even question whether such representations *usually* play this kind of causal role. The most important point, though, is that introspection may not be the right tool for separating those cases in which our representations of mental states play a direct causal role in generating our behavior, from those cases in which they do not. Furthermore, even if our ability to introspect could (on certain occasions) accurately determine that such states played at least *some* causal role in generating our behavior, we doubt whether this ability could isolate the exact nature of that role. Humans are well-known for their proclivity in generating rapid, after-the-fact (indeed, sometimes impossible) explanations for their actions. The reinterpretation hypothesis argues not simply that introspection is the wrong tool for recovering the correct causal relation between mental states and behavior, but that its inadequacy in this regard derives precisely from the fact that the ability to describe behaviors in mentalistic terms evolved well after those behaviors were already up and running and being generated by other psychological mechanisms unrelated to the representation of mental states.

An example may help us to illustrate our model by showing how other systems which possess higher-order representations (akin to second-order mental states) co-vary with, but frequently play no *direct* causal role in the production of a given behavior. (For a detailed treatment of this example, see Povinelli and Giambrone, in press.) For example, we can think of a speedometer as a device which represents, but does not directly cause, the motion of a system comprised of an automobile and its driver (here-after, we will simply refer to this as 'the automotive system'). We wish to make several points about this example. First, note that prior to the installation of a speedometer, the automotive system possessed a wide range of behavioral propensities (accelerating/ decelerating, starting/stopping, traveling along an infinite series of paths, etc.). Furthermore, installing a speedometer did not eliminate or fundamentally alter this initial set of behavioral propensities, nor did it suddenly endow the system with a wide array of new propensities. And, to think about it another way, the behavioral propensities of the system would not suddenly change if at some later time-point the speedometer was removed. After all, the relevant behavioral propensities were established by design constraints of the system that were in place long before the speedometer was installed.

But if a speedometer does not endow the automotive system with a variety of fundamentally new basic behaviors (behaviors that were impossible without this representational device), one may reasonably ask why it would be installed in the first place. The answer, of course, is that although the speedometer would not immediately lead to (or directly cause) the appearance of new basic units of behavior, its introduction would undoubtedly have indirect (but not negligible) effects on the timing, efficiency, organization, and interactions of the already-existing set of the automotive system's behavioral propensities. Just to use one example, prior to the addition of the speedometer it was certainly possible (at least in principle) to drive a specified distance in a specified period of time. However, a speedometer would make such an achievement easier, and perhaps even practical. Now, to be sure, one might wish to label this a 'new' behavior. But this does not detract from the central point which is that the new behavioral possibilities would be composed out of ancestral basic behavioral elements, thus making it difficult to characterize them as completely novel.

In order to appreciate the implications of this example for the case of the evolution of theory of mind (or second-order mental states), consider the following scenario. Imagine that in a particular community of automobiles, speedometers are added into some automotive systems but not others. Your assignment is to follow around all of the automotive systems in the community (without looking inside them), and then report back on which ones possess the speedometers and which ones do not. We expect that this would be an exceedingly tricky task. Indeed, no matter how certain you felt about your observational data and the conclusions you derived from them, we suspect that you would have a very difficult time persuading a naive audience that some of the automobiles possessed a special representational device that the others did not. After all, the automotive systems all look more or less the same, and they all exhibit the same set of basic behaviors. In contrast, imagine how easy it would be to make the very same discrimination if you were allowed to take all of the automobiles out to a racetrack and conduct a simple experiment with them. One by one, you tell each automobile to accelerate to exactly 60 km per hour. Obviously, all of the automobiles are capable of traveling at 60 km per hour, but only some have a special device that makes this behavior practical on demand without some kind of explicit training. We suspect that in very short order you would have the automobiles correctly sorted. The implications of this example for the use of naturalistic versus experimental data for making inferences about whether chimpanzees reason about mental states should be obvious.

As we have seen, the introduction of an explicit representation of 'speed' into the automotive system may not have immediately led to a noticeable expansion of behavioral patterns. However, over long periods of time, the operation of this new representational device might well have consequences in other areas. For example, the introduction of speedometers might indirectly lead to the invention of new social institutions such as speed limits, as well as entire bureaucratic structures dedicated to enforcing these new limits. Indeed, we believe that our species' ability to reason about mental states have indirectly resulted in the enormous differences between humans and chimpanzees in terms of material culture, ethical systems, and pedagogy (Cheney and Seyfarth 1990; Povinelli and Godfrey 1993; Premack 1984). In general, though, our example should illustrate how the addition of higher-order representations can have profound effects on a behavioral system through their indirect effects on existing behavioral propensities. The most important point is that such representations need not endow the system with a plethora of fundamentally new basic behavioral propensities in order to be extremely advantageous.

Likewise, the reinterpretation hypothesis proposes that the majority of the most tantalizing social behaviors shared by humans and other primates (deception, grudging, reconciliation) evolved and were in full operation long before humans invented the means for representing the causes of these behaviors in terms of unobservable mental states. In this sense, our reinterpretation hypothesis may be the evolutionary analog of Annette Karmiloff-Smith's (1992) concept of 'representational redescription,' which she posits as a major driving force in human cognitive development. Her proposal envisions a process in development whereby information implicitly *in* the mind is progressively recoded at increasingly explicit levels both within and across domains in ways that make this information increasingly available *to* the mind. One way of thinking about our proposal is that humans have uniquely evolved a psychological mechanism that allows for the most abstract levels of representational redescription (see Karmiloff-Smith 1992).

But if all of this is true, what causal role is left for our ability to reason about mental states? Indeed, some philosophers will already be wondering if we are advocating a form of epiphenomenalism—the idea that mental states co-exist with, but play no causal role in generating physical states such as overt behavior. To be clear, we reject the strong form of this argument. Instead, we argue that although mentalistic descriptions of behaviors may only rarely be the direct cause of the behaviors they attend, in many cases they may serve to indirectly regulate more fundamental behavioral units. In many other cases, however, they may merely be convenient (and useful) *ad hoc* descriptions of our behaviors—behaviors that both can and do occur without such descriptions.

Why evolve a theory of mind?

So far, we have refrained from offering our speculations about why only one lineage—the human one—evolved the ability to reason about mental states. As a consequence, some researchers will be unsatisfied with our account. They will want to know the exact selective forces that sculpted the human ability to reason about the mind. In short, they will want an 'adaptive scenario' for why humans, but no other primates, evolved a theory of mind.

We confess up front that we do not know the answer to this question. However, there are certain aspects of the reinterpretation hypothesis that may offer important clues. To begin, the reinterpretation hypothesis directs us away from an entire class of ideas related to the emergence of a particular and distinctive novel behavior or set of behaviors that could only have been possible by evolving a theory of mind (e.g. deception, reconciliation, cultural transmission of tool use). Our proposal shows that such ideas are too simplistic. Furthermore, if we are correct in asserting that the emergence of theory of mind was not initially associated with the appearance of new behavioral units, but rather with new efficiencies in organizing, planning, and deploying already-existing ones, then it becomes possible to see why, if mentalistic descriptions began to emerge for other reasons, selection would have acted to enhance them. If theory of mind (and related representational systems) initially offered only marginal—but not negligible—improvements in the efficiency of ancestral behaviors, then they might have rapidly come under strong selection pressures. Evolutionary biologists have long known that evolutionary novelties which are linked to even slight advantages over their alternatives can result in rapid selection, and ultimately lead to fixation of the trait in question (Fisher 1930; Haldane 1932; Wright 1931, 1932). Thus, if we are correct, once the ability to represent mental states was introduced into the human lineage, it was selected for not because it was the only means to be a successful social primate (witness the success of the myriad other social primates), but because once it was introduced into a particular lineage, it was just a bit better than its alternatives.

Although helpful, this account still begs the question of why such an ability first appeared in humans. One possibility is that, in its earliest forms, the ability was a by-product of selection for some other (perhaps more general) psychological system. Language seems like a likely candidate in this regard. At any rate, once the initial form of the ability appeared, it undoubtedly came under strong selective pressure, ultimately leading to the psychological system we call 'theory of mind.'

The end of the argument by analogy?

We began this chapter by showing how the argument by analogy had a profound influence on philosophical and scientific thinking about the mental lives of animals.

Little by little, throughout this chapter we have presented empirical and theoretical reasons to doubt the argument's validity. We now end this chapter by formally exposing its flaws.

First, recall that the argument (as applied to inferences about theory of mind in other species) is something like this:

P1 I (and other humans) exhibit bodily behaviors of type B (i.e. those normally thought to be caused by second-order mental states).

P2 Chimpanzees (and other species) exhibit bodily behaviors of type B.

P3 My own bodily behaviors (and those of other humans) of type B are usually caused by my (and other humans') second-order mental states of type A.

C   Therefore, bodily behaviors of type B exhibited by chimpanzees are caused by their second-order mental states of type A; and so, *a fortiori*, chimpanzees have second-order mental states of type A.

First, note that the argument relies heavily on its third premise (which in turns rests heavily on the accuracy of introspection). Indeed, Russell (1948) pointed out that there are actually two separate claims embedded in this premise, which when adapted to the case of second-order mental states become the following: (1) we claim to know (on the basis of something like introspection) that specific second-order mental states cause specific behaviors; and (2) we claim to know (again, through introspection) that this particular behavior is only (or at least generally) caused by this particular second-order mental state.

Now, how confident can we be of these two claims? With respect to the first claim, we are willing to accept that there may be some cases in which our second-order mental states directly cause our behaviors. We are all familiar with the experience of feeling as though our reflections on our own mental states (or those of others) directly lead us to act in a specific manner. To avoid becoming side-tracked, we are willing to grant that in at least some of these cases this introspective assessment is actually correct, and that these higher-order mental states are actually causing our behaviors.

The second claim, however, is far more dubious. It is not at all clear that introspection can confidently assure us that behaviors which are *sometimes* caused by our higher-order mental states are *usually* caused by them. This is because of the fallibility of introspection. Of course, there are a number of different ways of thinking about introspection. On one extreme, introspection is viewed as a kind perceptual faculty—one that accurately perceives the contents of our cognitive systems. On perhaps the other extreme, 'introspection' is viewed merely as a form of internal explanation (or story-telling) which is more or less simultaneous with the supposed events of the story. In this case, the explanations generated may range from sheer confabulation to relatively solid theoretical speculation. Indeed, in a related vein, some theorists have maintained that the common-sense belief that we have special, privileged access to our own first-person mental states is simply wrong (see Gopnik 1993).

We take the position that many of our self-reports about the causes of our behavior are not generated by self-observation at all, but rather by after-the-fact explanations which are constructed from our already-held, general beliefs about why we behave the way we do. Gaze-following provides an excellent example of this phenomenon. It seems likely to us that in some cases we follow the gaze of others precisely because we suddenly want to know what it is that they are looking at. In such a case, the representation of the other person's mental state may be part of a tight causal nexus leading us to turn and look where the other person is looking. But is this the typical case? Suppose, for example, you are in the middle of a conversation with a friend who suddenly glances behind you. Furthermore, suppose that you quickly follow his gaze, but then immediately return to the conversation with hardly a break at all. Now, what if you are later asked why you turned and looked away. Most likely you would confidently claim that you did so because you wanted to know what your friend was looking at. We contend that this self-report is often not derived from propositional memories of what you had earlier known through introspection, nor from a current, vivid recollection of the behavior and the mental states that purportedly attended it. Rather, we suggest that, at the time when it occurred, the behavior was generated by low-level psychological mechanisms unrelated to second-order mental states.

If we are correct that second- (or higher-) order mental states do not accompany and/or cause our behaviors nearly as often as we intuitively believe, then it directly follows that our confidence in the third premise of the argument by analogy must be substantially lowered. Similarly, our confidence in the conclusion needs to be substantially lowered.

Of course, some may argue that the third premise was overstated to begin with, and may suggest that the argument can be salvaged by simply noting that the conclusion of the argument needs to be understood as implying that the relevant chimpanzee behaviors are directly caused by second-order mental states *as much or as little as in humans.* However, to maintain this position would be to miss the central point of our analysis. After all, once one accepts the fact that behaviors which we typically think of as being caused by second-order mental states may have other, unrelated psychological causes, then the true significance of the reinterpretation hypothesis becomes glaringly apparent. Rather than dismissing the weakness of the third premise as trivial, the reinterpretation hypothesis highlights this as direct evidence for the idea that second-order mental states were added into a social fabric that already contained many or all of our most sophisticated behaviors. The fact that many of our behaviors are only sometimes directly caused by second-order mental states may be evidence in favor of the reinterpretation model's stance that human evolution featured the integration of a new psychological system into a more ancient one. *Thus, our model implies that the third premise of the argument by analogy is not simply false, it is false precisely because of the way in which second-order mental states evolved.* The bottom line is that the frequency with which human behaviors are caused (or attended) by second-order mental states may have absolutely no bearing on the probability that chimpanzees possess such mental states.

As we have just seen, the weakness in the third premise can be accounted for by the reinterpretation model. Nonetheless, we feel compelled to note that as a logical point, even if the third premise were true, the inference to the conclusion that chimpanzees possess second-order mental states would still be weak. It is an inherent aspect of arguments by analogy that their strength depends not simply on the extent of the similarities under scrutiny, but even more so on the relevance of those similarities. Likewise, of course, such arguments are weakened by relevant dissimilarities.

As we explored in the main part of this chapter, there is compelling evidence that humans and chimpanzees behave in strikingly different ways in controlled laboratory tests—that is, that they are dissimilar in ways that are relevant to the question of whether they possess second-order mental states. To begin with, their behavior reveals that they initially behave very differently from even young children. Second, the relatively slow rate of their learning, as well as the weak nature of long-term retention, are additional evidence of this dissimilarity. Importantly, there are also relevant and striking dissimilarities between humans and chimpanzees in their natural social behaviors and material culture—dissimilarities which, in the past, have been down-played for a variety of reasons (including Darwin's concern for establishing a chain of unbroken psychological continuity between humans and other animals). Finally, of course, there are obvious dissimilarities in overall brain size and brain structure as well (Preuss and Kaas 1999; Preuss *et al.* 1999). For example, humans have enlarged the overall size of the brain threefold since our divergence from the common ancestor of the great ape/human group. In contrast, modern chimpanzees may possess a brain which is not appreciably larger than the one possessed by the common ancestor of the great apes and humans. In summary, we believe that there are important, highly relevant dissimilarities between humans and chimpanzees which seriously weaken the inductive strength of the argument by analogy.

Given that scientists have known about many of the dissimilarities between humans and chimpanzees for quite some time, it is instructive to ask why they have not been emphasized. One reason, of course, is that researchers have felt that the similarities were more overwhelming—or at least more interesting. However, there is another reason as well. Because thinking in this area has been fairly informal, many theorists have conflated the argument by analogy with a somewhat different justification—namely, an argument to the best explanation. In short, although many scholars have relied on the argument by analogy, they have also felt that the inference that chimpanzees possess second-order mental states is more compelling *because there is no better explanation* for their behavior—especially because of the pervasive view that the best explanation of the behavioral similarity between humans and chimpanzees would have to maintain the intellectual continuity between humans and animals in which Darwin so fervently believed.

Reformulating the argument by analogy as an argument to the best explanation, then, turns the question around and asks, 'If chimpanzees do not possess second-order mental states (some kind of theory of mind), how else could they be generating behaviors so similar to our own?' The reinterpretation model not only answers this question, it also provides a *better* explanation (currently the best explanation), because it accounts not only for the relevant behavioral and neurobiological similarities between humans and chimpanzees, but for the relevant dissimilarities as well. Indeed, part of the point of our extended discussion of the experimental research on chimpanzee social under- standing was to make precisely this point: models which posit that chimpanzees reason about the behavioral propensities of others, not their mental states, have consistently done a better job of predicting how chimpanzees will behave in crucial experimental situations. At the same time, these models provide an account of how their natural, spontaneous social behaviors can be generated without appealing to second-order mental states. To reiterate, we believe that the reinterpretation model currently offers the best explanation for the behavioral similarities and differences that exist between humans and chimpanzees.

There is a final objection to our position that we need to address. Certain philos- ophers might concede that we have adequately defended our claim that there is no simple causal connection between second-order mental states and the behaviors that they tend to accompany. Indeed, they might go on to advance an epiphenomenalist revision of the argument by analogy. The traditional epiphenomenalist contends that both the behavior and the mental state are caused by a common third variable—a given neural state. Thus, unlike the idea that mental states interact with behavior, the epi- phenomenalist would contend that no such connection exists; the reason why certain mental states covary with certain behaviors is because both are caused by the same underlying neural state. However, a revised version of the argument by analogy (one which replaced interactionist assumptions about the connection between mental states and behavior with strictly epiphenomenalist ones) can be shown to suffer the same fate as the version of the argument that we examined earlier. After all, the epiphenomenalist must concede that to the extent that there are relevant behavioral differences between humans and chimpanzees, then there must also be different neural states which gener- ate them. And, once one concedes that there are different neural states in the two species, the floodgates are opened to the existence of different mental states.

———•———

Our exposition of the logical weakness of the argument by analogy places in a com- pletely new light all previous attempts to provide an a priori answer to the question of whether chimpanzees possess a theory of mind. The reinterpretation model reveals why each time we ask whether humans and other animals (even chimpanzees) share a common understanding of the world, we must turn to experimental studies for an answer. It is only these kinds of studies which can allow animals to express alternative ways of conceiving of the world. Not only is our *human* way of thinking about the rela- tionship between our mental states and our behavior not completely accurate, there is a significant chance that it is not the only game in town.

CHAPTER 3

CAUSALITY, TOOL USE, AND FOLK PHYSICS: A COMPARATIVE APPROACH

DANIEL J. POVINELLI

In the previous chapter, we showed how the natural, spontaneous social behavior of chimpanzees, no matter how similar it appears to our own, may be attended by very different kinds of psychological states. In this chapter, we set the stage for asking similar kinds of questions about chimpanzees' natural and spontaneous interactions with physical objects in the context of their use and manufacture of simple tools (see Chapters 4–11). We do so in two ways. First, we review the very limited experimental evidence which bears on the question of how nonhuman primates understand physical causality in the context of their use and manufacture of tools. We show how this evidence is ambiguous with respect to the question of whether or not species other than our own appeal to unobservable phenomena to assist in explaining or predicting interactions among physical objects. Second, and in contrast, we present evidence that human children, from a very early age, come to develop a folk physics which directly appeals to precisely these kinds of unobservable phenomena.

Tool use and manufacture as a window into folk physics

For over a century, we have known that a wide variety of animals are capable of using simple tools to mediate their actions on the world, typically in order to obtain food resources. Sea otters open mollusks by hammering on rocks that they place on their chests. The woodpecker finch uses small twigs to probe for insect larvae in small holes and crevices that it cannot reach directly with its beak. Even more striking, of course, is the fact that some species—such as chimpanzees and New Caledonian crows—not only use objects that they discover lying about in their natural environment, they even modify those objects in a manner that earns them the title of tool makers (e.g. Goodall 1968*b*; Hunt, 1996).

A number of authors have already reviewed the evidence for natural tool use in animals in general (Beck 1980), nonhuman primates in particular (Chevalier-Skolnikov 1989; Parker and Gibson 1979), and chimpanzees as a special case in point (McGrew 1992), and thus we shall not do so again. However, in order to provide some sense of the range of skills and activities involved, Table 3.1 offers a partial summary of some of the tool-using activities of chimpanzees that have been observed in the wild.

Table 3.1 Selected examples of tool use in wild chimpanzees.

Purpose	Examples
Extending reach	Sticks to bring food to within reach
	Sticks to knock down fruit
Probing into inaccessible areas	Stems/blades of grass for termites
	Sticks for dipping into bee hives
Weapons and displays of aggression	Shaking branches to intimidate others
	Throwing stones to intimidate or injure others
	Sticks as clubs to hit others
Amplification of force	Stones and anvils for nut-cracking
	Sticks to lever open logs or termite mounds
Sponging up liquids	Chewed up leaves as sponges to soak up water
	Leaves to wipe fecal material or blood from body

Sources: McGrew 1992; Tomasello and Call 1997.

However, despite the widespread documentation of tool use in animals, relatively little is known about how nonhuman species understand the physical or causal principles underwriting these activities (see Visalberghi and Limongelli 1996). It is possible, of course, that animals appreciate the underlying causal relations involved in tool use in virtually the same manner as humans; after all, as Euan MacPhail (1987) has noted, 'Causality is a constraint common to all ecological niches' (p. 645). On the other hand, other species may exhibit a different understanding of causality, in which case it would be instructive to know how their understandings compare with our own. Finally, it is possible that their use of tools may be devoid of any theoretical notions—perhaps based solely on the perceptually observable features of the world, without any consideration of unobservable variables such as gravity, force, space, and mass. As noted in Chapter 1, our project was designed to move beyond simple descriptions of tool use and tool making in animals, and to understand what animals, and chimpanzees in particular, know about the causal principles that effectuate their use and construction of tools.

Although it will ultimately be of interest to test a wide array of animal species for their understanding of the folk physics involved in tool use, we focus on chimpanzees because they represent a crucial test case for determining whether or not there are uniquely human aspects of folk physics. By comparing the similarities and differences between how humans and chimpanzees understand the basic causal principles that govern how objects interact with one another, we will ultimately be able to specify which kinds of understandings are restricted to the human species. (Of course, it is also possible that chimpanzees, as well as other species, may have evolved their own peculiar notions about the causal structure governing the interaction of physical objects.) To emphasize, the research we report in this book was not conducted to explore the ability, range, or even the upper limits of tool use and manufacture in our group of chimpanzees; rather, it was undertaken in an effort to explore what our seven apes—Megan, Mindy, Apollo, Jadine, Candy, Kara, and Brandy—understand about the physical principles that underlie their use and manufacture of simple tools.

Folk physics for apes?

Our project is not the first to consider what apes understand about tools. Indeed, 80 years ago, the German gestalt psychologist, Wolfgang Köhler, published a landmark excursion into chimpanzee psychology, *The Mentality of Apes*. In this work, he described experiments on tool use that he had conducted with his own group of seven chimpanzees on the island of Tenerife during the First World War. His aim was to explore how chimpanzees perceive the physical world—along with their ability to use objects to act creatively and insightfully within that world. Several generations of psychology students have now been introduced to his work—often through the photograph reproduced in Fig. 3.1. This particular photograph should be of special interest to us. After all, this is the photograph of Köhler's work that is most frequently reproduced in introductory psychology textbooks as allegedly supporting his belief that chimpanzees, like humans, are capable of 'insight learning'. Grande, the female chimpanzee who stands precariously atop her self-constructed tower of boxes, is cast (along with her peers), as an imagining agent—one who, after fumbling about foolishly for a time, is said to have suddenly and completely struck upon a novel solution to the problem of the out-of-reach bananas: 'Of course! Stack the boxes on top of each other!' As we shall see, however, this widespread interpretation of the photograph turns out to be a scientific legend—an incorrect idea based on a fundamental misunderstanding of Köhler's work.

Köhler's discovery that his chimpanzees were capable of insightful acts of both tool using and tool making was somewhat of a relief to the first generation of post-Darwinian evolutionary biologists, who found his results consistent with their master's notion of psychological continuity among species. As we saw in Chapter 2, establishing that there was complete psychological continuity among species had been a high priority for Darwin. In the case of the psychological faculties which make tool use and manufacture possible, Darwin was quick to assure his readers that tool use was well within the capacities of animals: 'It has often been said that no animal uses any tool; but the chimpanzee in a state of nature cracks a native fruit, somewhat like a walnut, with a stone' (p. 51). So much for tool use—but what about tool manufacture? Darwin was forced to at least partially concede to the Duke of Argyll, who had claimed that 'the fashioning of an implement for a special purpose is absolutely peculiar to humans' (p. 52). But even here Darwin attempted to minimize the differences between humans and other animals by asserting that although humans may have carried tool making to an extreme, the underlying psychological abilities which made such performances possible were nonetheless present in our closest living relatives such as chimpanzees.

It was in this sense, then, that Köhler's work was a relief to Darwin's followers—here at last were numerous clear demonstrations not just of intelligent tool use in animals,

Figure 3.1 Grande, an adolescent female chimpanzee studied by Wolfgang Köhler (1927), stacking boxes to obtain an otherwise out-of-reach banana.

but of creative and insightful tool manufacture as well. Viewed in this context, the later reports by Jane Goodall (1968b) and others which described chimpanzees engaging in termite fishing and nut cracking in nature were, in some sense, just completing the circle—not only were chimpanzees in principle capable of tool use and manufacture (as revealed by experiments in captivity), they also exhibited such behavior on a fairly regular basis in their natural habitats. Indeed, the more recent appreciation of tool use in species as diverse as capuchin monkeys, crows, and wasps (see Beck 1980) has just seemed to strengthen the claim for psychological continuity all the more. After all, if

Hume's intuitions were correct, evidence of widespread tool use in the animal kingdom would pretty much sew up the case that the kind of folk physics which seems to motivate our own species' use of tools must be shared by a wide array of species indeed.

If all of this is true, then it might seem that an experimental investigation of chimpanzee tool use at this stage of the game is a bit superfluous—a project best left to those who like to fiddle around with already well-established facts. The real work, on this view, has already been done. Chimpanzees have already told us what we wanted to know the most: 'Our ability to make and use tools', they appear to have pronounced, 'reveals quite clearly that we, too, see the world in terms of simple causal interactions involving everyday folk notions of weight, force, gravity, shape, and so on.'

Of course, this conclusion hinges upon the assumption that the use and manufacture of simple tools requires an understanding of the causal principles that do, in truth, underwrite such behaviors. And it is here—at the juncture between the form of a given behavior on the one hand, and its underlying cause on the other—that we re-encounter the argument by analogy. And so it is here that we must remind ourselves that only experiments (such as the ones reported in this volume) can make progress toward settling the issue one way or another. Indeed, viewed from this perspective, nothing seems less obvious than whether chimpanzees conceive of their use and manufacture of tools in terms of abstract causal variables such as those which comprise our human folk physics. Again, this is not to deny that there are striking similarities in the final behavioral and physical products achieved by humans and apes. *Indeed, a major part of our conclusion from the experiments to be presented in this volume is that many of the same perceptual–motor abilities are involved.* But do chimpanzees, like humans, come to understand their use of tools within a framework of a naive folk physics—a level of abstraction that provides a more flexible system for representing actions on the world prior to engaging in them, and for extracting and organizing the regularities in the world more rapidly?

In one sense, of course, chimpanzees' efforts with tools ultimately force them to cope with gravity, space, force, shape, and so on—but this may have no bearing on whether such concepts are explicitly present in their minds. *Indeed, a second major conclusion of our work is that chimpanzees do not represent abstract causal variables as explanations for why objects interact in the ways that they do.* For example, after they have achieved success on a particular problem involving transfer of force, our work directly addresses the question of whether they emerge with an explicit folk notion of 'force'—an abstract concept that can be invoked during attempts to solve perceptually novel problems. Far from the answer that seems obvious from their spontaneous, intelligent use of simple tools, the answer to such questions is not, 'Of course!' but rather, 'We do not yet know'. And, as we shall now see, some of the most persuasive reasons for approaching such questions with an open mind can be derived not from experiments conducted in modern research laboratories, but from Wolfgang Köhler's (1927) research on Tenerife almost a century ago.

Stacking boxes: a chimpanzee folk physics of statics?

A dispassionate assessment of Köhler's work reveals that although he believed that his apes were capable of insightful learning, he was equally struck by the differences between their way of conceiving objects and events in the world and our own. Indeed, his writing is laced with the musings of a scientist struggling to make sense out of a complex pattern of similarity and difference between human and chimpanzee psychology. On the one hand, his apes seemed to provide ample evidence that they could act creatively and insightfully, and that they possessed traits and characteristics which prior to his work had been heralded as exclusively human. On the other hand, he encountered numerous situations in which his chimpanzees absolutely failed to hit upon solutions that would seem, to us at least, quite obvious. For example, in a variety of tests in which the solution depended upon removing an obstacle (say, a box) in order to reach an objective, Köhler was struck by his apes' confusion. In some cases, the problems appeared so extremely simple that, Köhler noted, 'one is inclined to say, before the test: "here is something the chimpanzee can do at once."' To my astonishment this estimate is not correct' (p. 59). And ironically, despite the impressions created in the minds of many, perhaps no example better illustrates the apparent differences in the folk physics of humans and apes than Köhler's investigation of the process by which his chimpanzees learned to stack boxes in order to obtain otherwise out-of-reach bananas.

Initially, Köhler confronted his young apes with the following situation: a banana nailed to (or suspended from) the ceiling of a room containing only a large wooden crate. The problem was created, of course, by the apes' desire to retrieve the banana. The solution of interest to Köhler was the apes' ability to learn to place the box under the objective, thereby allowing them access to the reward. In describing the results of these first tests, Köhler singled out the performance of Sultan, his most gifted ape, for special mention because of his rather sudden solution to the problem. Köhler reports that after numerous attempts to retrieve the reward directly by jumping, Sultan 'suddenly stood still in front of the box, seized it, and tipped it hastily straight toward the objective, but began to climb upon it...and springing upwards with all his force, tore down the banana' (p. 40). Because the action was performed suddenly, and all at once, Köhler (perhaps justifiably) was convinced that Sultan's solution was 'genuine'—in other words, that it was achieved through insight.

Köhler was clearly impressed by the sudden and complete nature of Sultan's solution to the problem involving one box, as he also was by the sudden and complete nature of his others apes' solutions (even though these latter solutions appeared only after numerous seemingly stupid and irrelevant efforts). Indeed, it was precisely this kind of evidence that Köhler invoked in support of his general conviction that particular solutions had been achieved through insight. However, Köhler was even more impressed by the chimpanzee's *difficulty* in taking the very next step: placing a second box on top of the first when the objective was higher and thus out of reach from a single box. Here, even his star pupil, Sultan, seemed stumped. Although the ape immediately pushed one box beneath the objective, he quickly realized that he could not reach the objective. Köhler's descriptions of Sultan's actions from that point forward will ring true with anyone who has ever observed a chimpanzee struggling to derive a solution to a difficult problem:

> Presently [Sultan] took notice of the second box and fetched it, but instead of placing it on top of the first, as might seem obvious, began to gesticulate with it in a strange, confused, and apparently quite inexplicable manner; he put it beside the first, then in the air diagonally above, and so forth.

The other apes, too, approached the box stacking task as if it were an altogether different situation than the task involving a single box. Even his two most advanced apes appeared to completely disregard the principles of naive statics:

> Chica tries in vain…to attain the objective with one box; she soon realizes that even her best jumps are of no avail, and gives up that method. But suddenly she seizes the box with both hands, holds it by great effort as high as her head, and now presses it to the wall of the room, close to which the objective hangs. If the box would 'stick' to the wall, the problem would be solved… In the same experiment, later on, Grande puts the box under the objective, lifts her foot to climb, but then lets it drop again, discouraged… Suddenly she seizes the box and presses it, still looking up toward the objective, to the wall at a certain height, just as Chica had done. (pp. 156–7.)[1]

Here, then, was a puzzle for Köhler. Why did his apes have such a difficult time with stacking two boxes, when placing one box under the objective was so easily within their abilities?

With enough experience, of course, his animals did eventually learn how to stack the boxes on top of one another to reach the bananas. Indeed, Grande was sometimes even able to construct towers involving up to four boxes. However, it will be a great surprise to those who are only sketchily familiar with Köhler's work to discover that his central conclusion was that chimpanzees seem to understand the situation in a manner very different from humans: '…[T]he total impressions of all observations made repeatedly on the animals', Köhler noted, 'leads to the conclusion that *there is practically no statics to be noted in the chimpanzee*. Almost everything arising as "questions of statics" during building operations, he solves not with insight, but by trying around blindly' (p. 149; italics in original). Of course, once they discovered a given solution, the apes were apt to

---

1   Similar experiments involving orangutans, chimpanzees, and gorillas were conducted by Robert Yerkes and his colleagues in the United States (see Yerkes 1916; Yerkes 1927*a,b*; Yerkes and Learned 1925). Although Yerkes describes similar patterns as Köhler, he generally tends to emphasize the intelligent (or, as he put it, the 'ideational') quality of the apes' behaviors. And so, for instance, after a description of how one of his chimpanzees (Chim) came to solve the box-stacking problem, rather than offering a careful description of what happened on subsequent trials, we are left to imagine: 'Subsequent opportunities to meet the situation adequately resulted merely in the perfecting of the method. It is needless to describe the process. Chim had gained the necessary insight for the solution of the problem' (Yerkes and Learned 1925, p. 47).

repeat it, but even the nature of these repetitions suggested striking differences in the underlying conceptual knowledge of humans and apes.

One might wonder why Köhler reached the conclusion that chimpanzees and humans differ so greatly in this context, especially in the face of his apes' eventual success. Indeed, given Köhler's overall portrait of chimpanzees as intelligent, insightful beings, this would seem to be an especially interesting question. True, Köhler was poised, ready, and willing to attribute insight to apes where the evidence seemed to warrant it, but there were several aspects of the animals' solutions which gave him reason to pause. First, after their initial solution of placing one box on top of the other, Köhler repeated the tests, only to discover that their initial successes were neither easily nor immediately repeated. Even after modeling the correct solution for the animals ('reminding' them of the answer, so to speak), the solution of placing one box on top of the other was only gradually incorporated into their repertoire. Köhler described the process as one in which the apes were content to let 'everything depend on the success or failure of plan-less movements' (p. 145). He was ultimately forced to conclude that his chimpanzees perceived the box-stacking problems as altogether different from the ones which required placing a single box under the banana. Köhler explains:

> Adult human beings are inclined to overlook the chimpanzee's real difficulty in such construction, because they assume that adding a second piece of building material to the first is only a repetition of the placing of the first one on the ground (underneath the objective)... [T]herefore, in the building-up process the only new factor is the actual lifting up. So the only questions seem to be, whether the animals proceed at all 'tidily' in their work, whether they handle the boxes very clumsily, and so forth... [But] [i]f putting the second box on the first were nothing more than a repetition of the simple use of boxes (on the ground) on a higher level, one would expect—after the other experiences—that the solution once found would be repeated. ...[B]ut neither [Sultan or Grande] succeeded easily in reproducing his *building* methods, and one glance at the description of the experiments will show that...the animal does not behave then like somebody accomplishing the task clumsily, but like someone to whom the situation does not offer any definite lead toward a particular action. (p. 146.)

Indeed, Köhler was so struck by their lack of comprehension that he goes on to note that:

> ...[I]f you did not know that the animals see perfectly well in the ordinary sense of the word, you might believe that you were watching extremely weak-sighted creatures, that cannot clearly see where the first box is standing. Especially does Tschego keep lifting the second box over the first and waiving it about for some time, without either box touching the other for more than a few seconds. One cannot see this without saying to oneself: 'Here are two problems; the one ("put the second box up") is not really a difficult task for the animals, provided they know the use to which a box can be put; the other ("*add one box to the other, so that it stays there firmly, making the whole thing higher*") *is extremely difficult*' (p. 147; italics in original).

Even after considerable experience with this problem, and even after some of his apes had learned how to stack the boxes, Köhler noted that his animals persisted in making the most startling errors, such as removing boxes from the tower beneath them, causing the entire structure—themselves included—to collapse completely!

Köhler's second reason for concluding that '*there is practically no statics to be noted in the chimpanzee*' (p. 149) was derived from his qualitative observations of the highly dubious nature of the structures they constructed—even after a great amount of experience. He describes how his chimpanzees placed boxes on top of each other with complete disregard to the integrity of their balance:

> If by chance…the upper box comes into any position where it does not for the moment wobble, the chimpanzee will certainly climb up, even though a mere touch or friction…has momentarily steadied the box… Whether one box, for example, projects far out sideways from the rest of the structure or not, seems to be a matter of indifference to the chimpanzee. (p. 151.)

The results of his tests seemed to suggest that the chimpanzees were driven by an 'optically-led treatment' (p. 151) of the situation at hand—in other words, they were driven to create a certain visual form, but with complete disregard of the underlying physical principles involved. After having discovered how to stack the boxes, the apes in some sense knew what they were trying to achieve: placing successive boxes higher still. But their knowledge of how even the most elementary principles of statics were involved seemed to be very impoverished indeed:

> Structures grow under [the chimpanzee's] hand, and often enough he can climb them, but they are structures which, according to the rules of statics, seem to us almost impossible. For all structures that *we* know (and are familiar with optically) are achieved by the apes by chance at best, and, as it were, by the 'struggle for not wobbling'. (p. 151.)

But did the apes' seemingly impossible structures simply stem from their reliance on a principle of least effort, their carelessness, or perhaps even their lack of motivation to build structures that were more stable? 'The animals' work may make this impression on a novice,' Köhler admitted, 'but longer observation of the tireless energy which Grande displays—as much in pulling down well-built structures because one part wobbles, as in building up structures which do not statically balance—will convince anyone that the real explanation lies deeper…' (p. 152–3). Perhaps among the most common and striking errors made by his apes were their insistent attempts to balance one box on top of another along a diagonal edge—a completely impossible feat. Köhler aptly describes this as a 'good error'—in the sense that if it could work it would have the effect of creating a heightened pinnacle on which they could perch. Amazingly, however, this was not an occasional error, but rather one that was likely to be 'repeated *ad infinitum*'—indeed, Köhler remarks that his most able box-stacker, Grande, 'with amazing stubbornness and minute care…repeated this "good error" for years' (p. 158).

Perhaps Köhler's greatest achievement was to step outside his distinctly human way of seeing the box-stacking experiments, and realize that he had, in effect, posed two very different problems to his apes. In the case of one box, Köhler speculated, no problem of statics is involved because the 'homogenous and shapeless ground' effectively solves the problem for the ape. Here, the ape must only place a box close enough to the objective, but it really does not matter where, exactly, the box is placed. 'Quite different', Köhler observes, 'is the problem with *two* boxes...since the first and second box do not solve [the problem] by themselves, as the first box and the level ground did' (p. 148). In other words, Köhler was able to see that the question of statics could only arise when two objects are to be put into some special relation relative to one another so that gravity and transfer of force play an essential role. Once the problem of statics is introduced, Köhler concluded, 'the chimpanzee seems to reach the limit of his capacity' (p. 148).

In a particularly impressive attempt to test his interpretation of the discrepancy between the one-box versus multiple-box situation, Köhler set up tests in which stones were placed on the ground beneath the banana, thus creating an unstable building surface. In this situation, Sultan was again confronted with the one-box problem. And, not surprisingly, Sultan quickly retrieved the box and proceeded to place it directly beneath the objective. However, to Köhler's astonishment, Sultan made no efforts to remove the stones—despite several repetitions of the experiment—but rather proceeded in the most awkward manner to attempt to balance the box on top of them. In a further test, Köhler replaced the stones with a number of tin cans (placed on their sides so they would roll):

> Sultan immediately seizes the box and attempts to place it on the tins, whereat the box rolls off to the side over again. After fussing about with the box for some time, he pushes the tins (accidentally) a little sideways from the objective, so that a free place is made between them, big enough to place the box... But he makes further hard efforts to stand the box on the tins without paying the least attention to this free place. (p. 155.)

'Nothing in his behavior', Köhler observes, 'indicates any endeavor to remove the rolling tins, although he could do it in a few seconds without the least trouble' (p. 155).[2]

———•———

The antics of Köhler's apes during the box-stacking tests should not detract from the fundamental facts surrounding the manufacture and use of tools by chimpanzees, other primates, and a diverse array of other species: tool use is widespread; and tool manufacture, though generally rare among animals, occurs regularly among chimpanzees. Indeed, Köhler himself reports the construction of tools by one of his chimpanzees,

---

2   Köhler introduces this remarkably ingenious test with the following statement: 'Sometimes it seems advisable to take one of the facts developed by observation, and demonstrate it in sharp outline by an extreme test' (p. 154).

Sultan, who learned how to fit two hollow bamboo sticks together, and then used this longer probe to obtain an otherwise out-of-reach food item.[3] And clearly, these activities tempt the interpretation that the animals know something about the causal principles involved. At the very least, most researchers would be willing to conclude that, given the same general form and complexity of any given instance of tool use, the understanding of human and chimpanzees are probably similar. Of course, we have already seen that such an inference is based upon the persuasive force of the argument by analogy—an argument which is deeply flawed (see Chapter 2).

Nonetheless, this discussion naturally raises the question of how and when our own species develops the ability to reason about the causal mechanisms that we appeal to as explanations of the physical world. Do these concepts emerge late in development, or are they early-emerging abilities—abilities which may simply be elaborated in older children and adults? In the next section of this chapter, we show that from a very young age, children appear to reason about the physical world in terms of causes and effects, and even appear to know a fair amount about the nature of the mechanisms that allow causes to produce their effects—even mechanisms that are invisible.

Young children's understanding of causal mechanisms

Most of the early research on young children's understanding of causality was highly descriptive, using children's verbal explanations of real or hypothetical events to emphasize differences between their causal reasoning and that of adults (e.g. Piaget 1930). In contrast, in the past several decades researchers have sought to isolate the factors controlling young children's thinking about causal interactions, and in particular, their ideas about why one event 'causes' another. These more modern explorations of young children's understanding of causality, especially those which have focused on their understanding of causal mechanisms, are of special interest to us because these studies squarely address the nature of the young child's 'folk physics'.

The purpose of this section is not to provide an exhaustive review of young children's understanding of causality (for reviews see Shultz 1982a; Shultz and Kestenbaum 1985; White 1988). Instead, we seek to highlight the evidence that young children's understanding of the physical world includes the notion of 'cause'. To do so, we briefly review the major philosophical positions on the question of causality, and in particular

---

3   The conjoining of sticks to make a longer reaching stick should not be questioned, and indeed, the general effect has been replicated in both other apes and monkeys (e.g. Lethmate 1977). However, there is considerable mythology surrounding the evidence for insight in Sultan's actions. First, Köhler did not actually witness Sultan's solution (it was reported to him by one of the ape's trainers). Second, even as it is described, it does not seem to qualify as an action that occurred by insight. Rather, Sultan apparently discovered the fact that the sticks could be joined in play, and then, once having done so, used it to retrieve the reward.

the question of whether causal interactions can be directly perceived. Second, we selectively review the evidence that preschool children reason about both observable and unobservable causal mechanisms. Third, we review evidence that infants as young as six months may be sensitive to causal relations—although these latter findings may be more related to 'causal perception' than 'causal reasoning'.

Can causes be observed?

Perhaps the most well known philosophical position on the question of causality is the skeptical one espoused by David Hume (1739–40/1911). Hume explicitly denied that humans can directly perceive causal interactions. Although his ideas seem counterintuitive to the uninitiated, Hume offered a simple, coherent argument to support his contention that we do not directly observe one event causing another, but rather, we *infer* that one event has caused another. After all, Hume challenged, when we see a white billiard ball strike a red one, and then see the red one speeding away, what else do we observe but the movement of the balls; where do we observe a 'cause'? What we observe, Hume noted, is a mere succession of events: 'All events seem entirely loose and separate. One event follows another; but we can never observe any tie between them. They seem *conjoined*, but never *connected*' (Hume 1739–40/1911, section 7; italics in original). Granted, as adults we automatically interpret this succession of events within a causal framework, but Hume argued that this manner of thinking is an illusion created by the human mind. Indeed, as part of his general indictment of induction, Hume argued that our automatic and intuitive conclusion that the white ball has caused the red ball to move is logically indefensible.[4]

It is important to stress the fact that Hume did not deny that humans ascribe causes to the events that they observe. Rather, he argued that causal thinking is a logically flawed way of thinking that develops in the human mind through 'habit.' He suggested that our minds learn to form the conclusion that one event has caused another under a fairly specific set of conditions. In particular, he identified the following conditions as being especially relevant for ascribing cause–effect relations: (1) one event follows the other; (2) this order of succession occurs regularly; (3) there is spatial and temporal contiguity between the two events; and (4) there is a similarity between at least certain characteristics of the two events.

Despite the simplicity and force of Hume's position, it has not gone unchallenged. A number of theorists have argued either that humans can directly perceive that one event

---

4   The reader will note that there is a contradiction between Hume's general indictment of the notion of cause, and his reasoning in the argument by analogy. After all, in the argument by analogy, Hume claims not only that mental states cause behavior, but that we can know which of our mental states cause which of our behaviors through the act of introspection. Hume's extreme skepticism on the existence of causes in the *Enquiry*, alongside his calm use of the notion of causes elsewhere (as in the *Treatise*) is what earned him the label 'the congenial skeptic'.

causes another, or at least that our inferences about such causes are justifiable (Bunge 1979; Harre and Madden 1975; Kant 1781/1933; Michotte 1963; Piaget 1970/1972, 1974). This position has been described as a 'generative view of causation' because it maintains that causes generate (or produce) their effects through a process whereby one event necessarily leads to another, typically through some sort of transmission of energy between objects (see review by Shultz 1982a). Contrary to Hume, proponents of this view maintain that the world is not composed of a mere succession of essentially 'loose and separate' events, but that causes necessarily generate their effects through causal mechanisms, and, furthermore, that humans can obtain verifiable knowledge of these cause–effect relations.

However, even such causal realists exhibit disagreement on a point which shall prove to be pivotal for our investigations of chimpanzees' folk physics—the question of whether mechanisms of causal production can be directly observed. For example, when the white ball strikes the red one, causing it to move away (or 'launching' it), can we directly observe (and/or know) the nature of the causal mechanism which generates the movement of the red ball? Some researchers and theorists have argued that under certain conditions, at least, we can. Michotte (1963), for instance, conducted a large number of experiments showing that, when humans observe such prototypical 'launching events' using light-projected images, a very narrow set of conditions determine whether the initial event is judged to be the cause of the succeeding event. For example, when one image of a rectangle approaches and then 'contacts' a second, stationary one, if the second one begins to move away (is launched) within 250 milliseconds, adults typically perceive that the first object caused the second to move. On the other hand, if the interval between contact and movement is greater than 250 milliseconds, adults do not experience the sensation that the first object caused the movement of the second one. Furthermore, many observers in Michotte's (1963) experiments reported that they actually 'saw' aspects of a transmission process that were not there. For example, when one rectangle approached and stopped just short of a second, stationary one, and the second was nonetheless launched within the 250 millisecond window, human observers reported that they perceived some kind of medium in the narrow gap between the two rectangles which was compressed just prior to the second one being launched. A similar kind of illusion was reported by 6-year-olds in a study by Lesser (1977).

In contrast, other causal realists such as Piaget (1970/1972) have maintained that although the generative transmission process is real, the exact mechanisms involved cannot be directly observed, and must therefore be inferred. Thus, on this view, observers do not directly observe 'gravity' at work, nor do they directly see the transmission of kinetic energy from white ball to red ball. Rather, these mechanisms are inferred. To some extent, this was Hume's position as well. The difference, of course, is that these scholars have maintained (unlike Hume) that the inference of causality is a verifiable (or knowable) one (Bunge 1979; Harré and Madden 1975; Piaget 1970/1972, 1974).

The view that causal mechanisms are an inferred, but nonetheless 'real', aspect of the physical world is of special interest to us, because of our broader concern with the question of whether chimpanzees reason about unobservable causes in general. As we saw in Chapter 2, much of our previous work concerning the nature of chimpanzee social understanding has hinged on the question of whether they understand that the behavior of other organisms is caused by internal, psychological states. Such psychological states are not directly observable and therefore must be inferred from overt behavior. And, as we have seen, chimpanzees do not appear to reason about such unobservable states. On the other hand, they reason quite well about overt behavior. Much of our concern in Chapters 4–11 will focus on the extent to which chimpanzees reason about the unobservable causal mechanisms at work in object–object interactions. Thus, the parallel question we wish to address here is at what point young children develop the idea that there are unobservable causes of physical events.

In what follows, we explore young children's causal knowledge. First, we show that young children reason about events within a cause–effect framework, and second, we examine what they appear to know about the causal mechanisms which allow causes to generate their effects.

Children reason about cause and effect

A number of studies have established that even quite young preschool children respect some of the most important conditions for causal inference laid out by Hume (Bullock and Gelman 1979; Bullock *et al.* 1982; Keil 1979; Kun 1978; Mendelson and Shultz 1976; Shultz 1982*a*,*b*; Shultz and Coddington 1981; Shultz and Mendelson 1975; Shultz and Ravinsky 1977; Shultz *et al.* 1982; Siegler 1975, 1976). For example, under ideal conditions, children as young as three years of age will attribute a given effect to the potential cause which is its most consistent covariate. Consider a simple apparatus consisting of a box with two holes on the surface (one on the right, one on the left). Suppose a 3-year-old child is allowed to witness the following facts: (1) a particular effect (the ringing of a bell) occurs after a marble is dropped in the right hole (event A); (2) the bell also rings if separate marbles are dropped simultaneously into the right and left holes (events A and B); and (3) the bell does *not* ring if a marble is only dropped into the left hole (event B). Under these circumstances, the child will attribute the effect (the ringing of the bell) to event A and not event B (Shultz and Mendelson 1975; see also Siegler 1975; Siegler and Liebert 1974).

Young children also use both temporal and spatial contiguity between events to assist in their determination of which of several possible events is the 'cause' of some other event. In general, events which are both temporally and spatially closer to (more contiguous with) a given outcome tend to be selected by young children as the cause of the outcome. With respect to temporal contiguity, several studies have shown that children as young as three years believe, as do adults, that causes must occur prior to their effects (Bullock and Gelman 1979; Kun 1978; Shultz and Mendelson 1975). When confronted with two possible events as causes of an outcome, 4- to 5-year-old children are more likely to select the event that immediately precedes the outcome, than one that precedes it by, say, five seconds (e.g. Mendelson and Shultz 1976; Siegler and Liebert 1974).

Likewise, 3- and 4-year-olds also use contiguity between a particular effect and several other events in deciding which one is the cause. For example, Bullock and her colleagues showed children two boxes into which marbles could be dropped (Bullock *et al.* 1982). The boxes contained runways leading to a jack-in-the-box (see Fig. 3.2). When the marbles were dropped, and the jack popped out of the box, even 3-year-olds were more likely to select the marble that had been dropped into the box that was touching the jack-in-the-box, than the one that had been dropped in the box that was further away.

In addition to covariation, temporal ordering, and spatial contiguity, children also use several other rules to determine which events are the likely cause of a given outcome (for a review, see Shultz and Kestenbaum 1985). Thus, given that children have a number of rules at their disposal, it is worth asking how they go about deciding which rules to use if they are in conflict. So, for example, what if one potential cause occurs closer to the outcome than another, but it is less temporally contiguous with the outcome? Young children appear to have several heuristics available which allow them to select which rule to use in order to settle on the cause of a particular event (see, for example, Shultz *et al.* 1986*b*). The main point we wish to make here is that, by a very

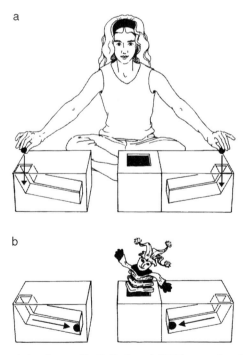

Figure 3.2 The experimental situation used by Bullock *et al.* (1982) to test for whether young children are sensitive to the spatial contiguity rule. The marbles are dropped into both runways simultaneously, followed by the jack popping out of the box: which marble was the cause? See text for details.

early age, children actively use a variety of rules to infer cause and effect, and exhibit structured ways of selecting among them.

There is, however, one principle which appears to be present earlier than all of the other rules just discussed, and furthermore, appears to be the one invariably preferred by children in situations where various causal rules are in conflict. This is the principle of *generative transmission*. Because this principle is intimately tied up with young children's knowledge about causal mechanisms, we now turn to a more general discussion of what children know about how causes produce the effects that they do. In doing so, we explore their appreciation of the notion that causes generate their effects through some sort of generative transmission process (or causal mechanisms).

Young children reason about causal mechanisms[5]

Several lines of evidence suggest that children as young as three years of age possess some knowledge of causal mechanisms—even ones that are not directly visible. For example, consider the simple situation depicted in Fig. 3.3 which consists of a starting ball, two ramps leading to intermediate balls, and finally to a target ball. Shultz *et al.* (1982) reported that, when confronted with this situation, 3- to 5-year-old children understood that the starting ball should be rolled down the ramp on the right in order to cause the intermediate ball to strike the target ball. Thus, the children appeared to

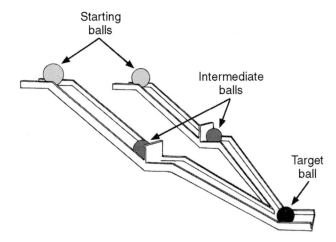

Figure 3.3 Apparatus used by Shultz *et al.* (1982) to determine if children understood the notion of a causal mediator in the context of transfer of force. Children are asked to dislodge the starting ball that will make the target ball move. Only the ball on the right can do so, by transmitting energy through the barrier to the intermediate ball.

---

5   Early studies of children's appreciation of causal mechanisms, conducted by Piaget (1971/1974), suggested that preschool children possessed little appreciation of causal mechanisms. However, because this work has been supplanted by more recent research it is not addressed in detail here.

grasp that in order to produce the desired effect (launching the target ball), there needed to be an appropriate causal mediator. They may have even appreciated that some kind of transmission process (what we would label transmission of energy) can occur through the barrier in front of the intermediate ball on the right.

In a similar fashion, Baillargéon and Gelman (see Bullock *et al.* 1982), using the apparatus reproduced in Fig. 3.4, showed that 4- to 5-year-olds who had initially seen this apparatus correctly predicted that the rabbit would fall if the rod was pushed toward the first domino-like block. In additional studies, 3- and 4-year-old children (who had already seen the general workings of the apparatus) were asked to predict whether the rabbit would fall down when confronted with several different manipulations to the basic apparatus (Bullock *et al.* 1982). Some of these manipulations were *causally-relevant* (e.g. the rod was made too short or was made out of a flexible material, the blocks were already down, or the rabbit platform was too far from the last block). Other manipulations were *causally-irrelevant* (e.g. the rod was a different color or made of a different substance, or a screen was placed between the children and the intermediate blocks). In all of the cases, even 3-year-olds proved to be very good at predicting the fate of the rabbit, appropriately distinguishing between the causally-relevant and the causally-irrelevant manipulations.

More direct evidence that children interpret physical events from the perspective of generative transmission comes from work by Thomas Shultz and his colleagues at the University of Toronto. In an extended series of studies, Shultz (1982*b*) pitted the kinds of rules that Hume believed to be at the core of our causal inferences (temporal succession, covariation, spatial contiguity, etc.) against the principle of generative transmission. In the studies conducted by Shultz (1982*b*), children as young as three years of age consistently preferred the generative transmission principle. Thus, they attributed the extinguishing of a candle to a blower that was turned on but further away rather than

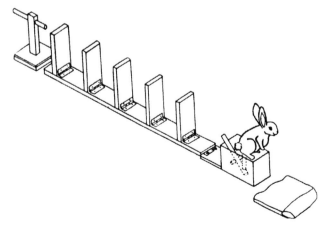

Figure 3.4 The 'Fred the rabbit' apparatus used by Baillargéon and Gelman (see Bullock *et al.* 1982) to explore young children's understanding of causal mechanisms. See text for details.

to a blower that was turned off but closer; they attributed the sound emanating from a hollow wooden box to a vibrating tuning fork as opposed to one that was not vibrating, even in the case where the vibrating one was further away from the box; they attributed a spot of light on a wall to a flashlight that had *not* produced this effect in the past, over one that had, but whose front was covered with an opaque disk (Shultz 1982*b*; Shultz *et al.* 1986*b*). Furthermore, when asked to provide verbal explanations of their choices, children overwhelmingly appealed to ideas related to generative transmission (see Shultz 1982*b*).

Perhaps the best illustration of children's preferences for explanations which appeal to causal mechanisms (even invisible ones) over other rules comes from a study conducted by Shultz (1982*a*, experiment 1). Two electric blowers faced a candle that was shield on three sides by a plexiglas box. The first blower was turned on and left on, but it did not extinguish the candle because of the plexiglas shield. Next, the second blower was turned on, but it too did not extinguish the candle because of the screen. However, immediately coincident with turning on the second blower, the experimenter rotated the screen so that the open side was facing the first blower, thus causing the candle to be extinguished. In this case, the child cannot use rules about spatial contiguity or covariation (neither is relevant here). However, the experiment neatly contrasts the temporal contiguity rule (which blower was activated shortly before the effect?) and the generative transmission rule (which blower could have actually generated some sort of transmission to the effect?). Even 2- to 4-year-olds chose the first blower as the cause, thus indicating their preference for focussing on causal mechanisms. Furthermore, their verbal justifications appealed to the idea of generative causes. Similar experiments have indicated that children base their selection of causes on their ideas about causal mechanisms (even hidden ones) when such concerns conflict with selections that would derive from rules about spatial contiguity (see Shultz 1982*a*).

One might wonder whether such results depend on familiarity with devices such as electric blowers, tuning forks, and flashlights. In an explicit test of this idea, Shultz (1982*b*) reported that when these studies were carried out with children growing up in a West African culture in which these implements were unknown, children performed in a nearly identical fashion. These results seem to suggest that the concern for causal mechanisms—that is, some sort of process which transmits substance or energy from one event to another—may be a universal feature of the human mind. (For other evidence in support of cultural universals of causality, see Atran 1990.) Furthermore, when children in Western cultures are presented with cause–effect relations that are known to be unfamiliar to them, and then asked to figure out how the effect is produced, they adopt strategies of searching for the underlying causal mechanisms—including ones that cannot be seen directly (see Shultz 1982*b*, experiment 5).

The idea of generative transmission is not only the most important principle used by young children in making causal judgements, it is also the one that develops the earliest. Shultz, Altmann, and Asselin (1986*a*) offered quite elegant data which supports the hypothesis that children use notions about causal mechanism before they are able to use other rules. They presented children with conditions involving the movement of two blocks (see Fig. 3.5(a)). In each case, the child was asked to judge which block had made the other one move. Each condition was designed so that a coherent answer could only be given if a child was capable of using a particular rule (in other words, no other rule could produce an answer to the question). For purposes of simplicity, we focus on two of the conditions: the temporal priority condition and the generative transmission (or causal mechanism) condition. Figure 3.5(b)–(e) presents a diagram of these conditions, which is useful in following the description of the experimental conditions.

In the temporal priority condition, the children were presented with a box with a slot on the top where two blocks (a red one and a blue one) sat about 11 cm apart from each other. As can be seen in Fig. 3.5(b)–(c), the blocks were partially obscured from the child, which provided the opportunity to link the blocks in ways that were unknown to the child. In the blue sub-condition (Fig. 3.5(b)), the blue block began to move first, and after it had traveled 3 cm, the red block began to move in synchrony behind it. In contrast, in the red sub-condition (Fig. 3.5(c)), the red block began to move first, and after it had traveled 3 cm the blue block began to move in synchrony in front of it. The purpose of this condition was to determine if children would identify the blocks that had moved first as the cause, and the blocks that moved second, as the effect. Notice that because there is no obvious mechanism, the generative transmission rule cannot be invoked as a causal rule. In contrast, use of the temporal priority rule can allow a consistent diagnosis of the cause–effect relation by appealing to the first event as the cause of the second.

In the generative transmission condition (see Fig. 3.5(d)–(e)), the situation allowed an attribution of causal mechanism.[6] In the blue sub-condition (Fig. 3.5(d)), the blocks were connected by a taut string (completely visible to the child) and both blocks moved together simultaneously to the left. In this case, a concern for causal mechanisms would consistently yield the attribution that the blue block was pulling the red block, even though both began to move simultaneously. In the red sub-condition (Figure 3.5(e)), a block was placed between the two blocks (again, in full view of the child) and the blocks moved together to the left. In this case, a concern for causal mechanism would consistently yield the attribution that the red block was pushing the blue block. Notice that the temporal priority rule could not allow a consistent causal attribution to one block over the other as the cause, because both blocks moved in unison.

The significant aspect of the results of this study is that 3- to 4-year-olds showed no ability to use the temporal priority rule (as well as other rules not discussed here), whereas the older children easily did so. In contrast, the 3- to 4-year-olds had absolutely no trouble in the generative transmission condition. Here, presumably because of their concern for underlying causal mechanisms, they consistently chose the blue block as the cause in the pulling condition and the red block as the cause in the pushing condition

---

6   In what follows, we combine the most important conditions from Shultz *et al.*'s (1986*a*) experiments 1 and 2.

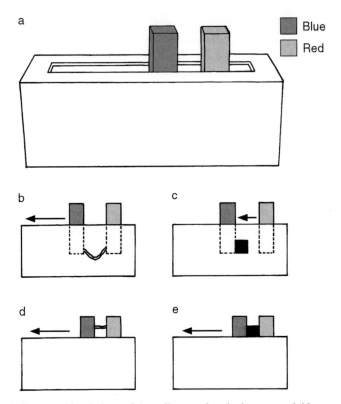

Figure 3.5 Conditions used by Shultz *et al.* (1986*b*) to test for whether young children use a temporal priority rule and/or a generative transmission rule in determining which of two events caused the other: (b)–(c) temporal priority condition, (d)–(e) generative transmission condition. See text for an explanation of the conditions and their significance.

(as did older children as well). Thus, contrary to what Hume would have predicted, the human mind's earliest concerns about causality seem to concern underlying causal mechanisms, not perceptual patterns of spatial and temporal contiguity.

Essentialism and the child's knowledge about hidden causes

Perhaps the most direct evidence that children appeal to non-obvious (invisible) causal mechanisms in explaining the physical world comes from research concerning whether children, like adults, hold 'essentialist' beliefs about the things they encounter. Essentialism is the belief that, first, the world has a real, underlying structure, and second, our categories map onto that structure.[7] On this view, people do not simply categorize objects based upon their surface or obvious features (although these features

---

7   The typical philosophical usage is similar, but does not insist that our categories map onto the underlying natures of things.

offer powerful clues as to an object's category), but rather they categorize things based on our beliefs about the underlying nature—or essence—of the object. This kind of thinking appears to be prevalent among adults and is found in cultures around the world (Atran 1990, 1994). Inherent in this kind of thinking is that there is an underlying causal structure to the world, and that it is this causal structure that is responsible for generating the surface or obvious features of things in the world (see Medin 1989). This view can be most clearly understood by thinking about how our belief about what a thing 'is' does not readily change even in the face of fairly dramatic alterations in its physical appearance.

Do children hold essentialist beliefs about the world? As part of a larger effort to answer this question, Susan Gelman and her colleagues have conducted a number of studies to determine whether children believe that natural events are caused by underlying, invisible mechanisms (Gelman and Kremer 1991; Gelman and Medin 1993; Gelman and Wellman 1991; Gelman et al. 1994). In one set of studies (reported by Gelman et al. 1994), preschool children were shown brief videotapes of animals, wind-up toys, or transparent human artifacts (e.g. a clear plastic pepper shaker). In some cases, the animals and artifacts were moved across a table surface by a human hand; in other cases the animals and objects began in a stationary position, but then began to move on their own (even though a hand was still visible at all times in these videotapes as well). After viewing each event, the children were asked about the causal mechanism responsible for the movement of the object. For the cases in which toys and artifacts were moved by a human hand, the children appealed to the obvious, external cause (the hand). However, in the cases where the toys and transparent objects appeared to move on their own, children generated accounts of the causal mechanisms involved which appealed to unobservable, internal mechanisms. The most significant results concern the children's explanations of the movement of the transparent objects. Here they appealed to hidden mechanisms such as magnets, electricity, 'invisible batteries'—one child even explained the movement of a transparent object by claiming that an 'invisible person' was present.

Other research on children's essentialist beliefs have shown that they appreciate that organisms (for example, a puppy or kitten) will remain the same individual even when it becomes an adult and looks very different; they seem to believe that individual organisms have internal, unobservable essences which persist even when the surface features change (see Gelman and Wellman 1991; Keil 1979; Rosengren et al. 1991). In short, by three to five years of age, children seem to hold the belief that the surface, observable properties (including both physical appearance and behavior) of things in the world are somehow generated or caused by underlying, nonobservable 'essences.'

The power of causal attributions

Not only do young children seek to predict and explain casual events within a framework that is centered on how one event generates another, but their quest for causal structure also appears to spill over into many aspects of their reasoning, including their classification of objects and their inferences about their causal properties. For example, Alison Gopnik and David Sobel, at the University of California at Berkeley, recently reported a study which elegantly illustrated the spontaneous ability of young children to reason about the causal properties of objects (Gopnik and Sobel, in press). Children were introduced to two different sets of four blocks. In the first set, the perceptual features of the blocks (their color, shape, and size) did not conflict with their causal powers (see below). In the second set, the perceptual features and the causal features conflicted.

The children were exposed to several conditions, but to illustrate our point we focus on the *induction* condition. As a first step in this condition, the experimenter picked up two of the four blocks and told the child they were 'blickets'. Next, the experimenter held up the other two blocks and told the child that they were not blickets. Immediately after this, the experimenter picked up one of the two blocks that had been labeled as a blicket, and set it on top of a (bogus) machine. As soon as the block touched the surface of this machine, a conspicuous light on the front of the machine was activated, accompanied by music. Thus, it appeared that the block had somehow activated the machine. Next, the experimenter picked up one of the two blocks that had not been labeled as a blicket and set it on top of the machine. This block did not activate the machine. Finally, the child was asked to show the experimenter another block that would light up the machine. In some conditions, even 2-year-olds selected the block that had previously been labeled as a blicket. In other words, the children seemed to extend novel causal powers to another object simply based on the fact that it shared a common name. Three- and 4-year-olds did so even when the perceptual features of the blocks conflicted with their apparent causal powers. Likewise, in another condition (a *categorization* condition), when the children were shown the causal powers of the four blocks before the experimenter named any of them, children assumed that objects which had exhibited the same apparent causal powers probably shared a common name.[8]

A moment's reflection on this experiment reveals its relevance to the question of causal mechanisms. For example, the children were never told that *only* blickets make the light come on, and thus their use of this apparent causal power to infer the causal

---

8   In order to be sure the children were really making a causal diagnosis, an important control condition was conducted, with additional subjects, in which the block was placed over the machine (but did not touch it). Simultaneously, the experimenter touched the top of the machine. In this case the light went on as before. If the subjects were merely forming a general association of the light with a block, this condition ought to have led to the same effects that were obtained in the main conditions. On the other hand, if the children were making a causal inference, the block would not appear to have the causal powers because the experimenter's hand is a more plausible cause of the light being activated. And children who experienced this condition did not use the contingency between the block being held up and the activation of the light to infer that the other 'blicket' would cause the light to come on, nor (in the categorization condition) did they use this contingency to extend the label 'blicket' to the other block which had been associated with the activation of the light.

properties of other objects with the same name (as well as to infer, based on the causal properties, the likely names of other objects) suggests that young children's interest in the causal properties of objects are a major, driving force behind how they understand the physical world. Indeed, some of the children even went so far as to try to peel back the protective covering of the blickets in what appeared to be an effort to see what was hidden inside the block that made it light up the machine (Gopnik, personal communication, 1999)!

Causal attributions in infancy?

So far, we have restricted our discussion of the development of young children's understanding of causality to the preschool years. But what about human infants? After all, long before our second and third year of life we are already confronting the world of objects. Visually guided reaching for objects appears to emerge sometime around four to five months of age, and from that point forward the infant's interactions with objects become increasingly more complicated. In the traditional Piagetian analysis, by eight to twelve months of age infants begin to exhibit behaviors which reflect their understanding that one action is a means to some other ends (Piaget 1954). For example, by this stage children understand that pulling a cloth is a means of bringing a toy, which is resting on it, to within reach. In this sense, infants of this age seem to grasp simple cause–effect relations. Unfortunately, however, the relative physical immaturity of the infant and its limited or non-existent verbal skills make it difficult or impossible to apply some of the tasks that have been developed for use with preschool children (see Diamond 1988).

   However, the development of non-verbal experimental techniques for exploring the cognitive processes of human infants have offered another avenue for exploring the development of infants' causal understanding. Rather than using their verbal or manual behavior, these techniques rely on their emotional responses (expressions of surprise), or their visual behavior (where, and for how long, they look at particular events) as measures of what they know or do not know (see Spelke 1985, for a discussion of some of these techniques). Research using these methods has demonstrated that even very young infants are sensitive to many properties of the physical world that were previously assumed to be far beyond their understanding (e.g. Baillargéon 1986, 1987, 1991; Baillargéon and Hanko-Summers 1990; Spelke 1988, 1990, 1991). For example, in an early study of this kind, Keil (1979, experiment 2) measured the surprise reactions of groups of $1^{1}/_{2}$ and $2^{1}/_{2}$-year-old children to a scenario involving a block tower. The children were shown a simple block tower, constructed from two supports and a top laying across the two supports. Next, a small screen was placed between the child and the block tower and the supports were removed. The screen was then removed, revealing the top still in the same position—as if floating! The $2^{1}/_{2}$-year-olds (but not the younger children) exhibited clear evidence of surprise at this (seemingly impossible) outcome. Of course, the nature of the infant's 'knowledge' about the physical world that is revealed by responses such as the amount of time they spend looking at a display or

their surprise reactions, is hotly contested (see Karmiloff-Smith 1992), and is an important issue to which we shall return in Chapter 12.

Even more striking evidence for young children's understanding of causality comes
from work by Alan Leslie (Leslie 1982; Leslie and Keeble 1987). Leslie and Keeble (1987)
developed a method for testing 6-month-old babies for their understanding of the
launching effect that Michotte (1963), as we saw earlier, developed for use with adults.
In particular, Leslie and Keeble devised a technique which revealed that when infants see
a green block strike a red one, followed immediately by the red one moving away, they
'perceive' more than a series of 'loose and separate' events. Rather, they see one event as
the cause, and the other as the effect.

Leslie and Keeble (1987) compared the reactions of two groups of 6-month-old
babies to the following experimental manipulations. First, each group was shown a particular film over and over again. One group was shown the classic launching event: a
green block strikes a red block, followed by the red block moving away. As we have seen,
Michotte (1963) found that adults automatically perceive that the green block has
caused the red block to move. Thus, this film can be thought of as a *causal* sequence. The
second group of babies was shown a very similar film in which the green block
approaches and contacts the red block, but the red block does not begin to move away
until a half-second later. The significance of this film is that, for adults, the introduction
of this half-second delay between the two events eliminates the impression that the
green block has caused the red block to move. Thus, this sequence can be thought of as
a *non-causal* sequence. Both groups of babies repeatedly observed their respective films
until the amount of time they spent looking at the film declined significantly. At this
point, the critical manipulation occurred. After a brief delay, each group saw their film
again—but in reverse!

The logic of habituating the infants to the films and then playing them backwards is
ingenious. First, consider the infants watching the *non-causal* film. If these infants, like
adults, do not perceive a causal connection between the movements of the green and red
blocks because of the delayed reaction, then once they become habituated to the
sequence, playing it backwards is only mildly different. After all, the temporal and
spatial patterning is the same in the forward and backward versions of the films; only
the direction of movement has changed. More to the point, if nothing is perceived as
causing anything else, there is no *conceptual* difference between the sequence played
forward and the sequence played backwards. In contrast, now consider the infants who
were shown the *causal* film. First, let us imagine that they do *not* experience the causal
impression that adults do. If so, then like the infants watching the *non-causal* film, they
ought to be only mildly interested when this film is played backwards. On the other
hand, if these infants originally interpreted the causal sequence not merely as a set of
spatial, temporal, and directional patterns, but also as a causal sequence (the green
block as 'cause' and the red block as 'effect'), then this film played backwards ought to
be of special interest. After all, the roles of cause and effect have been reversed! What
was the cause (the green block) is now the effect, and vice versa. In two separate

studies, this is exactly the pattern observed by Leslie and Keeble (1987). The *non-causal* group showed a mild increase in looking time when their film was reversed, but the *causal* group exceeded that by three to five times (see also Oakes and Cohen 1990, for a replication of this effect with older infants).

Leslie (1994) has offered a proposal for the nature of the infant's representation of objects which seeks to account for their early sensitivity to causal impressions. His proposal begins by noting that other researchers who have used visual habituation–dishabituation techniques have shown that by three or four months of age infants perceive the world as being composed of cohesive, bounded, solid, three-dimensional bodies that are spatio-temporally continuous (see Spelke 1990, for a review). Leslie argues that not only do infants possess the ability to keep track of these objects and their motions in space, but that they also possess a dedicated system (or 'module') for mapping energy distributions onto these objects. In his terminology, these mechanical properties of objects are labeled as 'FORCE'. Thus, Leslie speculates that two systems operate in parallel—a general visual system (with its various sub-components) and a separate system (what he calls the 'Michotte module') for keeping track of energy dynamics. The Michotte module is envisioned as receiving inputs from the visual system concerning the surface layout of a scene, the geometry of the objects in the scene (including their arrangements relative to one another), and their motions. Having this information, the device then maps FORCE descriptions onto the objects. In simple terms, this module describes the objects in mechanical terms.

Leslie's (1994) proposal, then, suggests an alternative way of thinking about Hume's claim that causality cannot be directly perceived. If he is correct, and humans possess an insularized (perhaps unconscious) device for mapping energy distributions onto objects based on their motions, then Hume could be right in the narrow sense that we cannot consciously observe one event causing another. After all, our conscious perceptual experiences contain no descriptions of FORCE. However, if more primitive mechanisms are hard at work translating visual information into more abstract descriptions of FORCE (mechanisms that may not be available to consciousness), and then feeding these conclusions into our higher-order reasoning processes, then it is easier to see why the causal impression is automatic, pervasive, but nonetheless non-verifiable. Furthermore, it may well be the case that, in their earliest forms, these FORCE descriptions are not available to the higher-order cognitive systems of the infant. It may be only later, perhaps at around two or three years, that this information becomes more generally available to the infant. (For proposals that are compatible with this view, see White 1988).

Regardless of whether Leslie's (1994) proposal turns out to be exactly right, it offers an important way of thinking about the evolution of causal understanding—one that dovetails nicely with the reinterpretation model offered at the end of Chapter 2. After all, if he is correct, then there exist a large number of possibilities for similarity and differences in the understanding of the physical world between humans and our nearest living relatives. Simply to choose one of the most extreme possibilities, what if chimpanzees share with us many of the same perceptual mechanisms for keeping track of the location, movement, and even simple geometry of objects, and in addition share with us homologous visual–cognitive processing mechanisms for constructing a common set of assumptions about the properties of objects (solidity, boundedness, etc.), but never re-describe these objects in mechanical terms? What this would mean, of course, is that chimpanzees and humans would share a common core of visual information which they could both use to learn about the statistical regularities in the world, and ultimately arrive at a common set of 'expectations', but only humans would interpret these dynamics in causal terms. The advantage of such interpretations will become clearer in Chapter 12.

Tool use and causal understanding in young children

In the previous section, we presented several lines of evidence which suggest that children generate causal interpretations of the events they witness. Although such interpretations are of use to children in organizing their knowledge about the world, we would also expect this causal knowledge to be explicitly reflected in their interactions with the physical world. One arena for using such causal knowledge is in the case of making and using simple tools. Of course, tool use may occur without the kinds of appeals to causal mechanisms that we have been exploring, but such interpretations may make both the discovery and use of tools easier and more efficient.

The development of tool use in infants was considered by a number of early researchers, including Piaget (1954), who observed his infants, Jacqueline and Lucienne, using supports in their efforts to retrieve objects. By nine to twelve months of age, Piaget's observations indicated that infants come to understand the idea that one object can support another, such as a toy resting on a cloth. If the toy is out of reach, but part of the cloth is within reach, infants of this age appreciate that the toy can be retrieved by pulling the cloth. Piaget (1952) argued that such knowledge is quickly generalized to many similar situations, demonstrating the infant's generalized understanding of the need for a point of contact between a tool and a goal object. Indeed, the traditional analysis of this problem suggests that its mastery is evidence of the infant's growing understanding of the deep, causal structure of the contact between the cloth and the goal object (see Bates *et al.* 1980; Brown 1990). The same logic has been applied to the infant's ability to use a string to pull in a goal object at around the same age (Uzgiris and Hunt 1975; Willats 1984). This view can be contrasted with that of more traditional learning theorists, who have argued that transfer of learning depends not on the infant's understanding of the causal structure of the world, but rather on its visible, perceptual features.

Interestingly, however, there is a considerable developmental gap between the infant's ability to solve the support or string problem (solved by about ten months of age) and a seemingly similar problem involving using a stick to retrieve an object (typically not solved until about 18 months of age) (Uzgiris and Hunt 1975). Inspired partly by some of Köhler's (1927) observations on chimpanzees, Liz Bates and her colleagues explored why such a developmental gap is present between these situations (Bates *et al.* 1980). They presented 10-month-old children with a number of situations in which they could attempt to use a tool to retrieve a small, fuzzy toy. The conditions used in one of their experiments are reproduced in Fig. 3.6. The situations are arranged from left to right in an order of decreasing physical connection. And, indeed, at ten months of age, infants readily solve those problems in which the tool object is in contact with the goal object (conditions 1–4), but only accidentally solve those in which contact is only implied (conditions 5–8). These results lead Bates and her colleagues to conclude that problem solving is easier when the connection between two objects is directly given by the spatial configuration of the tool object and the goal object—but instead of concluding that the infant's understanding is strictly perceptually-based, they suggest that: 'the child may know something, at some level, about the causal relations that hold when two objects are connected. If she is reminded of the connection, she is more likely to use that knowledge.' (p. 136.) However, their data would not appear to directly address the difference between perceptual contact and underlying, causal structure (i.e. physical connection).

In an attempt to explore whether young children's tool-using abilities are dependent on their knowledge of surface perceptual features, or on their knowledge of causal structure, Ann Brown (1990) conducted a series of studies exploring very young children's ($1^{1}/_{2}$-, 2-, and 3-year-olds') use of tools. In a series of studies, Brown and her colleagues presented children with a number of different tools. Initially, the children were allowed to use a workable tool to retrieve a toy that was otherwise out of reach. Next, they assessed what would happen if they gave the children a choice between two novel tools. One of these tools retained the correct functional properties (e.g. it was rigid, or had an effective pulling end [like a hook or rake], or was long enough), but was perceptually different from the original tool in some obvious way (e.g. it was a different color, it had a different, but still functional, end [a rake instead of a hook]). The second tool was perceptually more similar to the initial tool (e.g. it was the same color or shape), but it was functionally ineffective (e.g. it was too short, it was made of a flimsy

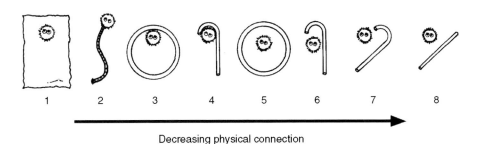

Figure 3.6 Various arrangements used by Bates *et al.* (1980) to explore the ability of 10-month-old human infants to retrieve a goal object (a fuzzy toy). See text for details.

material, or did not have an effective end). Brown reported that in the transfer trials, children as young as 24 months were almost completely unaffected by surface features such as color or the exact shape of the effective end of the tool. What did affect their choices were the rigidity, the length, and the presence of an effective end. In short, when confronted with novel tools, the children based their choices on the tool properties that were related to the causal structure of the task, not the perceptual aspects of the tools that were causally-irrelevant.

In considering the data on the development of infants' use of tools, Brown (1990) argued that although evidence from studies involving viewing time suggest that 6-month-olds seem to appreciate (at some level) that two objects must have a point of contact between them if one is to make the other move, they cannot actively use that knowledge (even at ten months) unless the tools are already in contact. Slightly later (at around 15 months or so, they can *learn* to apply this knowledge if they are given some demonstrations. By 24 months or so, children can easily apply this knowledge in tool-using tasks, even when the tool and object are not already in spatial contact. On her view, children possess the kind of causal knowledge which is crucial for tool use quite early in development, and they merely need assistance in applying it.

Of course, another possibility is that early causal knowledge is quite isolated from other cognitive systems, including general learning mechanisms, and only becomes explicit at around 24 months or so. On this view, the use of connected tools (e.g. Bates *et al.* 1980) to retrieve objects may say nothing about the infant's understanding of the causal principles involved. Furthermore, the early developmental progression outlined by Brown (1990) may involve the infant's detection of the regularities between certain spatial relations (or, after some experience, anticipated spatial relations) and certain outcomes. In any event, the work of Brown and her colleagues does provide fairly compelling evidence that, by about 24 months of age, children are attending to the underlying causal structures involved in tool use.

Tool use and causal understanding in nonhuman primates

Unlike research with young children, relatively little is known about nonhuman primates' understanding of causality. Furthermore, what is known is almost exclusively restricted to the context of tool use (see Bard *et al.* 1995; Limongelli *et al.* 1995; Mathieu *et al.* 1980; Natale 1989; Spinozzi and Potí 1989, 1993; Visalberghi and Limongelli 1994; Visalberghi and Trinca 1989; Visalberghi *et al.* 1995). By itself, this is not unfortunate, because tool use and manufacture, as we have seen, may be an excellent starting point for exploring chimpanzees' understanding of causality.[9] However, despite decades of research on the use and manufacture of tools by chimpanzees and other nonhuman

---

9   Other approaches to exploring chimpanzees' understanding of causality have been explored by Premack (1976) and Premack and Premack (1994). These shall be discussed in Chapter 12.

primates, there has been surprisingly little effort to experimentally probe what, exactly, these animals understand about the causal mechanisms that are involved in these inter-actions. There have been several explorations of the 'support problem' discussed in the previous section, but much of this work suffers from lack of controls, and sample sizes on the order of one or two animals (for a critique of this work, see Tomasello and Call 1997). We explore these particular studies in more detail in Chapter 10.

However, recently Elisabetta Visalberghi and her colleagues in Rome have pursued a productive line of research which has explicitly targeted the question of what non-human primates know about the causal interactions involved in certain aspects of tool use and modification. They have explored the distinction between performance and comprehension on tasks involving nonhuman primates' use and manufacture of tools (Limongelli *et al.* 1995; Visalberghi 1993; Visalberghi and Trinca 1989; Visalberghi *et al.* 1995). These studies have largely focused on capuchin monkeys and chimpanzees, mainly because of their reputations as excellent tool users.

In what follows, we focus on the studies of Visalberghi and her colleagues because they are, to date, the most programmatic of their kind. However, this is not to imply that there has been no other research on nonhuman primates understanding of causality. Although they are limited, we review other relevant studies in Chapters 4–11 as we introduce and discuss our particular experiments.

The tube problem

In a first set of studies, Visalberghi and her colleague, Loredana Trinca, re-considered the classic box-and-pole task (one early version of which we have reproduced in Fig. 3.7) that was originally devised by Haggerty (1913), and later systematized by Yerkes (1916, 1927*a,b*), Klüver (1933), and Yerkes and Learned (1925). The task simply consists of placing a desirable food item inside a long box or tube and providing the animal with a stick or pole to push it out. However, rather than merely asking whether their capuchin monkeys could solve the task, or describing qualitative changes in their behaviors as they arrived at the solution, Visalberghi and Trinca (1989) sought to probe the underlying knowledge possessed by the monkeys after they learned to solve the problem. For example, does the successful monkey learn a set of very general relation-ships about a stick and the hole into which it must be inserted, or does it appreciate the specific qualities (length, thickness, etc.) that a stick must or must not have in order to function effectively?

To investigate this, Visalberghi and Trinca (1989) first presented four capuchin monkeys with a clear plexiglas tube into which a peanut had been inserted (see Fig. 3.8(a)). They were also presented with sticks that could easily fit inside the tube to push out the peanut. Desirous of peanuts, three of the four capuchins spontaneously learned to insert the sticks and dislodge the reward. This allowed the researchers to ask the suc-cessful animals what they understood about their solution. To do so, the capuchins were presented with several different conditions in which a peanut was again placed inside the tube, but the nature of the potential tools was changed. On some trials, the monkeys

Figure 3.7 Dwina, a young female chimpanzee observed by Robert Yerkes (1943), solving the classic box-and-pole problem. Dwina (a) inserts pole into one end of the box, (b) pushes pole into the box, and (c) obtains food reward that emerges from the other end.

were presented with the usual tool, but on others they were presented with tools that were either too short (and hence needed to be inserted sequentially behind one another), too thick (and hence needed to be split apart), or inappropriately shaped (and hence had to be disassembled). These conditions are shown in Fig. 3.8(b).

The capuchins achieved solutions to all three of the relevant test conditions—typically within a matter of minutes. For example, when they were presented with bundles of sticks taped together, they eventually removed the tape and used the appropriate-sized sticks to dislodge the peanut. Or, in the condition in which they were presented with three short sticks, the capuchins were eventually successful in putting one stick behind the other, thus pushing the food out of the tube.

However, the nature and persistence of the errors made by their monkeys led Visalberghi and Trinca (1989) to conclude that their behaviors did not 'seem consistent with an understanding of the task' (p. 519). The capuchins regularly inserted short splinters which could not possibly dislodge the peanut, when a perfectly appropriate stick was available. On other occasions, they inserted a short stick on one side, and when the reward failed to move, they inserted the other short stick into the opposite opening. On still other occasions, they (appropriately) removed the crosspiece from one end of the tool, but then attempted to insert the other end (which was still blocked) into the tube! Not only did these errors occur on the first few trials, they persisted throughout the experiment. In short, their monkeys appeared to try every activity possible until they succeeded in dislodging the peanut. It is important to note that in scoring the 'errors' made by their monkeys, Visalberghi and Trinca (1989) were not concerned with those occasions in which the monkeys were trying to do something that might have

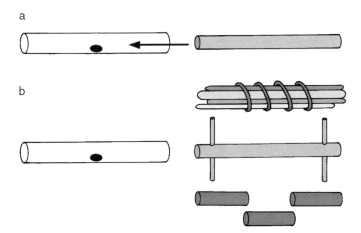

Figure 3.8 (a) The tube problem used by Visalberghi and Trinca (1989) with capuchin monkeys. (b) The implements offered to the monkeys after training.

worked, but then failed because they performed the action clumsily or inappropriately. On the contrary, they scored errors only when the animals were attempting solutions 'with things completely out of scale, and wrong' (p. 519).

The trap-tube problem

In a second test, Visalberghi and another of her colleagues, Luca Limongelli, returned to the tube situation, but in this case asked a slightly different question concerning capuchin monkeys' understanding of tool use. In this case, the investigators modified the plexiglas tube by affixing a trap to its center (see Fig. 3.9(a)). Again, a peanut was placed inside the tube, but either to the left or the right of the trap. A problem was thus created. To obtain the peanut they needed to avoid pushing it into the trap. Thus, the stick had to be inserted into the tube opening farthest from the peanut. Visalberghi and Limongelli (1994) administered this initial test to four capuchin monkeys (who were already proficient at using a stick to dislodge a peanut from an intact plexiglas tube). After 140 trials, only one of their monkeys learned how to solve the task—that is, learned to insert the tool into the opening farthest from the peanut, and thus avoid the trap. The rest of their monkeys persisted in two different strategies. They either inserted the tool into the same side on every trial, or switched sides randomly across trials. And, because the left/right position of the peanut relative to the trap was randomly varied across trials, these strategies lead to success on only half of the trials. In contrast, their single successful subject, Rb, learned how to avoid the trap after about 90 trials.

But did Rb's excellent performance suggest that he now understood the function of the trap, or, conversely, had he merely learned a rule of the type, 'insert the stick into the opening of the tube farthest from the reward' (Visalberghi and Limongelli 1994, p. 19)? Visalberghi and Limongelli devised several tests to probe Rb's understanding, the most compelling of which involved rotating the trap tube 180° so that it could no longer affect the peanut's trajectory—but again placing the peanut either to the left or right of the now ineffective trap (see Fig. 3.9(b)). The question was straightforward: would Rb continue to insert his stick into the opening farthest from the reward, despite the fact that the trap could no longer affect the movement of the peanut? Rb's answer was equally straightforward: he continued to use his strategy of inserting the stick into the opening farthest from the reward on 87 per cent of the trials, even though there was no need to do so. Furthermore, when he was confronted with both the trap-tube and the original plain tube, he now generalized his behavior to the original situation—even though no trap was present! On the basis of these (and similar) tests, Visalberghi and Limongelli (1994) concluded that, despite their excellent tool-using abilities, capuchin monkeys appear to understand very little about why their successful actions are effective. They explain:

> Capuchins have a high propensity to perform combinatorial behaviors and generate a variety of complex manipulative behaviors... This generativity can be viewed as a way of producing a variety of events, among which a winning association can be identified. In this sense, using a stick in the tube reflects an association between inserting the stick (no

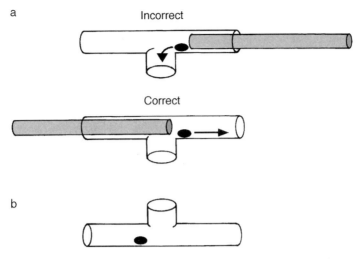

Figure 3.9 (a) The trap-tube problem devised by Visalberghi and Limongelli (1994) for use with capuchin monkeys. (b) The inverted trap-tube problem used to determine if the subjects understood how the trap functions.

> matter where) and getting the food, instead of comprehending why the side of insertion influences the outcome. (pp. 20–1.)

Although there is still much missing from this account, Visalberghi and her colleagues have clearly taken a major step forward in exploring the critical distinction between performance and comprehension in the context of tool using.

Are chimpanzees different?

In parallel to their studies of capuchin monkeys, Visalberghi and her colleagues have also investigated the reactions of chimpanzees (and other great apes) to the tube and trap-tube problems just described. Visalberghi, Fragaszy, and Savage-Rumbaugh (1995) investigated the reactions of common chimpanzees, bonobos, and an orangutan to the original tube study. As with the capuchins, these apes were initially presented with a clear plexiglas tube with a highly desired food item in the center, and a stick that could be used to dislodge it. As expected, the apes quickly figured out how to use the stick to push out the rewards. The critical testing occurred by presenting the apes with the taped-up bundles of sticks that were too thick to fit into the tube, as well as the inappropriately shaped sticks that could not be pushed into the hole until they were dismantled.

The results were as follows. In the bundle condition (where an error was defined only in those cases where the animals actually touched the tube with the bundle of sticks before breaking it apart), the apes were reported not to have made a single error. They untaped the bundles, and then proceeded to use one of the appropriate tools. In contrast, however, in the condition involving the inappropriately-shaped stick, in their initial block of trials the apes made just as many errors as had the capuchin monkeys. Just like the monkeys, the apes attempted to insert the tool in its inappropriate shape, they removed the blocking stick from one end only to go on to attempt to insert the other (still ineffective) end, and they sometimes even inserted the blocking stick (which was too short) after removing it from the main tool. Indeed, the initial appearance, type, and frequency of errors was indistinguishable from the capuchin monkeys. Notably, the apes were not administered the condition involving the three shorter sticks. Based on the results of these tests, Visalberghi and her colleagues concluded that with respect to an understanding of the causal relationships inherent in tool use, great apes 'appear to make greater progress [toward understanding causal relationships]…than do capuchin monkeys' (p. 59).

However, is it possible that apes simply uncover the relevant associations in such tests more quickly? Visalberghi and her colleagues acknowledge this possibility, but seem to favor the view that the differences uncovered in their tests 'are truly a reflection of qualitative differences in reasoning processes' (p. 59). However, given that the apes made numerous errors (indeed, as many as the capuchin monkeys) on one of the conditions, and the fact that the third condition was not administered, the exact differences between great apes and capuchin monkeys remain unclear (see also Tomasello and Call 1997).

Recognizing the ambiguity of these results, Visalberghi *et al.* (1995) appeal to 'convergent evidence' from other tests with chimpanzees—most notably, the trap-tube problem. They argue that the results of tests with chimpanzees involving the trap-tube problem reveal that some chimpanzees, at least, are able to relate their success on the trap-tube problem 'to an understanding of the causal relation between the tool-using action and its outcome…' (p. 59). We shall save our evaluation of this specific claim for the next chapter (Chapter 4), in which we not only examine in detail the evidence upon which their claim is based, but also present an extended series of more controlled empirical tests of chimpanzees' reactions to the trap-tube problem.

Here are the major themes to emerge from this chapter. First, many animals use objects that they encounter in their natural environments as simple tools, and some, such as chimpanzees, do so with a fairly wide range of objects in a variety of situations. In addition, although they are not the only animals to do so, chimpanzees do stand out as the most flexible of tool makers, regularly exhibiting evidence of applying simple modifications to objects found in their environments (McGrew 1992).

Having said this, however, some observations of chimpanzees suggest that our natural inclination to assume that they appreciate the underlying causal properties involved in tool use and manufacture may be misguided. For example, the dramatic solutions to artificially staged problems, such as Köhler's box-stacking tests, may not occur through the same processes used by humans. In contrast, a substantial amount of data suggests that by two or three years of age, human children come to appreciate the idea that the interaction of objects in the world are governed by underlying, and in some cases, invisible causal mechanisms. Indeed, using non-verbal techniques involving the amount of time infants spend looking at events, infants as young as six months of age have displayed some evidence of distinguishing 'cause' from 'effect'.

In contrast, the work of Elisabetta Visalberghi and her colleagues has suggested that at least certain instances of tool use (whether in monkeys or apes), which appear to be achieved on the basis of causal understanding, may turn out to be the products of rapid trial-and-error learning. Indeed, the obvious causal structure of the problems may be completely ignored, and perhaps never explicitly conceptualized by the tool-using animal.

We now move on to presenting our experimental attempts to assess to what extent chimpanzees and humans share a common folk physics. In Chapters 4–11, we report the results of two dozen experiments that we conducted with our seven chimpanzees to investigate their comprehension of tool use. Each chapter begins with a brief description of certain acts of tool use in wild or captive populations of chimpanzees that seem, on the surface at least, to involve an understanding of certain causal concepts that are under empirical scrutiny in the chapter. Next, the methods and results of our experiments related to this question are presented, along with a brief discussion of the implications of the specific findings.

In the final chapter of the book (Chapter 12), we critically evaluate the general approach used in these and related studies, and pay specific attention to the approach's strengths and weaknesses. In doing so, we identify a number of conceptual and empirical gaps in our knowledge of chimpanzees' understanding of causal relations among objects and use these to suggest an agenda for future investigations. Nonetheless, we conclude that, despite several limitations of the approach, it is thus far the single best available means of investigating the nature of other species' folk physics. Finally, we assess the broader implications of the findings reported here. We show how the differences between the psychology of humans and chimpanzees may transcend differences in specific domains of intelligence, and instead involve a distinction between reasoning about phenomenon that are, at least in principle, observable, versus those that are not. We suggest that this distinction may help to unify our approaches to understanding the evolution of folk notions of social cognition, on the one hand, and folk notions about physics, on the other.

CHAPTER 4

THE TRAP-TUBE PROBLEM

JAMES E. REAUX AND DANIEL J. POVINELLI

Termite fishing is perhaps the most emblematic form of chimpanzee tool use. Here, the chimpanzee inserts a probe—a long, thin, and pliant blade of grass, strip of bark, or piece of vine—into a narrow opening that he or she has exposed in a termite mound (see Goodall 1968b). This pattern of tool use was first documented by Goodall (1968b) at the Gombe National Reserve site in Tanzania, but has now been observed at other sites as well (Kasoje and Assirik; see McGrew 1992). Although there are numerous causal relations involved in the termite-fishing activity that are worthy of empirical scrutiny (see Chapters 5, 8, and 11), one of these dimensions involves the interaction between the tool (the probe), the substrate (the opening in the termite mound as well as the winding tunnel into which it must pass), and the food resource. It is of interest that a key aspect of the activity is not directly observed by the chimpanzee—namely, the termite seizing the tip of the probe with its mandibles. Nonetheless, the termite-fishing activity (along with other aspects of chimpanzee tool use) can be usefully thought of as a series of interlocking causal relations among the tool's interaction with the substrate, the tool's interaction with the food resource, and the food resource's interaction with the substrate. The animal's action on the tool provides a context for him or her to display some knowledge of these causal relations.

In this chapter, we report the results of an investigation of our chimpanzees' ability to solve the trap-tube task that was originally designed by Visalberghi and Limongelli (1994). As explained in Chapter 3, this task requires the subjects to insert a probe into one end of a tube in order to push out a food reward. Visalberghi and Limongelli (1994) originally designed the trap-tube task for use with capuchin monkeys. Their monkeys used a stick to push a reward out of a clear tube, but when the training tube was replaced with one that contained a trap in its center, only one of the monkeys learned to avoid the trap by pushing the food reward from the opposite side (see Chapter 3, Fig. 3.9). Recall that transfer tests to probe the successful monkey's understanding of his actions revealed that even this animal did not appear to be attending to the causal property of the trap. Rather, the results suggested that the monkey had learned a procedural rule of the type, 'insert the tool into the opening that is farthest from the reward'. For example, in one of these transfer tests the trap was inverted (thereby rendering the trap ineffective). Here, the capuchin monkey continued to insert the tool into the opening farthest from the reward, despite the fact that this strategy was no longer relevant.

Although Visalberghi and Limongelli's (1994) capuchin monkeys displayed little evidence of understanding the local causal interactions among the tool, the food object, and the trap, we felt that the natural proclivity for termite fishing among chimpanzees might offer this species a better chance of understanding of the trap-tube problem. However, although the trap-tube problem is similar in some ways to termite fishing, it also differs in several obvious ways. First, unlike termite fishing, the actions of the probe on the food resource and substrate are clearly visible at all times. Thus, in the trap-tube situation a subject can visually monitor the tool's moment-to-moment effect on the food reward. Second, in the trap-tube situation the means of obtaining the food reward is to push it out of an opening on the far end, not, as in the case of the termite fishing, having the food resource secure itself to the probe. Despite these differences, we sought to test chimpanzees on this task as a first step in exploring aspects of their causal reasoning in the context of tool using. After our tests began, an empirical report was published by Limongelli, Boysen, and Visalberghi (1995), who reported evidence that chimpanzees, unlike capuchin monkeys, understood the relevant causal interactions inherent in the trap-tube task. However, as we explain below, because they did not use the critical inverted trap condition of the original trap-tube study, it is difficult to interpret the results of their work.

Limongelli *et al.* (1995) tested five chimpanzees. Two of their apes successively learned (across 140 trials) to avoid the trap by inserting the tool into the side of the tube that would insure success. Next, to assess what these two apes had learned about the causal properties of the tool/trap/reward configuration, Limongelli *et al.* moved the trap from the center of the tube (Fig. 4.1(a)) to a location closer to one side of the tube opening, so that it was positioned between the reward and the end of the tube nearest the reward (Fig. 4.1(b)). Note that this was explicitly *not* the transfer procedure used by Visalberghi and Limongelli (1994), who inverted the trap, thus rendering it ineffective. Limongelli *et al.* argued that if the animals were relying exclusively on a distance-based empirical generalization, such as 'insert the tool in the opening farthest from the reward', then they would lose the reward because the trap was located on the other side of the reward (see Fig. 4.1(b)). And, in seeming contrast to the capuchin monkey studied by Visalberghi and Limongelli, both chimpanzees performed at levels far exceeding chance on this transfer test. Limongelli *et al.* concluded that their chimpanzees had demonstrated an understanding of the cause–effect relationships inherent in the trap-tube task.

However, Limongelli *et al.* (1995) excluded only one of several rules that the apes might have learned in their first experiment. Thus, although the transfer test they used was adequate to assess whether their apes were relying on a rule to insert the tool into the opening farthest from the reward, the transfer condition was not appropriate to test other associative rules the chimpanzees may have learned. For example, one rule that their two successful apes might have learned in the original training procedure was, 'push the reward (or tool) away from the trap'. Although this may appear to involve an

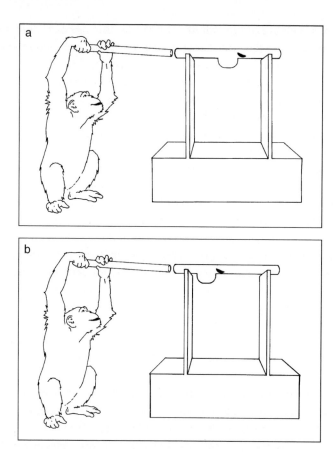

Figure 4.1 (a) Standard trap-tube problem of Visalberghi and Limongelli (1994). Two out of five chimpanzees tested by Limongelli, Boysen and Visalberghi (1995) learned to solve this version of the trap-tube problem. (b) Transfer test used by Limongelli *et al.* to determine if chimpanzees were relying on a rule: 'insert the tool into the opening that is farthest from the reward', or if they understood the causal properties of the trap. Although the chimpanzees successfully avoided the trap, this transfer test cannot adequately tease apart the apes' use of other procedural rules ('push the cookie away from the trap') from an understanding of how the trap functions. Limongelli *et al.* did not utilize the critical inverted-trap condition (see Fig. 4.5) used by Visalberghi and Limongelli with a capuchin monkey. See text for further details.

understanding of the causal properties of the trap/tool/reward relationships, this is not necessarily the case. Their chimpanzees might simply have learned to push the reward away from the general direction of the trap—even when it was inverted and thus clearly not able to interfere with the retrieval of the reward. Thus, although the performance of the chimpanzees tested by Limongelli *et al.* was consistent with the possibility that they understood the causal properties of the trap, the performance was also consistent with a simple rule that they did not address. Visalberghi and Limongelli's (1994) inverted trap condition, on the other hand, would appear to have the power to distinguish between these two accounts of the animals' performance.

The specific motivations behind the studies reported in this chapter were threefold. First, we initially explored this task because of its relation to aspects of chimpanzee tool use that develops in the wild. In particular, as outlined earlier, the task attempts to assess whether an organism can simultaneously keep track of the causal interactions among the tool, the substrate, and the food object to be obtained. Second, after the publication of what we considered to be a methodologically flawed empirical report claiming to have discovered a difference between how chimpanzees and capuchin monkeys understand the trap-tube task, we hoped to provide more rigorous tests of the chimpanzees' ability. To this end, we used the inverted trap condition employed by Visalberghi and Limongelli (1994), as well as several novel conditions that we developed. Finally, we sought to investigate whether, during the course of growing up, our apes would display evidence of maturationally- or experientially-driven changes in their understanding of the trap-tube task. We accomplished this by first testing our apes when they were juveniles (five to six years of age) and once more when they were young adults (ten years of age).

Experiment 1: the trap-tube problem, age 5–6

The purpose of experiment 1 was to test our chimpanzees on the diagnostic version of the trap-tube problem—a condition used by Visalberghi and Limongelli (1994) in testing their capuchin monkeys, but not used by Limongelli *et al.* (1995) in testing chimpanzees. In experiments 1(a)–(e) we applied novel transfer tests to further examine the nature of the chimpanzees' understanding of this task.

Method

Subjects and housing

The subjects were the seven chimpanzees described in Chapter 2. When this study began, they ranged in age from 5 years, 6 months (5;6) to 6;2. All of them had been born in captivity at the University of Louisiana. They had been peer-raised together in a nursery with several other chimpanzees. They were transferred to a specialized housing and testing facility when they were four years of age, where they lived together in an interconnected series of five indoor–outdoor enclosures. Details of their rearing histories and living environment are provided in Povinelli and Eddy (1996a). Prior to and during the tests described in this book, these chimpanzees participated in a number of different experimental protocols, none of which had investigated their tool-using abilities. The group consisted of six females (Kara, Jadine, Brandy, Megan, Mindy, and Candy) and one male (Apollo).

Apparatus and materials

The trap-tube apparatus consisted of a horizontal, clear tube (71 cm) with a diameter of 4.5 cm mounted onto a platform (91.5 × 61 × 25 cm) by two vertical plywood sheets (see Fig. 4.2(a)). The tube was later shortened to 51 cm and braced due to the animals' ability to crack the original tube. The design of the apparatus was very similar to that of Visalberghi and Limongelli (1994), but was adapted to test chimpanzees. A white PVC tube (71 cm in length; 3.5 cm in diameter) with end caps served as the tool.

Procedure

TRAINING. The chimpanzees were tested individually. First, each ape was transferred to an outdoor waiting area (connected to an outdoor testing area by a shuttle door) while the other animals remained together. The apes were intimately familiar with this process. The apparatus was placed in the center of the testing area and a reward was placed into the tube in plain sight midway between both openings. The ape was then let into the test unit. Several initial modeling sessions were administered during which the chimpanzee's trainer was inside the enclosure. The trainer placed the tool into the tube and pushed it to retrieve the reward (fruit or cookie) while the animal watched. Animals were allowed to try to complete the task with or without the help of the trainer. Two of the animals (Mindy and Apollo) refused to try to complete the task and were dropped from the experiment.

As soon as the remaining five animals displayed an ability to insert the tool and push out the reward, formal training began. The procedure was as follows. While the animal waited out of sight in the waiting area, the trainer entered the testing area, baited the apparatus, placed the tool in the neutral position (see Fig. 4.2(a)), and then exited the enclosure. The shuttle door was then opened, allowing the animal to enter the testing area and attempt to obtain the food reward from the tube. As soon as they succeeded,

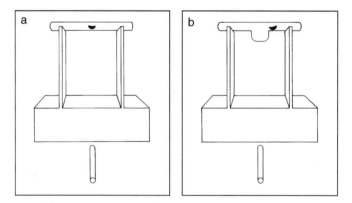

Figure 4.2 Setting and apparatus for our version of the trap-tube problem. (a) Training configuration (note the neutral placement of the tool along the midline of the tube). (b) Testing configuration using the trap-tube (again, note placement of tool along the midline of the apparatus).

the shuttle door was reopened and the ape was ushered back into the waiting area for the next trial. A maximum of ten trials per day were administered. We required the animals to perform 20 consecutive correct responses (with a minimum of 50 trials for each ape) before we advanced them to the trap-tube test. All five animals achieved criterion within 20 trials, and successfully completed every one of the 50 required trials.

TRANSFER TEST: TRAP-TUBE CONDITION. In this phase, the horizontal tube was replaced with a similar tube that contained a hole and a vertically oriented trap mounted in its center (see Fig. 4.2(b)). On each trial, a food reward was placed right or left of the trap according to a randomized schedule which was counterbalanced so that each ape received the same number of trials with the food to the right and left of the trap within each session. The tool was placed in a neutral position 3 meters directly in front of the midline of the apparatus. The trial began when the animal entered the testing area, and ended when the animal succeeded in obtaining the food, or pushed the food into the trap, or 2 minutes elapsed. An observer recorded the animal's latency to respond, the side into which they inserted the tool, and whether or not they obtained the reward.

The first 40 trials of the testing phase were used as a pilot study because several of the apes pushed the tool so quickly that they caused the reward (a vanilla wafer cookie) to skip over the trapping hole. None of the apes performed at levels exceeding chance across these trials. The tube was reconstructed by mounting the trap horizontally and enlarging the hole, which effectively eliminated this problem. Prior to restarting testing, each chimpanzee was administered one session of 10 retention trials, during which we used the horizontal tube (no trap). All five of the apes performed correctly on every trial. Another series of testing trials with the new trap tube was then conducted. One of the chimpanzees, Candy, refused to cooperate after she pushed the cookie into the trap on her first two trials, and was therefore dropped from the study. The remaining four animals were tested on 100 trials using the trap tube. They were tested once or twice a day in sessions of 10 trials.

Results

Table 4.1 presents the results of the 100 final trials of the trap-tube test for each of the four apes who were tested. Only one of the animals (Megan) performed at levels significantly above chance (see Table 4.1). Not only did the remaining three apes fail to learn to avoid the trap across 100 trials, two of them (Kara and Jadine) performed at levels significantly below chance. Figure 4.3 displays the individual performances of apes in blocks of ten trials. These data reveal that none of the unsuccessful chimpanzees performed above chance on any trial block.

The apes attempted a number of strategies in their attempts to retrieve the reward. The strategies of three of the chimpanzees (Kara, Jadine, and Megan) varied across blocks, whereas one of them (Brandy) consistently used the same strategy. The three unsuccessful apes either showed an initial bias toward inserting the tool on the same side as the reward (causing the reward to be lost every trial) or showed a preference for one side

Table 4.1 Performance of individual chimpanzee subjects in standard trap-tube test of experiment 1

	Percentage correct		
	Overall (N = 100)	Blocks 1–5 (N = 50)	Blocks 6–10 (N = 50)
Kara	38*	28*	48
Jadine	37**	28*	46
Brandy	51	52	50
Megan	80***	62	98**

For data below 50 per cent, significance values indicate a significant preference for the incorrect side (i.e. insertions of the tool into the opening closest to the location of the reward). All significance values are based on binomial tests. *$p < 0.05$, **$p < 0.01$, ***$p < 0.001$.

(resulting in being rewarded on half of the trials). Both Kara and Jadine used a combination of these strategies, initially choosing the same side, but later shifting to the right and left sides, respectively (see Fig. 4.3). Brandy consistently preferred the right side.

Megan was the only one of our chimpanzees who learned how to avoid the trap, and she averaged 80 per cent correct across the 100 trials she received (80/100, binomial test, $p < 0.001$). However, she did not understand the task immediately. Her performance in the first half of the study (trials 1–50) did not differ from chance (31/50, binomial test, ns). In contrast, she made only a single error in the second half of testing (49/50, binomial test, $p < 0.001$). Figure 4.3 depicts her learning curve in blocks of ten trials. During the first 30 trials, Megan almost exclusively inserted the tool into the same opening, regardless of where the reward was in relation to the trap (29/30 trials, binomial test, $p < 0.001$). However, she then began to vary the side of the apparatus into which she inserted the tool, and by the final 50 trials she made only a single incorrect insertion.

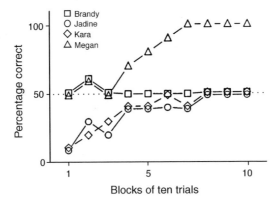

Figure 4.3 The performance of four chimpanzees who were tested on the trap-tube problem in experiment 1. The dotted line indicates the level of performance expected by chance responding or by a consistent bias of inserting the tool into either the right or left opening of the trap tube.

To investigate whether Megan's success on the task was accompanied by a significant difference in latency to respond on successful (as compared to unsuccessful) trials, an analysis of her mean trial duration in the first and second halves of the experiment was conducted utilizing a paired, two-tailed t-test. Results yielded a significant difference, $t(8) = 6.188$, $p < 0.001$, and an examination of the raw data indicated that this was because Megan took significantly longer to respond on each trial in the latter half of the experiment ($M = 21.3$ seconds, $SD = 3.95$) as compared with the first ($M = 9.1$ seconds, $SD = 1.95$). A significant correlation was found between her success rate and trial duration across the blocks of 10 trials (Spearman's $r^2 = 0.75$, $p < 0.05$).

Discussion

In their efforts to obtain the reward from the trap tube, our chimpanzees employed three distinct strategies: (1) always insert the tool on the same side (correct on half of the trials); (2) insert tool into the opening closest to the reward (always incorrect); and (3) insert the tool into opening farthest from the reward (always correct). An examination of the strategies used by the three unsuccessful apes (Brandy, Jadine, Kara), and the manner in which they appeared, suggests that these animals did not appear to understand that success was dependent first on the tool's interaction with the reward, and second on the reward's interaction with the substrate along which it moved (the trapping tube). Within the limited number of trials we administered ($N = 100$), these apes did not learn to use the successful strategy. In contrast, Megan learned to vary the insertion side of the tool, which in turn may have led to the ability to learn the correct strategy. Of course, it is important to emphasize that we administered only 140 trials of the trap-tube problem to our apes. We suspect that with enough experience most of our chimpanzees would have learned how to avoid the trap as well.

Although Kara, Jadine, and Brandy did not learn how to avoid pushing the reward into the trap, there was at least some evidence that these unsuccessful apes may have learned that they would not be rewarded on certain trials. For example, on several trials where Jadine inserted the tool on the wrong side, she immediately returned to the shuttle door to be let back into the adjoining unit, without ever pushing the tool—as if she recognized that the reward would be lost to the trap. Thus, Jadine may have learned to recognize the circumstances for failure, yet lacked the capacity to use this knowledge to exploit other possibilities for success.

This initial test addressed whether our apes would learn to solve the task by avoiding the trap tube. If the successful animals had succeeded from the outset, this may have implied a deeper understanding of the consequences of the causal structure of the task. However, it is clear that Megan, the only ape who did learn how to avoid the trap, did not do so immediately. This raises the difficult question of what to make of the kind of understanding that she developed during the course of learning how to solve the task. Clearly, at least two distinct possibilities exist. On the one hand, she may have learned a procedure based upon the distance of the reward from the openings of the tube, which could be described verbally as 'insert the tool into the opening farthest from the reward'. On the other hand, as an alternative (or in addition) to this rule, Megan may have learned something about the causal structure of the task. In particular, she may have represented the connection among the three central elements of the task: (1) her actions on the tool; (2) the tool's action on the reward; and (3) the trap's action on the reward. Indeed, it is the last relation in which we are most interested here, because it was this relation that was crucial to solving the transfer test. (However, as we shall see in later chapters, the nature of the chimpanzee's understanding of the other relations is equally open to question.) Throughout the remainder of this chapter, we shall refer to the hypothesis that Megan had simply learned a procedural rule, with no accompanying appreciation of one or more of the causal relations involved, as the *low-level model*. In contrast, we shall refer to the idea that she understood the relations involved as the *high-level model*. We appreciate the vagueness of these labels, and we realize that they may be misunderstood. However, it is necessary to have some shorthand labels to refer to these alternative accounts of Megan's understanding of her performance.

We should note that we have illustrated the low-level model with only a single rule type. In fact, as we noted in the context of critiquing the Limongelli *et al.* (1995) study, it is possible that a successful animal such as Megan may have learned a different rule, such as 'push reward away from the direction of the trap'. However, any such rules may or may not have been accompanied by an explicit representation of the various causal relations inherent in the trap-tube situation. As we shall see, however, the transfer tests we designed and conducted (experiments 1(a)–(e) to probe Megan's understanding of her behavior allowed us to determine whether she was relying on any such procedural rule, or whether she was attending to the specific interaction between the reward and the trap.

Experiment 1a: inverted trap condition, Megan, age 6

We first tested Megan on the transfer test used by Visalberghi and Limongelli (1994) in the capuchin study. Procedurally, experiment 1a was similar in all aspects to experiment 1 testing, except that the trap tube was inverted, rendering it ineffective in trapping the reward (see Fig. 4.4). Here, Megan could obtain the reward no matter where she decided to insert the tool. In this way, the predictions of the low- and high-level models were directly pitted against each other. If the low-level model were correct, and Megan was using a rule to insert the tool into the opening farthest from the reward, without considering how the trap functioned to capture the reward, she could be expected to continue to use this procedure *even when the trap was inverted*. Alternately, if the high-level model were correct, Megan could be expected to either insert the tool at random into either opening in the tube, or always insert it into one opening, because with the trap inverted it made no difference where the tool was inserted.

Method
This experiment was conducted six days after the completion of experiment 1. Experiment 1a consisted of four blocks of ten trials in which the tube was rotated so that

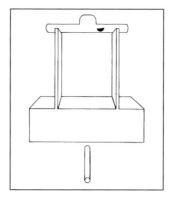

Figure 4.4 Configuration of the trap-tube apparatus for the inverted-trap condition used in experiment 1(a) (and later experiments). Note that the tool is placed neutrally along the midline of the trap tube.

the trap was inverted (facing up) and thus unable to affect the reward (see Fig. 4.4). A new schedule of reward placement was created using the same randomization and counterbalancing procedures described earlier. Otherwise, the testing procedures remained the same as experiment 1.

Results

Megan used the procedural rule strategy on 39/40 trials ($p < 0.001$, binomial test). Thus, she behaved as if the trap was still able to affect the reward, despite the fact that it was inverted. Another way of considering this result is to note that she behaved in exactly the same manner as she had when the trap was down and could affect the reward. These results are exactly those predicted by the low-level model, and imply that she was not attending to how the trap functioned to capture the cookie.

Experiment 1b: biasing the position of the tool, Megan, age 6

Although the results of experiment 1a support the notion that Megan was relying exclusively on a procedural rule to insert the tool into the opening of the tube that was farthest from the reward, it was possible that Megan understood that in its inverted position the trap could not affect the reward, but simply had no compelling reason not to use her procedural rule. After all, at the start of each trial, the tool was positioned equidistant from both openings in the trap tube (see Fig. 4.4). Thus, it required exactly the same amount of physical effort to use the procedural rule as to change to some other strategy (e.g. 'insert the tool at random into one of the openings').

We conducted experiment 1b to determine whether Megan's behavior on the inverted trap condition would change if their were a cost associated with the continued use of the rule (e.g. if the tool were placed on the base of the apparatus closer to one of the two openings of the tube). If she was relying exclusively on the procedural rule, we expected that, despite the extra effort required, she would carry the tool to the opposite side so that she could continue to insert the tool into the opening farthest from the reward. Alternatively, if she understood that the trap could not affect the reward in the inverted position, she could be expected to exert less effort and just insert the tool into the nearest opening.

Method

The experiment was conducted five days after the completion of experiment 1a. The same general testing procedure described earlier was used in this test. The new experimental treatment used in this test was termed the *tool-biased* condition. In this condition, the trap remained in the inverted position (unable to affect the reward) but the tool was placed on the base of the apparatus closer to the tube opening to which the food reward was closest. The low-level model predicted that Megan would continue to use the procedural rule, and therefore pick up the tool and carry it to the other side of the apparatus before inserting it. In contrast, the high-level model predicted that Megan, understanding that the trap could not affect the reward in its inverted position, would simply insert the tool into the opening that was closest to her (a response inconsistent with the procedural rule). Figure 4.5 depicts these predictions.

Megan was administered 20 trials. Ten consisted of the tool-biased condition (five on each of the two sides), and ten consisted of the experiment 1a test trials (trap up, tool in neutral position). In order to allow a direct comparison of Megan's reactions to the two conditions, administration of the 20 trials was randomized within the constraint that each of two ten-trial sessions contained five trials of each type, and that the tool (and reward) were placed on both sides of the apparatus equally often across the 20 trials.

Results

Megan behaved in accordance with the predictions of the low-level model. On 9/10 of the tool-biased trials ($p < 0.01$, binomial test), and on 10/10 trials where the tool remained neutral (experiment 1a trials), she used the procedural rule of inserting the tool into the opening farthest from the position of the reward. Thus, despite the fact that there was no reason to do so (the trap was inverted), Megan exerted the extra effort to insert the tool according to the procedural rule. These results are consistent with the predictions of the low-level model and are therefore consistent with the idea that what she learned in experiment 1 was not related to the specific local interactions of the reward and the trap.

Experiment 1c: trap-tube condition retention, Megan, age 6

The results of experiments 1a and 1b indicated that Megan was using a very general empirical generalization (the procedural rule) to solve the task. Before we could further probe her understanding it was necessary to determine if she would continue to use this

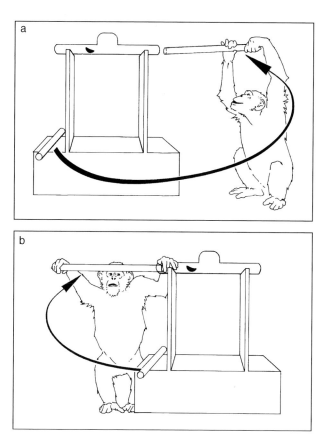

Figure 4.5 Configuration of the trap-tube apparatus for the tool-biased condition used in experiment 1(b) (and later experiments). Note that the tool is placed nearer to the opening of the tube that is closest to the reward. The predictions of the two models are shown. (a) The low-level model predicts the ape will expend the extra effort to carry tool to the opposite side of the apparatus to follow a procedural rule learned during the original trap-tube testing (e.g. 'insert tool into opening farthest from the reward'). (b) The high-level model predicts that the ape will not expend the extra effort because she understands that in the inverted condition the trap cannot affect the reward.

same strategy in the original condition from experiment 1 when the trap was actually in effect.

Method and results

Megan was tested five days after the completion of experiment 1b on two blocks of ten trials. The apparatus was configured as in experiment 1 with the trap in effect on all trials. A new schedule of reward placement was created using the same procedures described above. Megan obtained the reward on all 20 trials ($p < 0.001$, binomial test). Thus, she still consistently used the procedural rule when the trap was in effect.

Experiment 1d: tool-in-tube condition, Megan, age 6

The purpose of this experiment was to determine whether Megan would continue to use the procedural rule in an even more extreme version of the tool-biased condition from experiment 1b. In particular, we investigated how Megan would react to a tool-in-tube condition where she would encounter the tool already inserted into the opening of the tube that was incorrect from the standpoint of the procedural rule. This condition would present Megan with a situation in which the decision of where to insert the tool had, in effect, already been made—although in order to complete the task it would still need to be pushed. The trap was placed in the inverted position in this condition, rendering it ineffective. Thus, this condition tested the low-level model's prediction that Megan would inspect the apparatus, determine that the tool was in a position that violated her rule, and then retract it, carry it to the other side, and insert it in the opposite opening. If the trap were in effect, this would be a logical correction for Megan to make. However, because the trap was in the inverted position, no such correction was necessary, and therefore the high-level model would predict that she would not make the additional effort to change the side of insertion, and instead would simply complete the task of pushing the tool.

Method

This test began two days after completion of experiment 1c. Four sessions of 12 trials ($N = 48$ trials) were administered over a one-week period. Sixteen of these 48 trials consisted of the tool being placed in the neutral position, half with the trap in effect (down) and half with the trap not in effect (up). An additional 16 trials were administered using the tool-biased condition, in which the trap was not in effect and the tool was placed on the apparatus base, biased toward one side or the other. On half of these trials ($n = 8$), the tool was placed on the base of the apparatus closest to the reward, and on the other half ($n = 8$) it was placed on the side farthest from the reward. Finally, 16 trials of the new *tool-in-tube* condition were administered in which the trap was inverted (not in effect) and the tool was inserted 6 cm into the tube. On half of these trials the tool was inserted into the same side as the reward, whereas on the other half the tool was inserted into the side opposite from the reward. The 48 trials were randomly assigned across four sessions. Counterbalancing procedures were used within conditions to ensure that the tool position and reward locations occurred equally often on both sides (within the constraint that an equal number of the three general types of treatments be given within a session).

Table 4.2 summarizes the different predictions generated by the two competing hypotheses for each of the conditions used in this test. The low-level model predicted that Megan would continue to use the procedural rule of inserting the tool into the side opposite the reward regardless of treatment. Thus, the model predicted that on those tool-in-tube trials where the tool and the reward were on the same side; Megan would remove the tool and reinsert it into the opposite side; but on those tool-in-tube trials where the reward and tool were on opposite sides, Megan would simply push the tool.

In contrast, the high-level model predicted that, because the trap was inverted, Megan would simply push the already inserted tool, regardless of where the reward was positioned relative to the tool. The predictions of the two models for the tool-biased and tool-neutral conditions were the same as those derived in experiments 1, 1(a), and 1(b) (see Table 4.2).

Results

Curiously, the results provided support for both models. First, on all 16 of the tool-neutral trials, Megan performed in a manner consistent with the low-level model by selectively inserting the tool into the side of the tube opposite the reward, regardless of whether or not the trap was in effect ($p < 0.001$, binomial test). In addition, on all 16 of the tool-biased trials, Megan again inserted the tool into the side opposite the reward ($p < 0.001$)—despite the extra effort that was required on eight of these trials. Thus, she transported the tool to the opposite side even when it made no difference to the outcome. These two results provide support for the low-level model and suggest that she did not understand the specific causal principles of the trap.

On the other hand, in the new tool-in-tube condition, Megan simply pushed the inserted tool on every trial ($p < 0.001$, binomial test)—a behavior that had been

Table 4.2 Conditions and predictions for experiment 1d (with Megan)

Condition	n	Predictions of models	
		Low-level model	High-level model
Tool-in-tube			
	8	Ape will retract tool and insert on opposite side	Ape will push tool
	8	Ape will push tool	Ape will push tool
Tool-biased			
	8	Ape will carry tool to opposite side	Ape will insert tool on the side presented
	8	Ape will insert tool on the side presented	Ape will insert tool on the side presented
Tool-neutral			
	8	Ape will insert tool on opposite side from reward	Ape will insert tool randomly
	8	Ape will insert tool on opposite side from reward	Ape will insert tool randomly

predicted by the high-level model. Thus, regardless of whether the tool was inserted into the opening consistent with the procedural rule, Megan never retracted the tool to reinsert it on the opposite side. This performance is consistent with the idea that she understood that the trap could not affect the reward. However, the results from the other conditions cloud this interpretation. For example, if Megan was reasoning about how the trap affected the retrieval of the reward, then she should have responded differently than she did on the tool-biased trials.

The fact that Megan only seemed to understand the role of the trap in the tool-in-tube condition implied one of two alternatives. First, some aspect of this condition might have allowed her to demonstrate an existing understanding of how the trap worked. Perhaps the fact that she did not have to decide where to insert the tool allowed her to focus on the relevant causal interactions. Alternatively, however, this result might indicate that, far from appreciating the causal properties of the trap, Megan simply possessed a more structured set of procedural rules for solving the task than we had previously imagined. Experiment 1e was conducted to allow us to intelligently assess these two alternatives.

Experiment 1e: testing the revised procedural rule model, Megan, age 6$^{1}/_{2}$

A refined version of the procedural rule model (the low-level model) was developed which envisioned that on all trials Megan was following a deterministic order of steps: (1) obtain the tool; (2) locate the position of the food reward inside the tube; (3) determine the reward position in relation to the trap; (4) insert the tool into the opening of the tube that is farthest from the reward; and (5) push the inserted tool until the reward is obtained. This model envisioned that whereas Megan could begin from any one of these steps, she could only move forward in the sequence. If true, then in the case of the tool-in-tube condition, Megan would enter the testing area and immediately proceed to push the already inserted tool (step 5)—regardless of whether it was consistent with the rule she had learned—because the first four steps of the sequence had, in effect, already been executed. If correct, this condition would cause Megan to begin on step 5. And, if she could only move forward in the sequence, she would not have been able to retract the tool and insert it into the opposite side of the apparatus (which on half of the trials would have been consistent with the 'insert tool in opening farthest from the reward' rule).

The tool-in-tube condition of experiment 1d did not have the power to distinguish between this version of the low-level model and the high-level model because the trap was up (not in effect) on all trials, and therefore there was no cost associated with *not* removing the tool. In this experiment, we imposed such a cost by including a version of the tool-in-tube condition in which the trap was in effect (down) and the reward was on the same side as the tool. Thus, if the high-level model were correct, and Megan genuinely understood how the trap functioned to capture the reward, she ought to retract the tool on these trials, but not on the companion trials when the tool was inserted into the side opposite the reward (or, for that matter, on those trials when the trap was up). In contrast, the revised low-level model predicted that Megan would never retract the tool, because she was simply following the deterministic order of steps outlined above.

Method

The experiment was conducted approximately six months after the completion of experiment 1d. Because a considerable amount of time had elapsed, we conducted two phases of pretesting before beginning the experiment. Phase 1 of pretesting consisted of one session of ten trials using the original experiment 1 testing condition. Phase 2 of pretesting consisted of one session of ten trials in which the trap was in the up position. These were conducted to verify that Megan would continue using the rule about inserting the tool into the opening farthest from the reward, despite the fact that six months had elapsed. Experiment 1e followed these sessions.

Table 4.3 presents the conditions used in testing and the predictions of the two models. Four versions of the tool-in-tube condition were created by crossing the trap position (up or down) with the position of the tool relative to the reward (same versus opposite side). Thus, in two of the versions, the tool was inserted on the same side of the tube as the reward, with the only difference that the trap was up in one of these versions ($n = 8$) and down in the other ($n = 8$). In the remaining two versions, the tool was inserted on the opposite side of the tube as the reward, again with one version where the trap was up ($n = 8$) and the other where it was down ($n = 8$). We tested Megan on these 32 trials in two sessions consisting of 16 trials each. Each session contained four of each of the four trial types described above which were assigned in a random order.

The revised low-level model predicted that when the tool was in the tube Megan would simply push it (regardless of whether the trap was in effect). In contrast, the high-level model predicted that Megan would push the inserted tool only in those

Table 4.3 Conditions and predictions for experiment 1e (with Megan)

Condition	n	Predictions of models	
		Low-level	High-level
	8	Push tool	Push tool
	8	Push tool	Push tool
	8	Push tool	Retract tool/ reinsert on opposite side
	8	Push tool	Push tool

versions of the test where the trap was unable to affect the reward. In contrast, in those cases where the trap was down, and pushing the tool would cause it to fall into the trap, this model predicted she would retract the tool and then reinsert it on the appropriate side.

Results

The results of phase 1 of the pretest (with trap down, tool neutral) showed that Megan inserted the tool in the opening farthest from the reward on 8/10 trials ($p < 0.054$, binomial test). Megan did not follow the procedural rule on the first two trials, and therefore she lost the reward. After this, she followed the rule for the remaining eight trials. Grant's (1946) runs analysis indicated that this result was significantly different from chance ($p < 0.05$, where chance $= 0.5$).

In phase 2 of pretesting (with the trap up, tool in neutral position), Megan performed in a manner consistent with the procedural rule on 9/10 trials ($p < 0.01$, binomial test). She failed to use this rule on the first trial. In principle, this might have helped her to learn that in its inverted position the trap could not capture the reward, since she succeeded in obtaining the reward on this trial. However, this appeared not to be the case, as she reverted back to her strategy of inserting the tool into the opening farthest from the reward on all of the remaining nine trials of this type—despite the fact that it was not necessary to do so.

The crucial results of this experiment concern her performance on those tool-in-tube trials where the trap was up and the tool was inserted on the same side as the reward, versus those tool-in-tube trials where the trap was down and the tool was inserted on the same side as the reward. Megan's performance was exactly as predicted by the revised low-level model, and not as predicted by the high-level model. The most diagnostic trials ($n = 8$) were those in which the tool was inserted into the same side of the apparatus that the reward was on, and the trap was down. On these trials, Megan pushed the tool and therefore lost the reward to the trap on every trial—exactly as predicted by the revised empirical generalization hypothesis. Indeed, on 32/32 trials ($p < .0001$, binomial test), regardless of the trap configuration, Megan simply pushed the inserted tool. These results indicate in a very dramatic way that Megan did not understand the difference between the trap-up and trap-down versions of the tool-in-tube condition, thus indicating that her performance in experiment 1d should not be interpreted as supporting the high-level model.

Experiment 2: the trap-tube problem revisited, age 9–10

Four years after the beginning of experiment 1, we returned our animals' attention to the trap-tube task. In the interim, the chimpanzees had participated (or were currently participating) in a wide variety of tests related to tool use (see Appendix I for a timetable of these experiments). Thus, we sought to determine if our apes, now full adults and far more experienced at tool use, might display a better understanding of the trap-tube problem. For example, if additional animals learned to avoid the trap, perhaps they would show better evidence of comprehending the nature of how the trap actually functioned than had Megan four years earlier. Indeed, Megan herself represented an especially interesting case. Would her age and increased experience manifest itself as a deeper understanding of the problem than she had exhibited four years earlier? Of course, if some animals (including Megan) did perform differently at this time-point, it would be difficult to know whether this result ought to be attributed to individual, maturational, and/or experiential factors. However, in light of their more mature age, and considerably greater experience on other tool-using problems, an absence of such differences would be quite striking—as well as suggestive of deep, conceptual differences between humans and apes in the manner in which this problem is understood.

Method

Subjects
The subjects were the same seven chimpanzees (six females, one male) that began experiment 1. They ranged in age from 8;8 to 9;7 when the study began.

Apparatus and procedure
ORIENTATION. The same trap-tube apparatus and tool were used in this study. The study began by reorienting the animals to the apparatus with the baited straight tube (no trap). This orientation session consisted of placing the apparatus and two tools in the outdoor testing area, and allowing the animals to freely interact with it as a group for two hours. No food rewards were placed in the tube during this session.

TRAINING. The apes were individually trained on the problem of inserting the tool into the straight tube to dislodge the reward from the center. They entered the enclosure with the apparatus and the tool in place and were given 3 minutes to solve the problem. Each ape received three trials. From the exterior of the enclosure, the chimpanzees' trainer verbally encouraged the animals to solve the task. The purpose of this phase was: (1) to ensure that the animals who had previously mastered this part of the task (Jadine, Megan, Candy, Kara, and Brandy) still knew how to perform correctly; (2) to determine if the two apes (Mindy and Apollo) who had not previously learned to insert the tool would learn to do so spontaneously; and, if needed, (3) to train all of our apes to perform correctly. Those animals who did not perform correctly on all three trials were later paired with animals who did, and were allowed to observe and interact with these knowledgeable animals as they solved the task. They were then re-tested. This procedure was repeated until they successfully completed a three-trial session. Using various combinations of the procedures just described, all of the chimpanzees completed this phase by successfully completing a three-trial session

Next, a formal assessment of the apes' abilities was conducted in which the trainer did not interact with the animals. Each animal was tested in a session of ten trials. On each trial, a food reward was placed in the center of the tube and the tool was placed approximately 2 meters away in the neutral position (see experiment 1a–e). The animal was then let into the enclosure and was allowed up to 2 minutes to insert the tool into the tube and obtain the reward. The apes were required to complete a session of 10/10 correct responses before advancing to testing. All seven apes met this criterion in their first session.

TRANSFER TEST 1: TRAP-TUBE CONDITION. The straight tube was replaced with the trap tube for transfer test 1. The apes were administered 100 trials of the standard trap-tube condition, using the same randomization and counterbalancing procedures as in experiment 1. Thus, in order to be successful, the apes needed to insert the tool into the opening farthest from the reward. All aspects of testing proceeded as in experiment 1. Those animals that performed at levels exceeding chance were immediately advanced to Transfer Test 2. Only Megan met this criterion (see Results, below). The animals that were not responding at above-chance levels were provided with additional training in order to teach them how to avoid pushing the reward into the trap (see below).

ADDITIONAL TRAINING. The six apes that were not performing at levels exceeding chance by the end of the scheduled 100 trials of transfer test 1 underwent additional, more active training in an attempt to teach them how to solve the standard trap-tube task. These animals were trained across a variable number of sessions, with each session consisting of five trials. It should be noted that this training was approached with the idea of teaching the apes how to avoid pushing the reward into the trap, not of teaching them a specific rule. To this end, we used a variety of training methods, each tailored to the temperament of the individual chimpanzee. These methods consisted of shaping techniques (from outside the enclosure) that we designed to build upon the strategies that the individual animals were attempting to use to solve the test. For example, some animals were biased toward always inserting the tool into the left (or right) opening of the trap tube. In this case, we placed the reward in the tube in a position relative to the trap so that the ape would lose the reward on every trial if the ape persisted in his or her side bias. In addition, we frequently placed the tool nearer the correct opening in an attempt to break the animals' habits of always inserting it into the same opening. Where the apes would tolerate it, we also increased the number of trials per sessions. Verbal and gestural direction and encouragement (from outside the enclosure) were used throughout these training sessions. Those apes that eventually appeared to learn the task were formally assessed across 30 trials in which no prompting was provided. We required them to perform correctly on 90 per cent (27/30) of these trials to advance to transfer test 2. Two animals (Brandy and Candy) met this criterion (see Results below).

TRANSFER TEST 2. In order to assess the successful animals' understanding of the trap-tube problem, transfer test 2 was designed to test the apes in the same manner that Megan had been tested in experiments 1(a)–(e). Thus, we manipulated various aspects of the tool and trap positions, ultimately creating ten different conditions. These conditions, along with the predictions of the two models we were testing, are depicted in

Table 4.4. Each animal received eight trials of each condition, resulting in a total of 80 trials. The trials were administered in blocks of ten, with each session containing one trial of each of the ten conditions (and with the order of individual trial types assigned randomly).

Results

Transfer test 1
Table 4.5 presents the result of the trap-tube condition for each of the seven chimpanzees ($N = 100$ trials per ape). Perhaps the most striking finding was that Megan, who

Table 4.4 Conditions, predictions, and results for transfer test 2 of experiment 2

Tool/Trap Orientation	n	Subject's Behavior	Subject		
			CAN	BRA	MEG
(diagram)	8	Push tool	7	2	8
		Retract/reinsert	1	6	0
(diagram)	8	Push tool	8	8	8
		Retract/reinsert	0	0	0
(diagram)	8	Push tool	8	3	8
		Retract/reinsert	0	5	0
(diagram)	8	Push tool	8	8	8
		Retract/reinsert	0	0	0
(diagram)	8	Same side as food	0	2	0
		Opposite side of food	8	6	8
(diagram)	8	Same side as food	0	0	0
		Opposite side of food	8	8	8
(diagram)	8	Same side as food	2	1	0
		Opposite side of food	6	7	8
(diagram)	8	Same side as food	1	0	0
		Opposite side of food	7	8	8
(diagram)	8	Same side as food	1	0	0
		Opposite side of food	7	8	8
(diagram)	8	Same side as food	1	0	0
		Opposite side of food	7	8	8

had learned the task four years earlier, did not make a single error across the 100 trials. Her retention of the task thus appeared to be immediate and complete. Five of the other apes (Brandy, Candy, Jadine, Kara, and Mindy) performed at chance levels. Three of these animals displayed a strong side bias for inserting the tool into the left tube opening; the other two animals displayed the opposite bias. Thus, these subjects obtained the reward on roughly half of the trials. The final animal, Apollo, performed significantly *below* chance levels. He displayed a strong preference for inserting the tool into the opening of the tube that was closest to the reward, thus pushing the reward into the trap. As can be seen from Table 4.5, this preference to insert the tool into the incorrect opening grew even more pronounced in the second half of the test trials (despite the fact that this caused him to lose the cookie to the trap more frequently).

Additional training on the trap-tube condition

As described above, we attempted to teach the six unsuccessful animals how to solve the basic trap-tube task. Some of these animals were more conducive to this training than others and were able to learn how to avoid the trap within the relatively few additional training trials that we administered. Once a particular chimpanzee appeared to know how to solve the task, we assessed their performance in sessions of ten trials identical to those of transfer test 1. We required a criterion of 27/30 correct trials in order for them to advance to transfer test 2 (see below). Of the six apes who received this additional training, two (Brandy and Candy) reached the formal assessment and both met the criterion. Brandy had received 30 modeling/training trials prior to the criterion trials, whereas Candy required 80 such trials. Both of these animals were correct on 29/30 of the criterion trials.

Table 4.5 Performance of individual chimpanzee subjects in standard trap-tube test of experiment 2

| | Percentage correct | | |
	Overall (*N* = 100)	Blocks 1–5 (*N* = 50)	Blocks 6–10 (*N* = 50)
Apollo	17***	24***	10***
Brandy	48	46	50
Candy	49	48	50
Jadine	50	50	50
Kara	50	50	50
Megan	100***	100***	100***
Mindy	48	50	46

For data below 50 per cent, significant values indicate a significant preference for the incorrect side (i.e. insertions of the tool into the opening closest to the location of the reward). All significance values are based on binomial tests. *$p < 0.05$, **$p < 0.01$, ***$p < 0.001$.

The remaining four chimpanzees either did not show evidence of learning how to solve the task, became uncooperative, or both, and were therefore dropped from the study. At the time we made the decision to discontinue testing these four apes (Apollo, Kara, Jadine, and Mindy), they had received an average of 69 trials (range = 25–110).

Transfer test 2

Three chimpanzees (Megan, Brandy, and Candy) advanced to transfer test 2. The critical test concerned whether the animals understood the difference between the trap-up and trap-down versions of the tool-in-tube condition with the cookie on the same side as the tool (see Table 4.4).

As can be seen from Table 4.4, Megan and Candy responded in a very similar manner. On all trials of these two types, Megan simply pushed the tool, exactly as she had done four years earlier. Candy behaved in the same fashion on all but one trial of these two types. Thus, both animals lost the cookie to the trap on nearly every tool-in-tube trial where the trap was down and the tool was already inserted on the same side as the reward. Candy did retract the tool and replace it on the correct side on one of the eight tool-in-tube conditions when the trap was down, and never did so when the trap was up. This could be taken as some very limited evidence that she understood that the trap could only affect the reward when it was in the down position. However, it should also be noted that this occurred on trial 15 (out of 16) of the tool-in-tube conditions. In any event, with the exception of this single trial on Candy's part, the behavior of these two apes was consistent with the hypothesis that they were simply following a series of learned procedural steps—a sequence that could not easily be reversed in order to allow them to remove the tool from the tube to execute the general procedural rule they had learned to use to avoid the trap (see experiment 1e).

Brandy's performance differed from Megan's and Candy's. Although in the majority of the conditions her behavior was indistinguishable from Megan's and Candy's, in the critical tool-in-tube conditions with the reward on the same side as the tool and the trap either up or down, Brandy responded in a different manner. On 6/8 trials in the tool-in-tube, *trap-down* condition (see Table 4.4), Brandy retracted the tool, and then reinserted it into the correct side. On the surface, this behavior would seem to be consistent with the high-level model, and clearly inconsistent with the revised procedural rule model which had correctly anticipated Megan and Candy's behavior. However, Brandy performed in an almost indistinguishable manner in the comparable tool-in-tube, *trap-up* condition! Thus, she retracted the tool and reinserted it on the 'correct' side (that is, the side consistent with the procedural rule) on 5/8 trials, *even though there was no reason to exert this extra effort*. In short, although Brandy's behavior was inconsistent with the specific revised procedural rule hypothesis outlined in experiment 1e, she displayed no better evidence of distinguishing between the trap-up and trap-down versions of the tool-in-tube condition in which the reward was on the same side as the tool than did Megan or Candy. Rather, she can be thought of as being better able to execute the general procedural rule ('insert the tool into the opening farthest from the reward') than either Megan and Candy (who both appeared to have a much greater difficulty in reversing the steps in their procedures to obtain the cookie).

General discussion (experiments 1–2)

In experiments 1 and 2, three of our apes (Megan, Candy, and Brandy) learned how to successfully insert a tool into the opening of the trap tube that would allow them to avoid having the reward fall into the trap (that is, into the side opposite the reward). However, further tests (experiments 1a–e; experiment 2, transfer test 2) indicated that these animals were not conceptualizing the trap's up or down configuration as being relevant to their actions with the tool. Rather, they were relying on a rule which required them to insert the tool into the opening of the tube that was farthest from the reward. In addition, these tests suggested that the behavior of two of the animals (Megan and Candy) was guided by a set of difficult-to-reverse, procedural steps (see experiment 1e). The other ape that learned to solve the standard trap-tube task, Brandy, seemed to be able to reverse the order of steps in her learned actions, but even this animal provided no evidence that she was taking into account whether the trap was in effect in planning her actions.

We can summarize what the successful apes learned during the original trap-tube task as follows. They began by preferring to insert the tool consistently on one side of the tube, thus losing the reward on exactly half of the trials. Gradually, they began to vary the side into which they inserted the tool, thereby learning a rule to insert the tool in the tube opening farthest from the reward. In the case of Megan and Candy, once this behavior had been reinforced, the rule appeared to become routinized as a series of discrete, non-reversible steps. However, it is possible that these animals' apparent lack of understanding could be related more centrally to an inability to inhibit a learned sequence of actions. Thus, Megan and Candy may have been able to mentally represent the result that their actions would have, but were unable to inhibit carrying the tool to the side consistent with the rule, or, in the tool-in-tube conditions, pushing the already inserted tool. If true, this inhibitory problem would set limits on their ability to exploit other possibilities for success.

Brandy differed from Megan and Candy only in that she was able to implement the core procedural rule ('insert the tool into the opening farthest from reward') even on those trials where we had already inserted the tool into one of the openings. Brandy's results also cast doubt on attributing Megan and Candy's behavior strictly to inhibitory problems. After all, Brandy was at least somewhat capable of inhibiting the prepotent action of pushing the tool in the tool-in-tube condition, yet her underlying rule structure nonetheless appeared to be unrelated to the orientation of the trap.

In brief, the task can be thought of as requiring the animals to: (1) imagine a placement of the tool; and (2) imagine the effect of that tool placement on the fate of the reward. Although our procedure does not bear directly on this issue, it is possible that executing the rules that the apes learned through trial and error may take precedence over certain cognitive abilities (such as imagining the outcome of their actions) of which they may be capable.

In general, the results of these tests favor the hypothesis that our chimpanzees did not understand how the trap functioned in the context of the causal interactions among the tool, the reward, and the trap itself. Clearly, there are any number of reasons why this may be true. One reason (that we shall explore more thoroughly in Chapter 12) is that chimpanzees do not invoke a priori theoretical concepts (such as gravity) to mediate their use of tools. Indeed, Köhler noted that it is unclear 'how much the chimpanzee knows about the gravity [sic] and falling of objects. All this must be treated in greater detail in further experiments' (p. 116). A second possibility, though, is that something about the nature of the trap-tube task is artificially difficult. For example, one might question the logic of using a clear substrate which embeds a food resource. Indeed, one school of thought, which might be labeled 'hyper-naturalism', would assert that chimpanzees have not evolved to cope with problems related to obtaining resources embedded in clear substrates, and therefore cannot reasonably be expected to solve them with ease. Although we find such an objection implausible, and, futhermore, almost beside the main point under investigation by our project, it is nonetheless worth asking whether our chimpanzees could fare better on a task in which the causal interactions are, in some sense or other, more obvious. And to be fair, a weaker version of the objection just raised is that captive chimpanzees do not have enough direct *experience* coping with such problems, and therefore have not yet constructed an understanding which is, in principle, within their abilities. In effect, this discussion points to a slightly different objection, one which sees something about the nature of the trap-tube task itself that obscures the causal interactions involved. Indeed, the general difficulty that capuchin monkeys and chimpanzees alike have shown in learning to avoid the trap could be used to bolster this view (although we provide a different account of this difficulty in Chapter 12). Only 1/4 (25 per cent) of the capuchin monkeys tested by Visalberghi and Limongelli (1994), only 2/5 (40 per cent) of the chimpanzees tested by Limongelli *et al.* (1995), and only 3/7 (43 per cent) of our chimpanzees learned to avoid the trap (within the limited number of trials administered).

We close this chapter by emphasizing that we have little doubt that, with considerably more experience on their part, and considerably more patience on ours, most of our apes (as well as Visalberghi's monkeys) could have learned to solve the basic trap-tube problem. The fact that the majority of them did not learn to do so within 100 trials, and in some cases well over 200 trials, may suggest (for whatever reason) that this is not a task that nonhuman primates learn with ease. As we have seen, however, one possible reason for this is that the task either obscures the causal relations involved, or perhaps requires too many hypothetical scenarios ('if tool is placed in that opening, and if it is pushed, then…'). A related idea would be that it requires keeping too many causal principles (and too much other background knowledge) in mind at the same time. In the next chapter, we report a series of studies we designed to assess whether these ideas have predictive merit.

CHAPTER 5

THE TRAP-TABLE PROBLEM

DANIEL J. POVINELLI AND JAMES E. REAUX

As with any single task, there are several methodological limitations of the Visalberghi trap-tube problem that make it difficult to settle on the best interpretation of the results we obtained in experiments 1, 1(a)–(e), and 2. However, one means of addressing the inherent limitations of any single task is through *construct validity*—that is, developing multiple procedures for assessing the same psychological abilities. With this in mind, we constructed another tool-using task—the trap-table problem—in which our chimpanzees were again required to reason about the interaction between a simple tool (a rake), a goal object (a food reward), and the substrate (the table surface) along which the goal object moved. We designed the trap-table task so that it would embody the same logical causal interactions inherent in the trap-tube problem, but would present these interactions in a manner that might be more obvious to our apes.

Recall that, in the basic version of the trap-tube problem, one interpretation of the task was that the apes would have to execute two mental operations *before* acting on the tool. First, they would need to consider a particular tube opening into which they could insert the tool, and second, they would have to consider what the outcome would be if they pushed the tool into that opening. In contrast, we designed the trap-table situation so that the apes were confronted with a less complicated choice. In this task, they were confronted with a choice of pulling one of two rake tools, one of which would lead to a successful retrieval of the reward, the other of which would cause the reward to fall into a trap. Thus, the apes did not have to imagine both the placement of the tool and the outcome that would ensue if it were used in that location. In addition, we used substrates (flat surfaces) with which the apes were extensively familiar. In this way, we sought to test the generality of the difficulties that our apes had experienced with the trap-tube problem.

Experiment 3: the trap-table problem, age 6–7

The purpose of this experiment was to further examine the ability of our chimpanzees to anticipate the causal interactions between a tool, a goal object, and a substrate. A simple task was devised whereby our apes could choose which one of two rake tools to use in order to obtain a food reward. The selection of one of the tools would allow the ape to retrieve a food reward by dragging it along a solid, uninterrupted surface, whereas the selection of the other tool would result in the loss of a food reward into a large hole that we had cut into the surface. We designed this new tool-using system to help us assess the chimpanzees' understanding of the trap problem in a situation where the causal implications of their actions were, hopefully, more obvious.

Method

Subjects

The same seven chimpanzees who participated in experiments 1 and 2 were used. At the start of this study the animals ranged in age from 6;2 to 7;1.

Apparatus and materials

A wooden table (91 × 86 × 30 cm) was constructed and painted a neutral color. The length of the table was divided by a rail that allowed two identical sections to form the table surface (see Fig. 5.1(a)–(b)). The table was constructed so that these two surfaces could be taken out and replaced with other table surfaces as required in testing (for example, see Fig. 5.1(c)).

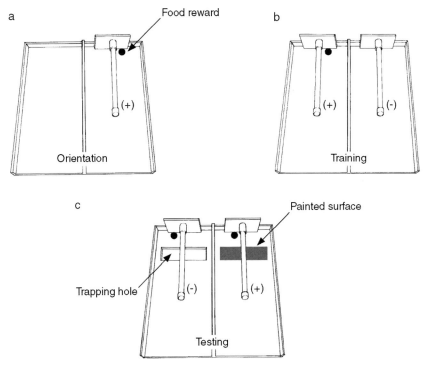

Figure 5.1 Experiment 3. (a) Configuration of the rake-and-table apparatus that was used to orient the chimpanzees to pulling the rake and retrieving the food reward. (b) Configuration of the rake-and-table apparatus that was used to formally assess the chimpanzees' abilities to select the rake that could retrieve the reward. (c) Trap-table setup that was used to test the apes to determine if they would select the correct option.

Two sets of surfaces were constructed. In the first set, the table surfaces were continuous and covered the entire table length and width (Fig. 5.1(a) and (b)). These surfaces were used in the training phase to familiarize the apes with the task. (They were also used in the testing phase to provide baseline trials to monitor the subjects' motivation.) The second set of surfaces consisted of one continuous surface and one surface in which a rectangular hole was cut into one side 15 cm from the far end of the surface (see Fig. 5.1(c)). The hole measured 10×30 cm, so that it spanned the majority of the surface width. The continuous surface contained a painted rectangle of the same dimensions that was located in a position analogous to that of the hole (see Fig. 5.1(c)). In an attempt to emphasize the solidity of the painted surface, we painted the rectangle blue to match the color of many apparatuses that the animals had used previously and extensively. This set of surfaces was used during probe trials in testing. The tools were rakes that could be used by the subjects to obtain a food reward that was placed out of their immediate reach (see Figure 5.1(a)–(c)). The rake handle was made out of white PVC tubing with a diameter of 2 cm and a length of 58 cm. The base of the rake was a plywood square (25×15 cm) that was mounted to the handle. The base of the tool was later lengthened to 41 cm $\times$ 15 cm to enable it to cover the entire width of the table surface (see Results section below). One rake was used in the orientation phase of the experiment, whereas two identical ones were used in the training and testing phases.

Procedure

TRAINING. Each ape was individually ushered into an outdoor waiting area that was connected by a shuttle door to an indoor testing room. The shuttle door was operated from the indoor testing room. The testing room was divided into a testing area (the 'test unit') for the animals (consisting of a clear plexiglas divider with a wire mesh top), and a working space for the experimenters (see Fig. 5.2). The plexiglas divider contained several holes that were 14 cm in diameter. Our apes were very experienced with being separated from their peers, entering the test unit, and manipulating apparatuses through the holes in the plexiglas to obtain food rewards. The apparatus table sat flush against the plexiglas partition just below the holes, making the rakes easily accessible. The holes were aligned with the table surfaces so that the apes could reach through and grab the rake handle and use it to pull in food that was positioned out of reach near the head of the rake (see Fig. 5.1(a) and 5.2).

We separately familiarized each animal with the apparatus, and provided them with a modeling session in order to orient them to the proper use of the tool. Only one rake was used and it was alternated between sides of the table so that the apes used the tool equally often on both sides. All of the apes readily learned to pull the rake and obtain a reward.

After the initial orientation session, formal training began. At the start of each trial, an experimenter entered the indoor test room, prepared the table surfaces by placing the tool and reward in their predetermined positions, and then exited the test room. The

Figure 5.2 Indoor testing unit with trap-table apparatus in place for orientation for experiment 3. Note location of shuttle door which was used to control the apes' entry into the testing unit.

trainer then opened the shuttle door via a pulley system on the back wall of the testing room and remained facing the wall during the trial. The apes entered the indoor test unit, reached through the holes, grabbed the rake handle, and pulled until the reward was within reach. The apes retrieved the reward and returned to the exterior waiting area and the shuttle door was closed behind them. The entire process was repeated for each trial.

Once our apes were proficient at using the tool, we implemented a criterion phase in which the apes were given a choice between two rakes, only one of which had a reward in front of it (Fig. 5.1(b)). The criterion phase consisted of 20 trials in which the apes were required to enter and pull the correct rake to retrieve the reward. We administered the criterion phase in four sessions, each of which consisted of five trials. We required the apes to perform 18/20 consecutive correct choices before we advanced them to testing.

TESTING. Testing consisted of baseline trials and probe trials. Baseline trials were identical to the trials used in the criterion phase (i.e. continuous table surfaces, a rake on each surface, but a food reward in front of only one of them). On probe trials, we replaced the solid surfaces with the testing surfaces (one with a hole, the other with a painted rectangle; see Fig. 5.1(c)). Each rake had a reward against its base on the far side of the hole or painted surface (see Fig. 5.1(c)). Each probe trial began by allowing a subject to enter the test unit and choose a rake to pull. For each trial, a choice was defined as pulling one of the rakes until the reward was either obtained by the ape or lost to the trap. Thus, the apes were allowed to switch tools until a reward was either lost or retrieved.

Each of the chimpanzees were administered ten testing sessions. Each session consisted of a total of six trials: four baseline trials and two probe trials. The probe trials were randomly assigned to occur between and including trials 2–5. Thus, a total of 20 probe trials and 40 baseline trials were administered to each ape across the ten sessions. The side of the correct choice for the baseline trials was randomized within the counterbalancing constraint that each side was correct on an equal number of trials within each session. The side of the correct choice on probe trials was randomized within the constraint that both sides were correct equally often across sessions.

We allowed the apes to make two choices on each probe trial if they chose to do so. For example, if an animal entered and chose the incorrect rake, the reward would fall through the hole rendering it inaccessible. At that point, they were allowed to pull the other rake if they so wished and obtain the reward. Alternatively, if a subject chose correctly on the first try, they were allowed to pull the incorrect rake if they so wished. However, in each case, the first choice was used as the main measure of their performance.

Predictions

We tested the predictions of two broad models. A *perceptual-motor* model envisioned that in the course of learning to use the rake tool in training, the apes learned a simple two-step rule: (1) 'locate the side of the table with the food reward'; and (2) 'pull tool to retrieve reward'. According to this model, the apes would not automatically assume that the nature of the surface was relevant to whether the reward was obtainable. Because there were two choices, the perceptual-motor model predicted that the apes' performance would not exceed 50 per cent correct (chance performance) on the probe trials. In contrast, a *high-level* model envisioned that, in addition to the procedural rules just described, the chimpanzees would integrate, before they acted, the effect of their own action on the tool, the tool's effect on the goal object, and the goal object's interaction with the table surface—thus causing them to choose the rake resting on the continuous surface.

Results

Training

When confronted with the choice depicted in Fig. 5.1(b), all of the apes met the criterion of 18/20 correct trials within their first 20 trials. As a group, they averaged 99 per cent correct. Thus, all of them advanced directly to the testing phase.

Testing

All apes responded on every baseline and probe trial. The baseline trials (which involved a choice between a baited and unbaited rake, both on continuous, solid surfaces), were used to assess whether all of the apes were sufficiently motivated to retrieve the food reward during test sessions. The apes made only a single error on the baseline trials (239/240 correct). These results indicate that the apes were highly motivated to obtain the rewards.

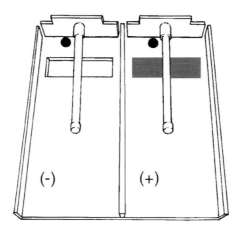

(-)   (+)

Figure 5.3 Modified rake tools used in experiment 3 testing. Note widened bases which prevented the incorrect rake from falling into the trapping hole.

The first ape to undergo testing was Candy. In her first probe trial, Candy made an incorrect choice. As she pulled the rake over the hole, the base of the rake fell into the hole and startled her. Due to the possibility that she would retain an irrelevant bias against the surface with the hole during the remaining probe trials, we decided to eliminate her from the study without further testing. Before testing any other apes, both rakes were modified by extending the base length to match that of the width of the table surface so that the rakes could not drop into the hole (see Fig. 5.3). At this point, the remaining apes were familiarized with the new tools on the continuous surfaces for one session, and then tested as described above.

The results for the remaining six apes are presented in Table 5.1. They reveal that Megan was the only ape in the group who consistently chose the correct rake as her first

Table 5.1 Number (and percentage) of correct solutions of each subject in experiment 3 testing

	Number (and percentage) correct		
Subjects	**Overall**	**First half ($N = 10$)**	**Second half ($N = 10$)**
Successful			
Megan	*16/20 (80)	8/10 (80)	8/10 (80)
Unsuccessful			
Jadine	13/19 (68)	5/9 (56)	8/10 (80)
Brandy	10/20 (50)	5/10 (50)	5/10 (50)
Mindy	10/20 (50)	5/10 (50)	5/10 (50)
Apollo	14/20 (70)	6/10 (60)	8/10 (80)
Kara	13/20 (65)	7/10 (70)	6/10 (60)

*$p < 0.01$ (binomial test).

Table 5.2 Trial-by-trial results for each subject in experiment 3 testing

Subject	Trials																			
	1	2	3	4	5	6	7	8	9	10	11	12	13	14	15	16	17	18	19	20
Jadine	−	+	+	+	+	−	X	−	+	−	+	+	+	−	+	+	+	−	+	+
Brandy	+	+	−	−	−	+	−	+	+	−	+	−	+	−	+	−	+	−	−	+
Megan	+	+	+	+	+	+	−	+	−	+	+	+	+	+	+	+	−	−	+	+
Mindy	+	−	+	−	−	+	−	−	+	+	−	+	−	+	+	+	−	−	−	+
Apollo	−	−	+	+	+	−	−	+	+	+	+	−	−	+	+	+	+	+	+	+
Kara	+	−	−	+	−	+	+	+	+	+	+	+	−	+	+	+	−	+	−	−

'+' = Correct trial; '−' = Incorrect trial; 'X' = Trial omitted due to subject pulling both rakes simultaneously.

choice, and she did so from trial 1 forward (see Table 5.2). She chose the correct tool on 80 per cent of the trials (16/20, $p < 0.01$, binomial test). None of the other animals performed at levels exceeding chance. An examination of the data from the second half of the testing phase (trials 11–20) indicate that two of the apes (Apollo and Jadine) may have been in the process of learning to select the correct tool (both 8/10 correct). The performance by trial for all apes is presented in Table 5.2.

Discussion

Five of the six apes who completed testing performed in the manner predicted by the perceptual-motor model. Indeed, only Megan displayed the ability to select the correct option to obtain the food reward; furthermore, she did so from trial 1 forward. Her results were consistent with the predictions of the high-level model.

How are we to interpret the difference between Megan's behavior and the rest of the group? On the one hand, this result may be taken to indicate that an understanding of the local causal relations of the trap-table task are not beyond the ability of chimpanzees. However, it is also possible that Megan's performance had little to do with an understanding of the causal relationships in the task. For example, she may have possessed an initial preference for the painted surface due to prior experience with the color. During previous experiments (none of which were related to the understanding of tool use or causality), all of the apes, including Megan, were tested using other apparatuses that were painted the same color as the painted table surface. Indeed, we had *intentionally* painted the surface this color in the hopes of assisting the apes in understanding its solidity (see above). Another possibility is that she may simply have chosen correctly on the first trial, and, unlike the other three apes who did likewise (Brandy, Mindy, and Kara), Megan may have formed an immediate association between the colored rectangle and successfully retrieving the reward. Because the procedures used in experiment 3 did not possess the controls necessary to rule out these possibilities, and because we hoped to explore possible developmental changes in the apes' understanding of the task, experiment 4 was conducted one year later.

Experiment 4: the trap-table problem revisited, age 7–8

This study was designed with two purposes in mind. First, as indicated above, we sought to test the idea that Megan's performance in experiment 3 was governed by an attraction to the surface with the colored rectangle, and not an a priori understanding of the causal interactions of the tools, rewards, and substrates involved in the task. Our second goal was to train all of the apes to respond correctly (through trial-and-error learning) and then, once they could successfully avoid the trap, assess what they understood about the task. Both of these goals were achieved by constructing five new configurations of the trap-table apparatus, each of which offered a choice between two surfaces. These configurations were explicitly designed to allow us to make inferences about the features of the surface, tool, and reward movement to which the apes were attending. The individual conditions are described in detail below.

Method

Subjects

The same seven apes that participated in experiment 3 served as subjects for this study. At the time of testing, the apes were approximately one year older (7;1 to 8;0).

Models to be tested

The purpose of this study was twofold. First, we sought to teach all of the apes how to solve the trap-table task (as presented in experiment 3) by giving them repeated trials until they became proficient at selecting the correct option as their first choice. Second, we sought to then test the animals on a series of experimental conditions that could allow us to evaluate three models of their understanding of their behavior. One model envisioned that the apes would learn a rule that invoked a simple association between the blue rectangle and successful performance (the *color-bias* model). A second model envisioned that the apes would learn a rule that invoked an association between the hole (the trap) and failure (the *avoid-side-with-hole* model). Finally, a *high-level* model envisioned that the animals would learn a more specific relation between the position of the goal object relative to the trap, or, even more advanced, would learn about the relation between the projected path of the objects and the position of the trap. Five different testing conditions were created to test the predictive power of the three models (see below).

Apparatus and materials

The same general apparatus and tools used in experiment 4 were used in this experiment, with the exception that new table surfaces were created to administer the new experimental conditions (see Fig. 5.4). In general, however, the task remained one in which the apes had a choice between two tools to aid them in retrieving a food reward.

Procedure

TRAINING. We trained the chimpanzees (including Megan) to choose the correct option by administering repeated trials using the testing condition from experiment 3 (one surface with a hole, the other with a blue rectangle, see Fig. 5.1(c)). The general procedures were the same as in experiment 3, with the exception that there were no baseline trials and, in order to speed the learning process, differential reinforcement was used. Thus, when the apes chose incorrectly, their trainer immediately ushered them out of the test unit before they could make a second choice. The apes were administered multiple sessions consisting of five trials each. Before we advanced them to testing, we

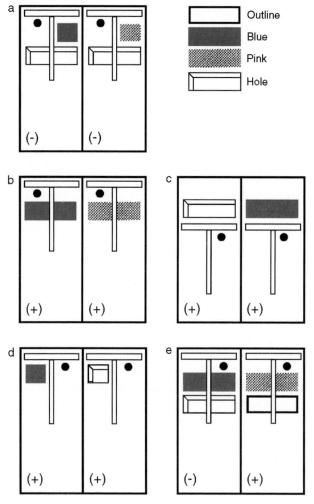

Figure 5.4 (a)–(e) Five testing conditions used in experiment 4. The text provides a detailed description of the logic of each condition

required the apes to reach a criterion of 14/15 correct choices (across three consecutive 5-trial sessions). All apes achieved this criterion, with some apes requiring more training sessions than others (see Results).

TESTING. Testing consisted of ten sessions, each containing six trials. Each session consisted of four baseline trials and two probe trials. The baseline trials were identical to those used in experiment 3 (two tools on solid surfaces, only one tool baited). The probe trials were used to administer five different experimental conditions (see Fig 5.4 and below). Each ape received four trials of each of the five conditions in a random order. The left/right positions of the table surfaces within each condition were counterbalanced across sessions within apes. A diagram of the testing apparatus for each condition can be found in Fig. 5.4. Placement of the probe trials within sessions was randomly determined within the constraint that they occur between and including trials 2–6. The remaining trials were baseline trials (with the correct side determined randomly, within the constraint that each side be correct equally often within each session).

TESTING CONDITIONS AND PREDICTIONS. Condition A (see Fig. 5.4(a)) consisted of an impassible hole (identical to experiment 3) cut into both table surfaces. Additionally, a small square (11 × 11 cm) was painted above the right half of the rectangular hole on each of the surfaces, one colored blue and the other colored pink. In this condition, it was impossible to retrieve the reward because each surface contained a trap in front of the reward. Both the high-level model and the avoid-side-with-hole model predicted that the apes would choose randomly, make no response at all, and/or hesitate longer (as compared to baseline trials and other conditions) because it was impossible to avoid the hole and succeed. In contrast, the color-bias model predicted that the apes would choose the tool that rested on the surface with the blue square.

Condition B (see Fig. 5.4(b)) consisted of the two table surfaces with blue and pink painted rectangles. In this condition, pulling either tool would allow the ape to successfully retrieve the reward; therefore, the high-level model predicted a tendency toward random choices by the apes. In contrast, the color-bias model predicted that apes would choose the tool that rested on the blue surface. The avoid-side-with-hole model made no predictions because there were no holes in the surfaces.

Condition C (see Fig. 5.4(c)) consisted of one surface with an impassible hole and the other surface with a blue painted rectangle. This condition was a duplicate of the original condition employed in experiment 3, except that the rakes were positioned in front of the trapping hole and the painted rectangle. Because either choice would lead to success, the high-level model predicted that the apes would tend to choose randomly. In contrast, both the color-bias model and the avoid-side-with-hole model predicted that the apes would choose the tool on the surface with the painted blue rectangle surface.

In condition D (see Fig. 5.4(d)), an 11 × 11 cm hole was cut into one surface and a blue square of identical dimensions was painted on the other. The hole and the painted square were located directly in front of one side of the base of the rake. The reward was placed near the opposite side of the base of the rake. As can be seen in Fig. 5.4(d), the rewards would easily avoid the hole or the painted square when the rakes were pulled. Because of this, the high-level model predicted that the apes would tend to choose randomly, whereas both the color bias model and the avoid-side-with-hole model predicted that the apes would choose the rake on the surface with the blue square.

Condition E (see Fig. 5.4(e)) consisted of one surface with a blue rectangle and immediately in front of this rectangle was an impassible hole. The other surface contained a pink rectangle and immediately in front of this rectangle was the painted outline of a rectangle. Both the high-level model and the avoid-side-with-hole model predicted that the apes would choose the tool on the surface with the pink rectangle and outline, thereby successfully retrieving the reward. In contrast, the color-bias model predicted that the apes would choose the tool on the surface containing the blue rectangle and impassible hole.

A description of the five conditions just described, along with the predictions generated by the three models, is provided in Table 5.3.

In all cases, a choice was defined as the first tool that a subject moved. The apes were allowed only one choice per trial.

Data analysis

In addition to the main dependent measure described above, the latency to respond for all testing probe trials was scored from videotape by a main rater. Latency to respond was defined as the elapsed time from the moment a subject's body broke the plane of the shuttle door as they entered the test unit until the reward was successfully retrieved by the subject or fell into a trapping hole. Twenty per cent of the data was scored from videotape by a second rater to assess reliability of the latency measures. Pearson's correlation between the two raters' data sets yielded a coefficient of determination, r^2 of 0.98. The results of the main rater were used for data analysis.

Results and discussion

Training

The number of sessions to achieve criterion ranged from 4 to 55 sessions ($M = 20.4$, $SD = 17.6$) and 20 to 275 trials ($M = 102.1$, $SD = 88.1$ trials). Perhaps the most interesting aspect of the training results came from Megan, who had performed above chance on her first block of trials of this condition in experiment 3. She performed randomly (2/5 correct) in her first session (although she performed flawlessly to criterion from that point forward).

On the other hand, Jadine, who had displayed some evidence of learning by the end of experiment 3 (see Table 5.1 and 5.2), met criterion in the minimum number of sessions possible, scoring 19/20 correct responses (only trial 5 was incorrect). The remaining five apes all displayed clear learning curves across the training sessions before achieving criterion (see Fig. 5.5).

Table 5.3 Predictions of three models of the trap-table problem (experiment 4) and empirical results

	Condition A		Condition B		Condition C		Condition D		Condition E	
	(-)	No Response	(+)	(+)	(+)	(+)	(+)	(+)	(-)	(+)
Predictions of models										
High-level	50 (33)	0 (33)	50	50	50	50	50	50	0	100
Avoid-trap	50 (33)	0 (33)	—	—	0	100	100	0	0	100
Color-bias	100	0	100	0	0	100	100	0	100	0
Empirical results										
Mean =	**35.7**	**21.4**	**50.0**	**50.0**	**39.3**	**60.7**	**46.4**	**53.6**	**25.0**	**75.0**
SEM =	37.8	26.7	20.4	20.4	19.7	19.7	17.3	17.3	28.9	28.9

Testing

The overall results of each condition can be found in Table 5.3. The results of each condition were separately analyzed using paired *t*-tests (two-tailed) to determine if the apes displayed a preference for choosing one of the two options. For conditions A, B, C, and D, no significant differences were found between the two options. In condition E, however, where there was a penalty for choosing incorrectly, the apes approached a significant preference for choosing the correct rake, $t(6) = 2.291$, $p = 0.06$.

In order to determine if some of the conditions were marked by longer response latencies than others, the mean response latency for the apes for each condition and for baseline trials were analyzed. A one-way repeated measures ANOVA indicated a significant main effect of condition, $F(5,30) = 6.247$, $p = 0.0004$. This was due to the fact that the apes took longer to respond during condition E than they did on every other condition including the baseline trials (Tukey-Kramer Multiple Comparison Tests, $p < 0.05$, in all cases). This effect may be due to the fact that in both the training trials and conditions A–D the trapping hole and the blue rectangle were always separated. In contrast, in condition E the trapping hole and the blue rectangle were present on the same surface. This may have been inconsistent with their general expectations from the training and other probe trials. No other conditions differed from each other.

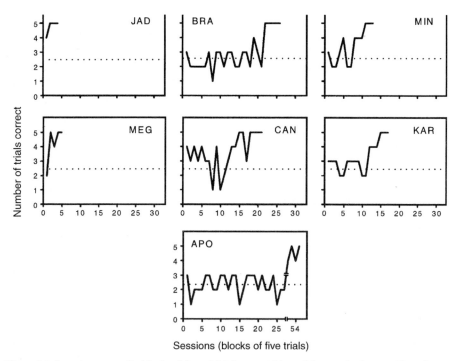

Figure 5.5 Learning curves (in blocks of five trials) for acquisition of the standard trap-table task (see Fig. 5.1(c)) in the training phase of experiment 4. Note especially Megan's initially random performance and Jadine's apparent retention from experiment 3.

How do these findings relate to the models that we set out to test? First, the fact that the animals did not have a preference for one option over the other in conditions A–D indicates the poor predictive power of the color-bias model—training the apes on the original trap-table condition did not appear to teach them to use a narrow rule that relied solely on pulling the tool on the side that contained a blue surface. If they had learned this, they ought to have displayed a preference for the side with the blue square or rectangle in all four of these conditions. Additional evidence against the color-bias model can be derived from condition A, where success was not possible. In this condition, Megan, Jadine, and Kara did not make a choice on half of their trials. Although this effect was not statistically significant, it is inconsistent with the a priori prediction of the color-bias model, and consistent with the predictions of both the avoid-side-with-hole model and the high-level model.

Next, certain aspects of the findings suggest that the apes were not relying on a simplistic 'avoid-the-side-with-a-hole' rule. After all, if this had been the basis for their decisions, they ought to have shown a clear preference for one side over the other in both conditions C and D, which they did not.

Overall, the results are most consistent with some version of the high-level model. The findings indicate that, after considerable training on the basic trap-table task, our chimpanzees learned more than a simple rule such as avoiding surfaces with holes or choosing surfaces with blue areas. At the very least, they appeared to learn that the only holes that were relevant were those that lay directly in front of the reward. This can be inferred from their random performance on condition D versus their preference for the correct option in condition E. Although this fact might seem to imply that the apes understood that the cookie would move along a path that would cause it to fall into the hole, careful reflection reveals that this is not necessarily so. Indeed, our data do not bear directly on this issue one way or the other. For example, our apes may have learned a rule that had nothing to do with the projected movement of the reward or its ultimate fate of being swallowed by the trap. Rather, they may have learned a rule about the perceptual alignment of the reward relative to the trap.

Despite the fact that the apes appeared to understand some very specific aspects of how the rake, reward, and trap functioned, the prediction of the high-level model that the apes should respond more slowly in condition A as compared to the baseline trials was not upheld. However, the fact that apes took longer in condition E as compared to any other condition shows that the animals were sensitive to the test. This outcome can be interpreted as indicating that the animals may have been confused by the fact that the two possible choices given them during training were combined, and then pitted against a novel choice. Thus, the animals may have required additional time to evaluate the consequence of choosing a side that contained a trap (despite the fact that it was ineffective).

Megan's data indicates that she did not prefer the surfaces with the blue color. Megan chose randomly in every case except condition E, where there was a penalty for choosing incorrectly. In this condition, Megan made no errors. Thus, these data indicate that neither Megan nor the other apes held a bias towards the color with which they have had prior experience. Furthermore, these results indicate that the apes' success after training was due to a fairly specific understanding about the position of the trapping hole, relative to the position or projected path of the reward.

General discussion (experiments 3–4)

In the first administration of the trap-table problem (experiment 3), only one of our chimpanzees, Megan, performed at above-chance levels in the initial exposure (20 trials) to the trap-table problem. And, unlike her performance on the trap-tube problem, she performed correctly from her first test trial forward. On first glance, two potential explanations suggest themselves. On the one hand, perhaps the trap-table problem, as we had imagined, embodies the causal relations among the tool, the goal object, and the substrate in a more transparent fashion than does the trap-tube problem. Although both tasks require the chimpanzees to anticipate the outcome of their actions before initiating a choice, the trap-table task simultaneously presented two options, one in which the reward could be retrieved using an existing procedural rule (*pull rake*), and the other in which the existing procedural rule would be ineffective. Thus, in the trap-table task, the animals had the opportunity (potentially, at least) to imagine what would happen in each case by envisioning the outcome of pulling each tool. In contrast to the trap-tube task, the apes did not have to imagine some starting position that was not perceptually present. On the other hand, it is possible that the trap-table task was not easier in any real sense, but rather that some aspect of what Megan had learned in the trap-tube task transferred to the trap-table task. Given the logical similarities of the two problems, this does not seem implausible.

Although these differences may account for Megan's apparent ability to succeed on the trap-table task, the results of the retention trials in the training portion of the follow-up experiment (experiment 4) raise questions about even her level of understanding in the original trap-table experiment (experiment 3). Recall that, when we returned to the basic trap-table problem a year later (experiment 4), Megan responded randomly (2/5 correct) in her initial block of trials. One interpretation of this surprising result is that Megan's initial performance in experiment 3 may have been due to a chance association on the first trial between the color and the reward, or to other, lower-level perceptual features of the task. For example, she may have favored the correct option because after she made her initial choice (determined randomly) she happened to attend to the right perceptual feature of the task (i.e. the relative position of the reward to the hole)—as opposed to interpreting the system ahead of time as a series of causal interactions. Her failure to show clear evidence of retention on this problem a year later would seem to highlight this possibility. Certainly, the data from the other chimpanzees reveal a clear pattern of trial and error learning across experiments 3 and 4 (see especially Fig. 5.5).

The results reported in this chapter emphasize two separate issues related to the nature of chimpanzees' understanding of tool use. First, chimpanzees are capable of learning to control the interactions among a tool, a desired goal object, and a substrate which affects the movement of both, and some of them may learn to do so fairly quickly. Furthermore, in the context of doing so, chimpanzees appear to learn a number of relevant, and very specific relations among the tool, the reward object, and the substrate. For example, in experiment 4, the effect of training our apes to solve the original trap-table problem was not merely that they learned to avoid the side with a trap, or to favor the side with a particular colored surface. Rather, they at least learned to judge the position of the reward relative to the hole, and possibly even to calculate whether the projected path of the reward would bring it into contact with a trap. Thus, after some extended training, our chimpanzees learned to use some of the perceptual relations that we as humans base our causal judgements upon.

We have devoted two chapters of this volume to understanding how chimpanzees reason about tasks which require coordinating an understanding of their own actions on a particular tool, the tool's action on a goal object, and the goal object's interaction with the substrate along which it moves or is embedded. Reflecting on the results of both the trap-tube and trap-table tasks, it seems clear that chimpanzees will uncover the regularities inherent in such simplistic problems. For example, Megan, Candy, and Brandy's skilful deployment of an empirical rule structure in experiments 1, 1(a)–(e), and 2 epitomizes how adept chimpanzees can be at learning and generalizing. At the same time, however, those results also emphasize that such learning need not occur within the framework of a set of abstract concepts related to physical causality. Likewise, our apes' performances in the testing phase of experiment 4 demonstrate that, regardless of whether chimpanzees make theoretical interpretations (i.e. causal judgements) about these kinds of situations, they nonetheless certainly reason about the causally-relevant features of such situations. Even here, however, the learning curves displayed by all of the apes across the trap-table experiments (experiments 3 and 4) highlight the central role that direct feedback through trial-and-error plays in their acquisition of such competencies.

One might be tempted (as are we), to give our chimpanzees the benefit of the doubt by recognizing that they are, after all, chimpanzees. As humans, we are able to visually survey the basic trap-table problem and easily diagnosis the solution: 'If I pull that rake, the cookie will fall into the hole'. But our ease in reaching this conclusion may obscure the multiple steps and possible actions that are, in fact, part of this seemingly simple diagnosis. It may be the case that our apes, with arguably far less experience on problems of this type, genuinely reason about abstract causal concepts, but have their nascent causal understandings overwhelmed by the multiple causal interactions embedded in our tasks. For example, perhaps they can hold in mind only one *explicit* causal relation at a time (e.g. *pull rake* ⇒ *make cookie move* or *cookie moves in direction of trap*

⇒ *cookie falls into trap*), and when called upon to keep two in mind simultaneously they become confused. These are issues which we shall explore in several of the following chapters. We emphasize, however, that these are merely possibilities to be empirically tested. For it is equally possible that they simply do not represent the movements of objects in causal terms. In any event, the combined results of the trap-tube and trap-table experiments provide little direct evidence that our apes were able to survey a novel problem involving tool–object–substrate interactions, and then invoke causal concepts to determine the correct solution. Nonetheless, our results do reveal that these apes can be quite adept at learning to solve such problems.

CHAPTER 6

THE INVERTED- AND BROKEN- RAKE PROBLEMS

DANIEL J. POVINELLI AND JAMES E. REAUX

In the experiments described in Chapters 4 and 5, we tested our chimpanzees on two different tool-use systems that required them to understand and coordinate two separate causal relationships: (1) the relationship between their manipulation of a tool and the movement of the desired object; and (2) the relationship between the trajectory of the reward and the nature of the substrate along which it moved. In both the trap-tube problem and the trap-table problem, the apes' responses provided little reason to suppose that they were using a priori conceptual understandings to anticipate the outcomes of their actions.

However, there are aspects of the trap-tube and trap-table problems that may have artificially obscured at least certain aspects of what chimpanzees understand about the causal relations involved in such situations. For example, although they may have difficulty keeping in mind both causal relations simultaneously (e.g. 'pull rake to make the cookie move' and 'avoid pulling the cookie into the trap'), they might, nonetheless, understand each relation separately. For example, consider the relation, 'pull rake to make the cookie move'. Given their ability to pull the rake to obtain the food (which is typical of many species of nonhuman primates), it may seem obvious that apes understand this relation. However, although we effortlessly assume that they understand this general relation, it may be instructive to ask more specifically what exactly they know about it. One possibility is that they explicitly understand that the base of the rake moves forward, drawing it into contact with the cookie, thus providing the force necessary to make the cookie move. In addition, they may also explicitly understand that pulling the handle of the rake causes the base of the rake to move in the first place.

For many observers, evidence from both naturalistic and experimental settings would seem to leave little room to doubt that chimpanzees understand both aspects of the 'pull rake to make the cookie move' relation just described. For example, at four distinct field sites, chimpanzees regularly dip the ends of sticks into paths of driver ants (see McGrew 1992). Once the ants have charged up the stick, the chimpanzee will lift the stick out of the ants and quickly run his or her hand along its length to gather them for consumption. Another widespread example involves chimpanzees' use of sticks to probe, flail, or club potentially hazardous objects or animals (see McGrew 1992). Furthermore, in captivity, chimpanzees and other nonhuman primates have frequently been observed or trained to use sticks or rakes to retrieve otherwise out-of-reach objects (e.g. Birch 1945; Guillaume and Meyerson 1930; Köhler 1927; Schiller 1957). (Indeed, the fact that our apes rapidly learned to use rakes in experiment 3 to obtain out-of-reach rewards is just more evidence to support this already widely known fact.) In all of these cases, it seems undeniable that the apes explicitly understand how their own actions on one end of the tool may directly control its distal end, ultimately resulting in the movement of the desired object. As we shall see, however, such assumptions may be mistaken. Indeed, there are several different kinds of understandings that may mediate and/or attend the exact same behavioral performances, not all of which require an abstract understanding of causal principles. For example, the ape may readily learn a procedural rule of the type, 'pull the rake and then grab the reward'. We can be sure that the ape will see that the rake makes contact with the reward, but whether the animal appreciates the significance of such contact within a folk physics of transfer of force is another matter entirely—one that we begin to address in the experiments reported in this chapter.

In this chapter, we simplified the trap-table situation in order to ask about one of the causal relations just described. In particular, we explored whether chimpanzees might exhibit a better a priori understanding of the causal aspects of tool use in a case where they only needed to attend to the interaction between the tool and the goal object, as opposed to simultaneously keeping track of the substrate upon which the tool and goal object were operating. By testing our chimpanzees in this manner, we sought to determine which aspects of the relation between pulling on a rake and the reward's subsequent movement they understood.

Experiment 5: the inverted- and broken-rake problems, age 8

Method

Subjects

The same seven chimpanzees participated in this study. At the time of this study, the animals ranged in age from 7;8 to 8;7.

Apparatus and conditions

The table apparatus that was used in experiments 3 and 4 was modified for use in this study. Two intact surfaces were placed on the apparatus to produce a continuous solid surface. On baseline trials, one of the standard rake tools was placed on the apparatus with a food reward in front of it. On probe trials, two sets of novel tools were placed on the apparatus. These sets of tools were used to create two conditions: the broken-rake problem and the inverted-rake problem (see Fig. 6.1(a)). The broken-rake problem pitted a broken, familiar tool that could not be used to retrieve a reward against a novel tool that could be used to retrieve a reward. The inverted-rake problem pitted a novel tool in an orientation that easily allowed it to be used to retrieve a reward, versus an identical novel tool that was oriented in a manner that did not easily allow the retrieval of a reward.

Procedure

ORIENTATION. Each chimpanzee initially received a single orientation session containing six baseline trials. These trials required the ape to enter the test unit after the shuttle door opened, approach the table, pull the baited rake, and retrieve the reward. All of the apes responded without error during this orientation session, and therefore advanced to testing (in which probe trials of the conditions described above were interspersed among baseline trials).

TESTING. We administered four test sessions to each ape, with each test session consisting of six trials. Baseline trials were administered on trials 1–2 and 4–5. The side that was correct on each of these baseline trials was determined randomly, within the constraint that each side be correct equally often within each test session. We designated trials 3 and 6 as the probe trials for confronting the animals with the experimental conditions. Across the four test sessions, each ape received a total of eight probe trials, half of which were of the broken-rake type, and half of which were of the inverted-rake type (see Fig. 6.1(a)). We constructed a master list which consisted of each condition repeated four times (twice with the correct option on the right, twice with it on the left),

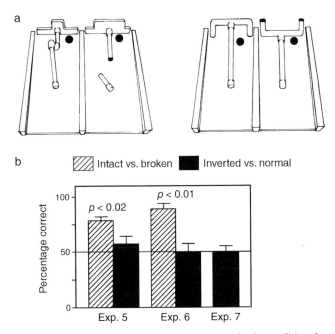

Figure 6.1 (a) Broken-rake condition shown on the left and inverted-rake condition shown on right. (b) Mean per cent correct (±*SEM*) for broken-rake and inverted-rake conditions in experiments 5 and 6, and inverted-rake condition in experiment 7. Dotted line indicates level expected by chance.

and then randomly and exhaustively assigned each trial type to each ape across the eight probe trials. The animals were allowed only one choice per trial. A choice was defined as moving one of the tools.

Results and discussion

The main results of this study are depicted in Table 6.1 and the extreme left-hand panel of Fig. 6.1(b). The most striking result is that the apes performed significantly differently in the two conditions (paired t-test, two-tailed, $t(6) = 3.286$, $p = 0.0167$). More specifically, they responded at levels well exceeding chance (50 per cent) on the broken-rake problem (one-sample t-test, two-tailed, $t(6) = 8.00$, $p = 0.0002$), but not on inverted-rake trials (n.s.). There was substantial inter-individual variability in how the apes responded to the inverted-rake problem (range = 25–75 per cent correct; see Table 6.1, results of experiment 5), suggesting possible individual differences in comprehension. On the broken-rake problem, the apes did not display evidence of immediate comprehension, as only 3/7 animals chose the correct tool on trial 1 (although by trial 2 they were responding at stable, above-chance levels).

Table 6.1 Summary of results from experiments 5 and 6 for individual subjects by trial

| | | Probe trials | | | | | | | | |
| | | Experiment 5 | | | | Experiment 6 | | | | |
	Condition	1	2	3	4	5	6	7	8	total
Apollo	Broken	+	+	+	+	+	+	+	+	8/8
	Inverted	+	+	+	−	−	−	+	−	4/8
Kara	Broken	−	+	+	+	+	+	+	+	7/8
	Inverted	+	+	+	−	+	−	+	−	5/8
Candy	Broken	+	+	−	+	+	+	+	−	6/8
	Inverted	+	+	−	−	+	+	−	+	5/8
Jadine	Broken	−	+	+	+	+	+	+	+	7/8
	Inverted	+	−	−	−	−	+	+	−	3/8
Brandy	Broken	+	+	+	−	+	−	+	+	6/8
	Inverted	+	−	+	−	+	−	−	+	4/8
Megan	Broken	−	+	+	+	+	+	+	+	7/8
	Inverted	−	+	+	−	+	−	+	+	5/8
Mindy	Broken	−	+	+	+	+	−	+	+	6/8
	Inverted	+	−	+	+	−	+	−	−	4/8
Grand M	Broken									6.7
	Inverted									4.3
Trial Ms	Broken	3/7	7/7	6/7	6/7	7/7	5/7	7/7	6/7	
	Inverted	6/7	4/7	5/7	1/7	4/7	3/7	4/7	3/7	

Broken = broken-rake condition. Inverted = inverted-rake condition.

A qualitative assessment of the animals' behavior on trial 1 from the broken-rake problem suggested that the animals may have been drawn to the broken handle as an object in its own right. In several cases, contact with the broken handle appeared to reflect a desire to obtain this object (as they grabbed it and brought it into the test unit), as opposed to an unsuccessful attempt to retrieve the food reward. Thus, it seemed likely that the rapid acquisition curve for this condition (as opposed to the flat performance on the inverted-rake problem) might have been somewhat artificial. In other words, despite our attempt to make the intact tool appear perceptually distinct from the rake used on baseline trials, the animals may have perceived the situation as a rake that was within their reach on one side, and a shorter rake that was out of their reach on the other side. However, some of the animals may have been drawn to inspect and/or retrieve the other object (what we had initially conceived of as the broken handle) also present within their reach on the incorrect side. This possibility suggested that our chimpanzees' relatively poor performance on the inverted-rake trials may have been a more valid diagnostic tool for assessing their understanding of the connection between their action on the tool, and the tool's action on the reward.

Experiment 6: replicating the inverted- and broken-rake experiments, age 8

Before directly exploring why our apes had performed so poorly on the inverted-rake problem, we first attempted to replicate the findings from experiment 5. We did so for two reasons. First, we wanted to determine if the apes' difficulty with the inverted-rake problem was robust, or whether they might rapidly learn to solve the task. Second, we wanted to determine if their excellent performance on the broken-rake problem was reliable.

Subjects and method

The same seven animals participated in this study. They began this study seven weeks after they completed experiment 5. At the start of the study their ages ranged from 7;11 to 8;10.

The procedures were virtually identical to those used in experiment 5. Each animal received one initial orientation session consisting of six baseline trials (one rake present). All of the apes performed without error and were therefore advanced to testing.

For testing, new schedules were created using the same counterbalancing and randomization procedures described earlier. As in experiment 5, each animal received four test sessions, each containing two probe trials which were used to deliver the two types of experimental conditions (broken-rake problem and inverted-rake problem). Thus, each animal received four trials of each of the two conditions. The decision rule for when the animal had made a choice was the same as in experiment 5.

Results and discussion

The main results are depicted in Table 6.1 and the middle panel of Fig. 6.1(b). Consistent with our expectations, the chimpanzees responded significantly differently in the two conditions (paired t-test, two-tailed, $t(6) = 4.260$, $p = 0.0053$). As in experiment 5, they responded at levels significantly exceeding chance on the broken-rake trials (one-sample t-test, one-tailed, hypothetical mean $= 50$ per cent, $t(6) = 7.778$, $p = 0.0002$), and did so from trial 1 forward (see Table 6.1). In direct contrast, the apes' performance did not differ from chance (50 per cent) on the inverted-rake trials (n.s.), nor did it improve across trials (see Table 6.1). In general, these results confirmed our earlier findings and established that the chimpanzees were interpreting the two conditions differently.

Experiment 7: an exaggerated look at the inverted-rake problem, age 8

We next sought to determine if our chimpanzees were experiencing difficulty with the inverted-rake problem because they failed to notice that the horizontal aspect of the incorrect rake would not make contact with the food reward when the tool was pulled (see Fig. 6.1(a)). In order to test this idea, we altered the rakes by substantially lengthening the vertical prongs, thus exaggerating the distance between the elevated horizontal aspect of the incorrect rake, and the position of the reward.

Subjects and method

The same seven apes that participated in the previous experiments were used. They began the study one week after completing experiment 6.

In preparation for the study, the tools used in the inverted-rake condition were modified by increasing the length of their vertical prongs by 137 per cent (from 7.5 to 17.8 cm). This modification was intended to make it more obvious that when the handle was pulled forward, the horizontal aspect of the incorrect rake could not make contact with the food reward.

We administered four test sessions to each chimpanzee, with each session consisting of five trials. Four of these trials were baseline trials (one rake present with food in front of it), and one was a probe trial of the inverted-rake problem using the modified tools. The probe trials were randomly assigned to trials 2–4. The same counterbalancing and randomization procedures described for the previous studies were used to produce the testing schedules. As before, only one choice was allowed (defined as above).

Results and discussion

Despite the exaggeration of the non-functional nature of the incorrect tool, and despite the fact that after the completion of this experiment each ape had received 12 total trials of this general condition, the apes' performances did not differ from that expected by chance (one sample t-test, two-tailed, hypothetical mean $= 50$ per cent, n.s.; see extreme right-hand panel of Fig. 6.1(b)). The data were also examined for individual differences (see Table 6.2). None of the apes (with the possible exception of Megan) appeared to learn the critical functional distinction between the two different orientations of the otherwise identical tools.

Experiment 8: reconceptualizing the inverted-rake problem, age 8–9

In this experiment, we tested two different conceptual accounts of our apes' failure to readily appreciate the difference between the two tools in the inverted-rake condition. First, we reasoned that perhaps chimpanzees tend to perceive the connection between a tool and a reward in a more gestalt manner than humans. Instead of understanding a tool contacting a reward object as a particular class of causal interactions resulting in the movement of the reward object, chimpanzees may perceive a tool, a reward, and a general *in front of* relationship with respect to the reward relative to the tool. In both of the options in the inverted-rake problem, the reward was (in this sense) perceptually contained by the space immediately in front of the tool. Thus, prior to learning any specific contingencies (through trial-and-error), our chimpanzees may have perceived a general connectedness between the tool and reward in both cases, and therefore may not have preferred one tool over the other. Of course, the alternative account of their behavior is that our chimpanzees can understand causal relationships in much the same way as humans, but simply require additional experience to focus their attention on the relevant features of our laboratory tasks. This experiment was designed to test these ideas in the context of the tool-use system of experiments 5–7.

Table 6.2 Summary of results from experiment 7 for individual subjects by trial

Subject	Trial Number				Totals
	1	2	3	4	
Kara	–	+	+	–	2/4
Candy	–		–	+	1/4
Jadine	–	+	+	–	2/4
Brandy	–	+	+	–	2/4
Megan	–	+	+	+	3/4
Mindy	–	+	–	+	2/4
Apollo	–	+	–	+	2/4
Grand mean					2/4
Trial means	0/7	6/7	3/7	4/7	

Subjects and method

The seven chimpanzees used in the previous studies were tested one month after completing experiment 7 (age range = 8;1 to 9;0). The same apparatus and general procedures were used. The animals were initially given a single orientation session of four baseline trials. All of the apes performed flawlessly and we therefore advanced them to testing.

Models to be tested

As generally described above, we sought to test the different predictions of two distinct models of the chimpanzees' understanding of the inverted-rake problem. First, the *perceptual containment model* posited that the apes were attending to whether the goal object was within a general area of space in front of or underneath the tool (see Fig. 6.2(a)), rather than along the projected path of a solid aspect of the tool. In contrast, the *physical contact* model posited that the apes were reasoning about whether the tool could (or would) make direct contact with the object (see Fig. 6.2(b)).

Experimental conditions and predictions

Six experimental conditions were created to pit the perceptual containment model's predictions against those of the physical contact model. In general, these conditions

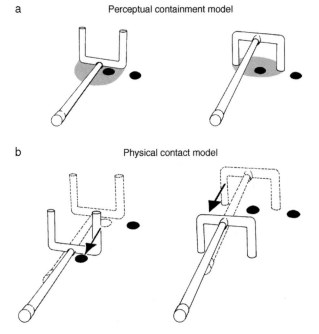

Figure 6.2 (a) The perceptual containment model's interpretation of correct versus incorrect choices. (b) The physical contact model's interpretation of correct versus incorrect choices.

varied the position of the reward (from in front of the tool's path to outside of its path) and the orientation of the tool. Each of the six conditions is visually depicted in the left-hand column of Fig. 6.3. Each ape received four trials of each of the six conditions across 12 testing sessions. Each testing session consisted of six trials: four baseline trials (counterbalanced within sessions for side correct) and two probe trials used to deliver the conditions. The order of administration of the condition types was random within the constraint that all condition types occurred twice within groups of six sessions. The side associated with each of the options in each of the conditions was counterbalanced across the two blocks of six sessions.

Predictions

The physical contact model predicted that the animals would attend to the relationship between the orientation of the tools and the position of the rewards, and, in particular, would select those tools whose horizontal aspect could make physical contact with a goal object. This model also predicted that the animals might (at least occasionally) not respond during conditions B, D, and E, given that there was no correct alternative in these cases. In contrast, the perceptual containment model predicted that the apes would focus on the degree of perceptual containment of the reward in front of the tool. As can be seen from the middle column of Fig. 6.3, the two models generated different predictions for three of the experimental conditions: A, B, and E. However, given that at this point the apes had experienced a total of 12 differentially reinforced trials of condition A (the inverted-rake condition from experiments 5–7), this condition (A) seemed less diagnostic than the others (B and E).

Results and discussion

Unlike in the previous three experiments, two of the chimpanzees occasionally entered the test unit, but after surveying the tool system, failed to make a response. Although somewhat infrequent, these no-response trials ($n = 6$) were limited precisely to the three conditions (B, D, and E) in which, from the perspective of the physical contact model, there was no correct option to choose (see middle column of Fig. 6.3).

The main results of this study are presented in the right-hand column of Fig. 6.3. We initially examined the three conditions (A, B, and E) for which the two models generated different predictions. First, although 5/7 apes now preferred the correct option in condition A, a two-tailed, one-sample t-test indicated that as a group their selection of the correct option did not exceed that expected by chance (50 per cent). In condition B, the apes performed in accord with the prediction of the physical contact model. A one-way repeated measures ANOVA indicated an overall effect ($F(2, 12) = 4.769$, $p = 0.0299$), and Tukey-Kramer posttests revealed that this effect was due to the fact that the animals made fewer no responses than responses to the uncontained, incorrect option ($p < 0.05$). As predicted by the physical contact model, however, the apes did not prefer the contained, incorrect configuration over the uncontained, incorrect configuration. In contrast, in condition E the animals performed according to the predictions of

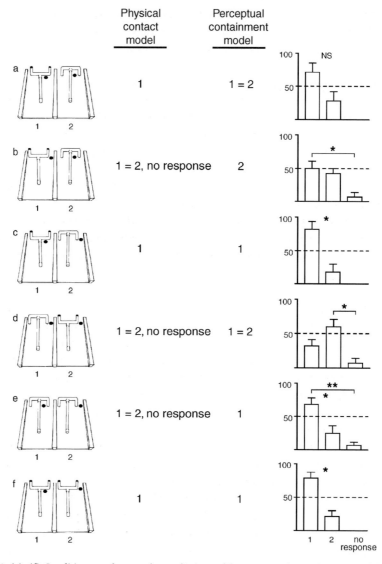

Figure 6.3 (a)–(f) Conditions used to test the predictions of the perceptual containment model and the physical contact model, predictions of the two models, and empirical results obtained. See text for additional details. * $p < 0.05$; **$p < 0.01$.

the containment model. A one-way repeated measures ANOVA indicated an overall effect ($F(2, 12) = 7.763$, $p = 0.0069$) which was due to the fact that the apes made significantly more responses to the contained, incorrect option than they made to the uncontained, incorrect option ($p < 0.05$) or no responses ($p < 0.01$). Thus, even though neither option was correct, the apes preferred the option in which the reward appeared contained by the space in front of the tool (although in accordance with the physical contact model, 'no responses' also began to appear in two of the apes).

The results from the remaining three conditions (C, D, and F) generally matched the predictions that both models generated in common. The only possible exception was condition D, in which the animals were confronted with two incorrect, uncontained options, with the only difference being the (irrelevant) orientation of the tool (see Fig. 6.3). Here, the apes tended to prefer the option in which the tool was in the correct orientation, despite the fact that the reward was not along the projected path of the tool. A one-way repeated measures ANOVA indicated an overall effect ($F(2, 12) = 5.828$, $p = 0.02$), but posttests revealed that this was due to the fact that the animals made fewer no responses ($p < 0.05$) than responses to correctly oriented, but uncontained options. No other contrasts differed from each other.

The mosaic of results obtained in this study can perhaps be best understood by imagining a more sophisticated model which considers additional features of the task about which the chimpanzees might have learned something during experiments 5–7. For example, the perceptual containment model might be a reasonable account for naive chimpanzees upon first confronting this task. Indeed, a general disposition along these lines appears to persist when other task features are equated (i.e. condition E). However, the pattern of results suggest that our apes learned something additional about the proper orientation of the tool, irrespective of the location of reward relative to the tool. This could explain (albeit in hindsight) why the apes chose randomly between the non-functional, contained option and the functional, uncontained option in condition B, but then preferred the non-functional, contained option in condition E. In effect, condition B pitted not just the contained versus uncontained location of the reward, but also the functional versus non-functional orientation of the tool, perhaps creating a competition among two prepotent responses. Thus, based on their previous experience, it may be that on some trials the apes attended to the appearance of containment, but on other trials they attended to the tool orientation.

In contrast, condition E varied only the reward location. In this case, even though the apes had ample experience from experiments 5–7 that the non-functional, contained option did not yield a reward, they significantly preferred it over the other option (presumably due to the superiority of its perceptual appearance). Some additional support for this idea can be derived from the results of condition D, in which the position of the reward was held constant (uncontained), but the orientation of the tool was different. Here, the animals displayed some preference for the correctly oriented tool—even though they almost never attempted to use it correctly by sliding it toward the reward (see Fig. 6.3).

A final set of data that may bear on determining which of the two models was best supported can be derived from an analysis of the videotapes that was conducted by a main rater. The rater was issued an instructional set which requested that she note each trial on which the apes selected an incorrect option, but then appeared to manipulate the tool in an effort to retrieve the reward using the extended prongs. A second rater used the same instructional set to code 20 per cent of the same trials and obtained perfect agreement with the main rater. The main rater's results reveal that such manipulations were restricted to two of our apes, Jadine and Brandy, who attempted such manipulations on 81 and 100 per cent of all probe trials, respectively. Despite these manipulations, however, Jadine and Brandy were only successful in retrieving the reward on 22 and 18 per cent of these trials, respectively. Although such manipulations might be thought of as implying some level of understanding of the causal interaction between the tool and reward, this idea is difficult to reconcile with the fact that these were the only two of our apes that did *not* learn to select the correct tool in condition A! Indeed, on the half of the trials that they happened to choose the inverted rake in this condition, they tried to use it to attempt to gain the reward. A retrospective analysis of such manipulations was also conducted for experiments 5–7 using the same procedures described above, with perfect agreement among the two raters. These results reveal that there was only a single previous instance of such manipulation (by Jadine, and it was unsuccessful).

Although the manner in which Jadine and Brandy manipulated the tools does not bear directly on the containment model, we have several reasons for interpreting them as additional evidence that the apes were extracting a series of perceptual generalizations from their interaction with the task, as opposed to relying on an abstract understanding of the causal interactions between the base of the rake and the reward. First, Jadine and Brandy attempted such manipulations equally often whether a correct option was available or not (Jadine: 100 and 100 per cent, respectively; Brandy: 78 and 83 per cent, respectively). Thus, this was not a strategy reserved for those probe trials where there was no correct option. Second, in conditions B and D there were two 'incorrect' options, but one of these options (the one with the tool in the correct orientation) could have easily been manipulated to retrieve the reward (see Fig. 6.3). Yet Jadine and Brandy showed no systematic preference for manipulating this correctly-oriented tool over the inverted one. Indeed, this partially explains why their manipulations of the tools so rarely led to success; when the opportunity was available, they failed to manipulate the tool that was at least in the correct orientation. One interpretation of these results is that the manipulations were the result of their frustration at not receiving the reward, or a general manipulatory tendency, as opposed to an alternative means of obtaining the reward on trials where there was no correct option available.

Finally, a qualitative micro-analysis of both Jadine and Brandy's earliest non-pulling actions on the tools suggests they were exploring their movement, as opposed to actively attempting to use it to rake in the reward. It appeared that only later, after such actions accidentally resulted in some movement of the reward, that the manipulations began to approximate retrieval attempts. Yet even at this point, the two apes persisted in such ineffectual tool manipulation on those trials where a clearly effective means was available (e.g. condition A). This emphasizes our apes' atheoretical understanding of the task. Thus, Jadine and Brandy's superficially intelligent behavior must be tempered by the realization that their tool manipulations appear to have emerged as a consequence of undirected tool manipulations which resulted from frustration at not receiving the rewards. However, once the prongs of the inverted rake had accidentally moved a reward, for example, they appeared to fixate on recreating this movement—despite the fact that there was often a much easier option available (see condition Λ).

General discussion (experiments 5–8)

The results presented in this chapter both extend and temper those reported in Chapters 4 and 5 in several important ways. First, the difficulty that our apes experienced in learning to select the properly oriented tool (correct) over the obviously improperly oriented one (incorrect), suggests that the results of our previous tests were not obtained solely because they required the chimpanzees to attend to two causal relationships simultaneously. In the tests presented in this chapter, success was possible by focusing exclusively on the connection between the manipulation of a tool and the resulting movement of the reward. There was no additional requirement, as in experiments 1–4, for the apes to attend to the connection between the substrate along which the reward was moving and the reward's ultimate fate. Despite this, our apes initially responded as if they were not attending to one very obvious aspect of the general relation between pulling a rake and retrieving a reward: whether or not the base of the rake would make contact with the reward once pulled.

Given the well-documented ability of chimpanzees to use tools such as sticks to make contact with specific objects beyond their reach (e.g. Köhler 1927), one may wonder why our apes behaved in the manner that they did. Indeed, like Köhler's chimpanzees, our apes had demonstrated on many occasions the ability to use a rake to pull in an otherwise out-of-reach reward. Such demonstrations, however, may merely show that the apes are able to learn to exploit the moment-to-moment kinesthetic and perceptual feedback involved in their actions in order to establish and maintain perceptual contact between the tool and the reward. In short, the apes may learn that contact between the tool and the goal object is important, without appreciating that such contact is important because it allows for the transfer of force. In the cases explored in this chapter, the chimpanzees must first pull the rake before noting whether the reward will move. However, at this point, a 'choice' has already been made. In contrast, once an expertise is achieved on this (or similar) tasks, using an implement to move another object may simply involve the on-line use of *in-front-of/behind* and *push/pull* judgements that are made at low levels of perceptual and kinesthetic information processing. Thus, it may be the case that efforts to assess whether an organism is relying on high-level cognitive judgements related to the folk physics of transfer of force will require testing them on systems where the causal judgements must be made ahead of time, as well as on systems where their motor actions are not highly sculpted through previous experience.

In closing this chapter, we must again be careful not to mislead our reader. First, we do not suppose that humans use high-level judgements related to the folk physics of transfer of force each time we use a stick to obtain an out-of-reach object. On the contrary, we suppose that on many occasions our actions are executed by fairly automatized procedures in which concepts related to folk physics are not involved. However, this should not obscure the fact that humans *can* invoke such concepts when circumstances demand it. Second, we are not implying that each time a chimpanzee uses a stick to retrieve an out-of-reach object they must rely on moment-to-moment feedback concerning their action on the stick and the goal object's movement. On the contrary, evidence from these, and previous, laboratory experiments shows that with sufficient experience these animals are able to execute their motor actions ballistically (see especially Birch 1945; Guillaume and Meyerson 1930; Yerkes 1927*a*,*b*, 1928–29). That is, with practice on general problems of this type, they need not fumble around blindly until the kinesthetic and perceptual information match the targeted perception (*behind the object*). Of course, some researchers will conclude that, once such learning has occurred, the ape must be displaying the same cognitive competence as the human who performs likewise. For reasons that shall become increasingly apparent, we are not comfortable with this conclusion.

CHAPTER 7

THE FLIMSY-TOOL PROBLEM

DANIEL J. POVINELLI, JAMES E. REAUX, AND LAURA A. THEALL

In their natural habitats, chimpanzees regularly make use of the differing rigidities of raw materials to obtain food resources. For example, chimpanzees use rigid probes (typically called 'digging sticks') to lever open beehives or the entrances to ant nests. The effectiveness of the probe will clearly depend on the strength of the tool in relation to the mass of the material to be moved. For other problems, however, the tool must possess the opposite qualities, of flexibility and resilience. For example, Teleki (1973) describes how termite-fishing probes must be flexible enough to wind their way through the termite passages, but then reassume their shape for the next insertion. Here, then, are two contexts in which opposite properties of a tool are exploited by chimpanzees in their quest to obtain food resources. In this chapter, we report the results of several studies that we conducted to examine whether our chimpanzees possessed a conceptual understanding of the relation between the rigidity of a tool and its ability to move an object. To this end, we confronted our apes with two similar rakes, one of which had a rigid base that could easily drag an apple to within their reach, and the other of which had a flimsy, pliant base that could not move the apple. After allowing our apes to play with these rakes freely for several sessions, we introduced the rakes into a formal testing situation to determine if the animals would select the one that could successfully retrieve the apple.

We used the rake-and-table situation as the context of these studies for two reasons. First, as the result of their participation in experiments 3–8, the apes had gained considerable expertise at this task. Thus, it seemed reasonable to pose the problem in the context of a tool-use system with which they were already familiar. Second, the results of experiments 5–8 revealed that our subjective impression that the apes were attending to the role of the base of the rake making contact with the reward (an impression fostered by the ease with which apes learned to use the rake in the first place) had been incorrect. Rather than attending to the importance of the rake making physical contact with the food, initially the apes appeared to know only that pulling the rake led to the reward's arrival. With training, however, many of the apes appeared to learn about the role of contact (see Results, experiments 7–8). As we explained at the end of Chapter 6, this result led us to ask whether this new-found competence reflected an understanding of the folk physics of transfer of force, or whether the animals had simply learned another specific procedural rule.

Now that we had clear evidence that our apes were attending to the importance of the base of the tool being in a certain spatial relation to the reward object, we asked our apes a slightly different (but intimately related) question concerning the nature of the base of the rake and its contact with food rewards. One way of thinking about this question is as follows. If, during the course of experiments 5–8, the subjects had only come to construct a procedural rule concerning the importance of the base of the rake being in such-and-such a spatial relation relative to the reward, or even physically contacting the reward, they would have no reason to appeal to a folk notion of transfer of force. On the other hand, if their ultimate success was framed in terms of an understanding that contact is necessary for the transfer of force, they might also be expected to appreciate that a highly flimsy object cannot effectively transfer force to an object of considerable mass. Thus, in this chapter, we asked our apes not about the possibility of physical contact between the tool and the reward, but about the relative effectiveness of such contact.

Experiment 9: the flimsy-tool problem, age 9

Method

Subjects

The seven chimpanzees who participated in the previous studies were used. This experiment began $6^1/_2$ months after the apes had completed experiment 8. They were between the ages of 8;7 and 9;6.

Apparatus

The rake-and-table apparatus from experiments 3–8 was used. Completely solid surfaces were placed into the table and used throughout the experiment. Two new rakes were designed and constructed for use in the testing phase. Both tools were superficially identical (57 × 40 cm), but differed in the following critical manner. The base of the rigid (effective) tool was constructed from solid plywood whereas the base of the flimsy (ineffective) tool was constructed from a thin strip of rubber. The tools and their differing rigidity properties are depicted in Fig. 7.1.

Procedure

Orientation to the tools. For the four days leading up to the beginning of the orientation phase (see below), we gave the apes experience with both the flimsy and rigid tools. The animals were ushered in pairs into the outside waiting area where both tools were present, and were allowed to freely play with the tools for 20 minutes. Four sessions of this type (one per day) were administered to the animals.

ORIENTATION. After being familiarized with the tools in the orientation sessions just described, each animal was administered a session consisting of six trials. On each trial one of the standard rake tools (see experiment 3) was placed either on the right or left

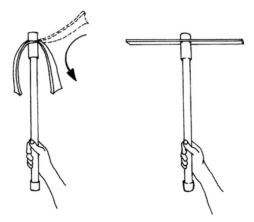

Figure 7.1 Flimsy and rigid rake tools used in experiment 9.

with food in front of it (the side was randomly determined within the constraint that the tool/reward appear equally often on each side within each session). We required each ape to enter the test unit, pull the tool, and retrieve the reward on at least 5/6 consecutive trials in a session before we advanced them into the testing session. All of our apes met this criterion in the first session.

TESTING. Testing consisted of eight sessions, each containing five trials. Trials 1–2 and 4–5 were identical to the orientation trials. The remaining trial (trial 3) served as a probe trial to deliver the experimental condition, which consisted of a choice between the flimsy and rigid tool. Thus, each ape received eight of the critical probe trials in which they had to make a choice between the effective and ineffective tools.

The procedure for each probe trial involved two phases: a *demonstration phase* and a *response phase*. In the demonstration phase, each ape entered the test lab and the shuttle door was closed behind them. The table apparatus was placed in front of the plexiglas partition as usual, and an experimenter sat directly behind the midline of the apparatus. However, in this phase a plexiglas screen covered the response holes in the partition so that the apes could observe, but not touch the apparatus or the experimenter (see Fig. 7.2(a)–(f)). As soon as the ape entered and the shuttle door closed, the experimenter lifted either the effective or ineffective tool, oriented it toward the ape, and then proceeded to demonstrate the properties of its base in an exaggerated manner for 15 seconds. (In the case of the effective tool, the experimenter shook the tool and repeatedly tapped on the base to demonstrate its rigidity (see Fig. 7.2(c)–(d)). In the case of the ineffective tool, the experimenter held up and shook the tool (causing the rubber stripping to flop up and down), and repeatedly lifted the stripping and let it drop (see Fig. 7.2(a)). The tool demonstrations always occurred from left to right (with the type of tool associated with each side counterbalanced as described above).

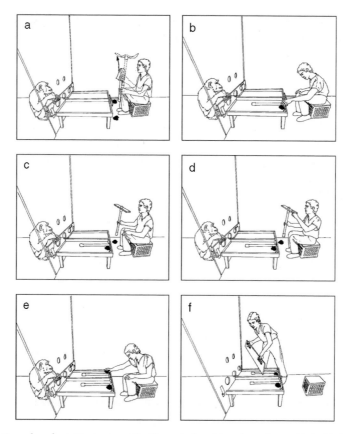

Figure 7.2 Procedure for testing apes on the flimsy tool problem (experiment 9). (a–b) Ape observes 'reminder' demonstration of the properties of the base of the flimsy tool by the experimenter. (b) Experimenter places half of an apple in front of the base of the flimsy tool. (c)–(d) Ape observes 'reminder' demonstration of the properties of the base of the rigid tool. (e) Experimenter places apple in front of the base of the rigid tool. (f) As ape waits outside for 15 seconds, experimenter removes plexiglas cover from response holes.

Immediately after demonstrating the property of a tool, the experimenter placed the tool on either the left or right side of the apparatus, and a half of an apple was set directly in front of it (Fig. 7.2(a)–(e)). In the case of the ineffective tool the rubber base had to be straightened as best it could, and so a similar (pointless) action was made as the effective tool was placed on the apparatus as well. During the demonstration phase, the apes were kept in the test unit for a total of 1 minute (which included the 30 seconds spent demonstrating the affordances of the tools). After 1 minute elapsed, the shuttle door was opened, the animal exited the test unit and the door was closed behind him or her.

The response phase of each probe trial began by the experimenter removing the plexiglas cover from the main partition (thus opening the response holes; Fig. 7.2(f)), reseating him/herself behind the midline of the apparatus, and fixing his/her gaze on a neutral point along the midline of the apparatus. The shuttle door was then reopened, allowing the animal to enter and respond. The interval between the end of the demonstration phase and the beginning of the response phase was 15 seconds. We defined a choice as moving one of the tools.

A master randomization schedule was constructed for the probe trials, which involved the following counterbalancing constraints. First, we equated the number of times each tool was placed on each side (and hence the order in which the two tools were presented) across trials for each animal. Second, within each session, three of our apes received the correct tool on one side and the other four received the correct tool on the opposite side.

Results and discussion

In the test sessions, the apes performed without error on the standard trials that surrounded the probe trials. Thus, the animals were highly motivated to respond and retrieve the food rewards. This finding is important, because it clearly establishes that the apes did not become bored or uninterested in the general testing procedures as the experiment continued.

The central results concern which tool the chimpanzees selected on the probe trials when they faced a choice between selecting the rigid or the flimsy tool. As a group, the animals selected the rigid tool on average in 57.1 per cent ($SD = 20.2$) of the probe trials. A one-sample t-test (two-tailed, hypothetical mean = 50 per cent) indicated that this performance did not differ from chance ($t(6) = 0.093$, $p = .386$). However, an examination of the trial-by-trial results of each of the seven animals (see Table 7.1) revealed that one of our chimpanzees, Jadine, performed flawlessly from her first trial forward (10/10 correct, $p < .001$, binomial test). This differs markedly from the other subjects. Indeed, if Jadine's performance is treated separately (see below), the group's performance was exactly what would be expected by chance (50 per cent correct).

Table 7.1 Summary of the performances of individual subjects (on each trial) for experiment 9

Subject	Session								Totals
	1	2	3	4	5	6	7	8	
Kara	+	−	−	+	+	−	−	+	4/8
Candy	+	−	−	+	−	+	+	−	4/8
Jadine	+	+	+	+	+	+	+	+	8/8
Brandy	+	−	+	−	−	+	+	−	4/8
Megan	+	+	+	−	−	+	−	+	5/8
Mindy	−	+	−	+	+	−	+	−	4/8
Apollo	−	−	+	−	+	−	−	+	3/8
Grand *M*									4.6/8
Trial *M*s	5/7	3/7	4/7	4/7	4/7	4/7	4/7	4/7	

For the majority of the apes, then, the results were straightforward. Neither their previous experience with the properties of the tools, nor the information provided in the demonstration phase, influenced their decisions about which tool to pull in the response phase. It is possible that they could not remember which tool was correct after re-entering the test chamber. However, Jadine's performance is at least some evidence against this. In addition, the bases of the two tools were visually distinct in that the flimsy one was not completely straight. It is possible that the reason they did not select the correct tool was because they did not (or were unable to) infer that the flimsy tool could not move the mass of the apple. On the other hand, Jadine's perfect results gave us reason to pause. Broadly speaking, two explanations of her results seemed possible. First, her results might be taken as evidence that, regardless of why the other animals performed at chance levels, the solution to the flimsy-tool problem is not beyond the intellectual capacity of the chimpanzee. In other words, by itself, her data could be used as evidence that chimpanzees are capable of inferring (either from direct experience and/or observational evidence) that a flimsy tool cannot move the mass of half an apple.

However, a second, more mundane interpretation of Jadine's results occurred to us. From previous research that involved exposing our animals to rubber snakes (L. Moses, D. Baldwin, and D. J. Povinelli, unpublished data), we had good reason to believe that, of all of our apes, Jadine was the most wary of snake-like objects. Thus, it seemed quite possible that, rather than actively choosing the rigid tool because of its causal properties (as the above account would suggest), Jadine may simply have been avoiding the flimsy tool because of its similarity to a noxious stimulus. Indeed, our informal observations of Jadine during the sessions in which she was exposed to the tools in free play seem to corroborate this idea. Although she observed the other animals playing with the tools, and occasionally sniffed or touched the tools herself, she was the only ape who was not observed to directly play with them.

Experiment 10: exploring Jadine's success on the flimsy-tool problem, age 9

In order to choose between the two competing accounts (see above) of Jadine's perfect performance in experiment 9, we devised a second experiment using hybrids of the rigid and flimsy tools. So, rather than confronting her with a tool with a flimsy base versus a tool with a rigid base, we constructed two identical tools. Half of the base of each tool was the same rigid construction used for the effective tool in experiment 9, and the other half was the flimsy rubber construction used for the ineffective tool in experiment 9 (see Fig. 7.3).

Subject and method
The single subject of the study was Jadine (age 8;11). She began this experiment seven days after completing experiment 9. Jadine was administered two 20-minute free play sessions with two of the hybrid tools in the exterior waiting area on the two days prior

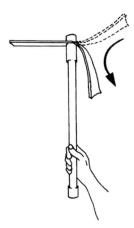

Figure 7.3 Hybrid tool designed for experiment 10 in order to test whether Jadine's performance in experiment 9 was due to a conceptual understanding of the flimsy tool problem, or an avoidance of the flimsy tool.

to beginning testing. Although she occasionally sniffed or touched the tools, she did not engage in play bouts with them.

Each test session was structured in the same manner as in experiment 9, with trials 1–2 and 4–5 serving as standard rake trials and trial 3 as the probe trial. Jadine received eight testing sessions and therefore eight critical probe trials. Each probe trial was again divided into a demonstration phase and a response phase. The manner in which the tools were presented, the manner in which their properties were demonstrated, and the manner in which they were placed on the apparatus were the same as in experiment 9, except that the flimsy and rigid portions of each tool were demonstrated for an equal amount of time.

For this study, the critical manipulation involved where the apple was placed relative to the two bases of each tool. On each trial, the apple was placed in front of the *rigid* half of the base of one of the tools, and the *flimsy* half of the base of the other tool. Eight possible combinations of the left/right position of the tool bases and reward combinations were possible (see Fig. 7.4). Thus, on each trial, the conceptual problem was identical to experiment 9. If Jadine selected the tool where the apple was in front of the rigid half of the base, the food would be pulled to within reach; if Jadine selected the other tool the flimsy base would not move the apple and she would be unsuccessful. Thus, if Jadine genuinely understood the importance of the rigidity/mass interaction of the tool and reward she could be expected to have no difficulty with this test. On the other hand, if her results in experiment 9 were merely the result of her avoiding the flimsy tool, she could be expected to perform randomly (as both tools contained an equal amount of the aversive material). She was randomly and exhaustively administered one of each of these conditions on the probe trials in sessions 1–8.

Results and discussion

Jadine performed flawlessly on the standard trials (only one rake present), thus demonstrating her continued interest and motivation in obtaining the rewards. More importantly, however, the results from the crucial probe trials offered clear support for the idea that Jadine had no better understanding of the importance of the rigidity/mass interaction of the tool and reward than her peers. She chose the correct tool on four trials and the incorrect tool on four trials—exactly what would be expected by chance responding. Indeed, some additional (albeit weaker) evidence in support of this idea can be derived from our measures of her latency to respond, which are presented in Fig. 7.5. (These data were coded separately by two coders after reading the same instructional set, by using a hand-held timer; Pearson's coefficient of determination, $r^2 = .999$.) These data reveal that during experiment 9, where Jadine selected the correct tool on

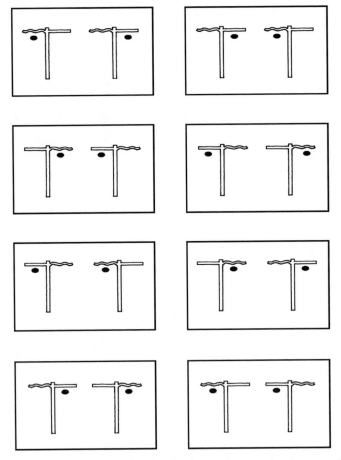

Figure 7.4 The eight specific test trials used with Jadine in experiment 10 showing counterbalancing for orientation of tools and placement of food rewards.

100 per cent of all probe trials, her latency to respond was stable. Presumably, this was because on probe trials she could enter the test unit and immediately select a tool with non-aversive qualities. As can be seen in Fig. 7.5, however, her latencies to respond in experiment 10 tended to be longer and more erratic. We interpret this as limited evidence that, in contrast to experiment 9, when Jadine entered the test unit on experiment 10 probe trials, *both* rakes were perceived to have aversive qualities (the flimsy rubber portion of the base), hence increasing her latency to respond.

General discussion (experiments 9–10)

The results of the experiments reported in this chapter offer interesting similarities to those presented in experiments 5–8. In the case of the inverted-rake problem, the apes did not initially attend to a necessary (and seemingly) obvious aspect of a simple tool system with which they were very familiar. Namely, they ignored (or did not appreciate) the fact that the inverted tool would not make contact with the reward and hence move it toward them. Of course, within about 16 trials, many of our chimpanzees learned to attend to the importance of at least certain perceptual aspects of this relation. Did they appreciate the more abstract, conceptual aspects? Although this question is difficult to answer, certainly the results from the studies reported in this chapter provide no evidence that our apes were recruiting conceptual knowledge of the connection between the rigidity of the rake tools and the mass of the apple which needed to be moved. Despite the extensive and specific experience that they received during the previous eight experiments, our apes appeared oblivious to the importance of a property of a tool that had obvious implications for retrieving an object—its rigidity. Even after allowing the animals to obtain direct experience with the nature of these tools in the context of

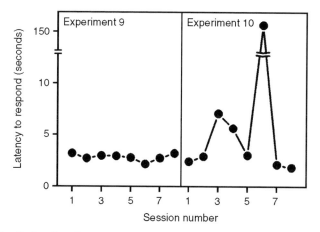

Figure 7.5 Jadine displayed an elevation in her latencies to respond in experiment 10 as compared with experiment 9, although the increase was not statistically reliable. See text for details.

free play, and further demonstrating the relevant properties of each tool immediately prior to allowing them to respond, our apes behaved exactly as if they did not understand how the significance of the differing properties of the bases would affect the movement of the apples. Perhaps even more interesting, the apes were remarkably insensitive to the differential feedback they received on each trial. Even after eight trials of this type the apes were still not showing evidence of learning. In contrast, Brown (1990) has summarized the results of studies showing that, by 24 months of age, human infants will avoid using non-rigid implements in simple reaching tasks (although aspects of the procedures used in those studies remain somewhat unclear).

Of course, we have no doubt that with enough trials of this type our apes would have learned to select the correct tool. The mere fact that they did not do so quickly—despite the clear feedback they received—further suggests that the nature of their learning about the physical relations between a simple tool and a reward may not be mediated by the same conceptual understandings related to folk physics that are present in human infants (see Brown 1990). Indeed, a fairly clear pattern can be seen in the results of each set of experiments presented thus far. Initially, our apes performed as if they had no understanding of the relevant folk physics of the problem at hand. However, with additional opportunities for learning, their performances improved, and indeed, in some cases there was evidence that the apes detected and used the same relevant perceptual features of the task as humans. However, in each case, transfer experiments revealed that this knowledge did not transfer easily to perceptually novel, but conceptually similar tasks. In contrast, research with children as young as two years of age suggests rapid transfer of learning in simple tool-using situations (e.g. Brown 1990).

CHAPTER 8

THE TOOL-INSERTION PROBLEM: THE QUESTION OF SHAPE

DANIEL J. POVINELLI, LAURA A. THEALL, JAMES E. REAUX, AND STEVE GIAMBRONE

In the wild, chimpanzees have been reported to use tools in ways that require them to learn about the interaction between the shape of a tool and the substrate around which the tool operates. Aspects of termite fishing can again illustrate this phenomenon. Goodall (1986) describes the mature form of the behavior: '…first, the chimpanzee, with index finger, second finger, or thumb, scrapes away the plug constructed by worker termites to seal a passage entrance. Next, a grass stem or other suitable implement is pushed down the passage. After a pause it is withdrawn, carefully, so as not to dislodge insects that have gripped the tool with their mandibles' (p. 251). Here, chimpanzees apparently learn to attend to several aspects of the tool–substrate interaction. Indeed, there can be no doubt that the chimpanzees learn to use their termite-fishing probes in a highly effective and efficient manner.

   In this chapter, we focus on just one of the causal relations involved in the interaction between the fishing tool and the substrate in and around which it must operate: namely, the size/configuration of the end of the tool and the opening in the termite mound into which it is inserted. Our research addressed this issue by asking whether chimpanzees possess an explicit understanding of this kind of relation. In order to do so, we created a simple context to elicit our chimpanzees' use of a straight tool to probe at a food reward through an opening. Next, we presented them with various tools as options, and examined the micro-genesis of their discovery of which tools to use, as well as how to use them.

Experiment 11: the tool-insertion problem, age 9$^1/_2$

Method

Subjects

We tested the same seven animals who participated in the studies described in the previous chapters. They were 8;8 to 9;7 when the study began, which began the day that experiment 10 (see Chapter 7) was completed.

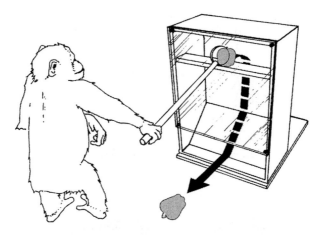

Figure 8.1 Apparatus and workings of the tool-insertion apparatus used in experiments 11–13. A female chimpanzee is shown using the training tool to dislodge the apple from the shelf, causing it to fall and roll toward her. Note that a plexiglas partition (not shown) separated the subject from the apparatus.

Apparatus

The apparatus shown in Fig. 8.1 was constructed using a plywood frame and a plexiglas front. The outside dimensions of the box were 80 × 60 × 32 cm. The box contained a narrow shelf at 61 cm from the base. The plexiglas front covered the upper two-thirds of the apparatus and contained a hole 9 cm in diameter that was positioned so that it was just in front of the shelf. This configuration allowed an apple to be placed on the shelf, just behind the hole, and rest there unless disturbed. The base of the apparatus was angled so that if the apple was dislodged from the shelf it would cause the apple to roll toward the ape (see Fig. 8.1). The apparatus was positioned out of reach of the apes in front of the plexiglas partition.

A total of five tools were constructed for the apes to use. The training tool was similar to the tool used in the trap-tube problem (experiments 1–2) and consisted of a straight, PVC tube with end caps (the tool was 2 cm in diameter and 45 cm in length). The tool was designed so that the apes could easily insert it into the hole and dislodge the apple. Four additional tools were constructed for use during testing and are depicted in Fig. 8.2. Two of the tools (⊥ and ⌐) were labeled as the *correct* tools because they could be used to retrieve the reward. Each of these tools had an 'easy' end (consisting of a straight length of PVC tubing identical to the training tool, and a 'difficult' end (consisting of a shorter projection of PVC tubing that was much more difficult to insert into the opening of the apparatus). The two *incorrect* tools (⊓ and ⊥) were constructed so that their ends could not fit through the hole and dislodge the apple.

Procedure

ORIENTATION TO THE TOOLS. Two days prior to the beginning of training, the five tools (the training tool plus the four testing tools) were placed in the outdoor waiting area of

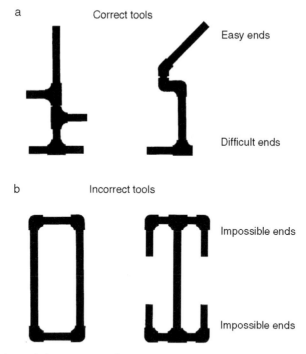

Figure 8.2 Four testing tools (two correct tools, two incorrect tools) used in experiment 11. The correct tools possessed easy ends (which could be inserted into the apparatus in the same manner as the training tool; see Fig. 8.1), and difficult ends, which could be used to dislodge the apple, but only with considerable effort and persistence. The incorrect tools possessed two ends that could not fit through the opening in the apparatus.

the testing unit. The animals were paired together, and these pairs were ushered in turn into the waiting area, at which point they were given 20 minutes to examine and play with the tools. Each animal received two such sessions (except for Megan who received four because she was paired with the odd-numbered animal). During these orientation sessions, the animals' trainer periodically gave the apes food rewards through the mesh as he encouraged them to interact with the tools.

TRAINING. Before testing began, the apes were trained to use the straight (training) tool to dislodge the apple from the shelf on the apparatus. The apparatus was placed 80 cm in front of the test unit (except for Brandy, where this distance was 70 cm) and the straight tool was placed on the floor directly between the plexiglas partition and the apparatus. All of the holes in the partition were covered except for the one directly in front of the tool and apparatus. Thus, the animals' task was to enter the test unit, grab the tool, and use it to dislodge the apple.

In the first session (consisting of two trials), each animal was individually ushered into the interior test unit and encouraged to use the tool to retrieve the reward. In the first training session, the trainer verbally encouraged the apes to use the tool to dislodge the apple, and modeled the task as needed. The apes were rewarded with food treats for any attempts to complete the task. After the first session, the trainer continued to facilitate the animals' performances, but the modeling was discontinued.

As soon as the trainer deemed that a given animal understood the general task, we advanced the ape to a criterion phase in which he or she was required to complete the task six times in succession (across three two-trial sessions) without any human prompting. Hereafter, these types of trials (with only the straight tool available and no human prompting) are referred to as *standard trials*. For these criterion trials, the apes entered the test unit, the shuttle door was closed behind them, and they were allowed 3 minutes to retrieve the apple. As soon as they did so, or as soon as 3 minutes elapsed without success, the door was opened and they were ushered into the outdoor area to await the next trial. The position of the tool alternated from left to right in front of the apparatus to accustom the animals to testing procedures. As soon as the apes met the criterion they were advanced to testing.

TESTING. We tested each ape across 20 sessions. The first trial in all test sessions consisted of a choice between two of the five tools (see below). For half of the sessions ($n = 10$) this was the only trial that was administered. In the remaining half of the sessions, the first trial was followed by a standard trial (i.e. only the straight tool was present). The purpose of these standard trials was to maintain the motivation of the animals by providing them with a certain frequency of trials that were easily within their ability. In addition, these trials served as control trials to ensure that any difficulties experienced on the main test trials were not due to a general lack of motivation.

The main test trials consisted of a choice between two of the five tools. The nature of these trials was determined as follows. First, each of the incorrect tools was paired with each of the correct tools, which resulted in four initial trial types (i.e. ⊥☐,⊥☐,☐,☐). However, each of these trial types had two variants, one with the correct tool (i.e. ⊥ or ⊊) on the right, the other with the correct tool on the left. Furthermore, because the correct tools had two different ends (an easy end and a difficult end) we chose to counterbalance the horizontal orientation of these ends to avoid systematically biasing the apes choice of one end over the other. This created two additional variants of each main test trial type. Thus, there were 16 possible trial configurations for the four main test trial types (four correct–incorrect tool pairings, with variants of each that differed in the side of the correct and incorrect tools and horizontal orientation of the correct tools). A fifth test trial type was created by pairing the training tool with the correct and incorrect tools. In each case, there was one instance where the straight (training) tool was positioned on the left and the other with it on the right.

In summary, this scheme resulted in five basic trial types and a total of 20 unique trial configurations. Each animal received each of these 20 trials one time so that they received the following: (1) four repetitions (varying in side placement and orientation of the tools) of four main test trial types (i.e. ⊥☐,⊥☐,⊊☐,⊊☐); (2) two trials where the training tool was paired with each of the correct tools; and (3) two trials where the training tool was paired with each of the incorrect tools.

   The order in which each ape received these 20 test trials was determined by randomly and exhaustively assigning one of each of the five kinds of trials, and then repeating the process until all 20 trials had been assigned. In this way, each animal received one of each of the five test trial types before repeating a type, and so on. Finally, the sessions containing a second trial in which only the training tool was present (the control trials) were determined by randomly selecting five sessions from the first half of the experiment (excluding those sessions in which the training tool had been one of the choices), and five sessions from the second half of the experiment (again, excluding those sessions in which the training tool had been one of the choices).

   Each trial proceeded as follows. The ape entered the test unit, the shuttle door was closed behind them, and a timer was started. During the ensuing 2 minutes, we allowed the apes to freely interact with the tools and make as many attempts to dislodge the apple as they desired with the tool or tools that were available. As soon as the ape retrieved the apple, or at the end of 2 minutes, the trial was ended and the ape was ushered outside.

Predictions

We examined three models of the chimpanzees' understanding of what they had learned during their initial training with the straight tool.

1. A *motor-action model* envisioned that the apes had simply learned a series of motor actions. These actions might be verbally described as follows: 'Reach for tool, orient its long axis toward hole/apple, and push'. If this were all that the animals had learned or understood, then on the probe trials involving a choice between a correct and incorrect tool they could be expected to exhibit a wide variety of behaviors, ranging from attempts to use the incorrect tools to using the correct tools in both their easy and difficult orientations.

2. A *perceptual similarity model* envisioned that, in addition to the general encoding of the relevant motor actions, the apes had also learned about the general perceptual features of the straight tool. If true, they ought to display a bias toward the straight (training) tool when it was available, and when it was not, they ought to exhibit some bias toward the novel tools which most closely visually resembled the straight tool. We believed that from a gestalt perspective, these were the two correct tools.

3. Finally, a *high-level model* envisioned that, during the original training sessions, the apes were encoding the causal structure of the task, including the relevant physical features of the straight tool and the opening in the substrate through which the tool needed to pass. If this were true, when faced with a choice between a correct and incorrect tool the apes ought to exclusively select the correct tools (presumably from trial 1 forward). However, as with the predictions of the other models, this model also predicted that on those trials when the straight tool was paired with

another tool, they ought to prefer to use it (although unlike the other models, this model expected that such a preference ought to be less on the trials when a correct tool was also present).

Videotape coding and data analysis

Two remote video cameras recorded all trials, creating a combined image which included a close-up view of the front of the apparatus as well as a general view of the subject. Two raters (a main rater and a reliability rater) coded the probe trials from the tapes using a set of standardized written instructions, which were designed to measure several aspects of the chimpanzees' tool use. The main rater coded 100 per cent of the trials ($N = 140$), and the reliability rater coded 20 per cent ($n = 28$). Primarily, the trials were coded according to bouts of the animals' manipulation of the two tools that were available on each test trial. A bout began when the ape grasped a tool and ended when the ape acted on the other tool which was present. Therefore, there could be multiple bouts of the same tool within a trial as the animals switched back and forth between the two tools. Perfect agreement (61/61 cases) was obtained in determining the bouts (Cohen's kappa, κ, = 1.00). Using hand-held timers, the raters obtained cumulative durations for each bout (pausing the timer at the intervals where the animal only temporarily ceased acting upon a tool without proceeding to manipulate the other tool), yielding a coefficient of determination (r^2) of .94. For each bout involving the correct tool, the raters listed the sequence in which the animals oriented the tool toward the apparatus using the easy and difficult ends and agreed on 34/38 cases ($\kappa = .80$). Next, the raters indicated whether or not the tool had contacted the apparatus in each orientation of the correct tool, as well as each bout with the incorrect tool, and they agreed on 68/69 cases ($\kappa = .97$). Finally, the raters agreed on 28/28 cases for whether or not the animal was successful in dislodging the apple from the shelf of the apparatus on each trial ($\kappa = 1.00$). Only the data from the main rater was used in the data summary and analysis.

Results

Training

Each chimpanzee received eight orientation sessions during which the trainer assisted them with the task. Once the criterion trials began, all of the apes successfully completed the task independently on six consecutive trials across three sessions. By the end of this criterion phase, the apes were entering the test unit, immediately picking up the straight tool, inserting it into the hole, and dislodging the apple from the shelf—all within 10–20 seconds.

Testing

During the test phase, the animals were allowed to manipulate either of the two tools as often as they wished within the two-minute duration of the trial. First, we examined those trials when the original training tool was paired with the testing tools, and then we examined the trials where a correct and an incorrect tool were paired together.

CHOICE OF TRAINING TOOL VERSUS THE NOVEL TOOLS. As predicted by all of the models, when the training tool was paired with a novel tool, the apes almost always selected the training tool (93 per cent of the trials), and then proceeded to use it to dislodge the apple. Thus, when available, the apes strongly preferred to use the tool with which they had been trained. Although this result by itself does not help to distinguish among the three models, a related finding is inconsistent with one of the weaker predictions of the high-level model. That is, the apes were no less likely to use the training tool when it was paired with a correct tool, than when it was paired with an incorrect tool.

CHOICE OF CORRECT VERSUS INCORRECT TOOL. We next examined those trials where a correct and incorrect tool were paired together and analyzed which tool the ape selected first. For these initial analyses, we focused on the subjects' attempts to use the tools, and we therefore grouped together those bouts on which the tool actually contacted the apparatus, and those on which it did not. (Below, we examine the data in a different manner, by focusing on just those bouts where the apes actually used a tool to make contact with the apparatus.)

Figure 8.3(a) displays the percentage of the apes who, on each trial, chose the correct tool first (although they may or may not have attempted to use it in the easy orientation, or succeeded in obtaining the reward; see below). As can be seen, the majority of the apes (5/7) chose the correct tools on the first two trials, and although their tendency to do so increased somewhat across trials, it was clearly erratic. A closer look at these results by individual condition reveals that the results of the first few overall trials (see Fig. 8.3(a)), were an effect of the animals avoiding a particular incorrect tool, $\mathbb{I}$, when making their first choice (see Fig. 8.3(b)–(e)). This can be inferred from the fact that, when we examined the apes' first choices in each condition, averaged across the four trials, we discovered that when tool $\mathbb{I}$ was paired with the correct tools, the apes chose the correct tools as their first choice more often than expected by chance (see Table 8.1), but when tool $\square$ was paired with the correct tools, the animals showed no such preference for the correct tools (see Table 8.1).

Next, we examined the data to determine whether, when the apes *did* select the correct tool as their first choice, they used it in a manner that allowed them to successfully retrieve the reward. Figure 8.4(a) summarizes these results by trial (regardless of tool), and indicates that for the initial four sessions approximately 30 per cent of the apes selected the correct tool first and were successful in using it to obtain the apple on that bout. This performance improved through session 16. Again, a separate analysis by condition (see Fig. 8.4(b)–(e)) reveals at least some differences among the conditions (compare Fig. 8.4(b) to Fig. 8.4(c)–(e)). Overall, however, the apes displayed a tendency

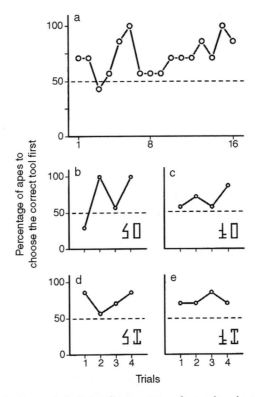

Figure 8.3 Experiment 11. (a) Graph depicting the percentage of apes who selected the correct tool as their first choice on a trial-by-trial basis regardless of condition. (b)–(e) Graphs depicting the percentage of apes who selected the correct tool as their first choice on a trial-by-trial basis within each of the four major testing conditions. The dotted horizontal lines depicts the percentage of apes who could be expected to choose the correct tool first due to chance alone.

Table 8.1 Overall means for the subjects' first tool choices, experiment 11

Condition	Percentage choices for correct tool	SD	p
ℐ vs. ৎ	75.00	13.93	.04[a]
ℐ vs. ⊥	74.75	7.50	.01[b]
◻ vs. ৎ	71.50	34.84	n.s.
◻ vs. ⊥	67.75	13.84	n.s.

One sample *t*-tests (two-tailed, hypothetical mean = 50.0) were used to examine whether the subjects exhibited a significant preference for one tool over the other in each condition: [a]$t[6] = 3.59, p < 0.04$; [b]$t[3] = 6.60, p < 0.01$.

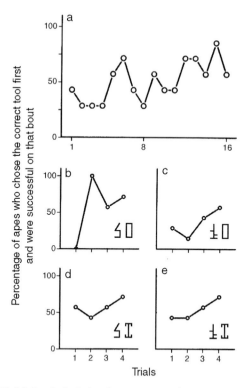

Figure 8.4 Experiment 11. (a) Graph depicting the percentage of apes who selected the correct tool as their first choice, and then went on to successfully dislodge the apple on that same bout, on a trial-by-trial basis regardless of condition. (b)–(e) Graphs depicting the percentage of apes who selected the correct tool as their first choice, and then went on to successfully dislodge the apple on that same bout, on a trial-by-trial basis within each of the four major testing conditions.

to improve in their ability to enter the test unit, select the correct tool, and then use it (in one way or another) on their first bout to obtain the apple.

Figure 8.5(a) reveals the average amount of time that the apes manipulated the correct and incorrect tools on each trial. Overall, the apes spent significantly more time manipulating the correct tool than the incorrect tool (paired t-test, $t[6] = 5.195$, $p = 0.002$, two-tailed). However, this overall difference was not present initially. As can be seen in Fig. 8.5(a), the mean durations of manipulating each tool were nearly identical on trials 1 and 2, although they diverged sharply thereafter. Thus, the apes manipulated the two tools equally at the beginning of the experiment, but then consistently spent more time using the correct tools than the incorrect tools. When we examined these data for each of the four conditions separately, averaged across the four trials, we discovered that, in three of the four conditions, there were significant differences between the mean durations of manipulations of the correct and incorrect tools (in each case higher for the

Table 8.2 Overall means (and standard deviations) for the subjects' durations of tool manipulations, experiment 11

| Condition | Mean duration (seconds) of tool manipulation | | |
	Correct	Incorrect	*p*
Ⅱ vs. ⌇	25.2 (6.6)	6.6 (9.0)	.03[a]
Ⅱ vs. ⊥	29.3 (10.2)	7.4 (6.3)	.01[b]
⎕ vs. ⌇	21.1 (5.6)	7.7 (7.0)	.02[c]
⎕ vs. ⊥	32.5 (18.6)	11.2 (14.9)	.06[d]

Paired *t*-tests were used to examine whether the subjects exhibited a significant preference for one tool over the other in each condition: [a]$t(6) = 3.097$, $p < 0.03$; [b]$t(6) = 3.744$, $p < 0.01$; [c]$t(6) = 3.703$, $p < 0.02$; [d]$t(6) = 2.375$, $p < 0.06$.

correct tool: Table 8.2). In the fourth condition, ⎕ vs. ⊥, the apes displayed a similar, but non-significant trend (see Table 8.2).

As a final analysis of our apes' use of the correct and incorrect tools, we examined the extent to which they switched from using one tool to the other during the two-minute duration of each trial (Fig. 8.6(a)–(b)). On those trials where tool ⌇ was present with an incorrect tool, the apes began by averaging 1.29 tool switches per trial, but this rate then gradually declined, until by the end of the study they were nearly always manipulating only a single tool (Fig. 8.6(a)). For those trials where tool ⊥ was present with an incorrect tool, the animals displayed much higher and sustained levels of tool switching throughout the course of the experiment, leveling off by session 3 at approximately one switch per trial (Fig. 8.6(b)).

Use of the correct tools. Until now, we have merely examined the apes' overall choices between the correct and incorrect tools. Of interest, however, is that the apes often initially attempted to use tools that could not possibly work, and this persisted at relatively high levels across the entire experiment (see Fig. 8.3(a)). However, given that there was some overall trend for our apes to select the correct tool as their first choice as the experiment progressed, we next asked how, exactly, the apes went about using the correct tools. In particular, we wanted to know if they tended to prefer the easy end over the difficult end. Recall that the perceptual similarity model had predicted that the apes would select the correct tools more often because they were more similar to the straight training tool. In contrast, the high-level model predicted that they would select the

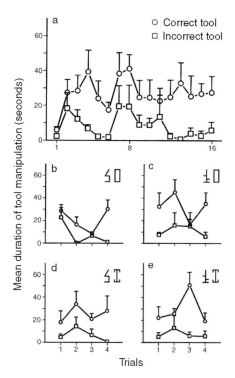

Figure 8.5 Experiment 11. (a) Mean duration of the subjects' manipulations of the correct and incorrect tool on a trial-by-trial basis, regardless of condition. (b)–(e) Mean durations of the subjects' manipulations of the correct and incorrect tool on a trial-by-trial basis within each of the four major testing conditions.

correct tools because they understood that only the correct tools could fit through the opening and dislodge the apple. Given that the animals did at least learn to select the correct tools more often than the incorrect tools as their first choice, we examined the

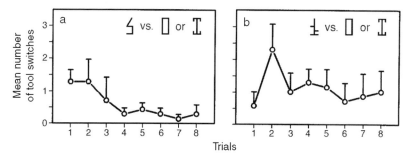

Figure 8.6 Experiment 11. (a)–(b) Mean number of times the subjects switched between the correct and incorrect tools on each trial. The data are depicted on a trial-by-trial basis, grouped by the correct tools.

more discriminating predictions of these two models by determining if the apes appreciated the difference between the easy and difficult orientations of the correct tools.

As a first approach to answering this question, we examined each animal's first eight attempts (regardless of trial number) to use the two correct tools, and noted whether they oriented them in the manner that we had envisioned as leading to the easiest retrieval of the apple (i.e. with the straight end directed toward the apparatus), or in the more difficult manner (i.e. with the angled end directed toward the apparatus). As is obvious from the results depicted in Fig. 8.7(a)–(b) and Table 8.3, the apes did not behave according to the predictions of the high-level model. For tool ∫, an equal number of apes used the easy orientation as used the difficult orientation. Worse yet for the predictions of the high-level model, when tool ⌐ was selected, the apes displayed a significant preference for grasping the straight end and using this tool in the *difficult* orientation (see Table 8.3). Furthermore, when we expanded our analysis to look at the average of all bouts using the two correct tools, the same effect was present (see Fig. 8.8 and Table 8.3). First, the apes oriented tool ∫ as often in the difficult orientation as in the easy orientation. Second, the apes exhibited a significant preference for orienting tool ⌐ in the difficult orientation of this tool type. Finally, we calculated the *percentage* of bouts for each trial in which the apes used the correct tools in each of the two orientations (Fig. 8.9(a)–(b)). This graph reveals that, as the experiment progressed, our animals learned to use the correct tools almost exclusively in the difficult orientation! Thus, even for tool ∫, in which the apes showed no overall preference for one orientation over the other (see Fig. 8.8), the apes came to prefer to use it in the difficult orientation (see Fig. 8.9(a)).

As we puzzled over these surprising findings (see Figs 8.7 and 8.9), we began to question whether the correct tools really did possess an easy and a difficult orientation as we had originally intended. Although in our pre-experimental design and testing of the apparatus it seemed clear to us that it was much easier to obtain the apple by inserting the straight ends of the correct tools into the hole in the apparatus, perhaps for some reason this was not true for the apes. To assess this question objectively, we calculated

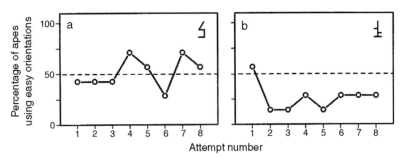

Figure 8.7 Experiment 11. (a)–(b) The percentage of apes who positioned the correct tools in the easy orientation across their first eight attempts (regardless of trial number). The data for each correct tool are depicted separately.

Table 8.3 Subjects' mean preferences for orientations of the correct tools, experiment 11

Tool type	Orientation		p
	Easy	Difficult	
Tool ⊊			
First 8 attempts			
M =	51.79	48.21	n.s.
SD =	15.12	15.12	
All attempts			
M =	48.09	51.91	n.s.
SD =	10.71	10.71	
Tool ⊥			
First 8 attempts			
M =	26.80	73.20	.01[a]
SD =	14.14	14.14	
All attempts			
M =	22.77	77.23	.002[b]
SD =	13.69	13.69	

One sample t-tests were used to determine whether the subjects displayed a significant preference (where chance = 50 per cent) for using the easy orientation in their first eight attempts (or all attempts): [a]$t(6) = 4.64$, $p < 0.01$; [b]$t(6) = 5.263$, $p < 0.002$.

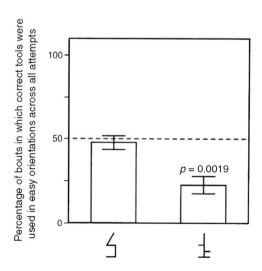

Figure 8.8 Experiment 11. The percentage of apes who positioned the correct tools in the easy orientation across all attempts. The data for each correct tool are depicted separately.

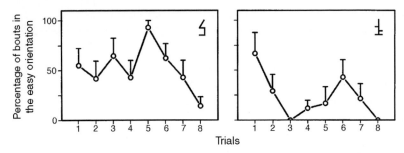

Figure 8.9 Experiment 11. The mean percentage of bouts on each trial on which the subjects used the correct tools in the easy orientation. The data for each correct tool are depicted separately.

how often the apes were successful when they used the correct tools in each of the two orientations (easy vs. difficult). To do so, we calculated a mean score for each animal consisting of the percentage of bouts in which they were successful in obtaining the apple using each of the two orientations for each of the two correct tools.

As can be seen in Fig. 8.10, the results supported our original assessment. The apes were considerably more successful when they positioned the correct tools in their easy orientations than when they positioned them in their difficult orientations (paired two-tailed t-tests: tool ⌐, $t(6) = 2.910$, $p < 0.03$; tool ⊥, $t(5) = 2.434$, $p < 0.06$). Indeed, for a given bout of using a correct tool, the apes were about twice as likely to succeed if they directed the straight end of the tool toward the apparatus. For example, in the case of tool ⊥, the apes attempted to use the tool in the difficult orientation 56 times, and in the easy orientation only 17 times, but they succeeded twice as often when they did position it in the easy orientation.

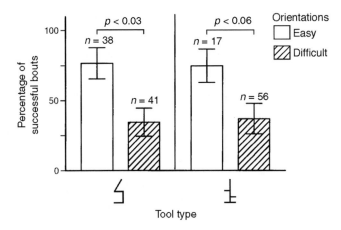

Figure 8.10 Experiment 11. The percentage of bouts on which the apes were successful while using the correct tools as a function of whether they oriented the tools in the easy or difficult orientation. The data for each correct tool are depicted separately.

USING THE TOOL TO CONTACT THE APPARATUS. As mentioned above, in the preceeding, analyses, we examined all deliberate orientations of the tools toward the apparatus. Do the patterns of results change if we distinguish between those bouts where the apes made contact with the apparatus versus those when they did not? We re-examined the data to determine if there was evidence that the apes at least perceptually recognized that the wrong tool was being used, or that the correct tool was in the wrong (i.e. difficult) orientation.

First, in Fig. 8.11(a)–(e) we show the percentage of apes who contacted the apparatus with the correct tool first. Note that this is the same general data set as was analyzed in Fig. 8.3, except that this graph depicts the first tool that the apes used to make actual contact with the apparatus (as opposed to holding it up and orienting it directly in front of the apparatus, without making contact). Although the overall pattern of results is similar to the data presented in Fig. 8.3, these data reveal a slightly higher overall tendency for the correct tool to be used for first contact (although several analyses revealed

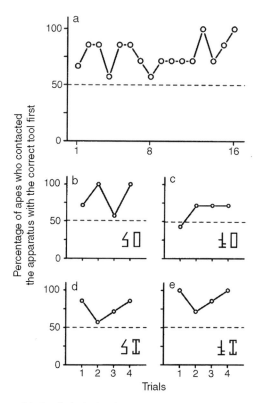

Figure 8.11 Experiment 11. (a) Graph depicting the percentage of apes who first contacted the apparatus with the correct tool. (b)–(e) Graphs depicting the percentage of apes who first contacted the apparatus with the correct tool on a trial-by-trial basis within each of the four major testing conditions. The dotted horizontal line depicts the percentage of apes who could be expected to choose the correct tool first due to chance alone.

that this effect was not statistically significant). The difference between the two analyses appears most pronounced in comparing Figs 8.3(b) and 8.11(b) (i.e. ⸦ vs. ⬚).

As a more general summary, we calculated the percentage of bouts in which the tool (and, in the case of the correct tool, each orientation of the tool) made contact with the apparatus and averaged these scores to obtain the values reported in Table 8.4. This analysis was conducted in order to determine if there was a significant difference in the frequency with which the apes made contact with the apparatus with the correct and incorrect tools, and/or the correct tools in their difficult and easy orientations. These analyses might reveal some underlying understanding (or at least perception) that the tools differed in being able to fit through the hole in the apparatus.

A one-way repeated measures ANOVA on the values reported in Table 8.4 yielded a strong overall effect ($F(2, 12) = 9.004$, $p = .0041$), and Tukey-Kramer posttests revealed that this was the result of the fact that the subjects tended to contact the apparatus with the incorrect tools significantly less often than they did with either orientation of the correct tool ($p < .01$ in both cases). Interestingly, the analyses also revealed that the apes did *not* differ in how often they contacted the apparatus with the correct tool in its two orientations.

In general, these restricted analyses provide some data to suggest that the apes displayed a difference in their actions on the correct and incorrect tools. In particular, having picked up a tool and oriented it toward the apparatus, they were less likely to contact the apparatus if it was an incorrect tool than if it was a correct tool. This may reflect an underlying recognition that the incorrect tool would not fit through the hole. On the other hand, the fact that they did contact the apparatus with the incorrect tools on almost 75 per cent of their bouts with these tools suggests that this was by no means a strong recognition.

Table 8.4 Percentage (and number) of bouts in which tool made contact with apparatus (averaged across conditions) by subject, experiment 11

Subject	Correct tools		Incorrect tools
	Easy orientation	Difficult orientation	
KAR	100 (9/9)	83.3 (10/12)	85.7 (12/14)
CAN	100 (4/4)	100 (17/17)	66.7 (6/9)
JAD	100 (12/12)	80 (12/15)	71.4 (5/7)
BRA	88.9 (8/9)	100 (11/11)	90.9 (10/11)
MEG	85.7 (6/7)	100 (9/9)	66.7 (4/6)
MIN	77.8 (7/9)	94.8 (17/18)	66.7 (12/18)
APO	100 (5/5)	100 (15/15)	75.0 (3/4)
Mean =	93.2	93.9	74.7
SD =	9.1	8.7	9.9

Discussion

The results of this experiment can be summarized as follows. In one, and possibly two, of the conditions, the chimpanzees displayed some initial evidence of choosing the correct tool as their first choice (Fig. 8.3(d)–(e)). However, these initial selections did not necessarily lead to success on that bout, often because the apes positioned the tool in the difficult orientation. Furthermore, as we described earlier, at least part of the apes' apparent initial preference for the correct tools is perhaps better described as an effect of avoiding tool $\mathbb{I}$, as opposed to a preference for the correct tools *per se* (see Fig. 8.3(b)–(e)). Nonetheless, by the end of the experiment, the apes were clearly tending to prefer the correct tools as their first choice across all conditions, even though their ability to solve the task on that bout lagged behind (compare Figs 8.3(a) and 8.4(a)), and even though they increasingly came to orient the correct tools in the most difficult manner. In general, the results seemed to best fit the predictions of the perceptual similarity model, coupled with learning that occurred across the course of the experiment.

One intriguing result of this study was that, having oriented a tool toward the apparatus, our apes were significantly less likely to use it to make actual contact with the apparatus if it was an incorrect tool (that is, if it could not pass through the hole). Does this imply that they understood the causal structure of the tool–substrate interaction? In isolation, these data could be used to support that view. However, we are cautious about rushing to such a conclusion for several reasons. First, on a full 75 per cent of the bouts involving an incorrect tool, the apes *did* use it to make contact with the apparatus. Second, there may be other differences between the correct and incorrect tools that may account for the result we obtained (i.e. differences in the nature of their grasping surfaces or centers of gravity). Indeed, as we show later, the animals' decision-making process about which tool to grasp may have been more influenced by the grasping surfaces of the tools, than whether or not the distal end of the tools could fit through the hole. Of course, after some experience on the task, the apes may have learned to perceptually recognize the incorrect orientations once they produced them, without explicitly categorizing the distinction between an easy, difficult, and impossible orientation. In other words, rather than seeing the problem as one of causal structure, they may have come to learn the perceptual regularities involved. Having said this, however, we should quickly add that, given the overall pattern of the results, even this learning was not dramatic within the trials we administered.

In any event, there are aspects of the results that raise problems for all of the models. For example, despite learning to enter the test unit and select the correct tool, the apes did not learn to position the correct tools in the easy orientation—despite their difficulty in obtaining the reward when these tools were oriented in the difficult orientation. Indeed, in the case of tool $\perp$, they preferred the difficult orientation almost from the very beginning of testing. These findings raise the following question: why did our apes increasingly select the correct tools as their first choice, but then increasingly prefer to use them in their difficult orientation?

As a general point, of course, it is hardly necessary to emphasize the fact that the chimpanzees only succeeded when they interacted with the apparatus using the correct tools. Thus, their increasing tendency to select the correct tools as the experiment progressed may be, at least in part, due to a general association between their manipulation of the correct tools and success in dislodging the apple. But what about their increasing insistence on orienting the correct tools in their difficult orientations?

Here, two possibilities occurred to us. First, the animals may simply have preferred to use the difficult ends of the tools to attempt to dislodge the apple. Despite our (admittedly subjective) impression that our apes' central objective was to retrieve the apple as rapidly as possible, it occurred to us that they might simply enjoy the challenge of attempting to dislodge the apple in the difficult manner, or indeed, they might 'see' this causal possibility more easily for some reason. A second possibility, however, was that the apes were, to a greater or lesser degree, basing their choices on which of the tools offered a grasping surface similar to the original, straight tool that they had used in training. In other words, it seemed possible that their choices were based on the nature of the end of the tool that they were grasping, not the end that interacted with the apparatus. In short, they might have been looking for a good 'handle' to grasp the tool. If this were true, it might go a long way toward explaining why the apes were so persistent in attempting to use the correct tools in their most difficult orientations. In addition, this idea offered another contributing cause for their increasing tendency across the experiment to select the correct tools in general—after all, these tools possessed the best 'handles'.

Experiment 12: testing the grasping-affordance hypothesis, age 9¹/₂

In order to test the idea that our apes' decisions were based more upon the grasping surface of the tool than upon the causal interactions between the tip of the tool and the substrate surrounding the apple, we modified the four testing tools in several specific ways. In particular, we added excellent gripping handles to the previously *incorrect* tools, and added additional complexity to the would-be handles of the previously *correct* tools. As we explain in detail below, this had the effect of turning the previously incorrect tools into *correct* ones (tools that possessed an easy/correct end as well as an impossible end), while turning the previously correct tools into *difficult* ones (tools with which either end could be used to dislodge the apple—but only with considerable difficulty).

Method

Subjects and apparatus

The same seven chimpanzees were used. Their ages ranged from 9;0 to 9;11 when the study began. They began this study approximately 3 months after completing experiment 11, and in the interim had participated in experiments 2 and 15 (see Appendix I).

The same apparatus and straight tool from experiment 11 were used. In addition, a new set of novel tools was constructed for the testing sessions by transforming the four testing tools that had been used in experiment 11 (see Fig. 8.12). This transformation resulted in the creation of two *correct* tools and two *difficult* tools.

Hypotheses and predictions

Consider the tools for this experiment that are depicted in Fig. 8.12. First, let us focus on the two *correct* tools. Note that one end of these tools (the impossible end) offers the same unworkable causal interaction between the tool and the substrate through which it must pass as the incorrect tools from experiment 11. However, also note that the other end (the easy end) offers the same easily workable causal interactions as the easy end of the original correct tools in experiment 11. Now consider the two *difficult* tools. Here, either end can be used to dislodge the apple, but only with the same level of difficulty as the difficult ends of the correct tools from experiment 11.

This study tested three models of our chimpanzees' behavior in experiment 11. We dubbed the first model the *chimpanzee-interpretation model*. It envisioned that our apes (for whatever reason) simply perceived the difficult ends as the appropriate means of dislodging the apple. If true, when presented with a correct versus a difficult tool, they ought to select the difficult one. In contrast, the *grasping-affordance model* envisioned that our apes were, to a large extent, evaluating the suitability of the tools by determining whether there was a portion of the tool that could be grasped in the same fashion as the straight tool used in the original training. We designed the novel tool set so that, if this model were true, the apes ought to largely ignore the difficult tools and, instead, prefer the correct tools. More importantly, *the surprising prediction generated by this model was that although the apes would prefer the correct tools, they would use them in the impossible orientation!* Finally, a *high-level model* envisioned that the apes were attending to the local interaction of the tip of the correct tool and the opening in the substrate, and would therefore use the correct tools in the correct orientation.

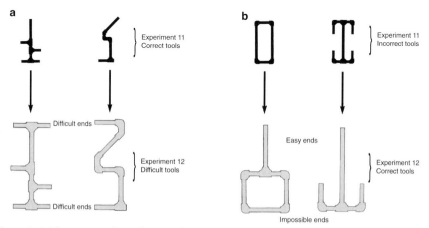

Figure 8.12 The process of transforming the original tool set from experiment 11 to the tool set that was used in experiment 12. See text for the details of the significance of these transformations.

Procedure

The general position of the apparatus relative to the testing unit, the placement of the tools, and the counterbalancing procedures were the same as those described for experiment 11.

RETENTION TRIALS. Each ape received sessions consisting of two trials with the training tool. The task was simply for the animal to enter the test unit, pick up the tool, and use it to dislodge the apple. We required each ape to perform correctly on four consecutive trials before they could advance to testing.

TESTING. Testing was very similar to experiment 11. It consisted of eight sessions per animal. Six of these sessions consisted of a single experimental trial consisting of a choice between one of the *correct* tools and one of the *difficult* tools. The remaining two sessions (determined randomly), consisted of an experimental trial (as just described) plus a standard trial (on which only the straight tool was present). These standard trials were included in the hopes of maintaining the motivation level for animals that might not perform well on the experimental trials, and who might thus become frustrated with the problem. Unlike experiment 11, we did not include trials in which the straight tool was paired with each of the novel tools. The reason was because they had exhibited such an overwhelming preference for the training tool (which they had selected on 93 per cent of all trials).

During each experimental trial a correct and a difficult tool were present. Both were positioned horizontally in front of the apparatus. The end-to-end orientation of the correct tool was counterbalanced so that it occurred equally often in the two possible horizontal orientations. Because both ends of the difficult tools were presumed to be comparably difficult, these tools were placed in a fixed horizontal orientation relative to the apparatus throughout the experiment. All possible correct–difficult pairs (and orientations, given the above constraints) were created and administered to the animals so that each of them received four trials each of each correct–difficult pair. The positions of the correct and incorrect tools were counterbalanced so that each tool appeared equally often on the left and right.

Videotape coding and data analysis

The trials were recorded in a similar manner to that in experiment 11. Two raters (a main rater and a reliability rater) coded the probe trials from the tapes using a set of standardized written instructions, which were designed to measure several aspects of the chimpanzees' tool use. The main rater coded 100 per cent of the trials ($N = 56$), and the reliability rater coded 25 per cent ($n = 14$). The trials were coded according to the same scheme as in experiment 11. Near perfect agreement (37/38 cases) was obtained in determining the bouts ($\kappa = .91$). The raters' coding of the cumulative durations for each bout yielded a Pearson's r^2 of .98. The raters exhibited near-perfect agreement on the orientation of the correct tool in each bout on 20/21 cases ($\kappa = .64$). (This κ is low despite the high agreement of the raters because of an inherent limitation of Cohen's kappa calculations which, in particular situations, causes the proportion expected by chance to be very high.) Next, the raters exhibited perfect agreement (37/37 cases) as to whether the tool had contacted the apparatus ($\kappa = 1.00$). Finally, the raters agreed on 28/28 cases as to whether or not the animal was successful in dislodging the apple from the shelf of the apparatus on each trial ($\kappa = 1.00$). Only the data from the main rater was used in the data summary and analysis.

Results

The main results provide support for the predictions generated by the grasping-affordance model and some possible support for the chimpanzee-interpretation model (although, as we shall see, these data are open to other interpretations). No support for the high-level model was obtained.

First, Fig. 8.13(a) displays the percentage of apes who selected the correct tools as their first choice by trial number, regardless of the specific condition. Although their

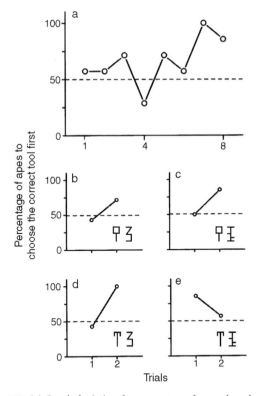

Figure 8.13 Experiment 12. (a) Graph depicting the percentage of apes who selected the correct tool as their first choice on a trial-by-trial basis regardless of condition. (b)–(e) Graphs depicting the percentage of apes who selected the correct tool as their first choice on a trial-by-trial basis within each of the four major testing conditions. The dotted horizontal line depicts the percentage of apes who could be expected to choose the correct tool first due to chance alone.

tendency to do so was not overwhelming in the first several sessions, by the end of the experiment the animals came to exhibit a clear preference for choosing the correct tool first. Indeed, as can be seen from Fig. 8.13(b)–(e), in three of the four testing conditions, the apes initially exhibited no preference for choosing the correct tool first on trial 1, but by trial 2 they clearly did so.

Despite the data concerning their first choices, the percentage of time they spent manipulating the correct and incorrect tools suggests that even on trial 1 the apes preferred the correct tools. As is clear from Fig. 8.14(a), on trial 1, the apes manipulated the correct tools for a significantly greater amount of time (over 2.5 times longer) than the incorrect tools, $t(6) = 3.424$, $p < .02$. However, by trial 2, the amount of time spent manipulating the correct tool declined to approximately the same level as the amount of time they spent manipulating the incorrect tool, which remained more or less constant (see Fig. 8.14(a)). How were the animals orienting the correct tool during their initial attempts? The data plotted in Fig. 8.15 clearly reveals that (for both of the correct tool types) the apes oriented the correct tools in their impossible orientations on the vast

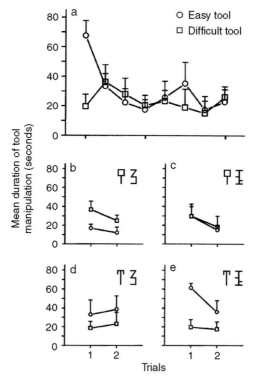

Figure 8.14 Experiment 12. (a) Mean duration of the subjects' manipulations of the correct versus difficult tools on a trial-by-trial basis, regardless of condition. (b)–(e) Mean durations of the subjects' manipulations of the correct and difficult tools on a trial-by-trial basis within each of the four major testing conditions

majority of their initial attempts. Figure 8.16 shows these data as the percentage of bouts in the correct orientation on each trial, and it reveals that the apes preferred to orient the correct tool in the impossible orientation across the entire experiment. Indeed, these data also reveal that even on trials 2–4 the apes continued to orient the correct tool in the impossible orientation. The reason for this, of course, was because the apes were grasping the straight (easy) end of the correct tool as a handle. Additional data on this point is provided in Tables 8.5 and 8.6, which present every attempt that each ape made with the correct tools and display whether the tool was oriented in the

Table 8.5 Orientations during all attempts with the correct tool type ⊤ in experiment 12

Subject	Attempt number							
	1	2	3	4	5	6	7	8
APO	−	+	−	−	−	−		
KAR	−	−	−	−	−	−	−	
CAN	−	−	−	−	−	−	−	−
JAD	−	−	−					
BRA	−	−	−					
MEG	−	+	−	−				
MIN	−	−						
Mean percentage of easy orientations =	0	29	0	0	0	0	0	0

A '+' indicates that subject oriented the tool in the easy orientation, whereas a '−' indicates that the subject oriented the tool in the impossible orientation.

Table 8.6 Orientations during all attempts with the correct tool type ⫟ in experiment 12

Subject	Attempt number								
	1	2	3	4	5	6	7	8	9
APO	−	+	−	−	+	−	−	−	−
KAR	−	−	−	−	−	−			
CAN	−	−	−	−	−	−			
JAD	−	−	−	−	+	−			
BRA	−	−	−						
MEG	−	−	+	−	+	−	−	−	
MIN	−	−	+	−	−	+	−		
Mean percentage of easy Orientations =	0	14	29	0	50	17	0	0	0

A '+' indicates that subject oriented the tool in the easy orientation, whereas a '−' indicates that the subject oriented the tool in the impossible orientation.

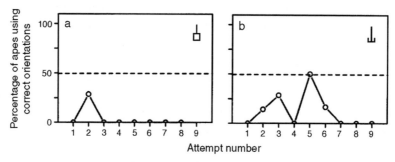

Figure 8.15 Experiment 12. (a)–(b) The percentage of apes who positioned the correct tools in the easy orientation across all attempts they made (regardless of trial number). The data for each correct tool are depicted separately.

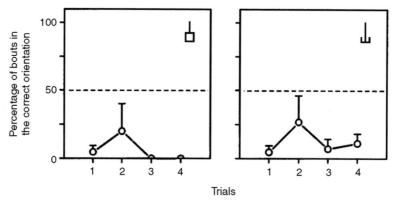

Figure 8.16 Experiment 12. (a)–(b) The mean percentage of bouts on each trial in which the subjects used the correct tools in the easy orientation. The data for each correct tool are depicted separately.

easy or impossible manner. The apes displayed an overwhelming tendency to use the correct tools in the impossible orientation.

One practical consequence of our apes' insistence on using the difficult tool as much as they did, as well their insistence on using the correct tool in the impossible orientation, was that the subjects were rarely able to retrieve the apple in this experiment. Indeed, across the entire experiment, there were only *three* trials on which animals obtained an apple: Jadine succeeded twice with a difficult tool, and Megan succeeded once with a correct tool.

Discussion

The results of this study can be summarized as follows. Contrary to the prediction of the grasping-affordance model, the apes' very first tool selection (on trial one) was essentially random; that is, they did not immediately grasp the correct tool by the easy end and orient it incorrectly. However, rather than providing strong support for the chimpanzee-interpretation model, this result appears to have been the result of the apes retaining a residual and transient preference for the tool that physically resembled the tool that they had grown accustomed to using in experiment 11 (i.e. the difficult tool). This idea is supported by two clear patterns in the data. First, even within the first trial our apes preferred to manipulate the correct tool (see Fig. 8.14(a))—which they did 2.5 times more than the difficult tool. This finding stands in clear contradiction to the chimpanzee-interpretation model as well as the high-level model. The second line of evidence is that, as the experiment proceeded, the apes displayed an increasingly strong tendency to select the correct tool as their first choice, but then persistently positioned it so that the impossible end was oriented toward the apparatus. In summary, the data suggests that once they overcame their initial tendency to choose the tools which most perceptually resembled those they had favored in experiment 11, they behaved almost exclusively in the manner predicted by the grasping-affordance model.

Experiment 13: further tests of the grasping-affordace model, age 9^1/$_2$

The results of the previous study provided support for the hypothesis that our animals' choice between tools, and how they oriented those tools, was more dependent on their understanding of how to grasp the tools than on the interaction of the distal end of the tools with the substrate through which they needed to pass. In this study, we attempted to simplify the situation by presenting them with only one (correct) tool on each trial. Each tool had an easy end and an impossible end (the correct tools from experiment 12). However, on each trial the tool was either oriented so that the straight end was positioned closest to the hole in the apparatus, or oriented so that the straight end was closest to the ape (i.e. it appeared to be a handle). In this manner, we attempted to determine if the apes could overcome a proceduralized rule about the grasping affordance of the tool when the causal affordance of the correct tool on the apparatus was made more perceptually obvious by its orientation.

Method

Subjects and apparatus

The same seven chimpanzees participated in this study, and were between 9;2 and 10;1 when the study began. This study began 1^1/$_2$ months after experiment 12 was completed. The subjects were simultaneously participating in experiment 2, and had participated in experiment 16 in the interim (see Appendix I). The same tool-insertion apparatus from experiments 11 and 12 was used. However, only the training tool and the two correct tools from experiment 12 were used.

Procedure

ORIENTATION. We reoriented our apes to the tool-insertion problem by administering a single session consisting of two standard trials (only the training tool present). The same procedure from experiments 11 and 12 was used. All of the animals met the crite-rion of responding correctly within 2 minutes on both trials, and we advanced them directly into testing.

TESTING. Testing consisted of 16 sessions per animal, each of which contained a single experimental trial. However, eight of these sessions (four in the first half on the experi-ment and four in the second half) also contained a second trial identical to the orienta-tion trials (only the standard tool was available) to maintain the subjects' motivation levels.

Each experimental trial proceeded as follows. First, one of the two correct tools was placed vertically on the floor between the test unit and the apparatus. It was either posi-tioned so that the correct end of the tool was closest to the apparatus (thus it did not need to be reoriented), or so that the incorrect end was closest to the apparatus (and thus did need to be reoriented) (see Fig. 8.17(a)–(b)). Hereafter we refer to these as the correct and incorrect orientations. Next, the shuttle door was opened and the animal entered the test unit. Upon entry, the ape was allowed 2 minutes to respond, during which time period they were allowed to manipulate the tool as often as they wished.

Each subject received eight experimental trials with each correct tool. We counterbal-anced the orientation of these tools so that each correct tool was placed with the correct end closest to the apparatus on half of the trials, and the incorrect end closest to the apparatus on the other half. In order to assign the exact sequences of tool types and ori-entations, the subjects were randomly divided into two groups. Group 1 (Apollo, Brandy, and Jadine) received the orientation sequence ⊤, ⊥, ⊤, ⊥, whereas group 2 (Kara, Candy, Megan, and Mindy) received the sequence ⊤, ⊥, ⊤, ⊥. In order to provide each animal with four trials of each tool in each orientation, we tested each animal on four repetitions of the sequence of the group to which he or she had been assigned. As the above sequences reveal, we began each ape with the incorrect

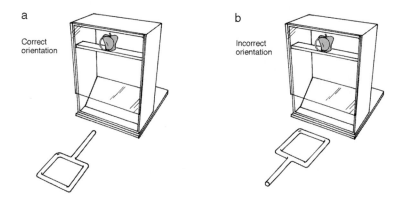

Figure 8.17 Critical manipulation used in experiment 13 involving (a) tools presented in the correct orientation; or (b) tools presented in the incorrect orientation. Note that only one tool type is shown. See text for details.

orientation. We did so because, given the apes' extensive experience with the general tool-insertion problem, and given the seemingly trivial nature of the problem, we felt that their first several trials might be more important for testing the predictions of the three models under consideration (see below).

MODELS TO BE TESTED. The *grasping-affordance* model was pitted against two alternative models (see Fig. 8.18). Recall that the grasping-affordance model predicted that the apes would perceive the correct (straight) ends of the tools as suitable handles, and thus consistently use the tools in the incorrect orientation. Indeed, this model predicted that on those trials where the tools were presented in the *correct* orientation, the apes would systematically reorient them into the impossible orientation before attempting to use them. In contrast, the *orientation model* envisioned that the apes would recognize the general vertical orientation as acceptable, and thus pick up the tools and attempt to use them in the orientation they found them. If true, they ought to perform successfully on the trials where the tools were initially presented in the correct (easy) orientation, but have difficulty on the trials where the tools were presented in the incorrect orientation. Finally, the *high-level model* envisioned that the apes would attend to the local interaction of the tip of the correct tool and the opening in the substrate, and would therefore use the tools correctly when presented in the correct orientation, and reorient the tools when they encountered them in the incorrect orientation.

Finally, both the grasping-affordance and orientation models generated a set of predictions about the apes' initial behaviors. Clearly, with repeated experience, both models left open the possibility that the apes could learn to perform in the manner predicted by the high-level model.

Videotape coding and data analysis
A main rater coded all 112 test trials (7 animals × 16 test trials = 112 trials) and a reliability rater independently coded 25 per cent of the total (4 test trials per animal). The

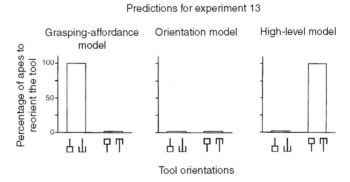

Figure 8.18 Predictions of three models of the chimpanzees' understanding of the tool-insertion problem in experiment 13. Each model predicts a different pattern of when, if at all, the animals would reorient the tools (from their experimentally presented positions) before using them.

written coding instructions required the raters to record the cumulative duration of time the apes spent manipulating the tool on each trial (Pearson $r^2 = 0.999$); the exact sequence of orientations for each bout of tool manipulation on each trial ($\kappa = .82$); whether the tool contacted the apparatus on each bout ($\kappa = 1.00$); and whether the ape succeeded in dislodging the apple on each trial ($\kappa = 1.00$). The main rater's data was used in all subsequent analyses.

Results and discussion

Overall success on the task

In order to provide some context for the apes' actions on the tools, we first describe their overall levels of success in dislodging the apple. (For this analysis, as well as all subsequent analyses in this study, within each orientation condition we combined the different tools because a preliminary analysis revealed that the subjects did not treat the two tools differently.) Figure 8.19(a) depicts the apes' overall success on each trial according to the initial orientation of the tool. As can be seen, the apes consistently exhibited higher levels of success in the condition where the tools were initially presented in the correct orientation ($M = 57.1$ per cent) than in the condition in which they were presented in the incorrect orientation ($M = 39.3$ per cent). Indeed, this difference is even more marked if we restrict our analysis to their success on the first bout within each trial (see Fig. 8.19(b)). The subjects' performances appeared to improve across trials (see Fig. 8.19(a)–(b)), and the basis of this learning will be discussed more below.

Reorientations of the tools

The main predictions of this study concerned the apes' understanding of the orientation of the tools, and hence we examined the overall frequency and patterning of the subjects' reorientations of the tools in the two conditions. The results were compared to the predictions generated by the three models depicted in Fig. 8.18 (see above).

Initially, we separately summarized each animal's data according to the overall percentage of trials on which they reoriented the tools in each condition. This allowed us to determine if the apes were applying a uniform strategy (reflected in the three models in

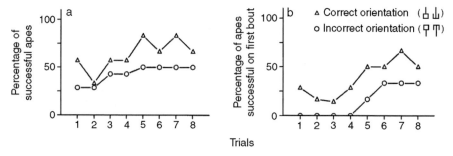

Figure 8.19 Percentage of apes who were successful in dislodging the reward as a function of initial orientation of the tools (a) on each trial and (b) on their first bout on each trial in experiment 13.

Fig. 8.18) in deciding whether to use the tools in the orientation in which they were presented or to reorient them. We structured these data in two ways. First, we examined whether they reoriented the tool on their very first bout on each trial, and second we examined whether they had reoriented the tool at the time they made first contact with the apparatus using the tool. These results are presented in Figs 8.20 and 8.21, respectively, and in each case both the overall group data are shown, as well as the data for each animal. Even at this level of analysis, it is quite clear that two of the subjects (Kara and Candy) were performing according to the grasping-affordance model and one subject (Brandy) was performing according to the orientation model. Three of the four remaining subjects (Apollo, Megan, and possibly Mindy) tended to perform according to a combination of the grasping-affordance model and the high-level model. The data reveal that these latter apes were just as likely to reorient the tool from a correct to an incorrect orientation as vice versa. This might either be because (1) the apes were reorienting the tools at random; or because (2) they understood the causal structure of the

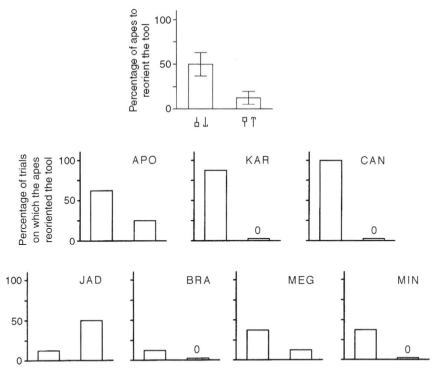

Figure 8.20 Percentage of apes who reoriented the tools on their first bout on each trial in experiment 13. The main graph depicts the overall results averaged across animals and trials, whereas the lower graphs show the results for the individual apes summarized across trials. Note that these reorientations may or may not have been associated with the ape contacting the apparatus with the tool.

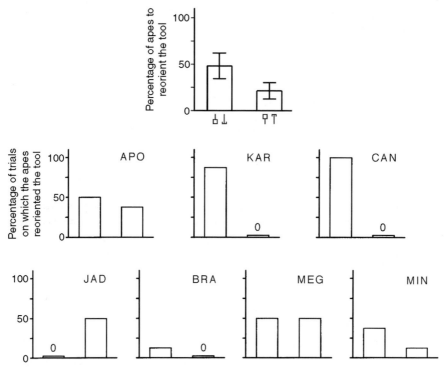

Figure 8.21 Percentage of apes whose first contact with the apparatus with the tool was with the tool in an orientation which was different from the manner in which it was presented to them in experiment 13.

problem but had difficulty escaping the grasping-affordance of the tools (when the tools were presented in the incorrect orientation). However, a closer analysis of the results (see below) clearly shows that the aspect of the data which implicates the high-level model was, in fact, learned across trials.

In contrast to the other apes, Jadine appeared to perform according to the high-level model (see Figs 8.20 and 8.21). However, a careful examination of the trial-by-trial data reveals that, in the initial half of the experiment, Jadine performed according to the orientation model, just as had Brandy. On her initial four trials, where the tool was presented *incorrectly*, Jadine did not reorient it, reflected in what she did both on her first bout and her first contact with the apparatus. However, on her second set of four trials in this condition, she reoriented the tool in every case on the first bout. Thus, Jadine's initial responses reveal that she performed exactly as predicted by the orientation model, and only *learned* to respond as predicted by the high-level model. Indeed, in this respect, Jadine was really just one of three apes (Jadine, Apollo, and Megan) who learned to perform according to the predictions of the high-level model—a trend reflected in the overall group data plotted in Fig. 8.22(a)–(b). (The trial-by-trial data for the individual apes, which reveal the individual learning trends, can be found in

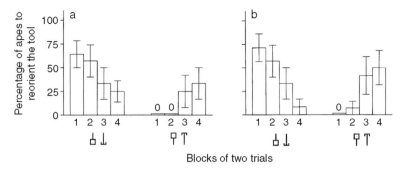

Figure 8.22 Learning effects across trials in experiment 13. (a) Percentage of apes who reoriented the tools on their very first bout on each trial as a function of trial number and the condition in which the tools were initially presented. (b) Percentage of apes whose first contact with the apparatus involved a reoriented tool as a function of trial number and the condition in which the tools were initially presented.

Appendix II.) The data just reviewed suggest that the apes, despite their previous experiences from experiments 11 and 12, did not initially appreciate the causal significance of the two orientations before acting with the tools. Two additional lines of evidence are consistent with this view. First, if we compare the mean number of tool reorientations (averaged across animals) in the correct orientation condition ($M = 1.214$, $SD = 0.790$) to that in the incorrect orientation condition ($M = 0.840$, $SD = 1.032$), they do not differ significantly, $t(6) = 1.160$, n.s.). This implies that the apes did not realize that the tools only needed to be reoriented when they were presented in the incorrect orientation. Second, the apes spent the same amount of time manipulating the tools regardless of their initial orientation (correct orientation: $M = 26.6$ sec, $SD = 14.02$; incorrect orientation: $M = 28.06$ sec, $SD = 13.46$).

In summary, within the first half of the experiment, not a single animal responded according to the pattern predicted by the high-level model. Rather, the initial performances of all of our subjects were best predicted by the grasping-affordance model or the orientation model. Three of the animals maintained their initial pattern of responding across the experiment (grasping-affordance model pattern: Kara, Candy; orientation model pattern: Brandy). Two others shifted from the pattern predicted by the grasping-affordance model to that predicted by the high-level model (Apollo and Megan). One shifted from the pattern predicted by the orientation model to that predicted by the high-level model (Jadine). And finally, one remaining animal (Mindy) essentially reoriented the tool randomly with respect to how it was initially presented. Thus, although three of the animals learned (at least with respect to their first bout and first contact data) to respond according to the pattern predicted by the high-level model, there is no unique reason to favor the idea that even these apes understood the causal structure of the problem over the idea that the causal structure of the problem sculpted, so to speak, the actions into a form that could allow the apple to be retrieved.

This is not to say that the apes were acting like unconscious Skinnerian learning machines, but rather that the information that they processed, stored, and came to act upon may have been about perceptual task features, not causal structure.

General discussion (experiments 11–13)

The studies reported in this chapter were designed to assess our apes' understanding of the causal interaction between a probing tool and a hole in a substrate through which the tool needed to pass to operate effectively.

As a general overview of the results, two things can be stated with certainty. First, our apes were highly interested in this problem across the three experiments we employed. They quickly learned to use the straight tool to dislodge the apple and, even on the most difficult trials, they were generally quite persistent in attempting to use the tools that were available to dislodge the apple. Second, because we allowed them to attempt to solve the task using whatever means they wished until the duration of the trial expired, in many cases the apes arrived at a solution. For example, in experiment 11, the apes were eventually generally succeeding well above half of the time on even the most difficult trials.

In considering how the apes eventually came to conceive of the problem, there can be no doubt that the training that the apes received with the straight tool provided them with some very general knowledge about how to approach the task. However, even here the exact nature of what they finally understood is unclear. It seems safe to say that they understood that the hole in the apparatus was the target for the action of the tool, and that the tool needed to contact the apple. It is even possible that they came to recognize the general perceptual form of the right kind of tool that needed to be directed toward the hole/apple (although it is of interest that we have no direct evidence for this).

However, the presence of more abstract levels of causal understanding (namely, that the tools need to 'fit through' the hole, or that the 'shape'—as opposed to the perceptual form—of the distal end of the tools set limits on their utility in contacting the apple) are not forced or even supported by the data we obtained. For example, in experiment 11 the apes initially chose tools which could not possibly fit through the hole as often as they chose tools which easily could. And, even after they learned to select the correct tools (presumably upon the basis of trial-and-error learning), they increasingly tended to use them in their most difficult orientations. Experiments 12 and 13 demonstrated that this rather odd finding could be explained by the fact that the apes were focusing on their own grasping actions on the tools, not how the distal ends of the tools interacted with the hole in the apparatus. It is of interest here that in his experiments involving box-stacking, Köhler (1927) argued that although his chimpanzees were able to intelligently correct numerous mistakes involving bringing one object of a particular shape into contact with another, they did not solve these problems by invoking the notion of shape at all. Rather, they appeared to rely on the structure of the problem itself to present the solution as they struggled with it. Having then seen the solution, they could learn the perceptual relations involved so that future solutions to the problem could be achieved with immediacy and fluidity. Indeed, Köhler (1927) argued that the concept of 'shape' was one of the places where 'the chimpanzee seems to reach the limit of his capacity' (p. 148).[1]

Despite the rather poor predictive power of the high-level model tested in this chapter, it is again quite clear that our apes' were not insensitive to the underlying causal structure of the problems we posed to them. In short, to some extent, they learned to behave in a manner that allowed them to effectively cope with the underlying causal structure of each test reported in this chapter. Two examples illustrate this point quite nicely. First, in experiment 11, the apes' initial tendency to choose the incorrect tools as frequently as the correct tools quickly dissipated. Thus, the apes learned that at least two of the tools were not effective in dislodging the apple. They may have either learned to avoid those particular tools, or learned to favor the correct ones. In either event, they displayed clear evidence of learning. Second, in experiment 13, several of the apes learned to reorient the tools only when they needed to be reoriented. Both of these facts show how the apes learned to behave in a manner that accounted for the causal structure of the problems at hand. But again, despite their ability to use their mental resources to develop appropriate behaviors, in no case did the apes initially behave according to the predictions of a model which assumed that the causal structure of the task was explicitly represented in their minds. In short, despite what the apes learned, we see no compelling evidence that they had such causal concepts to begin with, nor that they wound up constructing such concepts as the result of the repeated experiences they received.

---

1   The results of our tests with the tool-insertion problem suggest that, after considerable experience with the advanced forms of the problem, our apes still had little appreciation of how the shapes of the distal ends of the tools causally interacted with the problem. Nonetheless, we were left with the distinct impression that as the apes manipulated the tools and the correct ends passed in front of the hole, they seemed to 'recognize' this perceptual configuration and then acted upon it by pushing the tool toward the apple.

CHAPTER 9

THE ROPE, HOOK, TOUCHING-STICK, AND RELATED PROBLEMS: THE QUESTION OF PHYSICAL CONNECTION

DANIEL J. POVINELLI, JAMES E. REAUX, LAURA A. THEALL, AND STEVE GIAMBRONE

[The chimpanzee] will always pull the string if it visibly touches the objective. It appears doubtful whether the conception of 'connexion' in our practical human sense signifies more for the chimpanzee than visual contact in a higher or lower degree.

Wolfgang Köhler, *The Mentality of Apes*, 1927, p. 30.

When can two objects be said to be connected in the sense implied by Köhler? We submit that two objects appear to us as 'physically connected' when the following conditions are met or closely approximated: (1) there is a strong invariance between the movement of two objects; (2) as they move, the objects remain in physical contact; and (3) actions on one of the objects yields co-varied movement of the other. These *perceptual* conditions, we submit, trigger an ascription that there is some causal mechanism that connects or binds the objects in some intrinsic manner. It should be obvious from this definition that there may be greater and lesser degrees of physical connection.

One example of physical connection is a rope tied to a banana. Whether the rope is pulled straight ahead or to the side, or even lifted straight up, the banana will soon follow suit. Furthermore, we can imagine innumerable degrees of freedom between the movement of the rope and the movement of the banana. Of course, the nature of the frictional forces holding the rope upon the banana, and the rope upon itself, offers a scientific explanation for the covariation of pulling the rope and the movement of the banana. As we saw in Chapter 3, by at least two years of age human children appear to grasp the distinction between physical connection versus mere contact (see Brown 1990). Children younger than two appear to be sensitive to the presence or absence of perceptual contact between an implement and object to be moved (e.g. Bates *et al.* 1980; Piaget 1952), although it is unclear to what extent their understanding of 'contact' is grounded by the visual pattern (two objects in perceptual contact) versus a genuine appreciation of physical connection.

Importantly, however, covariation in the movement of two objects is not a *sufficient* condition for a folk physical ascription of a physical connection between them. Consider the rake-and-table problems described in the previous chapters. Here, the rake and reward move in concert, but we do not wish to say that this is a case of physical connection in any strong sense. In contrast to the rope-and-banana situation, there are far fewer degrees of freedom that can maintain the covariation of movement between the rake and the reward.

In this chapter, we attempted to test Köhler's (1927) claim that the chimpanzee has no explicit notion of physical connection, but merely sees contact to a greater or lesser degree. In order to explore our apes' ability to conceive of their solutions in terms of physical connection, we examined their reactions to a rope-and-banana problem (experiment 14), a hook retrieval problem (experiments 15 and 16), a touching-stick problem (experiments 17 and 18), and two problems that involved tools or substrates whose critical components were shown to be perceptually, but not physically, connected (experiments 19 and 20).

Experiment 14: the rope-and-banana problem, age 9

From the outset, we need to distinguish between the classic tests involving 'patterned-string problems' and the research reported here. Köhler (1927) presented his seven apes with patterned-string problems of the type depicted in Fig. 9.1. Since then, variations of this problem have been widely used with various species of nonhuman primates (Balasch *et al.* 1974; Beck 1967; Cha and King 1969; Finch 1941; Fischer and Kitchener 1965; Harlow and Settlage 1934; Settlage 1939), as well as with human children (Bates *et al.* 1980; Brown 1990; Richardson 1932; Uzgiris and Hunt 1975). Certainly, by ten months of age, human infants solve the basic task involving an attached versus an unattached string (Bates *et al.* 1980). By 14 months, however, human children are able to solve even the more difficult versions (see Fig. 9.2)—at least on transfer tests (see Brown 1990). However, many of these tests have focused on reasoning about more and more complex spatial relations among the strings (see Figs 9.1 and 9.2). In this experiment, we focused on a different question. We sought to ask our apes about their understanding of the *nature* of the contact (or potential contact) between a rope and a banana. That is, if we held the spatial arrangement of two ropes constant and unambiguous, could the apes distinguish between cases of physical connection versus cases of mere contact? In short, we sought to provide a critical means for testing Köhler's (1927) conjecture that apes understand connection as mere contact—an idea his own tests did not cleanly address. In this sense, this experiment had very little conceptual allegiance to classic patterned-string problems.

Method

Subjects
The subjects of this study were the same seven animals who participated in the studies described in the previous chapters. They were 8;7 to 9;6 when this study began. They began this study approximately 6 months after the completion of Experiment 8 (see Chapter 6).

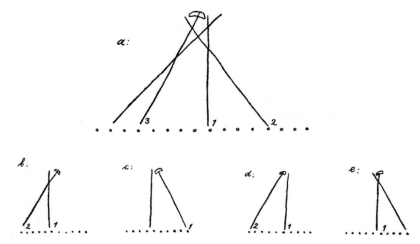

Figure 9.1 The string problem as originally implemented by Wolfgang Köhler (1927) to chimpanzees. Notice that the problem involves a kind of spatial confusion of crossing (or nearly crossing) strings with only a single objective.

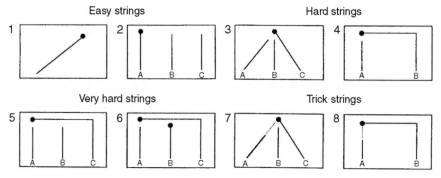

Figure 9.2 A modern version of the Köhler (1927) string problem as used with human infants and children (taken from Brown 1990). As with the original Köhler problem (see Fig. 9.1), the problem involves a successively more confusing series of spatial arrangements of strings.

Procedure

PREVIOUS FAMILIARITY WITH ROPES. All of the subjects had an extensive history with numerous kinds of ropes and their physical connection to various objects. For example, when these apes were six to eight years of age, they participated in several studies in which they used ropes to pull boxes to within their reach in order to retrieve food rewards or interesting objects. Further, beginning when they were four years of age (and intermittently earlier) they had permanent access to swinging ropes tied to the tops of their outdoor enclosures. Indeed, on occasion, the subjects had succeeded in untying the knots that held the ropes in place, although this appeared to occur fortuitously.

ORIENTATION TO THE ROPES. Three days before formal testing began, three lengths of rope (60 cm) were placed into each of the eight sections of the subjects' enclosure (a total of 24 ropes). In each section, one of the ropes was simply draped through the mesh (so that it could be pulled through easily), another was draped through but also tied to the mesh (using a simple knot identical to that used in testing), and the third rope was draped through the mesh with a knot tied on one end. The animals had free access to these ropes for the three days leading up to testing, as well as throughout the course of testing.

CONDITIONS USED IN TESTING. The apes were tested on seven conditions involving a choice between two rope-and-banana configurations. Figure 9.3 displays the six basic options (A–F) from which the seven conditions (see below) were composed. Each of the options had four perceptual variations in an attempt to minimize the rate of learning. In option A, the animals could always retrieve the banana if they pulled the rope, and in option D the subjects could retrieve the banana if they did not pull too quickly. In the remaining options (B, C, E, and F) the banana could not be obtained by pulling on the rope.

Seven conditions (1–7) were created by pairing these options together and presenting the animals with a choice between them. These conditions were designed to test the predictions of three different models of the apes' understanding of 'connection'. The

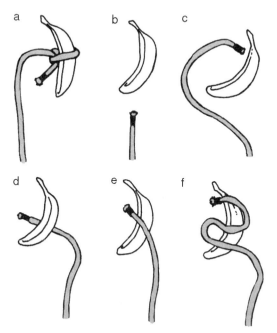

Figure 9.3 Experiment 14. The set of six basic options (A–F) from which conditions 1–7 were created. Note that the options instantiate different degrees of perceptual contact (or potential perceptual contact (C), whereas only option A offers a case of physical connection.

physical connection model postulated that the apes would appreciate that the banana would move toward them if they pulled the rope in option A (rope tied to banana) and option D (weight of the banana upon the rope), but not in the other options. In contrast, the other two models envisioned that the apes were responding to perceived visual contact of the rope with the banana. The *perceptual contact* model postulated that any perceived contact between the rope and the banana would lead the ape to expect the banana to move if the rope was pulled. Finally, the *degree of contact* model postulated that the apes' decisions would be influenced by the amount of perceptual contact between the banana and the rope (regardless of the actual physical connection). Four of the conditions (1–3 and 5) paired the rope tied to the banana with other options, and three others allowed some inferences about whether the amount of superficial contact would influence the apes' choices. Table 9.1 presents a graphic depiction of the options along with predictions of the apes' behavior generated by the three models.

Each animal received four trials of each of the seven conditions ($N = 28$ trials per subject). The animals received one trial of each of the seven conditions in a randomized order before being administered a second one, etc., until all of the trials types were exhausted. This process was then repeated until each ape had been assigned four trials of each of the seven conditions. Within each condition, the side of the specific option was counterbalanced so that each option occurred twice on the right and twice on the left. Finally, within each of the conditions, each trial was unique in that it consisted of a pairing of one of the perceptual variants and its counterpart for that condition (e.g. A_3–B_3, B_2–A_2, A_1–B_1, B_4–A_4).

Table 9.1 Conditions and predictions for which option(s) the apes should choose in experiment 14

	Conditions and predictions			
	1	2	3	4
Model				
Physical connection				
Perceptual contact				
Degree of perceptual contact				

TESTING PROCEDURE. One trial was administered per session, and typically each animal received one trial in the morning and one trial in the afternoon. As in experiment 9, each trial was divided into two parts, a *demonstration phase* and a *response phase*. For the demonstration phase, the response holes on the plexiglas partition were covered with a plexiglas screen, which prevented the animals from reaching through them (see experiment 9). The animal was then let into the test unit and the shuttle door was closed behind him or her. Upon entering, the animal encountered two bananas out of reach (100 cm) in front of the right and left response holes with two ropes laid out between the bananas (see Fig. 9.4(a)).

As soon as the door was closed behind the subject, the experimenter began the process of configuring the rope and banana while the subject observed (Fig. 9.4(b)–(d)). First, the experimenter took the rope on his left and began the process of configuring it and the banana in the fashion dictated by the experimental condition assigned to that trial. This process was carefully rehearsed and choreographed so that the rope and banana were manipulated for approximately 15 seconds. Once the left option had been configured properly, the process was repeated for the option on the right. The rope and banana were manipulated for the same amount of time that had been required to set up the left option. Once both options were laid out properly, the experimenter resumed his or her seated posture behind and midway between the two options and observed the subject for the remaining 30 seconds of the demonstration period. At this point, the shuttle door was opened, and the animal was ushered outside.

The subject waited outside for 15 seconds. During this brief waiting period, the experimenter removed the plexiglas screen from in front of the holes and then reseated

Table 9.1 (*continued*)

	Conditions and predictions		
	5	6	7
Model			
Physical connection			=
Perceptual contact	=	=	=
Degree of perceptual contact		=	

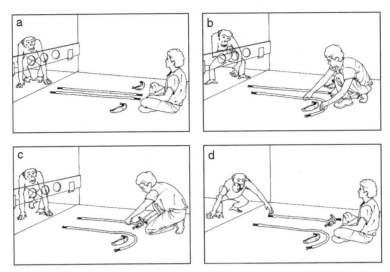

Figure 9.4 Experiment 14. Procedure for observation phase of the rope-and-banana problem. (a) Ropes, bananas, and experimenter in neutral position as ape enters test unit. (b)–(c) Experimenter arranges rope/banana relations according to predetermined condition. Ape exits test unit and plexiglas barrier is removed (not shown). (d) Ape re-enters test unit and responds (with experimenter in neutral position with gaze fixed on the subject).

him- or herself in the neutral position behind the bananas. After the 15 seconds had elapsed, the shuttle door was opened and the subject entered the test unit again, this time free to respond to either the left or right rope. The experimenter fixed his or her gaze upon the subject at all times. The subject was allowed one choice per trial, with a choice defined as the subject moving one of the ropes. If the subject attempted to reach for a second rope, the experimenter pulled it out of reach.

Results

The subjects were intensely interested in the rope segments that were placed in their enclosures during the orientation phase. We observed the subjects playing with them, chewing them, and carrying them around for the days leading up to the study, as well as throughout the duration of the study. In addition, the subjects pulled and chewed on the rope segments that we had tied to the mesh, and, after several days of efforts, succeeded in untying several of them (which we then reattached to the mesh).

The main results of the experiment concern the testing phase, and are summarized in Fig. 9.5. This figure depicts the mean percentage of choices (averaged across subjects) for each of the options within each condition. The only condition in which the apes displayed a significant preference for one of the options over the other was in condition 1. In this condition, one of the ropes clearly touched (indeed, was tied to) the banana, whereas the other was in front of it, and not touching it. Here, the apes selected the tied option on 82.1 per cent of the trials—a level significantly above that expected by chance

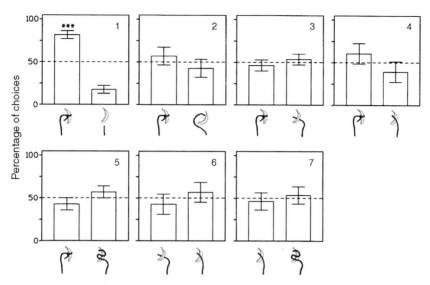

Figure 9.5 Main results from experiment 14. Each graph depicts a different condition, and percentages of choices (averaged across apes) are shown for each option within that condition.

(one sample *t*-test, hypothetical mean = 50 per cent, $t(6) = 6.971$, $p < 0.001$). This effect was present from trial 1 (7/7 apes correct) forward.

These data best fit the predictions of the perceptual contact model (see Table 9.1). Indeed, this model only generated a single incorrect prediction, in contrast to the physical connection and degree of perceptual contact models, which generated five and four incorrect predictions, respectively. The single incorrect prediction of the perceptual contact model concerned the apes' reactions to condition 2. However, the incorrect option in this condition consisted of the rope looped around the far side of the banana (see option C in Fig. 9.3). Although the rope was not touching the banana, the subjects may have anticipated that it would do so after they pulled it. Thus, the subjects may have anticipated contact, or indeed, may have failed to notice that it was not in contact. If either were true, our use of this condition may have been an inappropriate test of a more general version of the perceptual contact model (for example, one which incorporated the idea of 'potential' or 'imminent' contact).

However, several aspects of the results suggest that the subjects may have been influenced by the *degree* of perceptual contact between the rope and the banana. As can be seen from a closer examination of Fig. 9.5, in five of the six conditions in which the apes did *not* display a significant preference for one option over the other (conditions 2 and 4–7), they nonetheless tended to select the option with the greatest degree of perceptual contact. This result may suggest that although any perceptual contact is sufficient, more contact may be easier to recognize as fulfilling this condition. In general, these results provide little support for the idea that the apes recognized cases of physical connection between the rope and the banana, despite their fairly extensive previous experience with ropes.

At least one major objection might be raised against this kind of test. In particular, we might question whether apes should know anything about knots, and/or how they afford a physical connection between themselves and other objects. While an important issue, we designed the various conditions so that our interpretation of the results would not hinge solely on whether the apes possessed an understanding of knots *per se*. Indeed, the significant preference exhibited by the subjects in condition 1, but not in the other conditions, supports the idea that the subjects saw contact (or potential contact) as the relevant issue, not the particular nature of that contact. Consider, for example, the subjects' failure to distinguish between the two options in condition 6 (see Table 9.1). Here, the issue of relevance is less one of physical connection through a rope tied to a banana, as much as the question of a transfer of force from the mass of the banana to the rope. In this case, the subjects tended to prefer the option in which the rope rests over the banana (although this tendency was not statistically significant), providing a higher degree of perceptual contact. Nonetheless, addressing the question of physical connection in other ways seemed highly warranted.

Experiment 15: the hook-retrieval problem, age 9

In reflecting on the limitations of the rope-and-banana problem, we considered another case in which a tool can be said to physically connect to another object—in particular, a situation involving a hook and a ring (see Fig. 9.6). Chimpanzees in the wild have been reported to use sticks with hook ends to pull fig tree limbs to within their reach (Sugiyama and Koman 1979). Here, a very specific aspect of the tool (the hook portion) allows for a specific relation to that which is hooked—a relation which implies a strong invariance between actions on the tool and the movement of the other object. Thus, although the other object may be affected by mere contact alone, it is only when the hook is placed in a particular relation to the other object that a physical connection of sorts may be said to have been achieved. In the following set of experiments we created exactly such a situation. Initially, we trained the apes to use the hook property of the tool to secure a ring in the context of retrieving a reward. Having done so, we used a series of transfer tests to explore whether they had learned the concept of physical connection implied by a hook, or rather a series of specific empirical generalizations.

Method

Subjects and apparatus

The subjects were the same seven chimpanzees who participated in the previous studies. Their ages ranged from 8;9 to 9;8 on the first day of this study.

The subjects began this study approximately 3 months after the completion of experiment 14. In the interim they had participated (or were participating) in experiments 9, 10, 11, and experiment 2.

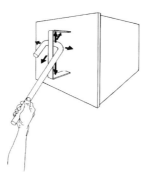

Figure 9.6 The degrees of freedom of a hook which maintain the covariation of movement between a hook tool and a ring.

The materials were several hook tools constructed from PVC tubing (1.3 cm diameter, 50 cm length) and platforms (a *training* platform and two *testing* platforms) that contained food rewards (see Fig. 9.7). As can be seen in Fig. 9.7, training platforms consisted of a flat wooden base (45.7 × 15.2 × 2.5 cm) with a post on one end and a ring on the other. The posts and rings were firmly attached to the platforms and served as locations where the hooks could be connected with the platforms. The testing platforms were identical to the training platforms except that the rings were removed.

Procedure

PHASE 1: ORIENTATION TO THE HOOK TOOLS AND PLATFORMS. In phase 1, six of the hook tools and three of the training platforms were placed inside the subjects' enclosure. The subjects were allowed to freely interact with these materials for five days. The purpose of this phase was to provide the subjects with extensive, but unstructured, first-hand experience with the affordances of the materials (for example, the solid attachment of the rings and posts to the base of the platform), as well as an opportunity to use the tools in a variety of spontaneous ways.

PHASE 2: LEARNING HOW TO USE THE HOOK TOOLS TO RETRIEVE THE PLATFORMS. After the five days of orientation to the materials, the subjects began phase 2. In this phase, the subjects were tested individually. While a subject waited outside, a platform was placed out

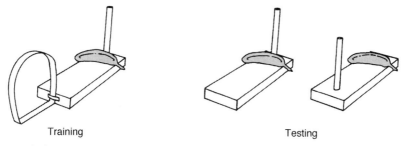

Training   Testing

Figure 9.7 Platform apparatuses that were used in the training and testing phases of experiment 15.

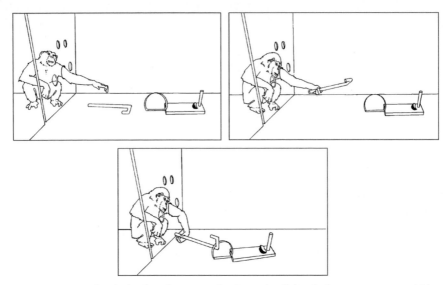

Figure 9.8 An ape using the hook tool to secure the ring and pull the platform apparatus to within reach in experiment 15.

of reach (90–110 cm, depending on the arm length of the individual subjects) in front of the middle hole in the plexiglas partition (all other holes were covered), and was baited with an apple or banana. The tool was placed within easy reach of the subjects, between the plexiglas and the platform (see Fig. 9.8). The task for the subjects was to grab the tool, use it to hook the ring, and then pull the platform to within reach so that they could obtain the food reward. In the first part of training, once the door was opened and the subjects entered, they were given 3 minutes to attempt to retrieve the reward. In this phase, the trainer stood behind the platform, and verbally encouraged the subjects to get the food reward, without demonstrating the solution. Each subject was administered two trials per session, and this training continued until he or she succeeded in retrieving the platform on four consecutive trials.

The second step in training was similar to the first, except that (1) the trainer did not interact with the subject after opening the door; and (2) four trials were administered in each session instead of two. As individual subjects successfully met a criterion of retrieving the platform and reward on 7/8 consecutive trials, they advanced to the critical testing phase.

PHASE 3: TESTING FOR TRANSFER FROM THE RING TO THE POST. In testing, we attempted to determine whether the apes, having just learned to use the tool to hook the ring and pull in the apparatus, would recognize a comparable physical connection between a hook tool and a post. We investigated this by confronting them with probe trials during which two options were available. One testing platform was placed in front of the left hole, and another was placed in front of the right hole (see Fig. 9.9). For the *correct* option, the platform was positioned so that the post was in the front, and the tool was placed so that

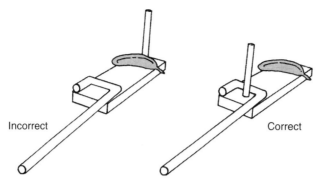

Figure 9.9 The configuration of the tools and platforms in the testing phase of experiment 15. The left/right position of the correct and incorrect choices were balanced across trials.

it was already hooked around the post. Thus, the only action that was necessary to retrieve the platform was to pull the tool. For the *incorrect* option, the platform was positioned so that the post was in the rear, and the hook tool was merely resting on the platform. In this case, pulling the tool was completely ineffectual.

Each test trial proceeded as follows. First, the subject waited outside until the trial was set up. The shuttle door was then opened, signaling the start of a trial. Once the subject entered the test unit, the door was closed behind him or her and he or she was allowed 60 seconds to make a choice. A choice was defined as touching and moving one of the tools. Once the subject made a choice, they were allowed to continue to use this tool as long as they wished until the 60 seconds had elapsed. If the subject discontinued use of the tool, but then came back to it again within the 60-second period, they were allowed to continue. However, if the trainer judged that the ape was about to reach through the other hole (in an attempt to grasp the other tool), the shuttle door was opened and the subject was ushered out of the test unit.

Each test session consisted of three trials. Two of these trials were designated as 'easy' trials, and were identical to the training trials (i.e. using the tool to hook the ring and pull the platform to within reach). The single probe trial per session was randomly assigned as either trial 2 or 3 (within the constraint that individual animals received an equal number of probe trials on trials 2 and 3 across sessions). Each subject was administered eight sessions; thus, each subject received eight of the critical probe trials. For each subject, half of the correct choices were on the right and the other half were on the left. During each session, three of the apes received the correct choice on the left, and four of the apes received it on the right.

Predictions

This test attempted to assess the chimpanzees' understanding of the underlying causal structure of the physical connection between a hook tool and another substrate. Here, we trained the apes to use a hook to connect with a ring—would this knowledge transfer to the hook's physical connection to a post? A *high-level* model of the apes' representation of how to succeed on the training task (i.e. using the tool to hook the ring) postulated that the subjects would recognize the logical similarity between hooking the ring and hooking the post (a certain degree of physical connection between the hook and the platform). On the other hand, a *procedural rule* model postulated that rather than learning about the notion of 'hook' or 'hooking' during the training phase, the subjects would learn a series of procedural steps (recognized and mediated by their perceptual–motor system) which consisted of positioning the hook portion of the tool through the ring and then pulling. If true, the procedural knowledge learned on the training trials would not be applicable on the test trials (there would be no ring into which the hook could be inserted). Thus, the procedural rule model predicted that the subjects' initial performance on the probe trials would be random.

Data analysis

Two raters coded the videotapes of each probe trial. A main rater coded 100 per cent of the trials and a secondary rater independently coded 25 per cent. The tapes were coded according to a set of detailed, written instructions, which asked the raters to observe each trial and answer several questions concerning the nature of the subjects' actions on the tools. First, they were asked to determine which tool (the correct or incorrect option) the subject moved first. Second, they were asked to determine the direction of motion of the first movement of the tool as being: (1) toward the subject; (2) away from the subject (toward the food); or (3) straight up. If the subject moved the correct tool first, the rater was then asked to decide whether the subject correctly pulled the tool forward, or dislodged it from the post before manipulating it further. Finally, the raters recorded whether the subjects were ultimately successful in obtaining the food reward. Because the main and secondary raters agreed on 100 per cent of the trials they coded, Cohen's Kappa values were not computed.

Results

Phase 1: orientation to the platforms and tools

Although no systematic data were collected during this phase, as soon as the materials were introduced, the subjects began to play with them in a variety of ways. In addition to carrying, sliding, dropping, chewing on them, and throwing them about their enclosure, the subjects were specifically observed to grasp the platforms by the posts and rings and drag them across the floor behind them. In other cases, they swung them about using the rings or posts. They also wound up with the platforms hanging from the various perches throughout their compound. Although their interest appeared to decline with time, they were observed to continue to interact with the objects throughout the five-day period.

Phase 2: learning to use the hook tools

In the first part of this phase, where the trainer verbally encouraged the subjects, the animals reached criterion in an average of 3.9 sessions (range = 2–4 sessions). In the second part, where the subjects were required to succeed on 7/8 consecutive trials with no interaction with the trainer, the subjects reached criterion within average of 4.3 sessions (range = 2–12 sessions).

Phase 3: transfer testing

The critical testing occurred over eight sessions. In each session, each subject received two standard trials (identical to those in the training phase) and a single probe trial.

The subjects were able to use the hook tool to retrieve the platform and reward on 95.5 per cent of the (easy) standard trials in which the ring was still present. This result demonstrates that the subjects remembered what they had just learned in the training phase (i.e. how to use the hook tool to retrieve the platform; but see Discussion). This result is important, because it reveals that in the very same sessions in which they received the diagnostic probe trials, the subjects were highly motivated to retrieve the platforms. Thus, any differential performance on the probe trials cannot be explained as the result of a purported general decline in interest or motivation across the course of the study.

The critical results concern the apes' behavior on the probe trials, where the rings were removed and the subjects were forced to choose between the two options depicted in Fig. 9.9. The results are presented for each subject on a trial-by-trial basis in Table 9.2. These results depict the subjects' first choice on each trial (defined as the first tool they touched and moved), regardless of whether they were ultimately successful in using it to retrieve the platform. (The trials on which the subjects chose the correct tool, but were not successful in retrieving the platform are noted in Table 9.2.) Averaged across trials and animals, the subjects chose the correct tool on 57.1 per cent of the trials, a level of responding that does not differ from that expected by chance (50 per cent), one-sample t-test, $t(6) = 1.922$, ns. Furthermore, a visual examination of Table 9.2 reveals that no individual apes appeared to appreciate that the only way to move a platform toward them was to pull the tool that was hooked around the post. Although

Table 9.2 Experiment 15, subjects' responses to probe trials on hook-retrieval problem

| | **Trials** | | | | | | | | |
Subject	1	2	3	4	5	6	7	8	Mean
Jadine	+	+	+	+	−	−	−	+	5/8
Apollo	+	−	+	−	−	−	−	+	3/8
Kara	+	+	+	−	−	+	−	+	5/8
Candy	−	+	+	+	+	−	+	−	5/8
Brandy	+	−	+	−	−	+	+	−	4/8
Megan	−	+	−	+	+	−	+	+	5/8
Mindy	+	+	−	+	−	+	−	+	5/8
Totals =	5/7	5/7	5/7	4/7	2/7	3/7	3/7	5/7	4.6/8

some of the animals (e.g. Jadine), displayed some initial behavior suggestive of comprehension, this was inconsistent across the eight sessions. These data supported the predictions of the procedural rule model and not those of the high-level model. They suggest that the apes did not, in fact, recognize the causal similarity between the hook-and-ring problem and the hook-and-post problem.

In order to explore more fine-grained aspects of how the subjects reacted to the probe trials, we examined the codings of the subjects' first movement of the tools and, when it was the correct tool, whether they dislodged it from the post. First, we examined the data to determine if the apes acted on the tools differently depending on whether their first choice was the correct or the incorrect tool. For example, even though the apes did not display a significant preference for the tool that was hooked around the post, perhaps aspects of their actions on the incorrect tool revealed that they thought they might be able to use it to retrieve the food from the far end of the platform (despite the fact that they had considerable experience during training that the food was out of the tool's reach). In other words, perhaps when they chose the incorrect tool they did so in an attempt to directly contact the food.

On those trials when the subject's first choice was for the *correct* option ($n = 31$), the subjects pulled the tool directly toward themselves on 81.7 per cent of the trials, pushed it away from themselves (i.e. toward the food) on 10 per cent of the trials, and lifted it straight up on 8.3 per cent of the trials. In the latter two cases (which comprised nearly 20 per cent of all trials) the subjects' actions resulted in dislodging the hook from the post. Generally speaking, this result can be summarized by stating that the apes' preferred motor action on the correct tool was to pull it toward them, thus retrieving the reward. However, the subjects displayed a nearly identical pattern of results on those trials ($n = 24$) on which they selected the *incorrect* option first! Thus, they pulled the tool directly toward themselves on 83.3 per cent of the trials, pushed it toward the food on 4.8 per cent of the trials, and lifted it straight up on 11.9 per cent of the trials. This micro-analysis reveals that the subjects' initial actions on the tools were the same whether the tool was hooked around the post or not; in particular, the majority of the time the subjects simply pulled the tool directly toward them. These results provide additional evidence that is consistent with the notion that the apes saw the two options as equivalent with respect to their expectations about retrieving the reward. It should be noted, however, that on the incorrect trials, once the subjects pulled the tool toward them, and the platform did not move, they then initiated a diverse set of actions. These included attempting to use the tool to reach the food and/or tapping the top or side of the platform.

A final aspect of the results worthy of mention concerns how the apes used the hook tool to retrieve the platform/reward. Our initial goal, of course, was to train the apes to use the tool to retrieve the platform by hooking the ring and then dragging the platform forward. Although it is clear that in general we were successful in teaching them this, there was evidence that not all of the apes learned the same thing. To explore this, we conducted an informal analysis of the manner in which the apes used the hook tools to retrieve the platforms on the standard trials that surrounded the probe trials during the testing phase. For this analysis, a rater simply noted whether, on their successful trials (which, as reported above, comprised 95.5 per cent of all standard trials), the apes used the tool as a hook as we intended, or used it in some other, more difficult manner, which ultimately resulted in success. The results revealed that although the apes used the tool as a hook on 78 per cent of the trials to retrieve the platform, there was considerable variation among the animals' performances (range = 23.1–100 per cent, SD = 25.6). Some of the apes (especially Apollo) often used far less efficient means of retrieving the platform (e.g. essentially using the tool as a stick by pushing the straight edge against the ring, and gradually moving the apparatus diagonally towards them). We attempted an *ad hoc* exploration of whether there was a relation between the individual apes' expertise in using the hook portion of the tool to retrieve the platforms on the standard trials and their success on the probe trials; there was not sufficient variation in both variables to allow a meaningful test. Nonetheless, in general the question of whether there is a relation between their expertise in using the hook portion of the tool to secure the ring and performance on the transfer test is an open and important one—especially given the fact that the ape that performed worst in testing (Apollo; see Table 9.2), also was a strong outlier in understanding the affordance of the hook aspect tool, using it correctly on only 23.1 per cent of his standard trials (as compared to the next least successful ape, Candy, who used it properly on 75 per cent of her trials).

Experiment 16: the hook-retrieval problem revisited, age 9–10

In the next study, we attempted to explore some questions that arose from the results from experiment 15. In particular, we designed several new conditions, using the general apparatus from experiment 15, in order to determine whether the subjects possessed an explicit concept of physical connection implied by a 'hook', or whether they were merely executing actions that the hook's properties had, in effect, led them to discover. Because we were especially interested in this question, we took additional steps to ensure that all animals were predominantly relying on the hook affordance of the tool when confronted with the standard problem involving the platform with the ring.

Method

Subjects and apparatus

The same seven chimpanzees were used. They began this study approximately $1^{1}/_{2}$ months after completing experiment 15. The subjects participated in experiment 12 (see Chapter 6) in the interim. The same platforms and tools from experiment 15 were used, with the addition of a straight tool (which was identical to the original hook tools except that the hook portion of the tool was removed).

Procedure

The study consisted of two phases, a training phase and a testing phase.

TRAINING. As noted in our discussion of experiment 15, by the end of training in experiment 14 there were still occasions on which a number of the animals were not using the hook's most obvious property to secure the platform. That is, on a number of trials, the subjects would extend the hook tool toward the ring, but rather than insert the hook portion into the ring and then pull, they would use the back lip of the hook to push the apparatus toward the side and slowly work it toward them, sometimes allowing them to retrieve the banana reward. In effect, this was no different than if they had been using a straight stick. In order to ensure that all of the apes were using the hook tool as we had intended (i.e. the easy way), we established an open-ended training procedure so that each subject's competence in using the tool could be assessed on a case-by-case basis.

On each trial the subjects were confronted with one of two versions of the hook tool problem in which the platform had the ring attached and facing them. In one case, the task was identical to the original training phase from experiment 15 (the tool lying between the ape and the baited platform). Thus, the ape merely had to pick up the tool, use it to hook the ring, and drag the platform to within reach. The second case was similar, except that the tool was already hooked into the ring; in this case, the apes merely needed to pull the tool. This latter type of training trial was designed to assist those apes who were still occasionally using the tool in an awkward manner to secure the platform. The subjects received multiple sessions consisting of two trials each (with one trial of each type, with the order of the trials counterbalanced across sessions). We continued to administer training sessions to each subject until he or she correctly used the hook tool in its easiest manner on eight consecutive trials. As each subject met this criterion, he or she was advanced to testing.

TESTING. Eight distinct conditions were created in order to probe the animals' understanding of the factors involved in using the hook tool to retrieve the food reward. These conditions, A–H, are depicted in Fig. 9.10. The questions addressed by these conditions are as follows:

1.   Conditions A and B addressed whether the apes were attending to both the interaction of the tool with the platform and of the food with the platform. Condition B was slightly more taxing than A, because here the ape would need to notice both the position of the reward and compute the placement of the tool.

2.   Condition C addressed whether contact of the tool with the post was sufficient for the apes to conclude that they could retrieve the apparatus by pulling on the tool, or whether they appreciated the physical connection implied by the hook's placement around the post.

3.   Condition D addressed whether the apes recognized the post (or at least the orientation of the apparatus) as generally important. Condition E also addressed this question, but simultaneously addressed whether the apes appreciated the specific implication of the hook portion of the tool for gaining a physical connection of the tool and platform (that is, whether they would reorient the tool into the better orientation).

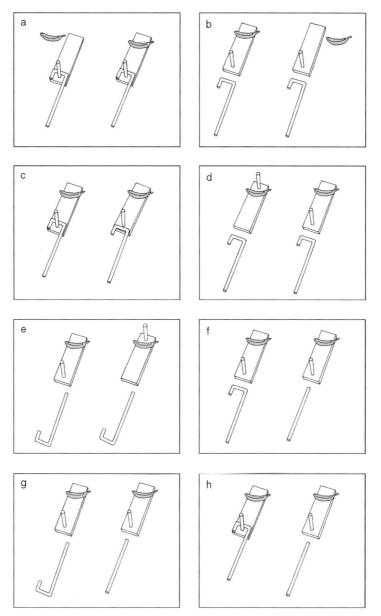

Figure 9.10 The testing conditions (A–H) used in experiment 16. The main text provides the rationale for each condition.

4. In condition F, the orientation of the platform was held constant, but the tools' affordances were pitted against each other. Thus, this condition probed whether the apes could distinguish between using a tool to contact the platform or the post versus the nature of that contact (a straight stick versus a hook). Condition G

addressed the same question, but was more demanding in that the hook tool needed to be reoriented in order to gain a degree of physical connection.

5. Finally, condition H addressed whether the subjects could either directly perceive the physical connection when the hook was already placed around the post or at least perceive the greater degree of contact between the hook option versus the straight stick option. (Regrettably, we failed to administer a companion trial type in which the stick tool was touching the post.)

Conditions A, B, C, and H were administered to each subject four times each, and conditions D, E, F, and G were administered to each subject two times each.

Each subject was tested across 24 sessions, and each test session consisted of three trials. Two of these were 'easy' trials (identical to the training trials) and one was a probe trial. The probe trials were randomly assigned to trial 2 or 3 within a session (within the constraints described below). The actual order in which the subjects received the probe trials was determined by randomly and exhaustively assigning one trial of each condition A, B, C, H, D, or E, and F or G, to each ape, and then repeating the process four times until all probe trials had been assigned. Across all sessions, for each ape the correct (or easiest) option appeared equally often in the right and left position. Additional constraints included the following: (1) in each ordinal position in their series of probe trials, three apes received the correct choice (regardless of condition) on one side (right or left) and the remaining four received the correct choice on the opposite side; and (2) each condition appeared equally often as the second and third trial within the test sessions. The apes were given 60 seconds to respond after they entered the test unit and, as described above, they were allowed to use whatever means they wished (including multiple choices) to retrieve the baited platforms.

Data analysis

Eight written sets of instructions were constructed for coding the videotaped probe trials of the eight conditions (A–H) depicted in Fig. 9.10. Each instructional set was comprised of a group of identical questions, with additional questions included or excluded because certain questions were only relevant for certain conditions. One rater was asked to code every probe trial of every condition and a second rater was assigned a subset of 33.3 per cent of the probe trials (comprised of one trial per condition per animal). Table 9.3 presents the reliability measurements for all questions that were used in the actual data analyses (see Results). These questions concerned the apes' first (and, in some cases, second) choices on each trial, as well as, whether they were successful on their first attempt; the general nature of their first actions; their ultimate success for each option; and, in relevant conditions, whether they reoriented the tools as needed (and whether the reorientations appeared to be deliberate). As can be seen from Table 9.3, the two raters displayed excellent agreement.

Table 9.3 Interobserver reliability summaries (Cohen's Kappa, κ) for experiment 16

Variable coded	Relevant conditions	Percentage agreement	κ
First choice	A–H	56/56	1.00
Second choice	A–H	56/56	1.00
First general action			
Side 1 / Tool 1	A, B, C, D, F, H	38/39	.90
Side 2 / Tool 2	A, B, C, D	16/17	.87
Success on first bout			
Side 1 / Tool 1	A–H	45/45	1.00
Side 2 / Tool 2	C, F, G, H	10/10	NA[a]
Overall success			
Side 1 / Tool 1	A–H	53/53	1.00
Side 2 / Tool 2	A–H	54/54	1.00
Tool Reorientations			
Side 1 / Tool 1	E, G	14/14	1.00
Side 2	E	5/5	1.00
Deliberate Reorientations	E, G	6/6	NA[a]

[a] For these variables, κ is undefined because all values are in a single cell of the agreement matrix.

Results and discussion

The results were analyzed in a series of steps. First, we conducted an overall repeated-measures ANOVA to examine whether the group's performance differed significantly across the eight conditions that were administered to them. Second, we examined the group data by condition in order to determine how (or whether) the apes appreciated the possibility of physical connection between the tool and the post that the hook portion of the tool offered. The first step in these analyses was to examine the apes' first choices on each trial. This analysis (the results of which are depicted in Fig. 9.11) focused on whether the apes chose the best option as their first choice. By 'best option' we simply mean whether the apes selected the tool/platform combination which offered the possibility for the highest degree of physical connection between the tool and the platform. In addition, in each case, we used one-sample t-tests (two-tailed) to compare the subjects' actual performance to that expected by chance (50 per cent). This analysis was followed by additional, more fine-grained analyses of the apes' second choices, their success in obtaining the rewards, how they initially made contact with the apparatus, and, in certain relevant cases, whether they reoriented the tools to make them more effective. In summary, in what follows we first present (1) the results of the overall comparison of the apes' performances across conditions; and (2) the condition-by-condition examination of the group's reactions to the eight testing conditions. Finally, we consider potential individual differences between the animals' performances and their implications for different kinds of understandings of the tests.

Overall performance

As a first step in assessing the subjects' reactions to the eight conditions, we calculated the percentage of trials in each condition in which each subject chose the best option as their first choice. These data were then structured into a one-way repeated measures ANOVA comparing all subjects' average scores across the eight conditions. The results indicated a strong overall effect of condition, $F(7, 42) = 5.588$, $p < 0.0001$. Tukey-Kramer Multiple Comparisons posttests were conducted and revealed that the subjects preferred the best option significantly more in condition A than in condition E ($p < .05$), condition F ($p < 0.001$), and condition G ($p < 0.001$). The only other significant contrast was that the subjects selected the best option significantly more often in condition B than in condition G ($p < 0.05$).

Conditions A and B

These two conditions can be thought of as control conditions to ensure that the apes minimally appreciated that the banana needed to be in contact with the platform. As can be seen from Fig. 9.11, these two situations posed little difficulty for the animals. Thus, when the physical connection (or possible connection) between tool and platform was held constant across the two options, the apes significantly preferred the option where the reward was supported by the apparatus (condition A: $t(6) = 13.000$, $p < 0.0001$; condition B: $t(6) = 3.361$, $p < 0.02$). This finding replicates previous work suggesting that several species of nonhuman primates appreciate the support problem in its simplest form (see Chapter 3). However, as we shall see in experiments 21–23, this does not guarantee an understanding of physical connection. Although the apes appeared to find condition A slightly easier (when the hook tools were already in place), the posttests for the overall ANOVA revealed no significant difference between the two conditions (see above).

Several additional comments about the apes' performances in these two conditions are warranted. First, as can be seen from the inset graphs in Fig. 9.11 for conditions A and B, the animals' preference for the best option was present on trial 1 and was more or less stable thereafter in both conditions. Second, on every trial where the apes choose the best option first in condition A, the apes' first action was to pull the tool directly towards them, thus correctly leaving the hook correctly positioned on the post. Third, despite their overall preference for the best option as their first choice, the apes frequently made a second choice by pulling the incorrect tool (80 per cent did so on trial 1[1] and 71.4 per cent did so on trial 2). Interestingly, on trials 1 and 2, 50 and 100 per cent

---

1   Due to experimenter error in implementing the protocol (which allowed for the apes to make second choices), two of the apes were inadvertently not allowed a second choice on trial 1. Thus, the figure of 80 per cent derives from the five apes who were allowed the opportunity to make a second choice (four of whom did so).

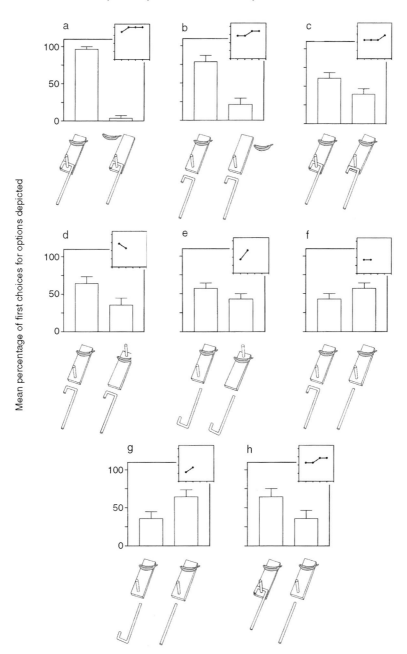

Figure 9.11 (Conditions (A–H).) Main graphs depict the mean percentage of trials (averaged across trials) that the subjects chose the options in each condition as their first choice (±*SEM*). The inset to each graph depicts the average percentage of subjects who chose the best option first on a trial-by-trial basis.

of the apes, respectively, who made a second choice in condition A, did so by simply pulling the empty platform toward them. Finally, with respect to condition B, on 95.2 per cent of the trials where the apes chose the correct option, their first action was to use the tool to contact the post. Similarly, on the trials that the apes chose the incorrect side as either their first or second choice, 83.3 per cent of the time their first action was to use the tool to contact the post. These later results would seem to suggest that, no matter what else the animals understood, they seemed drawn to make the tool contact the post—even when it was not relevant.

Condition C

This condition assessed whether the apes understood that a hook placed behind (as opposed to in front of) the post had a unique implication for physical connection (or, even more generally, transfer of force). Thus, if the apes had learned something about the importance of the post across the eight trials they received in experiment 15, this condition might allow us to ask exactly what the nature of that learning had been. As can be seen from the main portion of Fig. 9.11 for condition C, the apes did not significantly prefer the best option as their first choice ($t(6) = 1.441$, $p = 0.200$), and the inset reveals that any trend toward the best option is the result of an improvement toward the end of the experiment. However, the subject-by-subject data (see Table 9.4) reveals that one subject, Megan, was perfect across her four trials. If we remove her data, the subjects performed at exactly chance levels (50 per cent) across their first three trials in this condition. (We consider Megan's performance further below.)

Several more detailed aspects of the apes' behavior are of interest. First, the apes made a second choice on 82.1 per cent of the trials in this condition, and they were approximately equally successful in ultimately obtaining the reward from both options (92.9 per cent of all trials for the best option and 85.7 per cent of all trials for the other option). This might be interpreted as meaning that the apes realized that either option could be successful, and hence saw no reason to prefer one over the other. However, aspects of the nature in which the apes used the tools to act on the platforms offer at

Table 9.4 Percentage of first choices that were for the correct (or best) option for individual chimpanzees by condition in experiment 16

Subject	Condition							
	A	B	C	D	E	F	G	H
Apollo	100	75	75	50	50	50	0	50
Kara	100	75	50	50	50	50	50	25
Candy	100	100	50	50	50	50	50	75
Jadine	100	100	50	100	100	0	50	100
Brandy	100	100	50	50	50	50	50	50
Megan	100	50	100	100	50	50	0	100
Mindy	75	50	50	50	50	50	50	50
M =	*96.4*	*78.6*	*60.7*	*64.3*	*57.1*	*42.9*	*35.7*	*64.3*
SD =	*9.4*	*22.5*	*19.7*	*24.4*	*18.9*	*18.9*	*24.4*	*28.3*

least some reason to be cautious of this interpretation. In particular, when the apes chose the best option (hook behind the post), 85.7 per cent of the time their first general action was to pull the tool toward them. This can be contrasted with the fact that when the apes chose the other option (hook in front of the post), only 53.6 per cent of time was their first action to correctly place the hook behind the post. Indeed, only 20 per cent of the apes (who made this choice) correctly placed the tool as their first action on trial 1 and only 42.9 per cent did so on their final trial.

Condition D

Condition D was similar to the eight probe trials the subjects received in experiment 15; the only difference was that the tools were not in contact with the apparatus. The subjects did not significantly prefer the correct option (see Fig. 9.11, condition D; $t(6) = 1.549$, $p = 0.172$). Furthermore, the trial-by-trial pattern of results shown in the inset to Fig. 9.11 (condition D) leaves no reason to suspect that the apes were rapidly learning the correct choice in the condition, as the apes actually performed worse on trial 2. The more fine-grained analyses revealed two additional, important facts. First, on every trial, all but one of the apes ultimately succeeded in retrieving the food reward from the correct side (although only 64 per cent of the time was their first action on this side to hook the post and pull). Second, on all but two trials the apes (as either their first or second choice) attempted to retrieve the food from the incorrect side, but they were never successful.

Condition E

Condition E was identical to condition D except that the tools were oriented so that the hook portion was closest to the subjects, effectively asking the subjects if they understood that the hook portion of the tool was relevant to establish a degree of physical connection between tool and post on the correct side. First, as can be seen in Fig. 9.11 (condition E), the subjects displayed no significant preference for the correct option as their first choice ($t(6) = 1.00$, $p = .3559$), and the inset suggests that the apes were responding randomly on trial 1.

   With respect to more detailed analyses, several facts seem important. First, there were two cases (14.3 per cent of the trials) in which the apes reoriented the tool on the correct side so that the hook was oriented properly (in both cases the rater judged that the reorientation was deliberate). Although this might suggest some hint of understanding the unique affordance that the hook portion of the tool played in establishing a degree of physical connection, an identical result was obtained for reorientations on the incorrect side (two deliberate reorientations, comprising 14.3 per cent of the trials). Perhaps the best interpretation of this result is that the apes had some nascent understanding of the orientation of the tool that was associated with success, but did not appreciate why this particular orientation was necessary.

   With respect to the behavior they directed to the correct option, the apes made at least one attempt (as either their first or second choice) to retrieve the food on every trial (except on the two occasions where the subject was inadvertently not allowed a second choice; see Footnote 1). However, because they almost never reoriented the tool, they were successful only 57.1 per cent of the time (33.3 per cent on trial 1 and 71.4 per cent on trial 2), and only after great effort. With respect to the incorrect option, the apes attempted to retrieve the food at least once on all but one trial, although they never succeeded in doing so.

Condition F

Condition F asked whether our apes genuinely appreciated that the hook aspect of the tool offered the possibility for a greater (and also better) degree of physical connection between tool and apparatus than that possible with a straight tool. At least as measured by their first choices, our apes' response to this question was 'no'. As can be seen from Fig. 9.11 (condition F), our apes displayed no significant preference for choosing the hook tool over the straight tool ($t(6) = 1.000$, $p = 0.356$).

With respect to the more detailed analyses, every ape attempted to retrieve both platform on every trial (with only one exception). Significantly, however, although the apes were successful 92.9 per cent of the time with the hook tool (78.6 per cent of these successes were achieved by correctly hooking the post on their very first action with this tool), they were only successful 28.6 per cent of the time with the straight tool (14.3 per cent of the time on trial 1 and 42.9 per cent on trial 2). Coupled with their indiscriminate first choices (see above), this result strongly suggests that our apes perceived no difference between the two tools in terms of their potential for retrieving the platforms.

Condition G

Like the previous condition, condition G asked whether our apes appreciated the hook affordance of the tool (by having both platforms in the proper orientation), but was more difficult in that the correct tool was not oriented properly. As can be seen in Fig. 9.11 (condition G), the apes did not display a significant preference for one option over the other ($t(6) = 1.549$, $p = .172$), although the inset of this figure reveals that on trial 1 the apes may even have preferred the more difficult option (five of the seven apes chose the straight tool on trial 1).

Did the apes understand the necessity of reorienting the correct tool? Impressively, four of the apes did reorient the correct tools in the manner needed, and in each case they did so on one trial (in two cases it was their first trial, in two cases it was their second: in all cases the reorientations were rated as deliberate). In percentage terms, this meant that 28.6 per cent of the apes reoriented the tool in the appropriate manner on trial 1 and 28.6 per cent did so on trial 2. One interpretation of these reorientations could be that the apes understood the necessity of orienting the hook end toward the post in order to obtain a workable physical connection between the tool and post. On the other hand, such reorientations, although judged as 'deliberate' by the raters, might have been unrelated to this kind of understanding. As a control, we coded the number of trials in which the subjects reoriented the straight tool[2]—a tool whose orientation did not matter. Results of this coding revealed that three of the apes reoriented the straight tool on trial 1 (42.9 per cent of the apes) and one did so on trial 2 (14.3 per cent of the apes), and in every case the reorientations were judged as deliberate. Given that the apes reoriented the straight tool as frequently as the hook tool, there appears to be no compelling reason to think that those relatively few cases in which the ape reoriented of the hook tool reflected an understanding of the affordance properties of the hook portion of the tool. Rather, it seems likely, from the overall pattern of results, that having been unsuccessful with the tool (straight or hook tool) in one orientation, they simply reoriented it to try it again.

Finally, the apes attempted to retrieve the reward from both sides on every trial. With respect to their attempts on the correct side, only 28.6 per cent of the apes were successful on trial 1, although 71.4 per cent of them were successful on trial 2. It is important to note that the discrepancy between their trial 1 and trial 2 success in obtaining the reward was not the result of an increase in the number of apes who reoriented the tool and used the hook affordance; recall that two apes reoriented the correct tool on trial 1 and two apes did so on trial 2, and, furthermore, of these four instances of reorientation, only two resulted in the apes ultimately succeeding in pulling in the platform and obtaining the reward. Rather, their improvement was related to perfecting the very difficult technique of sliding the apparatus sideways and diagonally, with either the straight tool or a straight portion of the hook tool.

Condition H

As mentioned in the method, this condition was inferior to a condition which was not implemented: one with the correct option as depicted in Fig. 9.10, but the incorrect option having the straight tool in contact with the apparatus and touching the post. Nonetheless, the results of condition H as implemented revealed some intriguing variation among the subjects, even though as a group the apes did not significantly prefer one option over the other as their first choice ($t(6) = 1.333$, $p = 0.231$). However, three of the subjects (Candy, Jadine, and Megan) scored 75 per cent or better for the best option (Jadine and Megan always chose the best option; see Table 9.4).

Each ape attempted to retrieve the reward from both sides on 77.8 per cent of all trials (excluding one trial where the ape was inadvertently not allowed to make a second choice). On every occasion where the apes attempted to retrieve the food from the side where the took was hooked around the post, they were successful. In contrast, they were

---

2   For this coding, a main rater coded all 14 probe trials in this condition (two trials per ape) and a reliability rater seven trials (one per ape, chosen randomly). They were asked: (1) did the ape reorient the straight tool? (yes or no; the raters agreed on 7/7 trials, $\kappa = 1.00$); and (2) if yes, did they do so deliberately (yes or no; raters agreed on 2/2 cases). The main rater's data was used.

only successful on 38.1 per cent of the trials where they attempted to retrieve the reward using the straight tool (their ability to successfully retrieve the platform gradually improved from 20 per cent of the apes on trial 1 to 50 per cent on trial 4).

Performance of individual apes

The results and discussion above focused mainly on analyses of the performance of our apes as a group. We also analyzed the results to determine if the apes possessed a uniform interpretation of the general task, and, if not, what kinds of interpretations individual animals may have possessed. A quick glance at Table 9.4 reveals that although all of the apes understood most of the conditions in the same manner, Megan and Jadine appear to have performed better in some conditions than their peers. Interestingly, however, our conclusion is that they did not understand the issue of physical connection any better than their peers, and in Megan's case, even appeared to possess a more fragile understanding of all aspects of the test.

First, let us examine Megan's performance. A careful examination of her results reveals that in some ways Megan understood even less than the other animals. Our interpretation of Megan's results is that she possessed a highly specific understanding of the 'correctness' of the perceptual form of the hook around the post and the banana resting on the platform (that is, the correct option from experiment 15), but that she did not interpret this perceptual form as an instance of greater physical connection. We base this conclusion on the following rather striking pattern in her data (see Table 9.4). First, there were three conditions in which the perceptual pattern just described was available (conditions A, C, and H), and Megan chose that option on every trial (10/10 cases). Second, and in striking contrast, if we examine those conditions in which at least one hook tool was available and oriented properly in relation to the apparatus (conditions B, D, and F), Megan performed at chance levels (5/8 cases). What is most striking about this result is how poorly Megan performed in condition B—a condition that was relatively easy for the other apes! This can be interpreted as evidence that, for Megan, the task reduced to scanning the apparatus/tool combinations for one that matched the correct pattern from experiment 15. Further support for the idea that Megan did not genuinely understand the physical connection of the hook and post can be seen from the fact that she displayed absolutely no comprehension of the unique importance of the hook in condition F or G (she chose the best option on only 1/4 of these trials). Finally, Megan never attempted to reorient the hook tool when it was presented in the incorrect manner (conditions E and G).

Like Megan, Jadine's performance appears superficially better than her peers. However, also like Megan, a more careful examination of her responses across the eight conditions reveals that she, too, was following a very rigid rule structure which did not appear to rely on the concept of physical connection (albeit a rule structure different than Megan's). In particular, Jadine simply appeared to know two things. First, unlike Megan, she had a robust understanding that the food needed to be resting on the platform (hence her perfect performance in conditions A and B). Second, once this constraint was satisfied, the next most important issue of concern to her was whether one of the tools was or could be used to contact a post. Thus, across the condition where only one of the tools was in contact with a post (condition H) and the conditions (D and E) where it was only possible to contact one of the posts, Jadine always selected the actual or potential contact option first (8/8 correct). Although this is impressive in one sense, and may be thought of as being a step toward grasping the principle of physical connection, her performance in the remaining conditions reveal the shallowness of her understanding. First, in condition C, where both tools were already in contact with the post, but only one was positioned behind the post, Jadine chose randomly. Furthermore, on the three trials on which she chose the option where the hook was in front of the post (as either her first or second choice), her initial action on two of them was simply to pull the tool straight toward her! Second, and perhaps more revealing, in the two most important conditions with respect to the question of the unique importance of the hook for establishing physical connection (conditions F and G), if anything Jadine preferred the less desirable option (only 1/4 of her choices were for the best option). Furthermore, of the four occasions on which she could have reoriented the hook tool, she did so only once— and, as we saw earlier, these reorientations were just as frequent with the straight tool!

Experiment 17: the touching-stick problem, age 10

In reporting a task in which his apes were required to use sticks to knock down suspended food objectives, Köhler (1927) described how his animals occasionally attempted to use sticks that were too short. Köhler describes the efforts of one of his female chimpanzees:

> Suddenly, [Rana] changes her tactics, keeps only two sticks out of the bunch, and *puts them carefully end to end so that they look to the eye like a stick of twice the length;*…there is certainly no question of accident, for if the sticks slip and come together they are always put back into a position which makes them at least look like one long stick… It is astonishing to note how, apparently, the 'optics' of the situation is decisive for the animal, how the endeavor to solve the problem takes no account of the 'technically physical' point of view, but considers solely the optical aspect. (p. 125.)

After considering this idea, we designed experiments 17 and 18 to determine whether our apes would focus on the visual aspects of a test in which it was, from our perspective at least, obvious that the ape was confronted with a long, solid stick versus a perceptually similar form that was composed by simply setting three shorter sticks end-to-end as the apes watched.

Method

Subjects and apparatus

All seven chimpanzees participated in this study. They ranged in age from 9;10 to 10;9 when the study began. The apes began this study approximately $6^1/_2$ months after completing experiment 16. In the interim, they participated in experiment13 (see Chapter 8) and experiments 24–27 (see Chapter 11).

The apparatus used in this study was the small ramp depicted in Fig. 9.12. The ramp was positioned out of the subjects' reach and angled towards them. It contained a small elevated platform upon which an apple or orange could be placed. The apparatus was configured so that if the subjects used a stick to push the apple or orange to one side, it would fall off the platform, and roll down the ramp to within their reach. In addition to the platform, several types of straight tools were used. In training, two straight tools (constructed from 1/2-inch diameter PVC tubing) were used: one was too short to reach the apple (20 cm in length) and the other was long enough to easily reach the apple (62 cm in length). In addition to these tools, additional tools were constructed from 3/4-inch wooden dowels (painted blue) and were used in testing. One of these dowels was 62 cm in length, and three others were 20 cm in length.

Procedure

ORIENTATION. On the morning prior to introducing the animals to the apparatus and the general procedures (see below), a complete set of the tools (both the training tools and the testing tools) were placed in the subjects' enclosure and remained there throughout the duration of the study. The purpose of this procedure was simply to orient the apes to the particular objects that would be used in the study. As in previous studies, the apes took an immediate interest in these objects and were observed to play with them in a variety of ways across the period of time in which the study was conducted.

The orientation phase consisted of a series of sessions (two trials each) in which the apes learned how to use the long tool to dislodge the reward from the platform. On each trial, the apparatus (with an apple or orange placed on the platform) was positioned 110 cm from the front of the test unit, directly in front of the middle hole in the plexiglas. All holes except this one were covered. In addition, the plexiglas screen (which

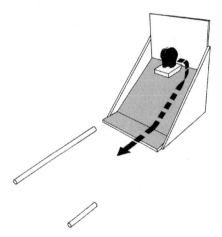

Figure 9.12 The ramp apparatus used in experiments 17 and 18. The standard condition is shown with a short tool and a long tool. Because of the distance between the plexiglas barrier and the apparatus, only the long tool can be used to dislodge the apple.

prevented the subjects from reaching through the plexiglas; see experiments 9 and 14) was in position. Finally, the two training tools were placed in the space between the apparatus and the test unit, vertically aligned toward the apparatus, and separated by 30 cm (see Fig. 9.12). The left/right position of the long and short tools on the first trial was determined randomly, and the second trial was assigned to the opposite configuration.

After the trial configuration was set, the shuttle door opened, letting the subject inside. Once the ape entered the test unit, the door was closed behind him or her, signaling the start of that trial. The trainer approached the plexiglas partition from the left side of the apparatus (from the ape's perspective) and removed the plexiglas screen. Upon removing the screen, he carried it to back of the room, set it down, and faced away from the subjects. The subject's task was to reach through the hole and use the long tool to dislodge the reward within 60 seconds of the trainer removing the screen. No assistance was provided by the trainer.[3] Each subject continued in this phase until they met a criterion of choosing the correct tool as their first choice and dislodging the apple on four consecutive trials. Upon achieving this criterion, they were advanced to testing. Four of the apes (Mindy, Brandy, Jadine, Candy) met this criterion within the minimum of 4 trials; two of the apes (Megan, Apollo) met the criterion within 8 trials; the remaining ape (Kara) met criterion within 10 trials.

TESTING. Testing involved comparing the apes' performances on two conditions, each involving a choice between the long testing stick and an arrangement of the three shorter sticks. In the 'aligned' condition, the animals watched as the experimenter held up and demonstrated the general properties of the long stick, and then placed it in front of the apparatus. Similarly, the experimenter demonstrated the properties of the three shorter sticks, and placed them in a straight alignment in front of the apparatus (Fig. 9.13(a)). This resulted in two perceptual forms that were identical in overall form and length, although the joints of the sticks in the aligned option were clearly visible. In the 'staggered' condition, the properties of the long stick were again demonstrated and then it was placed in front of the apparatus. The properties of the three short sticks were again demonstrated, but in this condition they were placed on the floor so that they touched, but were staggered as depicted in Fig. 9.13(b).

In order to compare our apes' reactions on the aligned versus the staggered conditions, we used an ABA design, where the A phases were composed of two trials using the aligned condition, and the B phase was composed of two trials using the staggered condition. In addition, a session composed of four standard trials (involving a choice between the short and long PVC tools) was interspersed between the initial A and B portion of testing as well as between the final B and A portion of testing, and served as

---

3   One subject, Kara, was assisted after trial 1 of Session 3. Unlike the other subjects, Kara did not seem to understand how to dislodge the apple. At this point, the Study Director authorized a protocol deviation in which Kara was brought into the test unit and the trainer showed her (using his hand) that if the apple were pushed off the platform it would roll toward her. After this, standard procedures were again implemented.

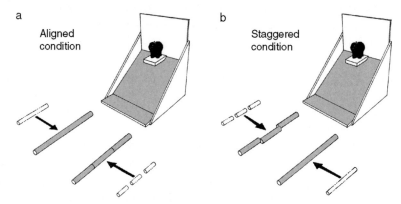

Figure 9.13 The two conditions used in experiment 17. (a) The aligned condition. (b) The staggered condition. In each condition, the ape has a choice between a tool of sufficient length and a perceptual pattern formed by three short tools which cannot be used to make contact with the apple. In each case the relevant properties of the tools are demonstrated and then set down in the positions shown before the ape is allowed to respond.

control trials. Thus, the complete design was A-s-B-s-A, where 's' denotes the sessions of standard trials.[4]

For all testing trials involving the aligned and staggered conditions, the testing room was configured in the same manner as for the orientation phase, except as described below. An experimenter was present and seated directly behind the baited apparatus. At the start of each trial, the four sticks used on test trials (the long stick, and the three short sticks) were all positioned behind the apparatus at the experimenter's feet. Each trial consisted of two parts: demonstration period and a response period. The demonstration period began as soon as the trainer opened the shuttle door and the subject entered the test unit. At this point, the experimenter reached down and picked up either the long stick or the three shorter sticks, held them up so that the ape could clearly see them, and conducted a choreographed demonstration of their general properties by waving them about, and in the case of the three shorter sticks touching them end to end to show that they would not stick together. After 15 seconds of demonstration, the experimenter moved to the appropriate side of the apparatus and placed the stick(s) in the pre-assigned left/right position and, in the case of the three short sticks, arranged them in the pre-assigned aligned or staggered configuration/pattern. Next, the experimenter returned to his/her seated posture behind the apparatus, and picked up the remaining stick(s) and demonstrated their general properties for exactly 15 seconds.

---

4   An additional 'A' phase (two sessions, each composed of one trial using the aligned condition) was implemented after the completion of this design to examine possible learning effects. See results for more details.

Again, at this point the experimenter placed the stick(s) in the appropriate position, and, in the case of the short sticks, in the appropriate configuration.

Having laid out both choices, the experimenter moved to a predetermined seated location against the back wall of the testing room. As soon as the experimenter was seated, the trainer approached the partition, removed the plexiglas screen, and immediately carried it to the back of the room. As in the first phase, the trainer always approached from the left side of the apparatus. With the plexiglas screen thus removed, the ape was free to reach through the single open hole in the partition and respond. The subjects were allowed to make as many choices as they wished, but we were mainly interested in comparing their first choices to their first choices on the standard trials. For the aligned and staggered trials, each ape was administered only a single trial per session. For the control sessions involving the standard trials, four trials per session were administered. Typically the apes received two test sessions per day on these procedures (once in the morning and once in the afternoon).

The following counterbalancing constraints were implemented. In the first phase of the aligned condition (the first A in the ABA design), on one of the two trials the experimenter demonstrated the long stick first, followed by the shorter sticks; the opposite order was followed on the other trial. On trial 1, three of the apes were shown the long stick first and the three short sticks second, whereas the remaining four apes were shown the tools in the opposite order. With respect to the left/right placement of the sticks, on trial 1, three of the apes received the long stick on the right, and four received it on the left, whereas on trial 2 this was reversed for each ape. In the subsequent phases (i.e. the staggered condition, and the second administration of the aligned condition), the same general counterbalancing constraints were followed, so that across all phases each ape received the correct (long) stick equally often in the left and right position. Also, this procedure ensured that in the demonstration period each ape was shown the correct (long) and incorrect (aligned or staggered) stick equally often in the first and second position. (Given these constraints, it was not also possible to counterbalance for the interaction between the tool that was demonstrated first and its left/right placement within each ape within each session. However, this factor was approximately counterbalanced across all apes across all phases.)

Video coding and data analysis

As usual, a standardized instructional set was created for coding the videotapes of the trials. A main rater coded all trials, including all probe trials. A reliability rater coded 25 per cent of the probe trials (two trials from each animal, randomly selected). The reliability coefficients between the two raters were as follows: first tool touched/moved by the ape ($\kappa = 1.00$), first tool grasped by the ape ($\kappa = 1.00$), and success on each trial (κ is undefined, 14/14 cases of agreement). The data from the main rater was used in all analyses.

Results and discussion

Overall success on the task

The apes were allowed to work freely (making as many choices as they wished) for the duration of each trial, and they ultimately obtained the reward on every trial. Clearly, the apes were highly interested and motivated to solve this problem.

Initial choice preferences

Although the apes were always successful, the main concern of this study was whether they appreciated the fact that the patterns that were composed from the three short sticks (both in the aligned case and in the staggered case) could not be effective in dislodging the reward from the platform. In order to address this question, we plotted the apes' first choices (the tool they touched/moved first) on each trial across the sessions for both the sessions involving the critical probe trials as well as the control sessions involving the standard trials (i.e. those trials involving a choice between the long and the short tool). (Of course, we focused on the apes' first choices, because once they touched/moved a stick, it became perceptually obvious whether the form was one stick or several.) These data are plotted in Fig. 9.14 and reveal two facts. First, the apes always choose the correct option (the long tool) in the sessions of standard trials (shown using open bars), and second, the apes reacted very differently to the aligned versus the staggered conditions (shown using solid bars). In particular, the apes exhibited a clear preference for the correct option in the staggered condition, but not in the aligned condition (where they chose randomly).

In both phases of the aligned condition, one sample t-tests (two tailed) confirmed the visual impression from Fig. 9.14 that the apes responded at levels which did not exceed

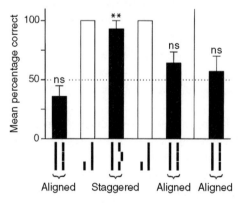

Figure 9.14 Mean percentage of trials (±SEM) on which the apes' first choice was for the correct tool in experiment 17. An ABA experimental design was used (aligned–staggered–aligned); these results are shown in the filled bars. Sessions composed of standard trials were interspersed between the experimental phases. These results are shown in the unfilled bars. Note that an additional aligned phase was administered after the main study was complete and is shown in the extreme right-hand panel.

chance (in both cases, $t(6) = 1.549$, ns). In contrast, the apes' performance was significantly above chance in the staggered condition, $t(6) = 6.000$, $p = .0010$. Their excellent performance in the staggered condition did not appear to be learned within the two trials that they received, as 6/7 apes were correct on trial 1, and 7/7 were correct on trial 2. Nor did this performance appear to be the result of learning that might have occurred during the first phase of the experiment. Recall that the A-B-A design used in this study allowed us to measure this by examining the apes' performance when we administered the second phase of the aligned condition. As can be seen in Fig. 9.14 the apes' performances fell to chance levels in the second administration of the aligned condition.

A one-way repeated measures ANOVA comparing the apes' performances in the three phases of the experiment tended to confirm this analysis. First, an overall effect of phase was detected ($F(2,12) = 9.931$, $p < .003$). Second, Tukey-Kramer posttests revealed that this was the result of the fact that the apes performed significantly better ($p < .01$) in the staggered phase (phase B) than in the first administration of the aligned phase. Notably, however, performance in the staggered phase was not statistically different from the *second* administration of the aligned condition (see further discussion of this point below). Third, the apes' performance in the first and second administrations of the aligned condition did not differ statistically.

Although the above results seem consistent with the idea that the apes immediately understood which option to choose in the staggered condition, but not in the aligned condition, the fact that there was no statistically significant decline from the administration of the staggered condition to the second administration of the aligned condition might be interpreted as meaning that the animals had transferred some learning across the phase of the experiment (even though each phase contained only two trials). As a first step in examining this, we administered two additional trials of the aligned condition to each animal following the final originally planned phase of the study. The results of this additional phase of the aligned condition reveal that if there were any learning effects they were extremely weak, as the animals performed at chance levels in this additional block of two trials of the aligned condition. Indeed, in absolute terms, they actually performed worse than in the immediately preceding phase of the aligned condition. Furthermore, if we examine the scores of the individual animals across the final four trials of the aligned condition, one animal (Mindy) performed perfectly, one scored 3/4 correct (Candy), and the remaining animals scored exactly at chance levels (2/4 correct in each case).

Finally, one might wonder if the apes' initial difficulty with the aligned condition might reflect a difficulty in realizing that the sticks needed to be a certain length in order to reach the apple, rather than reflecting the absence of an understanding that the sticks were not physically connected. Two facts mitigate against this interpretation. First, the apes had all met a criterion of 4/4 trials correct on the standard trials involving a choice between a short stick and a long stick, just before entering the testing phase, and always chose the long sticks as their first choice on the sessions of standard trials that were sandwiched between the testing phases (see Fig. 9.14). Second, and perhaps even more telling, when the animals did make an incorrect first choice, and thus found themselves picking up a short stick, they rarely attempted to use it to dislodge the apple by reaching toward the ramp. Rather, they typically set it down and immediately grasped the long stick. An informal assessment of this behavior was conducted by a single observer who observed the video record of each trial where an animal chose the incorrect option first. The results revealed that on 76.4 per cent of the occasions when the apes grasped one of the short sticks first, they immediately proceeded to set it down, without attempting to use it—in short, they seemed to instantly realize it was not a suitable length.

What then, can we make of our animals' very different reactions to the aligned and staggered conditions? On the surface, two different accounts are possible. On the one hand, the contrast between our apes' poor performance on the aligned condition and their excellent performance on the staggered condition could be interpreted as evidence that the aligned condition created a difficult-to-escape perceptual illusion for the apes (even though the edges of the sticks were very obvious to us). On this view, the results from the staggered condition could be interpreted as showing that when a strong visual reminder of the lack of physical connection is maintained (the staggered pattern of the three short sticks), the apes were able to hold in mind the fact that the three sticks were not, in fact, physically connected, and therefore avoided choosing that option.

Unfortunately, the design of the present study cannot rule out an altogether different account of the difference between the two conditions—an account which grants the apes little or no appreciation of the absence of physical connection among the staggered sticks. In particular, rather than diagnosing the absence of physical connection, our apes might simply have been avoiding the staggered option because it did not look like the straight tool that they had initially learned to use. In other words, all other things being equal (which, in this case, they were), the staggered tool would not be preferred over a straight tool—regardless of the nature of how the two perceptual forms were created. Clearly, choosing between these two very different interpretations required additional experimentation involving a contrast between the perceptual forms and physical connection. This was the purpose of experiment 18.

Experiment 18: the touching-stick problem revisited, age 10

Method

Subjects and apparatus

The same subjects began the current study 20–24 days after completing experiment 17. The materials used were the original long and short PVC tools, as well as the three short sticks used in experiment 17. In addition, another tool was constructed from three short sticks (identical to those just described) by physically connecting them with epoxy and internal screws. This created a staggered–connected tool. The long stick used in the previous study was not used.

Procedure

ORIENTATION. The apes were oriented to the new tool by placing it inside their testing unit and administering two consecutive sessions in which they were required to interact with the tool by picking it up from the back of the test unit, and then handing it to their trainer in front of the plexiglas. They were allowed to inspect and interact with the tool as long as they wished (up to one minute). This procedure was designed to provide them with direct experience of the solid nature of the staggered–connected tool. The subjects were not immediately rewarded for handing the tool to the experimenter, but were given several treats after both of these sessions were completed.

TESTING CONDITIONS AND PREDICTIONS. Two conditions were created in order to assist us in determining how the apes understood the staggered condition from experiment 17. In condition A, the new tool (staggered–connected) was one option and the aligned tool (composed from the three sticks set up so that they were perfectly aligned) was the other. In condition B, the staggered–connected tool was contrasted against the three separate sticks that were set down and composed (as the ape watched) into the staggered pattern (as in experiment 17). These two conditions are depicted in Fig. 9.15.

The significance of these two conditions was as follows. If the apes' performance in the staggered condition in experiment 17 reflected a genuine understanding of physical connection, then they ought to choose the staggered–connected tool in both of the conditions used in this study. On the other hand, if the apes had simply been avoiding the staggered option in experiment 17 because it was less perceptually similar to the tool that they were most familiar with in this context, they ought to display a significant preference for the aligned (incorrect) option in condition A (because the aligned option is straight), and yet choose randomly in the condition B (where both options are perceptually identical in that both are staggered). Thus, we reasoned that the *pattern* of results between the two conditions could allow for a critical inference as to whether the

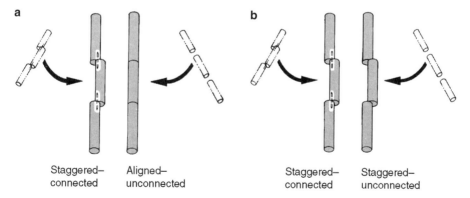

a   Staggered–   Aligned–   **b**   Staggered–   Staggered–
        connected   unconnected   connected   unconnected

Figure 9.15 Conditions used in experiment 18. (a) Condition A contrasts a staggered, but physically connected pattern of sticks with an aligned, but unconnected pattern of sticks. (b) Condition B contrasts the staggered, connected pattern with a staggered, unconnected pattern.

apes were attending to the physical connection among the elements of the two tools, or their perceptual form.

TESTING PROCEDURE. Testing consisted of eight sessions, each of which contained two trials. In each session, one trial was a standard trial involving the short and long PVC tools, and the other was a probe trial consisting of one of the two experimental conditions just described. Thus, each ape received four trials of condition A and four trials of condition B. The order of the probe and standard trials were counterbalanced so that each ape received as many sessions in which the probe trial was first and the standard was second as vice versa, and so that within each session three of the apes received the probe trial on one trial and the remaining four received it on the other trial. The actual condition that each ape received on each probe trial was determined as follows. First, each ape received each condition twice within the first block of four probe trials, and then twice again within the second block of four probe trials. In session 1, three subjects were randomly selected to receive condition A, with the remaining four receiving condition B. This order was reversed for session 2. The left/right placement of the two options in each condition was determined randomly across two-trial blocks for each animal.

As in experiment 17, each probe trial was composed of a demonstration period and a response period. The procedures associated with demonstrating each tool's properties, placing the tools on the floor, and removing the plexiglas screen were identical to the procedures used in experiment 17.

Video coding and data analysis

The coding was performed by a main rater, who coded all trials, and a reliability rater, who coded 25 per cent of the probe trials. The raters exhibited perfect agreement ($\kappa = 1.00$) for the question of which tool the ape touched/moved first, for which tool the ape grasped first ($\kappa = 1.00$), and for whether the ape was ultimately successful on each trial (κ is undefined, 14/14 cases of agreement). The data from the main rater was used in all analyses.

Results and discussion

Overall success

As in the previous experiment, the apes were allowed to work as long as they wished for the duration of the trial, making second (or even third) choices if they so desired. Thus, the apes were successful on every single trial.

Initial choice preferences

The main predictions of the study concerned which tools the apes would select first on each trial (their second choices were less relevant; see experiment 17). As can be seen in

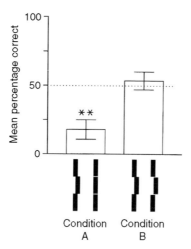

Figure 9.16 Mean percentage of trials (±*SEM*) on which the apes' first choice was for the correct tool in experiment 18. Note that in condition A, the apes preferred the incorrect (the aligned, unconnected) pattern, but in condition B they chose both options with equal frequency.

Fig. 9.16, in condition A the apes significantly preferred the *incorrect* (aligned) option (one sample *t*-test, $t(6) = 4.500$, $p = 0.0041$). Indeed, this preference was present immediately. On trial 1, all seven apes preferred the *incorrect* aligned option, and on trial 2, six of the seven apes did so. In condition B, they chose randomly between the two staggered options ($t(6) = 0.548$, ns). A paired *t*-test revealed that the apes' performance in the two conditions differed significantly ($t(6) = 3.333$, $p = 0.016$). These results exactly match the pattern predicted by the model which explained our apes' performance in experiment 17 on the basis of their avoidance of the staggered perceptual pattern (or preference for the straight perceptual pattern)—not their understanding that the staggered pattern was composed of three shorter sticks which were not physically connected. (Finally, although not depicted in Fig. 9.16, on every standard trial, involving the long and short tool, the apes selected the long tool as their first choice).

In summary, the results from the touching-stick problems (experiments 17 and 18) provide considerable evidence that, even after seeing the experimenter demonstrate the relevant properties of the sticks, and then lay them down in front of them, the apes did not appear to appreciate ahead of time the fact that although the patterns composed from the shorter sticks (whether they were aligned or staggered) were similar in their overall appearance to the straight (or staggered-connected) sticks, the individual elements from which they were composed were not physically connected to one another. In this sense, the results of the touching-stick problems strongly confirm Köhler's (1927) idea that the optics of the situation tends to control the apes' behavior.

Experiment 19: the rake-with-the-unconnected-base problem, age 10

We were deeply struck by the results of the touching stick experiments, and their wider implications for how our apes might conceive of the perceptual forms they encounter. In particular, we realized that many of the seemingly trivial aspects of our tasks—aspects that we had not directly manipulated—should be reconsidered within this framework. Thus, in experiments 19 and 20 we examined two tasks that our apes were now quite familiar with, and, indeed, were quite skilled at: (1) using a hook tool to secure a post on a baited platform so that they could pull the entire apparatus to within their reach (see experiments 15, 16, and 25)[5]; and (2) using a rake to pull a food reward to within reach (experiments 3–9). In the case of the rake problem, the question we addressed was whether the apes would immediately appreciate the difference between a rake with a physically-connected handle and base and one in which the base and handle were clearly two separate elements merely set into contact (see experiment 19). In the case of the hook-retrieval problem, we asked whether the apes would immediately appreciate the difference between a platform where the post was physically connected and one in which the post was merely set on top of the platform (experiment 20). We begin with our investigation of the case involving the rake problem.

Method

Subjects and apparatus

The same subjects participated in this study approximately nine weeks after they completed experiment 18. Between the end of experiment 18 and the beginning of this experiment, the animals had participated in several unrelated studies (not reported in this volume). They were between the ages of 10;1 and 11;0 on the day that this study began.

The materials used in this study were a functional rake (that is, a rake with its handle and base firmly attached to each other) and a non-functional rake (that is, a handle and base that were the same dimensions as the functional rake, but not physically connected). These materials are depicted in Fig. 9.17. The handles were constructed from 1/2-inch PVC tubing (55 cm long) and rectangular bases made from plywood (40 × 5 cm). The bases were painted different colors depending on the trials (see procedure explanation below).

Procedure

ORIENTATION. To orient the subjects to the test, we administered one session (consisting of four trials) in which the apes simply had to pull a rake to obtain a food reward. The rake sat on the floor in front of the middle hole of the plexiglas partition (all other holes

---

5 Note that, in the actual chronology of these studies, experiment 25 occurred before experiment 19. See Appendix I.

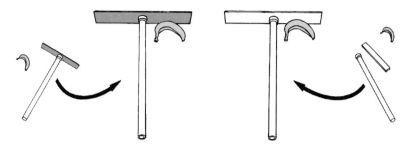

Figure 9.17 The construction process observed by the apes in experiment 19 (the rake with the unconnected base)

were covered). The rake was in a standardized position to the right or left of the midline of the hole. (This left/right position was randomized within subjects, within the constraint that it was in each position equally often.) The handle of the rake was 40 cm from the front of the plexiglas partition, meaning that the base of the rake and the reward were 95 cm from the plexiglas partition and out of the subjects' direct reach. The task for the apes was simply to enter the test unit, wait for the trainer to remove the plexiglas screen (which prevented the subjects from reaching through the open hole in the partition), pull the handle of a rake (which was baited with half an apple or its equivalent), and retrieve the reward. Once the trainer removed the screen (thus allowing the apes to respond) he returned to the rear portion of the test unit and faced the wall. The apes were given 60 seconds to respond once the screen was removed. Because all seven of the apes successfully completed the four trials in the single session they received, no further consideration is given to this phase.

TESTING. Testing consisted of four sessions, with each session containing three trials. Two of these trials were standard trials (identical to those used in orientation) and one was a probe trial involving the critical experimental manipulation. Probe trials confronted the apes with a choice between two rakes, a functional one (base and handle physically connected) and a non-functional one (base and handle merely placed in contact). (The procedure for these probe trials is described in detail below.) The first trial in every session was a standard trial. The probe trials were randomly assigned to occur as either the second or third trial (within the constraint that each ape received an equal number of sessions in which the probe trial was in each position).

  The general procedure on the probe trials was identical to the standard trials, except as follows. First, as in several of our previously described experiments, the probe trials were divided into a demonstration period and a response period. As the ape entered the test unit, the demonstration period began. An experimenter was seated facing the ape at a distance of 150 cm from the front of the plexiglas partition. A functional rake, the materials for a non-functional rake, and two food rewards were all positioned at the experimenter's feet. According to a predetermined schedule (described below), the experimenter first demonstrated, and then set up, either the functional rake or the materials which were used to compose the non-functional rake. For example, in the case where the functional rake was demonstrated first, the experimenter demonstrated the integrity of the handle and base for 5 seconds, set it down in either the left or right position in front of the response hole, and then placed half an apple in front of its base. Next, the experimenter picked up the unconnected handle and base, demonstrated that they were unconnected for 5 seconds, and then placed them in the opposite position from the functional rake. In this case, the base was simply set against the handle (and then baited with half an apple) so that perceptually this option looked nearly identical to the functional rake. The experimenter then returned to a neutral posture and fixed his or her gaze at a predetermined location on the floor exactly midway between the two options. The trainer then removed the plexiglas screen (allowing the animal to respond) and returned to the rear portion of the test unit and faced the wall. From this point, the apes were given 60 seconds to respond. The subjects were only allowed to make one choice (defined as touching a rake handle). Once a subject made a choice, the experimenter removed the option that the ape had not chosen to prevent him or her from making a second choice. On trials where the apes chose the functional rake, as soon as they obtained the reward they were ushered out of the test unit; on trials where they chose the non-functional rake, they were allowed to interact with the materials for the full 60 seconds if they so desired.

In an effort to assist the apes in keeping track of the properties of the two rakes during each trial, we painted the bases of functional and non-functional rakes distinctly different colors. However, as the apes received multiple trials, we did not want them to focus on the question of color alone (e.g. 'the red rake is always correct'). Thus, unique color contrasts were used on each trial. To mitigate against the possibility that uncontrolled-for color preferences might influence the results, the animals were randomly divided into two groups (group 1 = Kara, Candy, Jadine, and Mindy; group 2 = Apollo, Brandy, and Megan) and between groups the colors of correct and incorrect options were reversed. Finally, the side of the correct rake, and the order in which the rakes were demonstrated (left-to-right versus right-to-left), were counterbalanced so that each ape received an equal number of trials in which: (1) the functional or non-functional rake was demonstrated first or second; and (2) the first rake demonstrated (correct or incorrect) was placed equally often on the right and left.

ADDITIONAL TESTING. Following the four sessions of testing described above, each animal was administered an additional eight sessions of testing. Each of these sessions consisted of a single trial involving a contrast between a functional rake and a non-functional rake. Only two colors were used (red and silver). Each ape received four trials in which the rake with the red base was correct (twice on the right, and twice on the left) and four trials in which the rake with the silver base was correct (again, twice on the right, and twice on the left). The color of the correct rake, as well as the side on which it was positioned were counter-balanced across the eight sessions in two four-session blocks. In an attempt to maintain the apes' interest, the subjects' primary caretaker (their trainer) served as the experimenter who demonstrated the properties of the objects. Otherwise, the structure of the trials was identical to the original testing procedures (except that the food was placed on the floor first, followed by the tools).

Models to be tested

Two simple models were used to predict the apes' reactions to the experimental manipulation employed on the probe trials. The first model stipulated that the apes' reasoning about which rake to select would be governed by the overall perceptual appearance of the parts of the rakes, not whether the individuals parts were physically connected to each other. This model generated the prediction that, with respect to the functional and non-functional rakes, the apes would choose randomly. On the other hand, a second model posited that the apes would appreciate the significance of what they observed during the demonstration period for the functional integrity of the two otherwise similar perceptual forms. In particular, they would appreciate that pulling the handle of the non-functional rake would not cause the base (or therefore the reward) to move along with it.

Videotape coding and data analysis

A main rater coded the videotapes of all 84 probe trials (12 trials per animal; four from the original testing, plus the eight additional test trials). A reliability rater independently coded 25 per cent ($n = 21$) of trials. The raters exhibited excellent reliabilities on which tool the apes first moved ($\kappa = 1.00$); whether their first action on the tool handle was to pull it straight toward them, or slide it sideways toward the apple ($\kappa =$ undefined; 21/21 cases of agreement); and whether the apes were ultimately successful in retrieving the reward with the tool they chose first (recall that they were only given one choice; $\kappa = 1.00$).

Results and discussion

The most central question addressed by this study was whether the apes would choose the rake with the physically-connected base (the functional rake) over the rake with the unconnected base (the non-functional rake). The data on which rake the apes selected on each of their initial four trials is depicted in Fig. 9.18 (in blocks of two trials) and in Table 9.5 (on a trial-by-trial basis per subject). As can be seen, there is little evidence that the apes displayed an initial preference for the functional tool. On trial 1, only 3/7 apes selected the correct tool, and across the first two trials, the apes averaged only 50 per cent correct (exactly the level of performance expected by chance responding). This performance cannot be attributed to some general lack of motivation or interest on the part of the animals; they succeeded on 100 per cent of the easy standard trials that bracketed the probe trials during the first four sessions of testing.

In considering these initial results, we asked whether or not the apes' lack of preference for the functional tool might be because they envisioned a means of succeeding using either tool. In the case of the functional rake, they might have understood that they could simply pull the tool straight toward them. On the other hand, in the case of the unconnected rake, they may have understood that they could slide the handle sideways and retrieve the reward using, in effect, a stick. Two aspects of the data provide

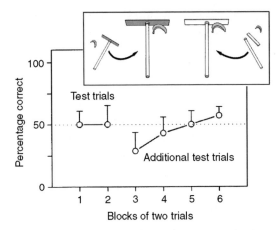

Figure 9.18 Mean percentage of apes (±*SEM*) to choose the correct option in experiment 19 in blocks of two trials.

good reason to doubt this conclusion. First, on 12/14 (86 per cent) of the trials in which the apes chose the incorrect rake, their very first action was to pull it straight toward them, not slide the unconnected handle sideways like a stick—exactly what one would expect if they had expected the base and reward to behave properly. (Indeed, across all sessions, including the eight additional testing sessions discussed below, this pattern held true on 85.1 per cent of the trials in which they selected the incorrect tool.) Second, the apes only succeeded on an average of 10.1 per cent of the trials in which they choose the incorrect rake. Thus, there is very little evidence to support the idea that the apes' lack of initial preference was because they envisioned alternative possibilities for success with the two different rakes.

Recall that after the original four sessions of testing, each ape received an additional eight trials of this task (administered in sessions containing a single trial) to explore

Table 9.5 Trial-by-trial results for the apes' first choices on the problem involving the rakes with the connected and unconnected bases (experiment 19)

Subject	Trial												
	1	2	3	4	5	6	7	8	9	10	11	12	*Mean*
APO	–	+	–	–	–	–	–	–	–	–	+	–	2/12
KAR	–	+	–	–	–	–	+	–	+	–	+	–	4/12
CAN	+	–	–	+	–	+	–	–	+	–	–	+	5/12
JAD	+	–	+	–	–	+	+	+	+	+	+	–	8/12
BRA	+	+	+	+	+	+	–	+	–	+	–	+	9/12
MEG	–	–	+	+	–	–	+	–	–	+	+	+	6/12
MIN	–	+	+	–	–	–	–	+	–	+	–	+	5/12
	3/7	4/7	4/7	3/7	1/7	3/7	3/7	3/7	3/7	4/7	4/7	4/7	5.6/12

how resistant they might be to learning the distinction in question. Despite these additional trials, the apes' performance did not improve (see Fig. 9.18 and Table 9.5), and did not exceed levels expected by chance (one-sample t-test, two-tailed, hypothetical mean = 50 per cent, $t(6) = 46.4$, $p = 0.651$). Indeed, only Jadine showed some evidence of learning across trials (see Table 9.5). Oddly, Brandy exhibited excellent performance across her first six trials, but was at chance levels on trials 7–12. Equally puzzling, Apollo exhibited a significant preference for the *incorrect* rake (10/12 choices for the unconnected rake; binomial $p = 0.02$). Although we have no doubt that given enough trials the apes could have learned the distinction in question, these additional trials suggest that, unlike some of the other tests that we presented to the apes, this was not something that was easy for them to learn. We discuss their resistance to learning this (and related problems) at the end of this chapter.

Experiment 20: the platform-with-the-unconnected-post problem, age 10

In this study we examined a question similar to the one we explored in the previous experiment, but in the context of the hook-retrieval problem. In particular, we asked whether our apes, in the context of needing to use a hook tool to pull in a baited platform, would understand the difference between a platform that possessed a post that was physically connected to it, versus a platform whose post had simply been set on top of it.

Method

Subjects and apparatus

The same subjects began this study approximately eight weeks after completing experiment 18. Between the end of experiment 18 and the beginning of this experiment, the animals had participated in several unrelated studies, as well as experiment 19, which overlapped with this study for seven days. The apes were between the ages of 10;1 and 11;0 on the day that this study began.

The materials used in this study were the two platforms (without the rings) and hook tools that had been used in experiments 15 and 16. One platform had a post that was rigidly attached (as in the previous studies) and the other was associated with a post of the same size and shape that was unattached. The posts were painted different colors across trials.

Procedure

TESTING. All aspects of the general procedure of this experiment were the same as in experiment 19. Thus, the animals were given an initial orientation phase in which they demonstrated an immediate competence at pulling in a platform (using a hook tool that was already attached around the post), and were then tested across four sessions consisting of three trials each: two trials identical to the ones used in orientation, and one

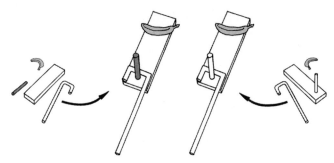

Figure 9.19 The construction process observed by the apes in experiment 20 (the platform with the unconnected post).

probe trial. The probe trials were divided into a demonstration period (where the relevant aspects of the posts and platforms were highlighted: see Fig. 9.19) and a response period (in which the apes chose between the two options). Thus, each ape received four probe trials involving the critical contrast between a platform where the hook was around a post that was connected to the platform and a platform where the post had simply been set upon it. All aspects of the experimental procedure, design, and counterbalancing procedures were the same as those described for the previous experiment.

ADDITIONAL TESTING. Also as in experiment 19, the apes were tested for an additional eight sessions after completing the initial four sessions described above. Only one color contrast was used between the connected and unconnected posts (yellow and green). The demonstration order, as well as the correct side and color, were counterbalanced as in experiment 19.

Videotape coding

The videotapes were coded in the same manner as the previous study. The two raters exhibited excellent agreement for their judgements of which tool the ape moved first ($\kappa = 1.00$); the ape's first general action on the tool (21/21 cases of agreement, $\kappa =$ undefined); and whether or not the subject was successful in retrieving the reward by the end of the trial ($\kappa = 1.00$).

Results and discussion

Similarly to the previous study, the central prediction we addressed was that the apes would prefer to pull the hook that contacted the platform with the physically-connected post as opposed to the platform with the post that simply rested on its surface. The results provide no evidence to support this prediction. On trial 1, only 2 of the 7 apes selected the tool that was contacting the physically-connected post, nor did the apes significantly prefer this option across their first four trials, where as a group they averaged only 53.6 per cent correct (one-sample t-test, two-tailed, hypothetical mean = 50 per cent, $t(6) = 0.420$, $p = 0.689$).

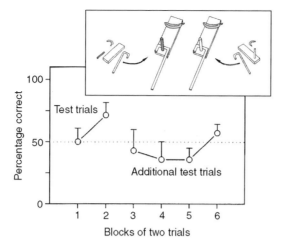

Figure 9.20 Mean percentage of apes (±*SEM*) to choose the correct option in experiment 20, in blocks of two trials.

The group data for both the initial test trials, as well as the additional eight test trials that were administered to each animal, are presented in Fig. 9.20. In addition, the trial-by-trial data for each subject are presented in Table 9.6. An examination of these data reveals that, as in the previous experiment, the subjects did not rapidly learn to select the correct option. Indeed, when averaged across the 12 trials that they received, the subjects averaged only 47.6 per cent correct, a level which does not differ significantly from chance (one-sample *t*-test, two-tailed, hypothetical mean = 50 per cent, $t(6) = 1.000$, $p = 0.356$). Furthermore, as Fig. 19.20 clearly reveals, the apes' performances did not steadily improve across the 12 test trials. Finally, as usual the apes performed excellently (100 per cent correct) on the standard trials which bracketed the more

Table 9.6 Trial-by-trial results for the apes' first choices on the problem involving the platforms with the connected and unconnected posts (experiment 20)

| Subject | Trial | | | | | | | | | | | | |
	1	2	3	4	5	6	7	8	9	10	11	12	*M*
APO	+	+	+	−	−	−	+	−	−	−	+	−	5/12
KAR	+	−	−	+	+	+	−	−	+	−	−	+	6/12
CAN	−	−	+	+	+	−	+	−	+	−	−	+	6/12
JAD	−	+	+	+	−	−	−	−	−	+	+	−	5/12
BRA	−	+	−	−	+	+	−	−	−	+	−	+	5/12
MEG	−	+	+	+	+	−	+	−	−	−	+	+	7/12
MIN	−	+	+	−	−	−	+	+	−	+	−	+	6/12
	2/7	5/7	5/7	4/7	4/7	2/7	4/7	1/7	2/7	3/7	3/7	5/7	5.7/12

difficult trials, and therefore it is difficult to attribute the results to some general lack of motivation or interest on their part.

As in the previous experiment, we systematically investigated whether the apes' incorrect choices simply reflected an alternative strategy for obtaining the reward (in this case, to push the tool toward the food). However, on 96 per cent of the trials where they selected the incorrect option, the apes' first action on the tool was to pull it directly toward them—as if they fully anticipated that the platform would move toward them. Furthermore, there was only a single trial where an ape (Jadine) was able to retrieve the reward after having selected the incorrect option (which she did by slowly poking at the base of the platform until she worked it close enough to grab the reward).

In summary, the results of both experiments 19 and 20 provide additional and striking evidence that, for the chimpanzee, the optical appearance of a form is far more important than the properties related to the physical connection among the form's constituent parts.

General discussion (experiments 14–20): toward a theory of the ape's understanding of 'connection'

The results of the experiments reported in this chapter provide converging and fairly persuasive evidence that our chimpanzees have a quite different appreciation of 'connection' than humans do. Indeed, the data provide strong support for at least some aspects of the Köhlerian view that chimpanzees do not have a notion of connection any deeper than mere contact.

If this is so, we might pause to ask two questions. First, how does the ape come to explain why in some cases their actions on an intermediary object (a tool) yield co-varied movements in a goal object, but in other cases they do not? Perhaps this question can be posed most succinctly by considering the apes' actions on objects in their world. When an ape grasps a hammer stone sitting upon a pile of rocks, surely the ape does not expect the other rocks to rise along with the hammer stone. One interpretation of this scenario is that the ape knows full well that the mere contact between the hammer stone and other rocks does not imply a kind of physical connection. On the surface, this would seem to raise trouble for the Köhlerian position.

However, such events are only problematic for the Köhlerian view if one assumes that chimpanzees seek coherent explanations among separate events in the first place. If, on the other hand, chimpanzees act upon objects in the world, detect specific regularities, and use them as default assumptions about how the world is likely to behave, then the kinds of effects we have reported in this chapter can rest quite comfortably alongside the sorts of actions chimpanzees perform all of the time. If the ape receives considerable experience (both through its spontaneous play and our experimental settings) that the post remains attached to the platform, but possesses no underlying explanation or account for why this is the case, then merely seeing a post set upon a platform may not initially offer any good reason (from their perspective) for believing that the resulting perceptual form has dramatically different affordances than the similar forms with which the ape is familiar.

The preceding example is a case where the ape is confronted with two options which, at the moment that a decision must be made, do not differ substantially in their perceptual appearances. Can a similar account be marshaled to explain their performances on tasks like the rope-and-banana and the initial hook-retrieval problems—cases in which the options do differ substantially in their perceptual appearances at the moment when the chimpanzee must make a decision? Consider one of the conditions from the rope-and-banana problem, involving the choice between a rope that is tied to a banana versus a rope that is merely draped over a banana. One might be tempted to think that this situation is very much like the example of the ape reaching for the hammer stone that rests upon a pile of rocks; after all, in one case the ape sees that a rope is merely placed over a banana, whereas in the other case a rope is actually tied to a banana.

However, consider our apes' previous experiences with ropes. In some cases, the ropes are in contact (in truth, physically connected) with other objects and the ape experiences that pulling on the rope co-varies with the movement of the object that the rope is contacting. But in other cases this is not so. An ape spies a rope lying in her compound among a pile of toys. She picks up the rope and carries it away. But, of course, the toys do not follow suit. Clearly, then, the ape receives both experiences. Sometimes ropes are intimately associated with movement of objects they contact, in other cases they are not. Armed with a theory of causal mechanisms, the human easily explains the difference within a coherent framework. Armed only with the perceptual evidence, however, the ape may merely assume that sometimes the association is present, and in other cases it is not. Indeed, it seems quite likely that the ape comes to expect that in situations in which a goal object is out of reach, but a rope (or some other intermediary object) is contacting the goal, the intermediary object can be acted upon to move the goal.

Thus, in summary, we envision chimpanzees as possessing excellent perceptual discrimination abilities, and thus able to make roughly the same 'contact' versus 'no contact' judgements as humans. Furthermore, we suspect that, with experience, their judgements about contact (or imminent contact) are used in generating robust expectations about the contingencies between their actions on an intermediary object and the movements of a goal object. Of course, as we saw in Chapter 6, factors other than direct contact may also play a role in their judgements. Nonetheless, we suspect that apes use their perceptual judgements about contact in formulating expectations about the interrelated movements of objects when they confront situations in which they must solve problems of the type we have outlined here. However, our results show that such judgements about contact need not be attended by parallel interpretations of underlying physical connection. We shall elaborate upon this idea further in Chapter 12.

However, in the meantime we move on to the next chapter, in which we continue to explore the chimpanzee's notion of connection in the context of several variations of the classic Piagetian 'support problem'—a related, but much-misunderstood task.

CHAPTER 10

THE SUPPORT PROBLEM: PHYSICAL CONNECTION REVISITED

DANIEL J. POVINELLI, JAMES E. REAUX, LAURA A. THEALL, AND STEVE GIAMBRONE

The final case of physical connection that we shall consider involves the classic 'support' problem, originally employed by Piaget (1952). Here, the problem involves a goal object (a toy) that is out of the infant's reach, but is resting on a support (a blanket) that is within reach. The question is whether the infant appreciates that the toy can be obtained by pulling on the support. This is typically described as a 'means–ends' problem, because it requires the infant to understand that pulling the cloth is the 'means' for achieving the desired 'ends' of bringing the toy to within reach. Piaget contrasted cases where the goal object was actually resting on a support versus cases in which the goal object was simply near or touching a support. In the past, researchers have used this task with different species of nonhuman primates, including chimpanzees, gorillas, several species of macaques, and capuchin monkeys (e.g. Mathieu *et al.* 1980; Spinozzi and Potí 1989, 1993). And, as we saw in experiment 16 (Chapter 9), our apes easily understood the contrast between an option in which a banana was resting on a platform and another option in which the banana was resting on the floor next to it.

Some researchers have continued to interpret the support problem as a test of an organism's understanding of 'means–ends' relations. Although we do not dispute this interpretation, it is also possible to view the problem along a different spectrum—in particular, as a special instance of problems related to physical connection (in this case, an instance of 'weak' physical connection afforded by the weight of the goal object resting upon the support). Note that, just as was true with the problems examined in the previous chapter, many actions on the tool object (in this case, the support) will yield co-varied movements on the goal object. However, if the Köhlerian position that we explored in the previous chapter is correct—that is, if the chimpanzee's understanding of connection is strictly related to visual 'contact'—then the most basic version of the support problem may be ill-suited to probe an organism's appreciation of the causal structure of the problem as it relates to physical connection. This is because the gross distinction between contact and no contact does not address the question of 'support'—a concept that lies at the very foundation of this task's ability to explore an organism's understanding of causal mechanism.

Viewed in this light, it is important to note that (to our knowledge) no previous researchers have systematically investigated chimpanzees' (or any other nonhuman primates') ability to distinguish between relevant and irrelevant kinds of *contact* between the goal object and support in the context of this problem. Several recent studies conducted by Marc Hauser and his colleagues at Harvard University (Hauser *et al.* 1999*a*) did, however, examine whether a nonhuman primate (the cotton-top taramin) could distinguish between relevant and irrelevant surface features of the support problem after having been trained on the basic version of the task. Indeed, because their work represents a way of thinking about the support (and related) problems in a way that has little or nothing to do with the concept of 'support', and thus deprives it of much of its theoretical significance, it is worth exploring in some detail. Furthermore, this provides an excellent opportunity to contrast traditional theoretical approaches to studying tool-use in non-human primates, to the one advocated here.

Initially, Hauser *et al.* (1999) confronted their monkeys with two versions of the support problem. One version was the basic support problem (food on a cloth versus food off a cloth; hereafter, 'ON' versus 'OFF'). The second version consisted of a correct option in which the cloth was a continuous strip, and an incorrect option where two cloths with a small gap between them were present (see Fig. 10.1). Although the second version of the problem is labeled the 'discontinuous cloth condition', another way of thinking about the incorrect option in this condition is that it consists of one piece of cloth within the monkeys' reach, and a second cloth out of the monkeys' reach; only the cloth that is out of reach is associated with food (see Fig. 10.1). Hauser *et al.* trained their monkeys until they were consistently selecting the continuous cloth. Following this, the animals were then confronted with hundreds of problems and sub-problems in which various nonfunctional aspects of the problems were altered, while the crucial features were left intact. So, for example, in the ON/OFF conditions, factors such as how far the food was from the cloth, the exact location of the food upon the cloth, the length, color, and shape of the cloth, the color and shape of the food, and the color of the table surface, were all manipulated. Likewise, in the discontinuous cloth condition, the same kinds of factors, as well as the exact width of the gap between the two pieces of cloth, were manipulated. Even the most challenging set of contrasts that were given to the monkeys merely contrasted the exact form and width of the gap between the two pieces of cloth. In many (but not all) cases, the monkeys were able to transfer what they had learned in their initial training to these new conditions. The researchers concluded that the ability of their monkeys to transfer across these various problem types revealed that they 'solve means-ends relationships, and that their ability depends on a discrimination between properties that are functionally relevant as opposed to irrelevant' (p. 565).

The manipulations employed by Hauser *et al.* (1999) undoubtedly assessed whether their animals were basing their selections on causally irrelevant features of the problems, such as the color of the cloth. However, in general their tests do not clarify whether

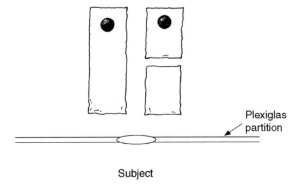

Figure 10.1 Discontinuous cloth option used by Hauser *et al.* (1999*a*). Note that the incorrect option can either by viewed as a 'discontinuous cloth' or as two cloths, one that is within reach but is not in contact with food, and one that is in contact with food but is out of reach.

the animals' decisions were based on an understanding of causal mechanism, or more straight-forward perceptual discriminations. Two perceptual discriminations are of relevance here. First, in the ON/OFF condition, the monkeys may have learned to choose the correct option not because they appreciated the idea of 'support', but rather because the correct option was always one continuous 'cloth-food' perceptual form, whereas the incorrect option always appeared as two distinct forms (see Fig. 10.1). Second, in the discontinuous cloth condition, the monkeys may have selected the correct option because it appeared as a single 'cloth-food' perceptual form that was within their reach, as opposed to the incorrect option, where the continuous 'cloth-food' form that was present (the more distant part of the option) was simply out of their reach (see Fig. 10.1). Rather than treating the incorrect option as a 'discontinuous cloth', the monkeys may have seen it as an irrelevant piece of cloth and a 'correct' option that was out of their reach. Recall that this is an exact analogue of the situation we had presented to our apes years earlier in the 'broken-rake' studies described in Chapter 6 (see Experiments 5 and 6).

If Hauser *et al.*'s (1999) monkeys were using the discriminations just described, then their study was only testing the animals' *perceptual generalization* abilities. This is a critical point. Every transfer test that Hauser *et al.* administered to their monkeys could have been solved on the basis of one of the two perceptual discriminations mentioned above. After the initial publication of this book, a possible exception to this was pointed out by Hauser (personal communication, letter to Daniel Povinelli dated 20 December 2000). He suggested that one or more of the sub-problems in their condition F did, in fact, address the ON/OFF (and hence, 'contact/no contact') distinction. To be fair, we had overlooked this sub-problem (mainly because it was never cast in terms of contact/no contact by the authors). However, even it is limited by the fact that it involves a *very small* generalization from what the subjects were initially trained to do.[1] Not even the conditions that the authors' describe as testing the tamarins' understanding of the 'type of connection' (their 'condition K') were really anything more than increasingly fine perceptual discriminations of the gap between the cloths.

The preceding discussion should illustrate that in order to be useful in exploring an organism's understanding of causal mechanism, the support problem must be cast in such a way that it actually addresses the issue of 'support' as a type of physical connection. In doing so, it must assess the Köhlerian possibility that the animals' choices are based simply upon visual contact. To be perfectly clear: every possible variation of the support problem can, with enough experience, be solved by perceptual discriminations. However, the presentation of appropriately designed variations of the task can allow for an initial assessment of whether the animals appreciate the distinction between physical connection and 'mere contact'. Although we have already demonstrated that our apes can immediately understand the support problem in the contact/no-contact contrast

---

1   For archival purposes, here is Povinelli's reply (in a letter to Hauser dated 4 January 2001) to the concern expressed by Hauser that we had not accurately characterized his research: '…if I have misrepresented your work here, I will certainly correct it in the soft cover printing of the book—which will be soon. Let me try to clarify what I think is the very confusing presentation of your work. Having reexamined condition F on the reprint you sent, I can now see that some of the sub-problems within condition F look like edge contact—they certainly did not look like that on…the photocopy that I received. From what I can make out from enlarging Fig. 2 by 400%…, what I have labeled as F1, F2, F3, and F6 involve the reward just touching at the edge, whereas the sub-problems I have labeled as F4, F5 and F8 do not. Is this correct? Unfortunately, this is not labeled or explained in the article. If you could clarify which of the F sub-problems involved edge contact that would be helpful. I [had] assumed that condition F was a uniform condition (ON versus OFF), something that seems to be implied in the description of condition F in Table 2, and from your definition of what ON versus OFF meant (see last paragraph on p. 567[)]. In Figure 4 and 5 you provide labels for F1 and F2—are these the two subtypes? Again, this terminology is not explained anywhere in the article that I can find. Indeed, a straightforward reading of the column headings in Table 2 would lead one to label the F sub-problems F4, F5, F6…F11, but I assume now that the column headers only apply to the first row (the A problems?).

  'Having said all that, from what I can tell from the tiny schematics in your Figure 2, even the sub-problems of F in which there is contact, do not draw the crucial distinction that we labor over in the book. Unless I missed something, these sub-problems merely involve[d] moving the [food] pellet a tiny distance (2 or 3 cm?) closer to the cloth (touching it at a point)—virtually indistinguishable from many of the incorrect options which the tamarins learned about in [the initial training of the] A and B series etc. So, what you have shown by the time you get to the F series is that they have generalized after a lot of training. Interesting from the point of view of stimulus generalization, but not the question of support (see our Chapter 11). To fairly consider the question of support, one would need to look at what they did right away, before any training and make the kinds of contact at least somewhat comparable: food on the cloth versus under the cloth (see our Figure 10.2b). Admittedly, ou[r] later tests are better (see Exps. 22 and 23), but again, in my opinion your tests are not strong ones for the issue of support.'

(see Chapter 9, experiments 14 and 16), the following studies were explicitly designed to examine their understanding of why the contact condition (the object resting on the support) is associated with obtaining the reward.

Experiment 21: the support problem as a case of physical connection, age 10

Method

Subjects and materials

Our seven apes were between the ages of 10;2 and 11;1 when this study began, which was two weeks after they had completed experiment 19. In addition, it overlapped with experiment 20 (see Chapter 9) by four days.

The materials used in this study were several pieces of rectangular pieces of heavy white cloth (50 × 20 cm). Although our apes had an extensive amount of experience with such cloths, the day before they began the orientation phase (see below), seven pieces of this cloth were placed inside the subjects' enclosures and they were allowed to freely interact and play with them throughout the duration of the experiment.

Procedure

ORIENTATION TO THE MATERIALS. The subjects were given an orientation session consisting of four trials to introduce them to the materials in the context of the test unit, as well as to teach them a simple task that we could use to surround the test trials. The task was simply for the ape to enter the test unit, pick up a cloth that had been set on the floor outside the test unit, and place it inside a bucket. Hereafter, these are referred to as *spacer trials*. Because they were intimately familiar with the idea of placing objects inside such buckets (in the context of unrelated studies), all of the apes entered the test unit, picked up the cloth and placed it in the bucket on all four trials. Their trainer handed them a food reward after each successful trial.

TESTING. Testing consisted of four sessions, with each test session composed of four trials. Trials 1 and 3 were spacer trials (the same as those used in the orientation phase) and were included for two reasons; first, to provide a background of easy trials for the animals, and second, to have the animals experience the properties of the cloth just prior to each crucial test trial. The remaining two trials (trials 2 and 4) were used to present two versions of the support problem to our apes (see Fig. 10.2). In the contact/no-contact condition, the incorrect option consisted of the cloth and an apple resting 5 cm away from it, as depicted in Fig. 10.2(a). In the contact/contact condition, the incorrect option consisted of the cloth draped against the side of the apple, as depicted in Fig. 10.2(b). The correct option was the same in both conditions (see Fig. 10.1(a)–(b)).

Each experimental test trial proceeded as follows. While the ape waited outside, an experimenter set up the two cloths, one in front of each of two holes in the plexiglas partition (all other holes were closed). The cloths were positioned 40 cm apart and the ends that would be closest to the apes were 40 cm from the partition. Two food rewards (either half an apple or half a banana) were placed in association with the cloths as dic-

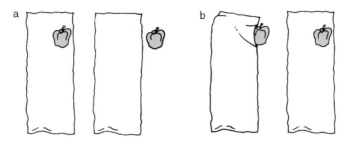

Figure 10.2 Conditions used in experiment 21. (a) Contact/no-contact. (b) Contact/contact.

tated by the particular condition that the animal was assigned to receive on that trial (see below). These rewards were 90 cm from the partition and out of the subjects' reach. Once the exact configuration had been set, the experimenter went to the rear wall of the test unit, faced away from the test unit, and opened the shuttle door, thus allowing the ape to enter and respond.

Each ape received four trials of each of the two conditions. They were presented in the following manner. Each ape received one trial from each condition in each session. The order of these was trials was randomly determined within the constraint that each ape receive the two possible orders an equal number of times across the four sessions. Also, within each session, three of the subjects received one order and four received the opposite order. The side of the correct option was also randomly assigned, within the constraint that each side was correct equally often within and across sessions. The animals were allowed one choice per trial, which was defined as the first cloth they moved.

Models and predictions

The test contrasted the predictions of two models. The *physical connection* model posited that the chimpanzees understood the relevance of a certain kind of contact between the cloth and the food reward (one which produced a degree of physical connection through the weight of one object resting on another). The *visual contact* model posited that the chimpanzees' judgements would be governed by the presence or absence of any contact between the objects. Thus, both models predicted success in the contact/no-contact condition, whereas they generated opposite predictions for the contact/contact condition. The physical connection model predicted success in this condition (after all, there was no physical connection between the apple and the cloth in the incorrect option), whereas the visual contact model predicted that the apes would choose randomly with respect to the two options (after all, in both cases the 'support' was touching the objective).

Videotape coding and analysis

A main rater coded all of the 112 test trials, and a reliability rater independently coded 25 per cent of these ($n = 28$ trials; four randomly selected trials for each animal). The raters exhibited perfect agreement on their judgements concerning (1) the cloth that the subject moved first (Cohen's $\kappa = 1.00$); and (2) whether the chimpanzee, if he or she moved the incorrect cloth first, attempted to 'use the cloth to contact the food as part of an effort to retrieve the food' ($\kappa = 1.00$).

Results and discussion

Figure 10.3 displays the subjects' choices, in both the contact/no-contact and the contact/contact conditions, in blocks of two trials across the study. As predicted by the visual contact model, the contact/contact condition appeared to be more difficult than the contact/no-contact condition.

Several statistical analyses support the interpretation that the two conditions differed in their difficulty level. First, although the apes performed at levels exceeding chance (50 per cent) in both conditions (one sample t-tests, $t(6) = 2.500$ and 5.347, $p = 0.047$ and 0.002), the apes scored better in the contact/no-contact condition ($M = 82.1$ per cent correct, $SD = 15.9$) than in the contact/contact condition ($M = 67.9$ per cent correct, $SD = 18.9$). However, a paired t-test indicated that this overall difference between the conditions was only marginally statistically significant, $t(6) = 1.922$, $p = 0.103$. A second reason for believing that the contact/no-contact condition was easier derives from a consideration of the learning that occurred across the eight trials that the apes received in each condition. In particular, when the data depicted in Fig. 10.3 were subjected to two separate one-way repeated measures ANOVAs, some evidence for learning appeared in the contact/no-contact condition ($F[3,18] = 2.842$, $p = 0.067$), but not in the contact/contact condition ($F[3,18] = 0.423$, $p = 0.738$). A third line of evidence that supports the idea that the contact/no-contact condition was easier can be derived from the animals' performances in their very first two-trial blocks in the two conditions (see Fig. 10.3). The apes performed at a level marginally above chance in the contact/no-contact condition ($t[6] = 2.121$, $p = 0.078$), but not in the contact/contact condition ($t[6] = 1.00$, $p = 0.356$). Finally, in the contact/no-contact condition, the apes performed at levels exceeding chance ($p < .05$) in trial blocks 2, 3, and 4, whereas they did not perform at above-chance levels in any two-trial block in the contact/contact condition.

Although the above analyses establish that the contact/contact condition was more difficult for our apes than the contact/no-contact condition, from the standpoint of the two models under consideration the most important aspect of the data concerns whether the apes performed at above-chance levels in the conditions. After all, the physical connection model predicted that apes would perform at levels exceeding chance in both con-

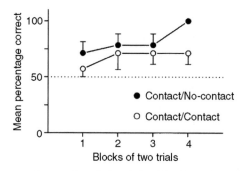

Figure 10.3 Mean percentage of correct first choices ($\pm SEM$) by the apes in experiment 21, in blocks of two trials.

Table 10.1 Performance of individual subjects by trial in the first support problem, experiment 21

Subject	Condition	Trial number								M
		1	2	3	4	5	6	7	8	
APO	1	−	+	−	+	−	+	+	+	5/8
	2	+	+	+	+	+	+	−	+	7/8
KAR	1	+	+	+	+	+	−	+	+	7/8
	2	+	−	+	+	+	+	−	+	6/8
CAN	1	−	+	−	+	+	+	+	+	6/8
	2	+	−	+	−	+	−	+	+	5/8
JAD	1	−	+	+	+	+	+	+	+	7/8
	2	+	−	−	−	−	+	+	+	4/8
BRA	1	+	−	−	+	+	−	+	+	5/8
	2	−	−	+	−	−	+	−	+	3/8
MEG	1	+	+	+	+	+	+	+	+	8/8
	2	+	+	+	+	+	−	+	−	6/8
MIN	1	+	+	+	+	+	+	+	+	8/8
	2	+	−	+	+	+	+	+	+	7/8

Condition 1 = contact/no-contact.

Condition 2 = contact/contact.

ditions, whereas the visual contact model predicted above-chance performance only in the contact/no-contact condition. The results support the prediction of the visual contact model. As described above, there is evidence to support the idea that the animals began the contact/no-contact condition at levels exceeding chance, and then continued at above-chance performance levels throughout the experiment. In contrast, the animals began the contact/contact condition at chance levels, and never exceeded chance in any individual two-trial block (although their mean percentage correct across all trials in this condition was higher than that expected by chance; see above).

So far, we have discussed the data for the subjects as a group. There were, however, several noteworthy individual performances (see Table 10.1). Mindy performed perfectly in the contact/no-contact condition and made only a single error in the contact/contact condition—notably, on her second trial. Megan also performed perfectly in the contact/no-contact condition. However, although she performed well overall on the contact/contact condition, her performance declined to chance levels in her final four trials of this condition. The only other particularly striking performance was by Apollo, who, surprisingly, performed better in the contact/contact condition than in the contact/no-contact condition.

Finally, four of the apes (Apollo, Mindy, Brandy, and Jadine) all exhibited at least one trial on which they made an incorrect choice and then proceeded to attempt to use the cloth to retrieve the apple by pushing the cloth toward it, or flapping at it. Given the flimsy nature of the cloth, these efforts were absolutely futile. Nonetheless, they are strikingly reminiscent of descriptions provided by Köhler (1927) of how his apes frequently used materials that could not possibly be effective in retrieving out-of-reach goal objects, but could make contact with them—even when more appropriate implements were nearby.

Experiment 22: a closer look at the support problem, age $10^1/_2$–$11^1/_2$

Although our apes' initial responses in experiment 21 supported the visual contact model's explanation of their reasoning about the support problem, the apes' *overall* performances in the crucial contact/contact condition were at levels exceeding chance (albeit only 67.9 per cent correct). In addition, two of the subjects (Mindy and Megan) displayed more impressive performances. In the next study, we attempted a more sophisticated test of the idea that the apes' judgements were based on the gestalt perceptual form of the support object and food reward, not the physical connection between the food and support afforded by the weight of the food. Several years earlier, during the conduct of experiments 5–8, we had confronted our apes with an option where there was no possibility of physical contact between a rake and a food reward (because the rake was inverted). In those tests, they displayed some evidence of responding on the basis of a kind of perceptual 'containment' of the food reward within the optical field of the tool (see Chapter 6, Fig. 6.2). Likewise, we reasoned that an even weaker version of the visual contact model might prevail as at least a partial explanation of the apes' behavior. Thus, in this experiment, we sought to create several versions of the support problem in which the contact that was relevant to physical connection was contrasted against mere perceptual containment.

Method

Subjects and materials

Our seven apes were between the ages of 10;3 and 11;2 at the beginning of this study, which began 18 days after the completion of experiment 21. No other studies that are reported in this book were conducted in the interim, although the apes were participating in an unrelated study at the time.

A number of white, rectangular cloths of the same dimensions as those used in experiment 21 were used as the supports in this study. They were cut into a number of distinct forms (see Fig. 10.4). Two of the cloth/reward options were 'correct' from the standpoint of the physical connection model. Option 1 was the same as the correct option used in the previous study. Option 2 was specifically designed so that the reward appeared less perceptually contained within the optical field of the support.

There were three options that were 'incorrect' from the perspective of the physical connection model. However, these options can be arranged in a linear order representing degrees of visual contact. Option 3, in which the cloth is draped almost fully around the apple, can be thought of as a case of *full contact*. Option 4, in which the apple rests not upon the support but rather inside a cut-out portion of the side of the cloth, can be

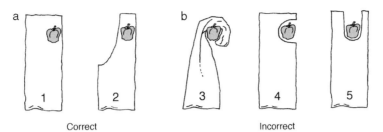

Correct   Incorrect

Figure 10.4 The individual correct and incorrect options used in experiment 22. The correct options (1–2) instantiate equal degrees of physical connection between the apple and the support, but at a perceptual level option 2 appears less engulfed in the support. The incorrect options contain two cases (3 and 5) where the cloth is either in contact, or will make contact once pulled, and one case where the apple is deep in the perceptual field of the cloth, but pulling the cloth straight ahead will not generate contact.

thought of as a case of *imminent contact*. Finally, option 5 can be thought of as a case of *no contact*, but because the apple sits well within the optical field of the cloth, can be thought of as a case of perceptual containment. Note that the apple could not be moved by pulling the cloth in any of the incorrect options.

Procedure

Each of the two correct options was separately paired with each of the three incorrect options, creating a total of six conditions (A–F: see Fig. 10.5). Each ape received four trials of each of these six conditions. The experimental procedures for testing the apes were the same as those used in the previous study (including the spacer trials in which the apes were simply required to enter the test unit and place a cloth inside a bucket). Thus, each ape received 12 sessions, each containing two spacer trials and two test trials. The trials were randomly administered to each subject within the constraints that (1) no correct or incorrect option was provided twice within a session; and (2) the incorrect

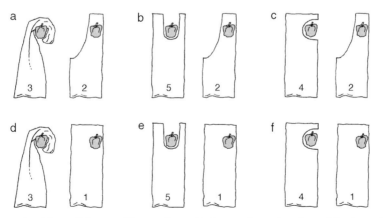

Figure 10.5 Specific conditions used in experiment 22. See text for explanations of the theoretical significance of each condition. Half of the conditions (a–c) involved pairing the new correct option (option 2) with the new incorrect options; the other half involve pairing the correct option from experiment 21 (option 1) with the new incorrect options.

options (3, 4, and 5) were administered once each before any of them was repeated. As in the previous study, the apes were allowed only one choice on each trial, which was defined as the first cloth they moved.

Predictions

Two broad models were considered. The first model was the *physical connection model*. This model was the same as in the previous study. It envisioned that the animals genuinely understood the idea of support as a form of physical connection, and thus would prefer the option which instantiated physical connection in all conditions. The second model was the *perceptual form model*. This model imagined that several factors related to the perceptual form of the cloth/reward forms were at work in controlling the animals' choices. First, it posited that the apes' experience with the correct form (option 2) from the previous study would cause them to prefer that option when it was available (conditions D–F), and that the apes ought to perform better in these conditions than in conditions A–C (which involved the new correct option). Second, and more importantly, it posited that, when the new correct option was paired with the incorrect options (conditions A–C), the apes would perform at chance levels. The reason for this prediction is that in each of the incorrect options the reward is perceptually contained within the general perceptual 'field' of the cloth. This is especially true for conditions A and C, where part of the cloth was behind the apple (thus allowing for imminent contact).

Videotape coding and data analysis

The coding procedures were the same as experiment 21. The main rater and the reliability rater exhibited excellent agreement for (1) the first cloth the subject moved ($\kappa =$ 1.00); and (2) whether the chimpanzee, if he or she made an incorrect choice, attempted to use the cloth to retrieve the reward (18/18 cases of agreement, κ is undefined).

Results and discussion

The main results of this study are presented in Table 10.2. These data display the percentage of trials in each condition on which the apes selected the correct cloth as their first choice. First, a one-way repeated measures ANOVA revealed that the apes' performances did not differ across the six conditions, $F(5,30) = 1.534$, ns. Second, individual one-sample t-tests for each condition revealed that the apes performed at chance levels in all conditions except condition E, in which the apes' performance ($M = 67.9$ per cent correct, $SD = 18.9$) was significantly above that expected by chance, $t(6) = 2.500, p < 05$. Notably, as predicted by the perceptual form model, this was one of the conditions involving the correct option with which the apes had previous experience (see experiment 21). Indeed, as predicted by this model, the apes performed better in the conditions (D–F) involving the correct option that had been used in the previous study than the conditions (A–C) involving the new correct option, 67.9 versus 53.6 per cent correct, respectively (although this difference was not statistically significant). This was an outcome predicted by the perceptual form model and no other model. In any event, the data provide no support for the physical connection model.

What about the two apes who had performed well in experiment 21? Perhaps most striking were the results for Mindy, who had made only a single error in the previous study; she performed at exactly chance levels in five of the six conditions in this study (see Table 10.2)! It seems relatively clear that, whatever the reason for her performance in experiment 21, she did not possess an understanding of support as an instance of physical connection. The other ape who had performed well in experiment 21 was Megan. An inspection of her data in Table 10.2 reveals a puzzling pattern. On the one hand, her overall performance is consistent with the predictions of the physical connection model (20/24 correct, $p < .001$, binomial test). Indeed, she performed without error in four of the six conditions. However, there were two conditions (C and E) in which she performed at exactly chance levels (50 per cent correct). The contrast between her excellent performance in conditions A, B, D, and F, and her random performance in conditions C and E, is not easily explained by any of the models—at least not in the forms that have been described thus far.

In contrast to the four apes who did so in the previous experiment, only one ape, Brandy, attempted to use the incorrect cloth in a futile attempt to retrieve the apple after making an incorrect choice. She did so on one trial in session 12.

Megan's data is of particular interest to us because her performance illustrates a difficulty common to all of our studies. Her performance may be explained in one of two ways. One possibility is that she understood the idea of support as physical connection. This would explain why she performed well in experiment 21, and why she performed well in most of the conditions in this study. It does not, on the other hand, explain why she performed randomly on her final four trials of the contact/contact condition in experiment 21, nor why she performed randomly in conditions C and E in this study. The other

Table 10.2 Percentage of apes who moved the correct cloth first in each condition, experiment 22

	Condition					
Subject	A	B	C	D	E	F
APO	50	50	50	75	75	75
KAR	50	75	75	75	75	50
CAN	25	50	75	25	50	25
JAD	50	75	50	100	100	100
BRA	0	50	0	25	75	75
MEG	100	100	50	100	50	100
MIN	50	50	50	75	50	50
Mean	46.4	64.3	50.0	67.9	67.9	67.9
SD	30.4	19.7	25.0	31.3	18.9	27.8
SEM	11.5	7.4	9.4	11.8	7.1	10.5

possibility is that Megan may have simply learned a much finer perceptual discrimination; namely, that the covariation of movement between the cloth and the apple was linked to a complete 'fusion of form' of the cloth and the apple. Unfortunately, both of these possibilities generate the same predictions in the conditions that we have used thus far. In the next experiment we uncoupled the predictions of these two general models in order to probe Megan and the other apes' understanding even further.

Experiment 23: final tests of the support problem, age $10^1/_2$–$11^1/_2$

This study continued to probe our apes' understanding of the support problem. First, we explored whether one of our apes, Megan, possessed an understanding of support as an instance of physical connection, or whether she was reasoning strictly about the visual fusion of form between the apple and the cloth. In addition, we sought to determine if the appearance of perceptual containment of the apple by the cloth was a stronger factor in governing our apes' choices than the fusion of form between the apple and cloth.

Method

Subjects and materials
The apes were between the ages of 10;5 and 11;4 on the day that this study began, which was approximately two months after the completion of experiment 22. No other studies that are reported in this book were conducted in the interim.

Several light blue, rectangular cloths were used as the supports in this study. They were cut into a number of distinct forms (see Fig. 10.6, options 1–4). Two of the cloth/reward options were 'correct' from the standpoint of the physical connection model, and two were 'incorrect'.

Procedure and Predictions
The correct and incorrect cloths were paired together to create the four possible conditions (A–D) which involved a choice between a correct and incorrect option (see Table 10.3). Each animal received each condition four times, using the same general counterbalancing and randomization procedures described for experiments 21 and 22.

There was one major difference in the procedure of the probe trials from the previous two studies. Because one of the options (see Fig. 10.6) involved the food was placed just over a gap in the cloth (a gap that could not be seen once the reward was set down), it was necessary to have the animals observe the food placement on each test trial. This was achieved by dividing each test trial into a demonstration phase and a response phase as we had done in several previous experiments (see Chapters 7 and 9). During the demonstration phase, the plexiglas screen covered the holes in the plexiglas and prevented the subject from responding as the experimenter (1) gained the subject's attention; and (2) placed the food rewards in the appropriate position on the two cloths (which were already in place as the subject entered the test unit). The experimenter was seated behind and exactly between the two options. The experimenter always placed the rewards from left to right. Once the rewards were in place, the exper-

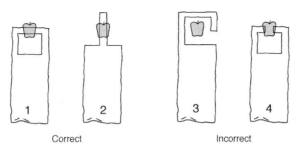

Correct   Incorrect

Figure 10.6 Individual correct and incorrect options that were used in experiment 23. See Table 10.3 for the actual conditions that were created by pairing each of the correct options with each of the incorrect options.

imenter fixed his or her gaze on a predetermined target midway between the two options. The trainer then removed the plexiglas screen (always from the right), faced away from the subject, and the animal responded by reaching through the open hole that was midway between the options (all other holes were covered). The only other differences in general procedure from experiments 21 and 22 were as follows: (1) duplicate copies of all *testing* cloths were introduced into the chimpanzees' living compound before the study began, and they were left there for the apes to explore and play with; and (2) the same cloths that were used on the test trials were also used on the spacer trials (the purpose of this was to provide the apes with even more opportunity to experience the properties of the testing cloths that they would confront on the test trials).

The ideas explored in the previous two studies were fleshed out in greater detail in order to create four models of how our animals understood the support problem, (see Table 10.3). First, the *physical connection model* was unaltered from its previous descrip-

Table 10.3 Conditions and predictions for experiment 23

Model	Conditions and predictions			
	A 1 3	**B** 1 4	**C** 2 3	**D** 2 4
Physical connection	1	1	2	2
Current contact	1	1 = 4	2	2 = 4
Current or imminent contact	1 = 3	1 = 4	2 = 3	2 = 4
Perceptual containment	3	1 = 4	3	2 = 4

tion. It predicted a pattern of responding indicative of an organism that could appreciate the idea of support as a form of physical connection. Second, the *current perceptual contact model* envisioned that the apes were basing their judgements on discrete contact/no-contact judgement at the moment of their response. Third, the *current or imminent perceptual contact model* posited that the apes would weigh current contact and imminent contact equally. Finally, the *perceptual containment model* posited that the apes would rely most heavily on perceptual evidence that the cloth was surrounding or containing the reward in making their decisions.

The particular options used in this study were designed so that four testing conditions could be created to test the models just described. As can be seen in Table 10.3, each model generated a unique pattern of predictions across the four conditions. We were especially interested in how Megan would respond to these conditions.

Videotape coding and data analysis

The coding and design were the same as in experiments 21 and 22. The main rater and the reliability rater exhibited excellent agreement for (1) the first cloth the subject moved ($\kappa = 1.00$); and (2) whether the chimpanzee, if he or she made an incorrect choice, attempted to use the cloth to retrieve the reward ($\kappa = 1.00$).

Results and discussion

The results concerning which cloth the subjects chose first are presented in Table 10.4. Because there were no learning effects either within conditions or across all trials as pre-

Table 10.4 Percentage of apes who moved the correct cloth first in each condition, experiment 23

	Condition			
	A	**B**	**C**	**D**
Subject				
APO	50	75	25	25
KAR	50	50	25	75
CAN	50	50	50	50
JAD	50	25	75	75
BRA	50	50	25	50
MEG	50	50	50	50
MIN	50	50	25	50
Mean	50.0	50.0	39.3	53.6
SD	0	14.4	19.7	17.2
SEM	0	5.5	7.4	6.5

sented (irrespective of condition), we present each animal's mean percentage correct in each condition. These data were used to assess the predictions from Table 10.3.

The most important results concern Megan, who had performed better than the other animals in experiments 21 and 22. In direct contrast to her previous results, she exhibited exactly chance-level performance in each of the four conditions used in this study. Her results fit the pattern predicted by the third model in Table 10.3, which envisioned that her choices were based on current or imminent contact.

The other animals exhibited performances similar to that of Megan (see Table 10.4), with the current or imminent contact model again providing the best prediction of the results. Two statistical analyses (using all subjects including Megan) confirmed this interpretation. First, as predicted by the current or imminent contact model, the apes did not perform better in one condition than another, $F(3, 18) = 1.00$, $p = 0.416$. Second, a series of one-sample t-tests indicated that the apes' performances did not differ from chance (50 per cent) in any of the four conditions.

Finally, after pulling the incorrect cloth the apes frequently attempted to use this cloth to retrieve the apple that, of course, remained out of reach. Averaged first across conditions within each subject, then across all subjects, they did so on 39.1 per cent of the incorrect trials ($SD = 34.6$). Individual animals ranged from doing this on 0 per cent of their trials (Kara) to 100 per cent (Candy). (Given our special interest in Megan's performance in this experiment, it is worth noting that Megan did so on 62.5 per cent of her incorrect trials.)

The results of this experiment are consistent with the idea that Megan's performance in experiment 22 was based upon some interaction of the local perceptual features of the arrangement between the cloth and the apple, not an understanding of physical connection. In addition, they also confirm this very same interpretation for the previous results of the other animals. It is important to note, however, that although the results of the current study were best predicted by the current or imminent contact model, it is possible that several of the perceptual factors are at work, competing for the animals' attention on any given trial. Below, we discuss this possibility further.

General discussion (experiments 21–23)

We believe that the studies presented in this chapter are consistent with the idea that chimpanzees solve the support problem on the basis of quite specific perceptual features related to the spatial arrangement of food and cloth. By itself this claim is fairly uncontroversial. However, our results also support the idea that these perceptual judgements do not interact with concepts related to physical connection as the animal makes a decision to select one of the two cloths. This means that, for chimpanzees, the support problem may have nothing to do with the concept of 'support'. The results of experiment 23, in particular, show that even Megan, who appeared quite sophisticated in experiments 21 and 22, was probably relying on extremely fine-scaled perceptual judgements about contact or imminent contact—not about support *per se*.

There are three general points we wish to emphasize in considering the results of these experiments. First, like any other problem, there are multiple ways of solving any variation of the support problem. Previous studies involving the support problem that have been conducted with nonhuman primates (and in some cases, human infants) have not employed the procedures that would allow them to demonstrate that the organisms were reasoning about support as an instance of physical connection (Hauser *et al.* 1999*a*; Mathieu *et al.* 1980; Piaget 1952; Spinozzi and Potí 1989, 1993). Simply demonstrating that an animal (or an infant, for that matter) can succeed on a particular variation of the task says little with respect to the question of how that solution was achieved. Furthermore, the rapid learning that can be displayed in such situations (see Fig. 10.3) reveals that it is necessary to probe what, exactly, is being learned by any given species or individual.

A second point we wish to address is the objection that we have recast the support problem in a way that it was not originally intended. In particular, some might argue that the support problem was never intended to assess whether an organism understands the physical connection between the cloth and the goal object. These theorists might argue that the problem's connection to the development of causality has to do with the organism's appreciation of the distinction between means and ends in problem solving, or an externalization of causality (see Piaget 1954). Of course, it is true that we did not directly test for our chimpanzees' appreciation of the means–ends distinction. However, a moment's reflection will show that the only way in which it makes sense to speak of Piaget's (1952) classic test as a 'support' problem is if it involves the subject reasoning about the physical connection between the object and the cloth as generated by the weight of the object resting on the cloth. Thus, what we have explored is whether chimpanzees interpret the support problem within the framework of unobservable causal phenomena. Our conclusion is that they do not.

A final point concerns the inability of the models we have outlined to capture fully the performances of our chimpanzees. Although it seems clear that the physical connection model was not useful in explaining our apes' reasoning about the support problem, a careful inspection of the data across the three experiments indicates that each of the other models may capture something about our animals' understanding of the task. From the perspective of Megan and her peers, contact, imminent contact, and perceptual containment may all be aspects of their perceptual world that have been useful predictors of covariation in movement in the past. This may lead them to see many options as equally viable. Furthermore, any given animal may be influenced by one principle more than another depending on any number of factors. Evidence for this view can be found in experiment 23 (see Table 10.4). For example, in condition C, four of the apes appeared to have a preference for the option which has the appearance of strong containment of the reward by the cloth; however, this same option did not appear to capture their responses in condition A. Why? Perhaps because of the different appearance of the options that it was being contrasted against in each case. In short, multiple and idiosyncratic concepts may be at work in controlling our apes' responses of such problems. Physical connection, however, does not appear to be one of them.

CHAPTER 11

THE QUESTION OF TOOL MODIFICATION

DANIEL J. POVINELLI, JAMES E. REAUX, LAURA A. THEALL, AND STEVE GIAMBRONE

One aspect of chimpanzee tool use that we have not yet experimentally considered concerns the ability to modify readily available raw materials in ways that transform them into effective tools. Again, the prototypical case involves termite fishing. Here, the chimpanzee may select a material to use as a fishing probe, and may alter the material in ways that tailor it to the causal structure of a particular problem, such as inserting a probe into a narrow opening in the termite mound and guiding it down a passageway. Goodall (1986) describes some of the types of modifications that occur:

> Some material, such as thin grass (green or dry) or a smooth stem or vine, is suitable for use as is. Other material must be modified before it can be used efficiently. Leaves must be stripped from small twigs, leaflets from a main leaf rib, and slender fibrous lengths from bark, thick stems, or frondlets of palm. Sometimes grass must be thinned down, and the chimpanzee removes blades from each side of the midrib. (p. 538.)

Other modifications include shortening or splitting inadequately-sized materials (McGrew 1992). It has even been reported that in some regions chimpanzees fray the ends of the probes by either chewing or pounding, possibly in order to provide a better gripping surface for the termites' mandibles (although it should be noted that this has not been confirmed through direct observation: see Sugiyama 1997). Another case of chimpanzees' modification of raw material in order to create tools involves their chewing of leaves to make simple sponges to dip into water that collects in basin-shaped holes in large trees (Goodall 1986; McGrew 1992; Sugiyama 1997).

Clearly, then, chimpanzees sometimes modify raw materials in ways that improve their suitability for the problem at hand. Thus, a chimpanzee selects a short twig, which possesses numerous leaves and smaller twigs protruding at right angles to the main axis. In this form, the would-be tool will not easily pass into the small opening (or, in many cases, will not fit at all). Thus, regardless of the chimpanzee's appreciation of why he or she is acting on the material, the modification itself serves to overcome a specific physical problem imposed by the physical structure of the elements involved.

As usual, of course, we are not interested in whether chimpanzees solve such problems, but rather in what they understand about the underlying causal structure of the problem. In the case of termite fishing, for example, we are interested in determining whether the chimpanzee's modifications are mediated by an explicit understanding of the connection between a given property of the material (its breakability, tearability, prunability, etc.) and the material's interaction with other physical aspects of the task (e.g. its ability to fit into a small hole), or whether such activities are governed by procedural routines or scripts. Thus, as an alternative to postulating that the chimpanzee explicitly conceives of the fact that the tool must be pruned in order to pass through the hole, it is possible that a young chimpanzee, from four or five years of observing her mother and other adults termite fishing, and from the direct feedback she has obtained through her own efforts, learns solely that, if such protrusions are present, they must be removed. Now, as we have seen in Chapter 2, using the behavior of wild chimpanzees to determine which of these alternatives best describes the true state of the chimpanzee's understanding will prove to be largely unsatisfactory—primarily because nature does not neatly carve apart the two critical issues: (1) conceptual knowledge of the causal structure of the problem in relation to the specific properties of the tools; versus (2) procedural or script-based knowledge of how to successfully solve the task.

In this chapter, we report the results of several experiments that we conducted to address these issues. The general logic of these investigations was as follows. First, we exposed our apes to specific properties of certain physical materials in non-tool-using contexts. Having exposed them to these properties, we then offered these materials in the context of two now-familiar tool-using problems (the tool-insertion problem and the hook-retrieval problem: see Chapters 8 and 9). Next, we created situations in which these properties offered the apes the opportunity to modify the material from an ineffective state to an effective state. In this way, we sought to distinguish between our apes' ability to construct detailed procedural knowledge related to the modification of materials for tool use, and their ability to understand why a given modification is necessary for a given causal structure.

Experiment 24: the bendable-tool problem, age 9^1/$_2$–10 years

In our first study, we allowed our apes to spontaneously explore the properties of individual pieces of bendable piping in play, for several days. To begin with, we documented their discovery and exploration of the relevant property of this material—namely, that it could be bent into different forms, and that it would maintain those shapes until bent again. Next, we offered them pieces of this material in the context of the tool-insertion problem to determine if they would transform the piping from an ineffective form to an effective one.

Method

Subjects and apparatus

Our seven chimpanzees were between the ages of 9;2 and 10;0 at the beginning of this study, which they began the day after completing experiment 16 (see Chapter 9). Four of the animals (Kara, Apollo, Candy, and Brandy) were still participating in experiment

2 (see Chapter 4) when this study began. We tested the apes using the tool-insertion apparatus described in Chapter 8 (experiments 11–13), although a different tool was presented. In this study, we used a 70 cm length (2 cm diameter) of a pliant, plastic-coated metal tubing as a potential tool. The nature of this tubing material was such that it could easily be bent into virtually any shape, and would retain that shape until it was deliberately bent again. Seven identical pieces were placed into the animals' enclosure in order to familiarize the apes with the unique properties of the material (see below). An additional piece was used in testing.

Procedure

ORIENTATION TO THE RAW MATERIAL. Five days prior to the beginning of the testing sessions, seven pieces of the tubing were placed inside the subjects' enclosure and the animals were allowed to freely interact with them. Thus, the apes were able to discover the pliant nature of the material. In addition, on days 1, 3, and 5 of this orientation phase, the apes were systematically observed for 45 minutes. During each observation session, an experimenter sat in front of their enclosure with an identical piece of the tubing and demonstrated its pliant nature. In addition, two observers scanned the subjects and documented up to five instances of each subject bending the tools, which all of the apes did. (This sampling procedure was not designed to provide detailed data on the form, frequency, or duration of our apes' modifications of the piping, but rather was to provide a general check that all apes had first-hand experience with modifying the material.) The pieces of piping were left in the enclosure 24 hours a day throughout the study.

RETENTION PHASE. Because the subjects had participated in other experiments since their last exposure to the tool-insertion problem, and because we were using a different material as the tool, we conducted a single two-trial session to ensure that the subjects understood that the new tool (in its straight form) could be used to dislodge the apple. The subjects entered the test unit with the tool-insertion apparatus positioned as in experiments 11–13. The tool was the piece of the pliant tubing. It was configured into a straight form and placed on the floor in front of the apparatus in the same manner as in experiments 11–13. On each of the two trials, the apes were required to enter the test unit, pick up the tool, and use it to dislodge the apple (within one minute of entering the test unit). They were required to perform correctly on both trials in order to advance to testing, which all of them did.

TESTING PHASE. We tested each chimpanzee across four sessions to determine if, after entering the test unit and discovering the tool bent into a simple shape that could not be inserted into the apparatus, he or she would modify its shape so that it could be effective. Each test session consisted of a single test trial, with the exception that two randomly predetermined sessions contained a standard trial which was administered after the test trial. As usual, this trial was included to both monitor and maintain motivation.

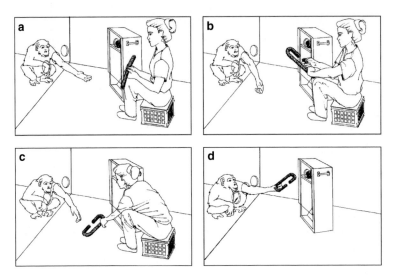

Figure 11.1 Experiment 24. Example of testing procedure for the bendable-tool experiment. (a)–(b) Chimpanzee enters test unit and experimenter demonstrates bendable property of tool by fashioning it into a C-shape. (c) Chimpanzee retrieves tool after experimenter slides it to within reach. (d) Experimenter backs away and chimpanzee attempts to dislodge the apple.

The test trials proceeded as follows. The trainer opened the shuttle door and the subject entered the test unit. Once the animal was inside, the door was closed behind them, designating the start of the trial. The baited apparatus was located in its standard position. An experimenter sat next to the apparatus (100 cm from the plexiglas), holding the tool in its straight configuration. As soon as the shuttle door closed, the experimenter held up the tool toward the subject and proceeded to bend it into one of two predetermined shapes (an S-shape or a C-shape). The experimenter manipulated the tool for exactly 30 seconds in all cases. At the 30-second mark, the experimenter set the tool on the floor, pushed it to within reach of the subject, and then pushed him- or herself away from the test unit (to a distance of 150 cm). The subject was allowed to freely interact with the tool and the apparatus for $2^{1}/_{2}$ minutes, or until they retrieved the apple, whichever occurred first. Because there was only one choice available, the experimenter was allowed (from their seated position) to gesture to the tool (by pointing) and verbally encourage the subject if he or she discontinued attempts to obtain the apple. Figure 11.1(a)–(d) depicts this process for a trial on which the experimenter bent the tool into a C-shape.

Each subject received two trials in which the tool was presented in the S-shape and two in which it was presented in the C-shape. We achieved this by alternating which shape they were given across consecutive sessions. Four of the subjects began with the S-shape, and the others began with the C-shape. If the subject intentionally or accidentally pushed the tool out of his or her reach during the $2^{1}/_{2}$-minute period, the experimenter slid it back to within reach (up to two times, after which the trial was ended).

Videotape coding and data analysis

A main rater was administered a set of standardized, written instructions which asked her to code each test trial for the information described below. A reliability rater was randomly assigned 25 per cent of the test trials (with an equal number randomly selected from each subject) and was asked to code them independently using the same instructional set. First, the raters were asked to record the cumulative duration of time that the ape spent grasping and manipulating the tool in any manner (out of the 2 1/2 minutes that the ape had access to the tool; Pearson's $r^2 = .999$ for the overlapping data sets of the two raters). Second, the raters were asked to record any attempts to manually unbend the tool by either (1) using the hands, feet, and/or mouth ($\kappa = 1.00$) or (2) hooking the lip of the plexiglas on the front of the apparatus and pulling ($\kappa = 1.00$). In all cases where the subjects attempted to unbend the tool, the raters were then asked to record which end of the tool the subject next attempted to use to contact the apparatus ($\kappa = 1.00$). Finally, the raters were asked to record whether the subject succeeded in dislodging the apple (the raters agreed on 16/16 cases, but because all cases were confined to one cell, κ is undefined).

Results and discussion

Only two apes, Kara and Jadine, displayed any attempts to modify the tool on the test trials, and each did so only once. When confronted with the tool in the C-shape on her first trial, Kara initially attempted to use the tool as it was presented. Following this, as she was in the process of sniffing the tool, she modified one end of the tool by partially straightening it out. However, Kara's modification of the tool seemed unrelated to her understanding of the problem at hand, reflected most obviously in the fact that she immediately attempted to dislodge the apple using the end of the tool that was still unmodified (and hence could not fit through the hole and dislodge the apple). She was not successful on this (or any other probe trial). Jadine's tool modification occurred on her fourth test trial when the tool was presented in the S-shape. Like Kara, she began with several attempts to dislodge the apple using the tool in its unmodified shape. She then hooked the tool under the bottom lip of the plexiglas front, and pulled the tool back toward her. This resulted in modifying the tool somewhat, and she repeated the general action several times. However, she did not successfully straighten out the tool and did not successfully retrieve the apple. No other apes exhibited any attempts to modify the tool from the shape in which it was presented.

One important question concerning the above results is whether the apes were motivated and interested in the problem at hand. There appeared to be ample evidence that, at least initially, they were. First, with respect to their general motivation during the experiment, it is important to note that the apes were immediately successful on every trial in which the tool was presented in its straight form. Thus, they appeared to be constantly motivated to obtain the rewards. However, what about on the test trials themselves? Did the unusual shapes of the tools discourage the apes from interacting with them? As reflected in the amount of time they spent manipulating the tools, this does

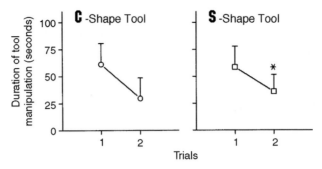

Figure 11.2 Mean cumulative duration that the apes spent manipulating the tool in the C- and S-shapes on each test trial in experiment 24.

not appear to have been the case. Figure 11.2 displays the mean cumulative duration per trial that the apes spent manipulating the tool that was presented to them on the test trials. As can be seen, on their initial trial in both conditions, the apes spent roughly one minute manipulating the tool. This typically took the form of the apes entering the test unit, grasping the tool, attempting to use it to dislodge the apple, followed by reorienting the tool repeatedly in their hands. However, presumably because they were unsuccessful at obtaining the reward, the apes' interest generally declined toward the end of the trials. Indeed, a comparable decline in time spent manipulating the tool can be seen across the two trials of each condition in Fig. 11.2. For the condition in which the tool was presented in the S-shape, this decline was statistically significant, $t(6) = 2.773$, $p = 0.032$.

This study provided little or no evidence that our apes appreciated that the bendable property of the tool was relevant to the solution of the task at hand. However, it occurred to us that several aspects of the procedure might have limited the apes' performances. For example, although having the experimenter bend the tool into a particular shape while the animals watched was intended to remind them of the relevant property of the tool (its pliability), it may have been the case that, for some reason or another, the apes assumed that because the experimenter bent it into a particular configuration, this was the way in which the tool needed to be used. Furthermore, it occurred to us that if we used the opposite procedure (that is, demonstrating how the tool could be bent from the incorrect shape into the correct shape), this might assist them on later trials in which the tool could be presented in the ineffective shape. In the next study, we explored this latter possibility in an explicit effort to scaffold their responses.

Experiment 25: demonstrating the solution to the bendable-tool problem, age 9¹/₂–10

Because the apes displayed no evidence of understanding the necessity of unbending the tool in order to dislodge the apple, we sought to scaffold their responses by explicitly demonstrating how the tool could be modified from an ineffective state to an effective state. After doing so, we then handed them the newly modified (and now effective) tool and allowed them to use it to obtain the apple. After two such demonstrations, we then offered them the opportunity to modify the tool in order to solve the task. In this way, we hoped to remind the animal of the tool's important property, but in a way that was consistent with the needed transformation (that is, from an ineffective state to an effective state).

Method

Subjects and apparatus

All seven animals participated in this study, which began the day after they completed experiment 24. The tools, testing apparatus, and experimenter position were the same as in experiment 24.

Procedure

The seven pieces of the pliant tubing that had been placed in the subjects' enclosure during experiment 24 remained there throughout this study. Thus, the subjects were able to continue to interact freely with these materials throughout the day while they were not being tested. In this experiment, each subject received four test sessions (no training or orientation sessions were administered). Each test session consisted of three trials. These trials were structured so that they proceeded from easy to difficult.

On trial 1, as the subject entered the test unit the tool was already bent into a C-shape and was sitting on the floor out of reach, and just in front of the experimenter. As soon as the shuttle door was closed behind the subject, the experimenter picked up the tool, showed it to the subject, and proceeded to straighten out both ends of the tool so that it was in the form of a straight tool. The experimenter verbally encouraged the subject to watch as he or she unbent the tool (a process that was choreographed to last exactly 15 seconds). After the tool was straightened, the experimenter placed the tool on the floor in front of the apparatus and within reach of the subject. The chimpanzees were then allowed 2 minutes and 45 seconds to use the tool to dislodge the apple from the apparatus.

On trial 2, the tool was again lying on the floor in front the experimenter in the C-shape as the subject entered. As soon as the shuttle door closed, the experimenter picked up the tool, showed it to the subject, and proceeded to straighten out one end of the tool, so that the straight end could fit through the hole and dislodge the apple, whereas the unmodified end could not. Again, the experimenter manipulated the tool for exactly 15 seconds, during which time he or she attempted to maintain the chimpanzee's attention. The experimenter then placed the tool in front of the apparatus in one of two predetermined horizontal orientations (in one case the hook portion was on the right, in the other case it was on the left). For each subject, the horizontal placement was alternated across sessions; within each session, three of the subjects received one orientation, whereas the remaining four received the other. Once the tool was placed on the floor in front of the apparatus, the subjects were again allowed 2 minutes and 45 seconds to respond.

Finally, on trial 3, the subject entered the test unit and discovered the tool, in the C-shape, on the floor within reach and directly in front of the apparatus. Of course, in this case, the tool was ineffectual unless the subjects unbent it in a manner comparable to what had been demonstrated on trials 1 and 2. The subjects were given 2 minutes and 45 seconds to attempt to retrieve the apple.

Videotape coding and data analysis

The trials were coded in a similar manner as in experiment 24. After reading a standardized set of written instructions, a main rater coded every probe trial and a secondary rater coded 50 per cent of the trials (two trials per animal). For trials 1 and 2, the raters were asked to measure the latency to success, beginning from the moment the tool was pushed to within their reach and ending when the apple fell from the apparatus (Pearson's $r^2 = 0.998$).

For trial 2, the raters were asked to record: (1) whether the subject first oriented the hook or the straight end of the tool toward the apparatus ($\kappa = 0.84$); (2) any attempts (as in experiment 24) to unbend the tool (14/14 cases of agreement, κ undefined); and (3) whether the subject was successful ($\kappa = 1.00$).

For trial 3, the raters were asked to measure and record, among other things: (1) the cumulative duration of time spent grasping the tool (Pearson's $r^2 = 0.999$); (2) attempts to unbend the tool (as above; $\kappa = 1.00$) and, if there were such attempts, which tool end was first oriented to the apparatus ($\kappa = 1.00$); and finally, (3) whether the subjects ultimately succeeded on that trial ($\kappa = 1.00$).

Results and discussion

Success on the task

As can be seen in Fig. 11.3(a), on trial 1 the apes easily solved the problem when the tool was unbent for them and then presented in its straight form. Likewise, on trial 2 they continued to succeed at relatively high levels when half of the tool was straightened out for them. However, on trial 3, when the tool was presented in its C-shape, the apes' success rate plummeted to almost zero. Was this because the apes became less interested across trials? The latency and duration data revealed that this was not the case. The apes took an average of 5.31 seconds ($SD = 1.90$) to dislodge the apple on trial 1, but on trial 2 their average latency to success increased to 42.49 seconds ($SD = 43.79$). However, even on trial 3, where the apes were almost never successful, they nonetheless averaged 71.93 seconds ($SD = 52.74$) per trial in time spent manipulating the tool as they attempted to solve the problem.

Evidence of tool modification

The central predictions of this study concerned whether the demonstrations we presented across the three trials in each session would assist the apes in realizing that the

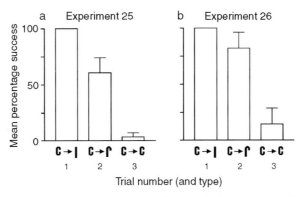

Figure 11.3 Success rate across the three trial types (reflecting the demonstrations shown to the ape before handing them a tool), in (a) experiment 25 and (b) experiment 26. The horizontal legend shows the shape that the tool possessed when it was first shown to the ape, and how it was modified (represented by the arrow) in the demonstration. When it was pushed to within the ape's reach it was in the final shape shown.

tool needed to be unbent. Thus, our main interest was not the apes' overall success rates. Rather, we were concerned with whether the apes would modify the tool's shape when necessary.

TOOL MODIFICATIONS ON TRIAL 2. Recall that, on trial 2 of each session, the tool was presented in the hook form (after the experimenter unbent one end). Across all of the relevant 28 trials of this type, there was not a single instance in which an ape unbent the tool using his or her hands, feet, and/or mouth. There were, however, two cases in which the apes did unbend the tool to some degree by hooking it under the plexiglas lip of the apparatus (Candy on trial 1 and Brandy on trial 2). Both of these cases involved pulling the tool against the plexiglas hole, which resulted in slightly unbending the tool. In both cases, the apes' first orientation after this modification was to orient the hook end of the tool toward the apparatus. Neither case led to successful retrieval of the reward.

The fact that the apes almost never unbent the tool on trial 2 raises the question of whether they immediately apprehended that one end was already effective. Two facts provide evidence against this view. First, the apes' success rate dropped from 100 per cent on trial 1 to 60.7 per cent on trial 2. Second, averaged across apes, the animals actually preferred (68.9 per cent of the time) to orient the tool *incorrectly* (chance = 50 per cent; one-sample t-test: $t(6) = 2.500$, $p < 0.05$). This means that the apes preferred to grasp the tool by the straight end, thus directing the hook end toward the apparatus (an outcome reminiscent of the results from experiment 11–13).

TOOL MODIFICATION ON TRIAL 3. Of the 28 cases of trial 3, there were only two instances in which an ape modified the tool by using the hands, and there were three cases in which an ape modified the tool by hooking it under the lip of the plexiglas or the edge of the apparatus. Three of the apes (Kara, Candy, and Jadine) accounted for all five of these instances of tool modification. However, as we now describe, there was little evidence that these modifications were related to their appreciation of the causal structure of the problem:

> Kara modified the C-shaped tool in sessions 3 and 4 by using her hands. In session 3, she first directed the end she had modified toward the apparatus, but because the modification was limited, she was not successful. In session 4, she first directed the end that she had not modified (the impossible end). She was unsuccessful on this trial as well.

> Candy modified the C-shaped tool in session 4. She hooked one end under the plexiglas front of the apparatus and pulled back. Although she first directed the modified end toward the apparatus, she was not successful in obtaining the reward.

> Jadine modified the C-shaped tool in sessions 1 and 2. In both cases, she hooked the tool on or under the plexiglas. Trial 3 of session 1 ended before she directed either end toward the apparatus. On trial 3 of session 2, she first directed the unmodified (impossible end) toward the apparatus.

Thus, the apes' behavior on the crucial third trials of their test sessions provided little evidence that they understood that one or both ends of the tool needed to be modified in order to allow the tool to pass through the hole in the apparatus. Indeed, in two of the five cases in which the apes did alter the shape of the tool, they appeared to be doing so to get a better grasping surface on the tool (Kara, trial 3 of session 4; Jadine, trial 3 of session 2).

In summary, the results of this experiment did not support the idea that demonstrating the correct behavior for the apes would improve their ability to understand the significance of modifying the tool's shape for dealing with the causal structure of the problem.

Experiment 26: further scaffolding on the bendable-tool problem, age 9$\frac{1}{2}$–10

The general purpose of this study was to determine if additional, explicit training on the pliable nature of the tool, in the context of the test unit itself, might assist the apes in understanding that the tool should be modified when confronted with the tool-insertion problem. Although we had ample evidence that the apes were bending and unbending the pieces of this material that we had kept in their enclosure, we sought to draw out this behavior in the context of the test unit itself, and 'remind' them of this property just seconds before testing them.

Method

Subjects and apparatus

All seven animals participated in this study, which began approximately three weeks after the completion of experiment 25. The tools, testing apparatus, and experimenter positions were the same as in experiments 24 and 25. In addition, a special box with two holes was constructed in order to facilitate training the subjects to bend the tool in the context of the test unit (see below).

Procedure

TEACHING THE APES TO BEND THE TOOL. Initially, an open-ended training protocol was established in which the trainer was allowed to work with each subject individually or in pairs to teach them how to bend and unbend the pliant material while they were inside the test unit. The tool-insertion apparatus was not present during this training. The trainer used a number of different methods to teach the apes, including repeated demonstrations, and placing the tool in their hands and molding their behavior. In the end, the most effective procedure was a slightly more structured task involving a small box with two holes (approximately 25 cm apart) cut into the surface. The trainer showed the apes how to bend the tool in a U-shape and place one end in each hole. Upon performing this action successfully, the trainer verbally praised the apes and gave them food rewards as he deemed appropriate. The apes were required to demonstrate a proficiency at performing this task before they were allowed to advance in the study. A video record was archived of each subject's maximal proficiency at the task.

RE-TESTING THE APES ON THE BENDABLE-TOOL PROBLEM. Each ape was then tested across four sessions, with each session structured exactly as in experiment 25. Thus, each session contained three trials, each of increasing difficulty (see experiment 25, Method, for a detailed explanation of each trial). The specific shapes used in each session were alternated across sessions so that each ape received two trials involving the S-shape and two involving the C-shape. Three of the apes began with the S-shape and four began with the C-shape.

Videotape coding and data analysis

The trials were coded in the same manner as experiment 25. A main rater coded every test trial and a secondary rater coded 50 per cent of the trials (two randomly-selected test trials per animal). For trials 1 and 2, the raters were asked to measure the latency to success, beginning from the moment the tool was pushed to within their reach and ending when the apple fell from the apparatus (Pearson's $r^2 = 0.98$ for trial 1 and 1.00 for trial 2). For trial 2, the raters coded (1) whether the subject first oriented the hook or the straight end of the tool toward the apparatus ($\kappa = 1.00$); (2) any attempts to unbend the tool ($\kappa = 1.00$); and (3) whether the subject was successful ($\kappa = 1.00$). Finally, for trial 3, the raters coded: (1) the cumulative duration of time spent grasping the tool (Pearson's $r^2 = 0.999$); (2) attempts to unbend the tool (as above; $\kappa = 1.00$) and, if there were such attempts, which end was first oriented to the apparatus ($\kappa = 0.72$, 6/7 agreements); and finally, (3) whether the subjects ultimately succeeded on that trial ($\kappa = 1.00$).

Results and discussion

Success on the task

Figure 11.3(b) shows the apes' average percentage correct as a function of trial (averaged across apes across sessions). As in the previous experiment, on trial 1 (when the tool was presented in its straight form) the apes solved the problem on every trial. Likewise, on trial 2 (when the tool was presented in the hook shape) most of the apes were successful in dislodging the apple by the end of the trial (see Fig. 11.3(b)). In fact, five of the subjects succeeded on every trial, and one succeeded on three-quarters of the trials. Only Kara continued to have difficulty on trial 2. However, it should be noted that, if we focus on their first attempt on trial 2, the apes oriented the tool correctly only 35.7 per cent of the time! Thus, although they were able to figure out how to dislodge the apple within the duration of the trial, as in the previous study (as well as experiments 11–13), they did not appear to grasp ahead of time that only the straight end would pass through the hole. On trial 3, however, when the tool was presented in the C-shape, the apes' mean success rate plummeted to 14.3 per cent. In fact, only a single animal—Jadine—ever succeeded on trial 3. We discuss her performance separately below.

As in the previous study, we examined the apes' latency to success and duration of tool manipulation to assess whether the apes' declining performance across trials 1–3 was due to declining motivation. On trial 1, when the tool was presented in the straight shape, the apes took an average of only 4.65 seconds ($SD = 1.27$) to dislodge the apple. On trial 2, however, their average latency to success increased considerably to 27.71 seconds ($SD = 31.15$), which can be expected from the fact (reported above) that their initial orientation of the tool was correct only 36 per cent of the time on this trial. On trial 3, where no apes, other than Jadine, were ever successful, they nonetheless spent an average of 54.86 seconds ($SD = 34.97$) per trial manipulating the tool in their efforts to solve the problem.

Evidence of tool modification

Recall that the central aim of this study was to determine if the experience of bending the tools just prior to needing to use them would bootstrap our apes' performance. Thus, as in the previous two experiments, our main concern was not about the apes' overall success rates, but rather whether they would modify the tool's shape by unbending it on trial 3 (and, to a lesser extent, on trial 2).

TOOL MODIFICATIONS ON TRIAL 2. On the second trial of each session, the tool was presented in the hook form (one end unbent). Across these 28 trials, there were no cases in which the apes unbent the tool using their hands, feet, and/or mouths. There was a single instance in which an ape did slightly unbend the tool. This case involved Kara (in session 1) pulling the tool against the plexiglas hole, which resulted in a small unbending of the tool. However, her first orientation after achieving this modification was to orient the hook end of the tool toward the apparatus. She was not successful on this trial.

One possible explanation for why the apes so rarely unbent the tool on trial 2 (when the tool was presented in its hook shape), was because they understood that one end was already effective. However, the fact that the apes did not initially prefer to use the straight (correct) end of the tool (they did so only 35.7 per cent of the time), strongly suggests that this was not the case. Rather, the absence of tool modification on trial 2 is probably the result of the fact that the apes continued to reorient the tool until they finally hit upon the correct solution.

Of course, the most crucial data are from trial 3, because here the apes could not succeed unless they modified the tool. First, and most striking, Jadine modified the tool appropriately (with her hands) on trial 3 in every session, and succeeded in retrieving the apple. In sessions 1 and 3, after she partially unbent the tool, her first attempt was to (correctly) use the end that she had straightened out. In session 2, her first attempt following the modification was with the (incorrect) end that was still curved. In session 4, her first attempt followed a modification of both ends of the tool.

If we examine the performance of the remaining animals, there were three trials (out of a possible 21) in which the animals modified the tool's shape at all, involving three of the animals (Kara, Candy, and Brandy). However, none of these instances appeared to be related to an appreciation of the causal structure of the problem. Candy and Brandy appeared to incidentally (and modestly) modify the tool's shape as they poked at the apparatus. Kara modified one end of the tool with her hands in session 1, but then used that end as a handle and oriented the still-curved (ineffective) end toward the apparatus.

Thus, with the very notable exception of Jadine, the evidence from the most important test trial (trial 3) suggests that the apes did not understand that one or both ends of the tool needed to be modified in order to allow the tool to pass through the hole in the apparatus.

In a minor study that immediately followed this one, we administered four additional sessions to all of the apes (except Jadine) using essentially the same procedures as the ones described above, but with one main alteration. On the crucial test trial, the apes entered the test unit and discovered the tool in its straight form lying on the box that had been used in teaching the apes to bend the tool while they were inside the test unit. The apes were required to pick up the tool and bend it into the inverted U-shape so that it would fit in the holes on the crate. Once they did so, the experimenter picked it up, and placed it on the floor in front of them (slightly closing the U-shape into a C-shape as he did so). The apes were then free to respond. Despite this strong 'reminder', only a single ape (Kara) modified the shape of the tool. However, although she did so on two of her four trials, in both cases she used the end that she had straightened as a handle and then unsuccessfully attempted to use the unmodified end to dislodge the apple.

In summary, only one of the seven apes (Jadine) was successful in learning to modify the shape of the tool in order to solve the problem at hand. Although Jadine's performance was solitary, it was nonetheless impressive. Indeed, her solution of using her hands to modify the tool's shape appeared quite suddenly in the context of the crucial third trials of the testing sessions of this experiment. Although she had exhibited some limited instances of tool modification in experiments 22 and 23, these were restricted to cases where the tool's shape was only slightly altered as she poked at the apparatus. Thus, it seems reasonable to suppose the elaborate scaffolding we used in this final study (experiment 25) may have assisted Jadine in appreciating the need to modify the tool. We discuss her performance further at the end of this chapter.

Experiment 27: the tool-construction problem, age 9¹/₂–10¹/₂

With the exception of Jadine, none of our apes learned to modify the bendable tool in experiments 24–26 in a manner appropriate to the task at hand—despite our extensive modeling procedures. In the present study, we attempted to simplify the problem of tool modification by teaching our apes how to assemble and disassemble a novel tool into two distinct forms. We worked with each ape individually until they were competent at both putting a novel tool together when it was in its unassembled state, and taking it apart when it was in its assembled state. The logic behind this study was that this tool needed to be in the assembled state in order to be effective at solving one familiar problem (the hook-retrieval task) and in the disassembled state for a different familiar problem (the tool-insertion task). The question, of course, was whether the apes, having just been trained how to assemble and disassemble the tool, would appreciate which modification was appropriate for each task.

Method

Subjects and apparatus

All seven animals participated in this study, which began two weeks after the completion of experiment 26. In order to counterbalance aspects of the experimental design (described below), the subjects were randomly divided into two groups (group 1 = Apollo, Candy, Jadine, and Mindy; group 2 = Kara, Megan, and Brandy). In this study, we used two tasks with which our apes were now intimately familiar: the hook-retrieval problem, involving hooking posts and rings (originally introduced in experiment 15), and the tool-insertion problem (originally introduced in experiment 11). The hook tool and the straight tool were used in connection with these apparatuses in the retention phase of the study and the standard trials in the testing phase (see below).

The crucial aspect of this study concerned the novel tool depicted in Fig. 11.4. It was composed of a main shaft which was 53 cm in length and 3/4 inch in diameter. Each end contained a hole into which the two shorter crosspieces (originally 25 cm and later shortened to 13 cm) could be inserted. The crosspieces were slightly tapered so that they could be inserted relatively easily, but would fit snugly once they were pushed to the center.

Procedure

TEACHING THE APES HOW TO ASSEMBLE AND DISASSEMBLE THE TOOL. The apes were initially familiarized with the properties of the tool in a series of informal sessions. During these sessions their trainer was allowed to use whatever training and demonstration methods he deemed most effective in order to teach each ape how to assemble the tool by inserting both crosspieces into the main shaft. The trainer worked with the animals until each ape could assemble the tool without the trainer's assistance. Next, a similar scaffolding procedure was used to teach them how to disassemble the tool, again culminating in their ability to disassemble the tool without the trainer's assistance. Once the trainer, study director, and principal investigator agreed that each ape knew how to assemble and disassemble the tool, a series of criterion sessions were implemented to formally assess each animal's ability.

Each criterion session was composed of four trials, two in which the tool was presented in its assembled form, and two in which the tool was presented in its disassembled form. The order of these trials was randomized for each animal within each session. While the subject waited outside, the tool was placed on the floor in front of the plexiglas panel in its pre-assigned form (either assembled or disassembled). The shuttle door opened, allowing the ape to enter, and then was closed behind the animal once he or she entered. The closing of the shuttle door behind the ape signaled the start of a two-minute period during which the ape was allowed to perform whatever actions he or she desired. As soon as the ape either inserted or removed one crosspiece from the tool, they were praised and offered a food reward. However, the apes were allowed to continue to manipulate the tool for as long as they desired during the two-minute period. If the subjects displayed the appropriate behavior of assembling or disassembling the tool on 7/8

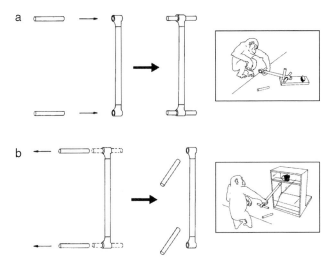

Figure 11.4 The modifiable tool used in experiment 27. (a) In its assembled form, it can be easily used as a hook, and is thus suitable to retrieve the platform apparatus. (b) In its disassembled form, such retrieval is extremely difficult. In contrast, with respect the tool-insertion problem, the tool is only suitable in its disassembled form; in its assembled form it cannot be used to dislodge the apple. The inserts show a chimpanzee having modified the tool to match the problem type *and* orienting the tool correctly. .

consecutive trials, they met the criterion to advance to the next phase of the study.[1] It is important to note, however, that, because we were simply interested in whether they knew how to assemble and disassemble the parts of the tool, we allowed the apes to perform any operation on the tools they wished during the two-minute period of each trial. Thus, they could both assemble and disassemble the same crosspiece in the same session and still be 'successful' on that trial.

RETENTION PHASE. To check that all subjects understood the basic tasks involved (the hook-retrieval problem and the tool-insertion problem), each subject was initially administered four sessions alternating between the tool-insertion problem and the hook-retrieval problem (which involved hooking the wooden post). Each session contained two trials of the relevant task. (The exact positions of the tools and apparatuses in each task were standardized and comparable to those used in previous studies, with appropriate modifications for distances from the plexiglas given the individual reaching lengths of the apes. A precise description of the configurations is provided in the protocol and is available from the authors.) Four of the apes began with the tool-insertion problem and three began with the hook-retrieval problem. The criterion for advancing to testing was that they be correct on both trials of each problem type in the final two sessions. Those apes that did not meet this criterion (Apollo, Brandy, and Mindy) were administered an additional session of the problem with which they had been unsuccessful. All three apes were correct on both of these trials and advanced to testing.

TESTING. The central questions we addressed in testing were: (1) whether the apes, when confronted with the hook-retrieval problem and the *disassembled* tool, would understand the utility of inserting a crosspiece into the straight tool in order to fashion a simple hook to secure the post; and (2) whether the apes, when confronted with the tool-insertion problem and the *assembled* tool, would understand the necessity of removing one of the crosspieces. Table 11.1 presents the general scheme we used to assess this understanding. The apes were each presented with two trials of each of the trial types represented by the four cells depicted in Table 11.1. The significance of this design is that for each task, there were two trials in which the tool was perfectly effective in the manner in which it was presented (in the case of the hook-retrieval problem, when the tool was assembled; in the case of the tool-insertion problem, when the tool was disassembled), and two trials in which it was not, and a modification was required. Thus, this design allowed us to assess whether the modifications of the tool that the apes

---

1   After meeting this criterion, the crosspieces were shortened from 25 cm to 13 cm, and all apes received one additional session, consisting of two trials in which the tool was assembled and two in which it was disassembled (administered in a random order). All apes displayed the appropriate behaviors on all four trials and advanced to the next phase. The crosspieces were shortened to minimize the possibility of the apes attempting to use them to dislodge the apple in the tool-insertion task.

Table 11.1 Testing design for experiment 27, the tool-construction problem

Task type	Tool form as presented	
	Assembled	**Disassembled**
Hook-retrieval	No modification required	Requires assembly
Tool-insertion	Requires disassembly	No modification required

undertook were tailored to the causal structure of the task at hand. In short, it allowed us to assess whether the apes genuinely understood that a given form of the tool was most appropriate for a given task (see Predictions, below).

The eight trials that we administered to each ape (spread across eight test sessions) were structured so that each ape received one trial of the four possible types during the first half of testing (trials 1–4) and a second trial of each type in the second half of testing (trials 5–8). This was achieved in the following fashion. First, the apes assigned to group 1 received the tool-insertion problem first, alternating thereafter between the two task types; the apes assigned to group 2 received the tasks in the opposite, alternating order. Half of the apes (selected at random) in group 1 were presented with the tool in its assembled form across the first two trials, followed by the disassembled form across the next two trials, with this process repeated for trials 5–8. The other half received the mirror image of this treatment. As above, two of the apes (selected at random) in group 2 received the tool in the assembled form followed by the disassembled form, and the other ape in this group received the opposite order. Each test session contained either the single test trial, or the test trial followed by a standard trial of the task matching the problem type faced on the preceding test trial, but with the standard tool present. Each ape received four sessions that included this second standard trial across the eight testing sessions); two involving the hook-retrieval problem and two involving the tool-insertion problem (within this constraint, the trial numbers were determined randomly). The purpose of these trials was (1) to maintain our animals' motivational levels in the event they experienced difficulty on the experimental trials and (2) to 'remind' the apes of the connection between the tool form and success with the task at hand.

Each experimental trial occurred as follows. The apparatus to be used on that trial was set in place and the animal was then allowed to enter the test unit. An experimenter (who was seated 100 cm from the plexiglas partition) held up the novel tool and proceeded to either assemble it from its parts, or disassemble it into its parts. This demonstration lasted exactly 15 seconds. At the 15-second mark, the experimenter placed either the assembled tool, or the disassembled pieces, on the floor and pushed it or them to within the subject's reach. The experimenter then backed up to a point 150 cm from the partition and allowed the ape to perform whatever actions they wished for the remaining 2 minutes of the trial.

Predictions

Our central objective in this study was to compare the apes' performances with three different models of their understanding of the problems. We describe these models below.

RANDOM TOOL MODIFICATION. If our apes' knowledge of how to assemble and disassemble the tool was not articulated to the tasks at hand, then we might expect that the apes would never modify the tool before attempting to solve the tasks, or if they did do so, they would modify them at random—without respect to either the task at hand, or the form in which the tool was initially presented. Furthermore, this model predicted that even when the apes did modify one part of the tool appropriately, they would not necessarily proceed to orient the tool correctly so that the functional end was directed toward the apparatus in question.

SYSTEMATIC TOOL MODIFICATION BASED ON ITS INITIAL FORM. A second model predicted that the apes would systematically modify the tool before attempting to solve the problem, but without consideration of the specific problem that needed to be solved. For example, when the tool was presented in the assembled form, the apes would disassemble it, and they would do so as often when they were being faced with the hook-retrieval problem as with the tool-insertion problem.

SELECTIVE TOOL MODIFICATION BASED ON THE CAUSAL STRUCTURE OF THE PROBLEM AT HAND. Finally, the apes might modify the tool only when needed (see Table 11.1). However, there were really two variations of the possibility. In one case, the apes might attempt a solution before modifying the tool, and only then, having visually perceived or directly experienced the inappropriate form of the tool, modify the tool appropriately. However, in the other case, they might modify the tool first (and only on those trials when it was necessary given the causal structure of the problem at hand), and only then attempt to use it in its modified form.

Videotape coding and data analysis

A main rater coded all 56 of the test trials ($n = 8$ trials per animal), and a reliability rater independently coded 50 per cent of the test trials ($n = 4$ trials per animal; these were randomly selected, within the constraint that the reliability rater code one trial of each problem/tool form combination). The written instructions given to the coders defined several target behaviors. Their task was to record each occurrence of these behaviors in the order in which they were performed, thus producing a sequence of behavior for each trial. For each trial, the raters coded: (1) the total amount of time the subject spent manipulating the tool (Pearson's $r^2 = 0.998$); (2) the latency to success ($r^2 = 0.999$); (3) the tool's orientation on the subject's first attempt ($\kappa = 0.79$); (4) whether the subject assembled the tool ($\kappa = 0.91$); (5) whether the subject disassembled the tool ($\kappa = 0.80$); and (6) whether the subject was successful in obtaining the reward ($\kappa = 1.00$). Only the data from the main rater was used in the analyses.

Although the data were analyzed in several ways, most of the analyses were derived from the results of several planned 2×2 (initial tool form $\times$ task type) repeated measures ANOVAs that used a 2-within and 0-between subjects design.

Results and discussion

Standard trials

The results are discussed in several steps. First, as described in the methods, in half of the sessions an easy trial followed the crucial test trial. These easy trials were of the same problem type as the animal had just faced, but with the standard tool for that particular task (as opposed to the modifiable tool; i.e. the straight stick for the tool-insertion problem, and the hook tool for the hook-retrieval task). The apes succeeded on 100 per cent of the easy tool-insertion trials, and 100 per cent of the easy hook-retrieval trials. These results show that when we provided the apes with the correct tool, they had no difficulty solving the two problems.

Test trials

OVERALL SUCCESS LEVELS. Although the main predictions of this study concerned the micro-genesis of the animals' attempts to solve the tasks, we first describe their overall success rates to provide a context for the information to follow.

The apes were highly motivated to solve the problem. Indeed, they typically worked at solving the tasks until they either arrived at a solution, or the two-minute trial duration elapsed. As might be expected, however, the apes performed better when the tool was presented in a form that was already well suited to the problem at hand. Thus, on the two trial types where tool modification was unnecessary, the apes' mean success rates in achieving the reward by the end of the trials were 100 per cent and 83 per cent (for the tool-insertion task with the tool presented in its disassembled state, and for the hook-retrieval task with the tool presented in its assembled state, respectively). In contrast, where tool modification was extremely helpful and/or necessary their success rates were only 57.1 per cent and 28.6 per cent (for the tool-insertion task with the tool presented in its assembled state, and for the hook-retrieval task with the tool presented in its disassembled state, respectively). Further evidence that it was indeed more difficult to solve the problems when the tools were presented in the incorrect form can be derived from the data concerning the amount of time the animals spent attempting to solve each problem (see Fig. 11.5). As expected, the ANOVA results revealed that there were no main effects of initial tool form or task type, but there was a significant interaction between the two, $F(1, 6) = 16.694$, $p = .0065$. This interaction was due to the significant contrasts shown in Fig. 11.5. In short, the apes spent much more time manipulating the tool (either modifying it or attempting a solution) when its initial form did not match the problem type.

In summary, these results show that the apes were interested and motivated to solve the task, and that the tasks were (as expected) much more difficult to solve when the initial tool form was not well suited to the causal structure of the problem at hand.

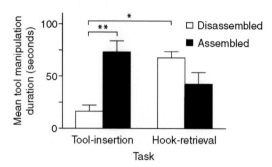

Figure 11.5 Mean duration in seconds (±*SEM*) of time spent manipulating the tool, as a function of the four conditions in experiment 27.

TOOL MODIFICATION. The most important results of this study derive from a series of comparisons (described above) which explored the interaction between the task (tool-insertion versus hook-retrieval), and the initial state in which the tool was presented (assembled versus disassembled). In particular, we focus on two key aspects of the apes' behavior: (1) the mean percentage of trials on which they modified the tool before attempting a solution; and (2) the mean percentage of trials on which their first attempt occurred with the tool oriented correctly.

Before we discuss these results, however, it is important to note that the animals generally continued to work with the tools until: (1) they arrived upon an effective tool modification; (2) they achieved the solution by some less efficient means; or (3) the trial duration expired. Because the apes continued to work throughout the trial, if one examines whether the apes engaged in tool modification *at any point* during a given trial, the apes behaved according to the predictions of the causal structure model—that is, on average a higher percentage of trials contained tool modifications when the initial tool form did *not* match the problem type than when it did (see Fig. 11.6). The ANOVA results again indicated, as expected, there was no main effect of initial tool form or task type, but there was a significant interaction between the two, $F(1, 6) = 67.50$, $p = .0002$. This interaction was due to the significant contrasts depicted in Figure 11.6. These results reveal that when the tool was initially presented to the apes in the disassembled form, the animals displayed higher levels of putting it together when they were attempting to solve the hook-retrieval problem than when they were attempting to solve the tool-insertion problem. In contrast, when they were presented with the tool in its assembled form, they displayed the opposite pattern of tool modification.

However, it is important to recognize that the significant interaction just discussed (see Fig. 11.6) only provides support for the weak version of the causal structure model (see Predictions, above). After all, if the apes had simply entered the test unit, attempted to use the tool in the form they found it, and then only later (if it did not work) modified it, then we would expect to see exactly the pattern that is evident in Fig. 11.6.

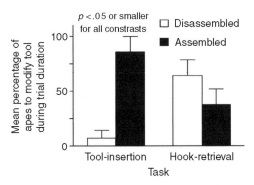

Figure 11.6 Mean percentage ($\pm SEM$) of apes who modified the tool *at some point during the duration of the trial*, as a function of the four conditions used in experiment 27.

Nonetheless, these results do establish that the apes were actively interested in solving the problem using means that were directly related to tool modification.

For this reason, the most revealing data concern tool modifications that the apes initiated *before they received feedback from the apparatus*. We explored these data in two steps. First, we plotted the mean percentage of trials in which the animals modified the tool from its initial state before attempting a solution (see Fig. 11.7). Again, as expected, the ANOVA results revealed no main effects of initial tool form or trial type, but did reveal a significant interaction between the two, $F(1, 5) = 10.0$, $p = 0.025$. This interaction is due to the significant contrasts shown in Fig. 11.7. These results reveal two important facts about the animals' tool modifications before their first attempt. First, when confronted with the tool-insertion task, they modified the tool before attempting a solution significantly more often when the tool was in its incorrect (assembled) state, than when it was in its correct (disassembled) state. Although this result would seem to be consistent with the strong version of the causal structure model, the comparable effect was not present in the case of the hook-retrieval problem (see Fig. 11.7). Also, although the main effect was not significant, there seems to be some evidence in Fig. 11.7 that the apes were simply more prone to modifying the assembled tool before acting on either apparatus, than they were to modifying the disassembled tool.

In considering which model is implicated by the data, it should be clearly kept in mind that the results just presented concern whether the apes modified the tool before their first attempt, and *not* whether their first attempt involved the tool in its proper orientation. It is crucial to consider these data for several reasons. First, although the apes may have modified the tool before attempting a solution, they may nonetheless have modified it back into its initial state before they actually attempted a solution. Second, they may have modified the tool in an inappropriate manner (e.g. when confronting the platform task, they may have disassembled the tool). Third, they may have modified one end of the

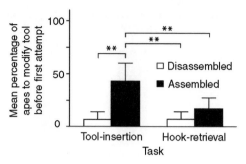

Figure 11.7 Mean percentage (±*SEM*) of apes who modified the tool *prior to attempting a solution*, as a function of the four conditions used in experiment 27.

tool in an appropriate manner, but then attempted a solution with the still-unmodified end. Thus, we analyzed the mean percentage of trials in which the apes' first attempt at a solution involved orienting a correct tool end toward the apparatus. The results are plotted in Fig. 11.8. The ANOVA results revealed an unexpected main effect of task type, $F(1, 5) = 10.0$, $p = 0.025$, such that the apes' first tool orientation was correct more often on the tool-insertion problem, overall, than on the hook-retrieval problem. However, there was also a significant interaction between initial tool form and task type, $F(1, 5) = 45.0$, $p < 0.002$. These results show that the apes' first orientations of the tool on each trial were virtually always correct when the tool was presented in the form that matched the task (see Fig. 11.8). However, when the tool was presented in a form that did *not* match the task, the apes' initial orientations were generally incorrect.

The results just presented, which concern whether the apes' first tool orientations were correct or not, suggest that the apes were not sensitive to whether the tool was oriented properly after they modified the tool—even in the case of the tool-insertion problem, where they displayed higher levels of tool-modification when the initial tool form did not

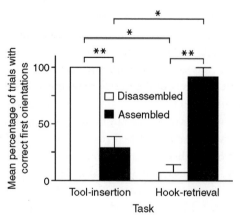

Figure 11.8 Mean percentage (±*SEM*) of trials in which the tool was oriented correctly on the apes' first attempt at solution, as a function of the four conditions used in experiment 27.

Table 11.2 Relationship between instances of deliberate tool modification which were followed by an attempt at solution, and whether tool was oriented correctly on the attempt.

Subject	n	Percentage of attempts	
		Correct	Incorrect
Apollo	5	20.0	80.0
Kara	7	57.1	42.9
Candy	6	33.3	66.7
Jadine	2	100.0	0.0
Brandy	4	25.0	75.0
Megan	2	0.0	100.0
Mindy	0	—	—
M =		39.2	60.8
SD =		35.1	35.1

Only those tool modifications which were followed by an attempt at solution are analyzed here. In addition, if the subject engaged in successive tool modification before orienting the tool toward the apparatus, only the modification just prior to the attempt is represented here.

match the problem type (see Fig. 11.7). Indeed, perhaps the strongest evidence that the apes' tool modifications were not directly related to the causal structure of the problem can be found in Table 11.2, which provides a condensed summary (data for the tool-insertion and hook-retrieval problems combined) of all deliberate modifications that the animals made to the tools *which were followed by an attempt to solve the task at hand*. The table shows the percentage of attempts that followed these modifications in which the tool was in the correct or incorrect orientation. As can be seen, the apes' modifications were not well articulated to an understanding of the causal structure of the problem; in fact, overall, the apes were more likely to modify the tool and then attempt to use it in the incorrect manner (60.8 per cent of all cases) than to modify it and use it correctly (39.2 per cent of all cases)—although a paired *t*-test revealed that this difference was not statistically significant. *Perhaps most significantly,* this same pattern held true if we examine only those modification-attempt relations from the trials involving the dislodging task and the assembled tool. Just as with the overall data, the apes were, if anything, more likely to modify the tool and then attempt to use it in the incorrect manner (63.9 per cent of all cases) than to modify it and then use it correctly (36.1 per cent of all cases). This is important, because this was the condition from which the only data in support of the causal structure model were obtained (see Fig. 11.7).

Appendix III provides a more detailed account of the first four modifications made to the tool on each trial by each ape in each condition, and thus offers the micro-behavioral evidence for the striking finding that our apes' tool modifications were not clearly linked to the causal structure of the task.

Finally, it is of interest to note that there were no striking individual differences among the seven apes on this experiment. Although Jadine, who had performed well in the final bendable-tool study (experiment 26), was correct on her first attempt at the mismatched tool-insertion problem, she was incorrect on the other trial of this type. Furthermore, she never modified the tool, and never succeeded, on the mismatched hook-retrieval problem.

General discussion (experiments 24–27): chimpanzees' understanding of tool modification

The experiments reported in this chapter were undertaken to determine if the chimpanzees' ability to modify tools reflects an underlying appreciation of the causal structure of the problems at hand. Experiments 24–26 explored the chimpanzees' understanding of modifications which would assist in a problem concerning the match between the shape of a tool and the shape (or size) or an opening in a substrate. Experiment 27 explored this relation also, as well as a problem involving the shape of the tool and its physical connection to another object.

Setting aside (for the moment) Jadine's performance in experiment 26, our results suggest that, although chimpanzees will modify tools if they understand their properties, these actions are only weakly related (if at all) to an understanding of the causal structure of the particular problem that they face. We acknowledge, of course, that with strong support and scaffolding our chimpanzees did provide evidence of ultimately modifying tools in ways that were appropriate to the tasks they faced. For example, in experiment 27 the chimpanzees modified the tools (by either assembling or disassembling them) on almost half of all of the crucial test trials. Second, in experiments 24–26 several of the apes showed limited evidence of unbending the pliant tool. However, with the exception of Jadine in experiment 26, our apes' modifications did not appear to be targeted toward the causal structure of the particular problem they faced. Kara, for example, who unbent the pliant tool with her hands at several points during experiments 24–26, consistently did so in order to create a more effective gripping handle, not in order to create a shape that would fit through the opening in the tool-insertion apparatus. Furthermore, the tool modifications that were observed in experiment 27 typically appeared to have been driven by a feedback process in which the apes first used the tool in the form in which it was presented and, when this did not lead to success, they then modified the tool using one of the skills (assembly or disassembly) that we had taught them. Although when the apes were confronted with the tool-insertion problem and the assembled (incorrect) tool form, they did modify at least one end of the tool before they made an attempt significantly more often than they did in all other conditions (see Fig. 11.7), following such modifications they were just as likely to use the tool in the incorrect as in the correct orientation.

Clearly, the best evidence in favor of the view that chimpanzees understand the underlying causal reasons for their tool modifications was exhibited by one of our female subjects, Jadine, who showed evidence for appropriate tool modification in the final bendable-tool experiment (experiment 26). However, although her performance was impressive, it needs to be viewed in the context of her other results. For example, her performance occurred only after she had displayed little evidence of understanding the necessity of unbending the tool in experiments 24 and 25, and she exhibited a decidedly unexceptional performance in the original tool-insertion problems (see Chapter 8). Thus, on the one hand, Jadine's knowledge of the properties of the tool object (its pliability), did not initially lead her to unbend the tool when it was clearly necessary (experiments 24 and 25), but, on the other hand, when she finally did arrive at the solution, it appeared suddenly and was quite robust. What, then, can we make of her performance?

There is one fact, in particular, that leads us to favor the idea that Jadine came to understand some very specific features of the tool configuration that was necessary to solve the tool-insertion problem, as opposed to reasoning about an abstract conception of 'shape' (see General Discussion in Chapter 8). First, in experiment 27 (which immediately followed experiment 26), on the two trials where Jadine was confronted with the tool-insertion task and the assembled tool (incorrect form), she appropriately modified the tool on the first trial before attempting to solve the problem, but did not do so on the next trial (see Appendix III). Furthermore, on the two trials where she was confronted with the hook-retrieval problem and the disassembled tool (incorrect form), Jadine never modified the tool—despite the fact that her repeated attempts to retrieve the platform never led to success. We admit, however, that this is a difficult assessment to make, especially because of the fact that we believe that 'genuine' solutions to these two tasks require slightly different kinds of causal understanding. The tool-insertion task requires a conception of how the shape of a tool interacts with the shape or size of a substrate opening (see Chapter 8), whereas the hook-retrieval task requires an understanding of how the shape of a tool can establish a greater degree of physical connection (see Chapter 9). Thus, it is possible that the fact that Jadine learned to modify the tool on the tool-insertion task, as opposed to the hook-retrieval task, simply reflects a better causal understanding of interactions involving notions of shape, than of notions of shape *and* physical connection.

In considering how the results we have presented in this chapter relate to the tool-modification abilities displayed by chimpanzees in the wild, the results of experiment 27 may be especially helpful. As we noted in the introduction to this chapter, young chimpanzees only gradually learn to use tools in the manner displayed by adults. Based on the results we have obtained, it seems quite likely to us that chimpanzees learn how to modify raw materials that are available, such as vines or twigs, without an explicit understanding of how the new perceptual forms that they have created causally interact with the world. Rather, it seems quite possible that, through a process of slow trial-and-error learning (a process that takes place throughout their infant and juvenile years), chimpanzees learn a series of procedural steps related to tool modification, each one matched appropriately to a particular context, and each one targeted toward creating a specific perceptual form. Although such a process will ultimately lead to successful performance, the route is developmentally long and, if we are correct, uninformed by explicit abstract causal concepts of 'shape', 'pliability' and 'physical connection'. As we suggest in the next chapter, this may be why chimpanzee material culture, although sufficient for their way of life—and impressive from the standpoint of other nonhuman primates—is so very limited when compared to that of our own species.

CHAPTER 12

TOWARD A FOLK PHYSICS FOR CHIMPANZEES

DANIEL J. POVINELLI

Having concluded our descriptions of the experimental portion of this project, we are now in a position to face some difficult theoretical issues which, up to this point, we have gingerly sidestepped. We address these issues in four steps. First, we offer our account of how chimpanzees interpret the interactions between the objects they use as tools and the effects that these objects produce. We illustrate the nature of this understanding by detailing one example of what we take to be a 'principle' of the chimpanzees' folk physics. Second, we compare and contrast our general theoretical stance with those of several previous theorists. Third, we outline a number of potential objections to our conclusions, and assess each one in turn. Finally, we conclude this project by offering a theory which may help to explain why chimpanzees and orangutans seem to make and use tools more than other nonhuman primates. Perhaps surprisingly, our explanation has more to do with the self-representational systems of these species than with their understanding of unobservable causal phenomenon.

Of course, we should begin by raising the general question of whether we are warranted in speaking of a chimpanzee 'folk physics' in the first place. For example, perhaps we should reserve the term strictly for those species that possess some kind of causal understanding? Although such an approach is tempting, it should be recalled that one of the major themes of our project is that, in its general use, 'causal understanding' is too broad an idea to capture interesting differences among species. An alternative approach, which is in keeping with our own particular research interests, would be to position the umbrella of 'folk physics' so that it covers only those species that reason about causes as unobservable phenomena. Or, in keeping with recent emphases in developmental psychology and other fields, we could seek to restrict the term 'folk physics' to those species that can produce reasonably organized ideas—or explanations—about how the world works (for a discussion of the role of 'explanation' in cognitive development see, for example, Carey 1985).

For the time being, we reject both of these approaches, and instead extend the term 'folk physics' to include all of those cognitive processes and concepts which are directly involved in a given species' reasoning about the regularities of physical phenomena. Conceiving of folk physics in this way allows us to elucidate certain 'principles' of the chimpanzee's folk physics, and at the same time leaves room for profound differences between humans and other animals. On the other hand, it allows us to exclude those motor procedures that are not explicitly 'reasoned about' in the organism's central cognitive processing system. In addition, it also allows us to entertain the possibility that many aspects of the chimpanzee's folk physics are *not* evolutionary precursors to high-level causal concepts used by humans (see Kummer 1995). Finally, it allows us to be more precise about the ways in which the chimpanzee reasons about what we understand as causality.

Chimpanzee folk physics is concerned with observable phenomena

The results of our investigations have convinced us that, although chimpanzees possess an excellent ability to reason explicitly about relations between objects and events that can be perceived, they appear to know very little (if anything) about phenomena that are, in principle, unobservable. Chimpanzees appear to share with us a common set of visual–cognitive processing systems which cohere a common set of object properties (such as solidity and boundedness), whereas systems which map unobservable causal descriptors onto these objects and their spatial relations may be a cognitive specialization of the human species. As we noted in Chapter 3, this would mean that humans and chimpanzees have access to the same kinds of perceptual information (both in terms of the kinds of objects in the world, as well as information of the statistical regularities that characterize their interactions), but that the two species interpret this information differently. This is not to say that chimpanzees are unaffected by unobservable phenomena; clearly they are. For example, the transfer of energy from one object to another gives rise to certain observable interactions that chimpanzees do detect and reason about. Nor does this mean that chimpanzees lack a visual imagination. Rather, we contend that their central reasoning systems do not reason about things which have the status of being 'hypothetical'. On our view, this is because the chimpanzee does not form such concepts to begin with.

We must be careful to emphasize that we are not claiming that chimpanzees (or other animals) fail to form concepts about the world. On the contrary, there is very good evidence that many nonhuman species form a variety of 'concepts' based on perceptual generalization gradients. (For a review of the evidence with respect to primates, see Tomasello and Call 1997.) Rather, we suggest that the range of concepts formed by the chimpanzee does not include concepts about entities or processes that have no perceptually-based exemplars. On our view, chimpanzees detect the regularities that exist between events, and learn to act on the basis of them, but they do not appeal to unobservable phenomena (force, gravity, etc.) to account for (or assist in their reasoning about) such regular associations of events.[1] Indeed, representations of hypothetical

---

[1]   In a different context, Premack (1976) proposed that '[t]he internal representations that the chimpanzee can generate must be reliable and of considerable tangibility for the

entities may be impossible without a human-like language, or perhaps more directly, language may have created such representations. Thus, we accept the claim that chimpanzees form concepts about the world, but that their folk physics does not suffer (as Hume would have it) from an ascription of causal concepts to events which consistently co-vary with each other. Later in this chapter, we shall offer a similar characterization of their folk psychology.

This conclusion stands in some contrast to a number of early interpretations of tool use in nonhuman primates which, using Piagetian approaches to understanding tool use, concluded that the spontaneous use of tools by nonhuman primates (and chimpanzees in particular) implies that they appreciate the underlying causal relations involved (e.g. Chevalier-Skolnikoff 1989; Parker and Gibson 1977, 1979; Parker and Potí 1990). Of course, part of the difficulty in comparing and contrasting ideas about causality stems from the ambiguities in what is meant by terms such as 'causal relations', 'causality', and 'cause-and-effect'. For example, if one uses the term 'causal understanding' to suggest that a chimpanzee, for example, represents in some fashion the more-or-less invariant event sequences that it detects in the world (for example, B usually follows A), then there is no room for argument (e.g. Dickinson and Shanks 1995; Premack 1976). However, if one means to imply that the chimpanzee is representing something more about the situation (such as an unobservable variable which mediates the sequence 'A followed by B'), then we need to be more cautious. Thus, it is not that we reject the findings of previous researchers, exactly; nor is it the case that we reject the usefulness of comparative descriptions of the feedback loops that exist between an organism's actions on its environment, on the one hand, and the environment's response, on the other (e.g. Chevalier-Skolnikoff 1989; Parker and Gibson 1979). Rather, we propose that chimpanzees (and other nonhuman primates) interpret those interactions differently from humans. In particular, we propose that they do not appreciate 'causality' as something distinct from the actions and events themselves.

We are not the first to suggest that chimpanzees differ from us in their understanding of causality. Others, including Köhler (1927), Premack and Premack (1994), and Tomasello and Call (1997), have all argued for differences between the nature of human causal reasoning and that found in chimpanzees. In what follows we highlight certain

---

animal…[to] operate on them with the same accuracy that it operates on external events… Intelligence involves, among other things, the ability to operate on internal events, in the ideal case to be able to carry out in the head all the operations one is capable of carrying out on external items. When the events in the head are fleeting or vague one cannot perform in this way. However, if the internal event has the tangibility of, say, a block of wood, one should be able to operate on the internal event almost as efficiency as the external one' (pp. 15–16). Given the general view expressed in this passage, two things are surprising about Premack's ideas about the mental lives of chimpanzees: first, that he saw no fundamental difference in the kinds of causal concepts formed by humans and chimpanzees (see below), and second, that he believed that chimpanzees could form concepts about unobservable mental states (see Premack and Woodruff 1978).

aspects of these proposals. But first we offer our own account of the folk physics of chimpanzees—an account that embraces both the similarities and the differences that have struck us in our extensive observations of our seven chimpanzees' interactions with the physical world.

Learning to make and use tools

In thinking about the evolution of causal understanding, we need to bear in mind that many tool-using and tool-making behaviors can be supported by psychological processes which do not involve representations of unobservable phenomena (e.g. gravity, force, shape, and mass). As Dorothy Fragaszy (1989) has put it: 'The similarities between the [tool-using] activities of humans and nonhumans can generate ideas about the processes underlying the similarity. But noting the similarity in *behavior* is not sufficient to show that the *cognitive processes* involved are the same' (italics in original, p. 596). A similar cautionary point has been made by numerous other researchers in thinking about the relation between tool use and causal understanding, including Köhler (1927), Premack (1976), Visalberghi and Limongelli (1996), and Tomasello and Call (1997).

However, after adopting such a cautionary stance, the question remains as to how we are supposed to think about the diversity of ways in which organisms may arrive at the same endpoint of using, and even making, simple tools. Perhaps the best place to begin is by squarely facing the fact that both cognitive and 'non-cognitive' mechanisms are likely to support even the most complex acts of tool use—including those displayed by our own species. Furthermore, in many instances (in both our own and other species) tool using and tool making will proceed without any explicit mediation by causal principles or concepts. We also need to take more seriously the role that other, more general cognitive and learning mechanisms may play in the development and use of tools. Indeed, prior to the emergence of humans, many species of animals possessed the ability to keep track of the temporal connections between closely connected, observable events, as evidenced by the almost universal presence of associative learning in the animal kingdom (see MacPhail 1987). Kummer (1995) has labeled the kind of knowledge that is generated by such mechanisms as 'weak causal knowledge' (see Kummer 1995). Such knowledge is described as 'weak' because learning to associate two events requires experience and, at least in principle, organisms can learn to associate any two events. (For a similar account, see Premack's (1976) notion of 'arbitrary' causality.)

On the other hand, it is now clear that many species of animals are born into the world pre-prepared to form certain kinds of associations as opposed to others (Bolles 1971; Garcia and Koelling 1966; Garcia *et al.* 1966; Pearce *et al.* 1978; Shettleworth 1975: see Domjan 1983). Thus, we can think about evolution as having sculpted the sensory and neural systems of various species to attend to, and learn about, certain relationships with little or no experience. Kummer (1995) has referred to this kind of knowledge about events as 'strong causal knowledge'—'strong' in the sense that evolution has directly selected for the neural systems that will guarantee that organisms will form these particular representations. As an example of this kind of 'hard-wired' knowledge, Gene Sackett (1966) has demonstrated that infant rhesus monkeys who have been reared in isolation from other monkeys will respond appropriately to images of adult males who are displaying threatening facial expressions, even though these infants have never had the social experiences upon which to learn such reactions. Presumably, responding appropriately to such social signals is so important that evolution has acted to guarantee that infant rhesus monkeys will react without any prior experience.

Of course, the fact that animals possess these kinds of 'weak' and 'strong' causal knowledge does not necessarily imply that they are reasoning about causes *per se* or, even more specifically, whether they are reasoning about unobservable causes. Indeed, part of Kummer's (1995) conclusion is that the kinds of causal knowledge possessed by animals should not necessarily be thought of as evolutionary precursors to the kinds of causal reasoning found in humans. In the present context, we can imagine that many species, especially certain nonhuman primates, may have evolved specific predispositions for learning to manipulate objects in ways that strongly facilitate (or, in some cases, even guarantee) the discovery and use of tools. As a simple example, consider the primate hand. Although other anatomical appendages can be used to manipulate tools (such as the raven's beak), the nature of the anthropoid hand may, by itself, increase the probability that certain contingencies inherent in tool use will be discovered, and hence exploited (see Brésard 1993; Jouffroy 1993). This is not to say that the mere presence of the primate hand will automatically lead to tool-using behaviors; however, coupled with selection for tendencies to manipulate objects, the possibility of tool discovery will be dramatically heightened. Our general point is this: there are many ways in which species such as chimpanzees may develop tool-using abilities other than by explicitly appreciating the kinds of unobservable causal variables that are of such interest to even very young children (see Chapter 3).

But what about the exact process by which chimpanzees and other nonhuman primates learn to use and make tools? With respect to chimpanzees, most researchers would agree that the following processes play at least some role in the development of chimpanzee tool use (e.g. Boesch and Tomasello 1998; Goodall 1986; Matsuzawa 1994; Tomasello *et al.* 1993). First, chimpanzees are born into the world predisposed to manipulate objects. Second, like many other species, they are predisposed to interact preferentially with objects that they have recently observed others interacting with. Third, they learn about the connections between manipulating objects in certain ways and specific outcomes that soon follow. Now, some researchers would even go further, arguing that chimpanzees imitate each other's acts of tool use, and in some cases adults even actively teach their young (for a discussion of these issues, see Boesch and Tomasello 1998; Whiten 1999). However, it should be noted that there is extreme controversy over the exact mechanism of learning that is responsible for transmitting tool use from one generation to the next. Some researchers maintain that genuine imitation is involved, whereas others hold out for lower-level mechanisms of social learning.[2] In addition, if active teaching is present in chimpanzees, it is very rare (indeed, we and others have questioned whether it exists at all; for a range of views see Boesch and Tomasello 1998; Cheney and Seyfarth 1990; Povinelli and Godfrey 1993; Premack 1984; Tomasello *et al.* 1993; Whiten 1999). Nonetheless, on this general account, it would seem that three factors—(1) a drive to manipulate objects; (2) social learning; and (3) individual learning—could, in combination, account for the gradual process that leads chimpanzees during their infancy and early juvenile years to become proficient at the tool-using traditions that are present within their community.

A different approach to understanding the development of tool use in chimpanzees has been advocated by Matsuzawa (1996), who devised a more formal account of the hierarchical nature of chimpanzee cognitive processes, and has attempted to explain the degree of chimpanzee tool use and manufacture in similar terms (e.g. Matsuzawa 1996). Based on fieldwork in which he has explored chimpanzees' use of stones to crack open palm nuts, Matsuzawa (1994, 1996) argued that there is a critical period between about three and six years of age in which young chimpanzees learn to become proficient tool users. Matsuzawa (1994) emphasizes the commonalities between the development of these abilities in human children and chimpanzees, arguing that the use of stone tools, for example, requires learning an 'action grammar' not so different from the grammar of human language (see Greenfield 1991; Matsuzawa 1996).

Although each of these general accounts of how chimpanzees learn to make and use simple tools seem to capture something that is correct, all of them also seem incomplete in that they do not elucidate any of the core heuristics that must guide tool use and manufacture in this species. For example, consider instances of tool modification by free-ranging chimpanzees. As we have seen, chimpanzees tailor the raw materials that are available in their environments to solve specific problems, and these activities may be supported by some kind of representation of a target tool form. To be sure, much of this activity may be governed by learned procedures that are fairly automatized and relatively insensitive to relevant changes in the causal structure of the problem. In addition, our tests also reveal that chimpanzees develop fairly coherent empirical generalizations, which guide their actions. *However, we contend that chimpanzees' generalizations are derived from surface features of the problem which do not*

---

2   Few researchers doubt that animals learn at least something from observing others. Indeed, classic experiments in the early part of this century established that naive monkeys who observe expert monkeys solve a problem learn to solve the problem faster than control animals who do not (e.g. Warden and Jackson 1935). However, there are numerous mechanisms by which such learning may occur, ranging from the observer simply having his or her attention drawn to the relevant objects more than controls (and hence discovering the contingencies faster), to more advanced forms of imitation (see Galef 1988; Whiten and Ham 1992). Shettleworth (1998) has provided a broad but thorough overview of the recent controversy surrounding social learning in nonhuman primates and other species.

explicitly incorporate an entire class of concepts that humans have about causation—even though they reason about surface features of the world which abut, as it were, very closely against such concepts. In practice, then, the results of our experimental work should allow us to explore the chimpanzee's alternative to human causal concepts, and in doing so, allow us to begin to articulate specific 'principles' of the chimpanzee's folk physics.

Principles of chimpanzee folk physics

Opening caveats

In what follows, we describe an example of a simple principle of the chimpanzee's folk physics. By 'principle' we mean a basic rule or heuristic about the regularities in the world that guide chimpanzees' interactions with objects. However, before we proceed, there are several general points that should be kept in mind. First, in thinking about the differences between how humans and chimpanzees understand any given act of tool use, we must recognize that these differences are embedded into a matrix of similarities. For example, many of the perceptual–motor skills which orchestrate any act of tool use are likely to be very similar (if not identical) in the two species. As we emphasized in Chapter 2, novel human cognitive specializations are likely to have been woven into the hominid brain without fundamentally disrupting or replacing the ancestral systems. Furthermore, the fact that humans have access to certain physical concepts that are not available to chimpanzees does not mean that these concepts are recruited each time a human uses a tool. Indeed, we suspect that most acts of tool use in humans are fairly automatized, and that it is only in novel contexts that these higher-order concepts directly influence our motor actions. Of course, many of the differences between humans and chimpanzees may be attributable to specifically human systems, which unconsciously translate visual or other perceptual information into neural codes that represent abstract causal information (such as Leslie's (1994) 'FORCE' descriptions; see Chapter 3). This information may be present in some implicit forms at a quite young age in humans, but only later 'redescribed' in more explicit codes that are available for general use (see Karmiloff-Smith 1992). In any event, a successful account of the chimpanzee's folk physics of tool use must work to integrate both the similarities and the differences that are likely to exist between their species and our own.

   The second point to keep in mind is that much of the chimpanzee's knowledge about the world will not be ensconced as 'principles' at all, but instead may be encoded as generalized action sequences (see Premack 1976; Tomasello and Call 1997)—perhaps instantiated in visual imagery (e.g. Kosslyn 1994). Furthermore, their understanding of actions that they have actively generated (such as those involved in their use of tools), may be confined to motor procedures that are mediated by other, more general representations of external objects and events. Thus, much of the information that chimpanzees possess about the workings of the physical world may not warrant inclusion in an account of the principles of their folk physics. Take, for example, cases in which adult humans attribute 'force' as causing one object to launch another one into motion. The chimpanzee, too, may anticipate that when one object comes into contact with a second, stationary one, the second one is likely to move away. However, this 'knowledge' may be restricted to the organism's perceptual–motor systems, thus making it unavailable for use in those central processing systems that are more directly responsible for planning and executing particular actions. Indeed, a difficult conceptual challenge arises from the fact that it is possible (intentionally or unintentionally) to train chimpanzees (and other animals) to attend to their own reactions which emerge from their low-level psychological systems. And, once trained to respond to their own behavior in this fashion, it becomes a nightmarish problem to determine whether the chimpanzee's new-found skill is based upon higher-order conceptual principles, or sensory–motor skills.

Perhaps equally vexing is that, in both chimpanzees and humans, the neural systems that are dedicated to detecting statistical regularities in the world may possess more detailed information than higher-level cognitive systems. This disparity may place organisms in the awkward position of detecting, but not being able to use, information about the regularities that exist in the world. Consider the following thought experiment related to our inverted rake experiments (see Chapter 6). Imagine that a chimpanzee named 'Kanzo' enters our test unit and sees one tool that is inverted and another that is in its normal orientation. In addition, he sees that there are cookies associated with each of the tools. Pulling the inverted rake will be of little help to Kanzo because the base of the rake will pass over the cookie. However, our results suggest that Kanzo will not initially perceive this functional difference between the two options, largely because at the highest levels of his cognitive system he equates 'imminent contact' and 'perceptual containment' as variants of 'contact' (see Chapters 6 and 10). Thus, on some occasions, Kanzo reaches out and pulls the inverted (incorrect) rake. The cookie does not move, and when it does not, Kanzo displays evidence that this is not what he expected (he looks longer, or perhaps even becomes startled or upset). Now imagine that we alter the causal relationship so that an invisible mechanism causes the cookie to move under the arch of the inverted rake—despite the fact that the rake does not physically contact the cookie. Here again, we can measure Kanzo's attention and surprise. This simple experiment has not been conducted either with chimpanzees or with human infants, and so we cannot know with confidence what its outcome would be. It is possible, however, that Kanzo would provide evidence that this event violated his expectations as well-after all, he has never before seen a cookie moving spontaneously!

At this point, our reader should be puzzled. Why should Kanzo be 'surprised' when the cookie moves under the inverted rake? After all, he purposely chose the inverted rake precisely because he did not yet see the functional distinction between perceptual containment and contact. How can we account for such a paradox? The solution becomes straightforward if we imagine that different parts of Kanzo's neural system contain different kinds of information about the statistical regularities of events in the world. In this case, Kanzo's high-level action planning and execution systems may lead him to intentionally select the inverted rake because these systems are operating on the basis of an abstracted set of perceptual parameters. In contrast, other aspects of Kanzo's neural system, perhaps ones more closely tied to primitive orienting mechanisms, may have access to a much larger set of information about the kinds of events that do occur and do not occur in the world. Thus, he looks longer (or is startled) as these systems register and process the atypical event. Kanzo's eyes may, in a sense, be smarter than he is.

The most troubling aspect of this thought experiment is that it reveals that Kanzo will stare longer at the result (or possibly exhibit surprise) both when there is a genuine causal irregularity and when there is not, even though he does not possess an explicit understanding of the causal principle involved. Worse yet, the subject who truly *does* have access to causal knowledge concerning the transfer of force through contact may exhibit the same response. After all, if Kanzo did possess such knowledge, would we not expect him to look longer when the cookie moves under the arch of the inverted rake? This example illustrates that behavioral evidence for the *detection* of causal irregularities can be prompted by knowledge about unobservable mediating causal concepts, or by other, lower-level psychological phenomena.

Our thought experiment highlights two key ideas. (1) the neural systems of animals represent the world at multiple levels, and these distinct levels of representation may differ from each other both qualitatively and quantitatively. (2) developing a proper theory of the chimpanzee's mind will require embracing the idea that the intelligent ways in which chimpanzees behave stem from both conceptual analyses (within the limits we have proposed) and from detailed perceptual analyses.

The principle of 'contact'

By now, it should be obvious that we are comfortable with the idea that as chimpanzees learn to use tools they construct guiding principles that are directly accessible to their high-level reasoning systems. In order to explore the nature of such principles, we now consider the notion of 'physical connection' that we examined in Chapters 9 and 10. In this case, humans appear to explain the covariation of movement between two objects as being the result of some kind of 'physical connection' between them. The experienced chimpanzee, in contrast, appears to attribute the co-varied movement of two physical objects to their contact. It seems to us that this constitutes a principled account of the covariation of movement between the objects. For example, as our chimpanzee Jadine attempts to use the straight stick (instead of the hook) to solve the hook-retrieval problem (see Chapter 9), she may be actively seeking to create an outcome that was planned in advance—establishing 'contact' between the tool and the platform. In short, she is attempting to create a perceptual configuration that she believes is necessary for the platform to move. If this is true, Jadine may prefer to use the straight tool, because for her the hook does not imply 'physical connection' (a concept that is not available in the chimpanzee's folk physics). Rather, for her, the hook portion of the tool is simply seen as an inconvenient obstruction at the very point where the tool needs to make contact with the platform. Thus, we may have identified a principle of the chimpanzee's folk physics: *contact is necessary and sufficient to establish covariation in movement.*

To what extent does this chimpanzee's principle of contact map onto the physics of the world as we understand it? To begin, the chimpanzee's principle of contact is at least partially correct. In the hook-retrieval problem, for example, contact certainly is necessary for co-varied movement. With additional experience on the hook-retrieval problem, the chimpanzee's principle may be refined further. For example, Jadine might learn that the hook must be positioned around the far side of the post—the perceptual configuration that would lead us to say that the tool is hooked around the post. But, on our account, Jadine would not necessarily have moved closer to the human notion of physical connection; rather, she would have constructed a more narrow perceptual target for the kind of 'contact' that is effective in moving the platform.

So far, we have been a bit loose about the term 'contact', treating it as if it were a unitary construct for the chimpanzee—and, for all we know at this point, it may well be. However, it is also possible that the chimpanzee possesses several separate representations related to contact which are not globally integrated. Imagine two related situations. First, suppose that one of our apes, say Mindy, enters the test unit and picks up a tool which must be moved some distance before it contacts the platform. In this case, Mindy will receive both visual and haptic information concerning the exact moment at which the tool 'makes contact with' the platform. A second, related case occurs when Mindy enters the test unit and sees two options confronting her—one in which the tool is already in contact with the platform, and another in which it is not. In this case, Mindy may immediately choose the first option, and if she does so, she has based her decision solely on visual information concerning contact.

This raises the question of whether Mindy finds an equivalence between the different kinds of sensory information which suggest contact. Given the evidence that chimpanzees are capable of some form of cross-modal matching (e.g. Davenport and Rodgers 1970), one might suspect that she does.[3] However, it is important to note that we have no direct evidence to support this claim. We do not doubt that with enough experience Mindy will come to coordinate her reactions to the two types of sensory information (visual and haptic). However, this fact alone does not guarantee that she understands both sources of information under a common conceptual umbrella such as 'contact'. Indeed, it could be that Mindy's visually-guided efforts to direct the tool toward the platform reflect her search for a kinesthetic target (the *feel* of the tool striking the target), as much as a visual/spatial target. Of course, this is likely to be true in the human case as

---

3   'Cross-modal matching' refers to the ability to translate sensory information across the different modalities (for example, matching the taste of a banana to its visual image. Although there are several reports of cross-modal mapping in nonhuman primates (see Tomasello and Call 1997, for a review), we have doubts about the meaning of these demonstrations. In most cases, the extensive amount of pre-training that has been involved suggests alternative accounts of how the animals came to exhibit the performances that they did. We emphasize that we are not specifically indicting the idea that nonhuman animals can transfer information across the sensory modalities (indeed, we think that it is possible that they may actually experience sensory information in less dichotomous terms than humans). Rather, the experimental demonstrations of cross-modal mapping in chimpanzees (and other nonhuman primates) may be tapping into a far less conceptual form of the phenomenon than is typically displayed by humans.

well, but in the human case we can be reasonably certain that both sources of information are ambassadors for the same conceptual notion of 'contact'. When humans face a novel task, higher-order causal concepts (such as the idea of physical connection) may be activated, and thus be available to guide the motor system toward establishing the particular type of contact that will ensure physical connection. Indeed, some support for this latter claim can be derived from recent clinical research which has shown that certain types of brain damage can result in the selective loss of a patient's ability to use the structure of a simple tool to infer its function (Goldenberg and Hagmann 1998).

One implication of the preceding discussion is that, in applying the principle of 'contact', the chimpanzee will rarely be fooled by superficial alterations of the task. Changes in the color, size, or even the general perceptual form of the tool or the platform will rarely befuddle the experienced chimpanzee (see especially experiment 4). This is because the experienced chimpanzee has already 'seen through' this level of surface features, and has localized the perceptual features and spatial arrangements of the objects that yield the outcome desired. This crucial point has been missed by some researchers who have been impressed at the level of perceptual generalization displayed by one species or another on a given tool-using task (see, for instance, Hauser *et al.* 1999*a*; see also Chapter 10). However, of equal significance is that the chimpanzee will not blindly choose a hook tool simply because this is the tool form that has always been used in the past when confronted with this particular task. No, in applying this general principle, the chimpanzee will freely substitute any tool that will generate contact, and indeed, may even avoid the hook tool if some other implement will make the requisite contact more effectively. And, as we have seen, in some cases this will actually lead the chimpanzee to avoid the tool that can establish what is, in reality, a more reliable form of physical connection.

This, then, is our most important theoretical conclusion: the principles of chimpanzee folk physics are founded upon things that can be directly perceived, including action sequences that can be generated from imagination or held in memory as visual imagery. Nonetheless, our work is still incomplete. First, we have glossed over those aspects of the chimpanzee's behavior that are not based upon principles at all, but upon sensory–motor procedures, and other less 'cognitive' mechanisms. In addition, there are many principles of the chimpanzee's folk physics that we have not yet systematically fleshed out (although our general discussions in Chapters 4–11 have offered a rough outline of several such principles). For example, when Apollo witnesses one object strike another, is his anticipation that the second object will move mediated by principles which relate the specific properties of the objects to their movement? If so, does Apollo reason solely about the obvious properties of the objects (e.g. their size), or does he also reason about the importance of their less obvious properties (e.g. their weight)? Although we have only recently begun to conduct the tests that will allow us to answer such questions, the proposal we offer here predicts that, in each relevant instance, the chimpanzee will use principles that are based upon patent object properties—even in those cases where focus on such properties generates predictions that are nonsensical from the perspective of our human folk physics.

A final limitation of our account is that we have presented the chimpanzee's principles of folk physics as if they existed within a phenomenological world that is equivalent to our own. Almost unavoidably, the language that we have used to describe the chimpanzee's principle of contact, for example, carries with it objects and events that exude a distinctively human 'feel'. This is only natural. After all, evolution has fashioned our minds to resist alternative kinds of interpretations or experiences, such as imaging the world as containing objects with distinct and coherent perceptual forms, but no 'shape'. And yet one of the most sobering consequences of studying the chimpanzee's mind is the realization that, despite the fact that their senses register most of the same regularities in the world as ours, and despite the fact that they behave in much the same manner as we do, their phenomenological experience of these objects and events may, in some ways, be radically different from our own.

Do chimpanzees excel at visual imagery?

Our proposal implies that humans have evolved certain ways of conceiving of the physical world that are not available to chimpanzees, such as explicitly representing unobservable causes. To some extent, this suggests that humans have discovered certain aspects about the way in which the world operates that chimpanzees have not. However, this human cognitive specialization in abstraction may not be without its own unique set of drawbacks. In fact, our species' penchant for abstract thinking may have resulted in leaving our perceptual and memory systems vulnerable to 'conceptual intrusions'. By this, we mean that if humans have specialized in quickly translating incoming perceptual information into more abstract conceptual codes, then we may sacrifice some of the local, perceptually-rich details about the world (or at least make that information unavailable to our higher-order cognitive systems). If true, it follows that chimpanzees, who we believe operate on a far less conceptual level, will consequently suffer less from such conceptual intrusions. Indeed, this may be an arena in which chimpanzees exhibit skills which are perhaps superior to our own.

This proposal stems from two sources. First, over the past eight years, we have been deeply impressed by the extraordinary sensitivity that our chimpanzees have displayed to very small details of their environment—details that seem of little or no importance to us. And in formal tests, we have been struck by how our apes have extracted highly specific rules from their experiences, as opposed to forming concepts about underlying psychological or physical phenomena. The second source for this proposal is a recent paper by Nicholas Humphrey (1998), who speculates that chimpanzees may have a better picture memory than humans—or at least that chimpanzees rely on picture memory strategies in situations where humans would rely on conceptual strategies (see Farrer 1967). We shall return to Humphrey's ideas on this point shortly. For the moment we note that the idea that chimpanzees may suffer less than we do from conceptual intrusions can be seen as an extension of the theoretical position that we presented in the first part of this chapter: chimpanzees form principles of folk physics that are grounded to the world of visual images, and do not 'cloud' their reasoning with concepts related to hypothetical entities or processes.

Is it plausible to suppose that chimpanzee cognition could be as concrete as we have just suggested? Certain aspects of the human developmental disorder of autism may help to illustrate such a proposal. Uta Frith (1989) has championed the idea that autism may be characterized as a disorder involving weak central coherence in cognitive processing. The term 'central coherence' was invoked by Frith in an attempt to capture the manner in which humans typically (and effortlessly) organize the stream of incoming perceptual information into more abstract levels of meaning. For our purposes, the most intriguing aspect of Frith's proposal is its recognition that, in our everyday lives, this drive toward 'central coherence' occurs at the expense of the perceptual details of what we have just seen or heard. There is a considerable amount of experimental evidence on this point. Evidence that humans tend to process information globally as opposed to locally can be derived from studies of reading comprehension, perception, and recall (see review by Happé, 1999). In contrast, autistic individuals appear to develop a preference for thinking about the physical world in terms of fragmented parts and details of objects and events, as opposed to a more globally integrated view. Indeed, Kanner (1943), who coined the term 'autism', noted that one of the typical characteristics of autistic individuals is their 'inability to experience wholes without full attention to the constituent parts)' and that for the autistic individual '...a situation, a performance, a sentence is not regarded as complete if it is not made up of exactly the same elements that were present at the time the child was first confronted with it' (p. 246). Frith has proposed that, unlike most people, autistic individuals do not favor globally processed, conceptually condensed interpretations of what they experience. Of course, none of this is to deny that there are other significant dimensions to the autistic syndrome, including profound impairments in social understanding and executive function (for overviews of these areas of research, see contributions to Baron-Cohen *et al.* 1993; see also Russell 1998).

Francesca Happé (1999) has recently summarized the evidence that autistic individuals exhibit weak central coherence, and has shown that it manifests itself in some rather surprising ways. There are several ways in which autistics focus on perceptual details in ways that distinguish them from other members of the population. They are better than most people at locating a small element within a whole picture (the embedded figure test); as a population they show an unusually high rate of individuals with perfect musical pitch; and they also exhibit superior performance on block design tasks that do not require an integration of features across blocks (see Heaton *et al.* 1998; Jolliffe and Baron-Cohen 1997; Shah and Frith 1983, 1993). Thus, considering autism as a case of weak central coherence—an over-emphasis on detail at the expense of higher-level organization and meaning—may be a useful way of thinking about some of the unique strengths and weaknesses exhibited by autistic individuals (see Frith 1989; Happé 1996).

We are not suggesting that chimpanzees reason exactly like autistic individuals, or vice versa. Autistic individuals are human beings, replete with the numerous specializations (including language, to greater and lesser degrees) that characterize our species. Although aspects of their emotional and higher-order cognitive processing systems may be different from the rest of the population, it seems unlikely that these systems are completely dysfunctional. Indeed, while some autistics are mentally retarded, others are not, and many exhibit quite remarkable skills in certain areas. In contrast, chimpanzees are another species, replete with their own modal developmental pathways. Thus, any aspects of their cognitive processing that parallel those found in autistic individuals exist within a normal, healthy organism—not an organism with a suite of behavioral and cognitive disorders. Nonetheless, some of the ways in which autistic individuals process information may offer a hint of what it would be like to be an organism that is fine-tuned to detecting detailed perceptual patterns and statistical regularities without interpreting them within a coherent explanatory framework. In his proposal, Humphrey (1998) has argued that the remarkable artistic, musical, and memory abilities so often exhibited by autistic individuals may reflect a more primitive way of thinking about the world that may be present in chimpanzees. Our conjecture is more limited, however; chimpanzees may rely on a kind of 'picture memory' without possessing the extraordinary abilities of, for example, the mnemonist studied by the Russian psychologist, Aleksandr Luria (1968), or the various 'idiot savant' skills displayed by some autistic individuals.

If humans have specialized in generating and reasoning about abstract interpretations of physical events, then our cognitive system may effectively 'crowd out' the most detailed levels of perceptual information in favor of more abstract, or even more prototype-based representations of a given scene, object, or event (for evidence of this phenomenon in speech perception, see Kuhl 1991). Such processes may be involved in phenomena as diverse as category formation, speech perception, and false memories. We are not suggesting that there is an unbridgeable dichotomy between humans and chimpanzees in their ability to form 'abstract' concepts. Rather, we suggest that humans have specialized in an ability to generate certain kinds of extremely abstract representations that refer to entities (or classes of entities) that are difficult or impossible to observe through our standard perceptual systems (vision, olfaction, audition, etc.), and that this specialization has left a clear stamp upon the way our brains process information.

The preceding discussion suggests that chimpanzees, like autistic individuals: (1) may perform better than most humans at embedded figure tasks; and (2) may suffer less from false memories generated from category-based inferences. These predictions seem perfectly consistent with our more general proposal that chimpanzees do not explain physical events in terms of unobservable physical phenomena, but instead are concerned with particular spatial arrangements of objects—as well as the flood of contingencies that seem to be released from them.

Some researchers will fairly object that many species of animals have demonstrated an ability to reason on the basis of categories, and even to reason about abstract relations (for a thorough and recent review of these abilities in primates, see Tomasello and Call 1997). In response, we would suggest that many comparative psychologists have assumed that there is only one psychological route to a given behavioral end. Typically, animals are trained on hundreds or even thousands of trials, and are then tested for their abstraction abilities using somewhat novel stimuli, or novel arrangements of familiar stimuli. In many cases, the species in question will display an impressive ability to generalize to the new stimuli, an ability which is interpreted as meaning that they have formed the relevant concept. However, even for those demonstrations that have been interpreted as the most persuasive evidence of conceptual abstraction (for example, the ability to use 'abstract' same–different relations), alternative accounts that focus on the interface between the perceptual dimensions of the stimuli and the attentional activities of the animal can easily be generated.

Previous proposals

At the outset of this chapter, we noted that a number of previous scholars have also attempted to characterize the similarities and differences between how humans and chimpanzees reason about 'causality'. Köhler (1927), for example, concluded that chimpanzees were capable of 'insight learning' about how objects can be used to solve specific problems. However, the conclusion that he highlighted in *The Mentality of Apes* was that there are strong limits on the ability of apes to form such insights—limits that are directly related to their focus on the visual characteristics of objects. 'One must learn,' Köhler argued;

> …within what limits of difficulty and in what functions the chimpanzees *can possibly* show insight…[T]he experiments in which we tested these animals brought them into situations in which all essential conditions were actually visible, and the solution could be achieved immediately… We do not test at all, or rather only in passing, how far the chimpanzee is influenced by factors not present, whether things 'merely thought about' occupy him noticeably at all… In the field of the experiments carried out here the insight of the chimpanzee shows itself to be principally determined by his optical apprehension of the situation… (pp. 265–7.)

In some sense, then, our conclusion is not so different from Köhler's, although we emphasize the chimpanzee's reasoning about 'observable' phenomena more broadly than just what is detectable through the visual system. Köhler's main objective was to explore the intelligent, insightful ability of chimpanzees, but he was nonetheless deeply impressed by their limitations. Thus, it is slightly ironic that, although our own research was designed to explore the ability of chimpanzees to use concepts related to real, but hidden phenomena, we have been left deeply impressed by their ability to extract powerful empirical generalizations from the world in the apparent absence of such concepts. Indeed, as we discussed earlier, it has even led us to suspect that, in some ways, the chimpanzee's mental representation of the world may be more accurate than our own.

Fifty years after Köhler's monograph was translated to English, David Premack (1976) also considered the similarities and differences between the causal reasoning of humans and chimpanzees. Premack argued that chimpanzees, like humans, possess a natural ability to make causal inferences, and therefore concluded that, as far as he could determine, there were no fundamental differences in this area between the two species. His claim, and later elaborations of it by Premack and Premack (1994), rest upon a set of experiments in which his 'language'-trained apes were presented with still reconstructions (see Fig. 12.1) of several events, and were then asked to make judgements about which of several implements had produced the transformation. So, for example, his chimpanzees were shown a whole apple and an apple cut in half, and were required to choose from among several candidate implements (e.g. a knife, a pencil, and a glass of water). The idea was to establish a way of asking the apes if they understood, for example, that the knife is what produced this particular transformation. His chimpanzees performed successfully on such tests without extensive training (including on 'verbal' versions of the tests, which used plastic language chips that they had been trained with for several years). Based on their performance, Premack concluded that chimpanzees naturally make causal inferences (e.g. 'the knife is what cut the apple'). Several variations of these tests were conducted in an attempt to rule out very simple-minded associative explanations of the results (e.g. 'the knife goes with the apple'; see also Premack and Premack 1983).

Do these results contradict the proposal we have made here? A moment's reflection shows that they do not. At best, what Premack's (1976) results demonstrate is that the chimpanzee understands how particular patterns in the world are associated with the actions of specific objects. Indeed, certain aspects of his results suggest that chimpanzees may understand the inherent asymmetry of many cause–effect relations—for example, that pencils generate marks on the paper, but not vice versa. However, his results do not address whether chimpanzees represent anything about the situation other than the events themselves (that is, whether they reason about non-obvious properties of the world). After all, a chimpanzee that is extremely familiar with a particular implement (for example, a pencil), may easily understand that certain actions with the implement (pressing on paper) are spatially and temporally associated with particular other events (marks emerging on the paper)—indeed, how could they not?—without understanding anything further about underlying causes.

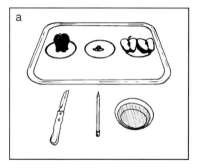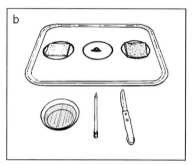

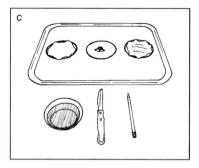

Figure 12.1 Several procedures used by Premack (1976) to determine if chimpanzees could select the implement that 'produced' the transformation of the objects presented. (a) A whole apple and an apple cut in half. (b) A dry sponge and a wet sponge. (c) A paper with no marks and a paper with marks. Premack interpreted the ape's ability to select the implement that generated the depicted event as evidence of causal inferences by chimpanzees. See text for discussion.

Premack (1976) himself might be among the first to agree with this interpretation, given his claim that he could find 'little difference between…functional knowledge and causal inference except in the generality of the latter' (p. 258). Indeed, Premack seems to adopt the view that Hume was correct in asserting that there is nothing else to causality other than the mere succession of events. But, regardless of what one thinks about Hume's position, humans certainly attribute causal forces to events. Thus, although many species may keep track of specific functional properties of objects, perhaps only humans have specialized in an ability to form representations of phenomena which do not have particular physical exemplars. Consider the idea of 'force', for example. Although there are an infinite number of cases in which humans can invoke force to explain events that have been observed, there are no cases (as Hume so clearly noted) in which force is actually observed. Thus, we disagree with Premack's (1976, p. 258) supposition that the human's theory of causality 'would seem to be a generalized version of the functional knowledge' possessed by other species. On the contrary, the human's 'generalized version of functional knowledge' may turn out to be composed of representations that are completely unrecognizable to the chimpanzee.

Recently, Tomasello and Call (1997) have speculated, contrary to Premack, that non-human primates do not understand causal relations at all. In particular, they argue that there is no necessary reason why tool use implies an understanding of causality. They speculate that:

> ....nonhuman primates understand causal relations only in the sense of one external event typically leads to another (the events are seen as ordered and therefore predictable), but they do not understand why one event leads to another in the human sense in which there is some force acting as an intermediary that may be manipulated in various ways to cause the effect. (p. 389.)

Although we are in general agreement with this claim, there is an aspect of their proposal with which we strongly disagree. Tomasello and Call suggest that the difference between humans and apes stems from the fact that apes possess a very limited understanding of how multiple actions can lead to the same effect. In emphasizing the idea that nonhuman primates do not understand the 'web of possibilities' that connect a given sequence of events together, Tomasello and Call offer the following thought experiment:

> ...[S]uppose that an individual ape, who has never before observed such an event, for the first time observes the wind blowing a tree such that the fruit falls to the ground. If it understands the causal relations involved, that the movement of the limb is what caused the fruit to fall, it should be able to devise other ways to make the limb move and so make the fruit fall. (p. 389.)

Because they believe that apes do not understand the web of possibilities between actions and outcomes, Tomasello and Call believe that most researchers 'would be astounded to see the ape, *just on the basis of having observed the wind make the fruit fall,* proceed to shake the limb, or pull an attached vine, to create the same movement of the limb' (italics in original, p. 389). Although we cannot speak for others, we would not be the least astounded to see the ape do so—not because we believe that the ape would perform a genuine causal diagnosis of the situation, but because this contingency can be represented on the basis of mental images which have concrete, observable referents. Even though the ape may not represent unobservable phenomena as generating the events that mediate the limb shaking, he or she can, on our view, appreciate the direct associations between limb-shaking and fruit-falling, and can also imagine alternative means of generating the antecedent of limb-shaking.

Furthermore, Tomasello and Call (1997) also propose that when apes are mere observers of a series of events such as those cited in the example cited above, they cannot grasp alternative means to reproduce the desired outcome:

The key issue in the human forms of intentional and causal understanding is that there is a web of possibilities that the intermediary constrains or determines. Understanding this web of possibilities and the relevant intermediaries in a particular case enables individuals to devise novel ways of producing the intermediary and thus the end result. (p. 390.)

They believe that the problem for the ape stems from the fact that the initial event (the wind) is independent of the animal's own behavior, and so it cannot use its own internal sensations (and the consequences that stem from them) to prompt novel ways to produce the desired effect. This is how Tomasello and Call reach the conclusion that performing a novel behavior to make the limb shake would require 'a deeper causal analysis' (p. 389).

For us, the key difference between humans and chimpanzees is not that humans alone understand that there is a web of possibilities connecting an antecedent event to consequent event, but rather that the two species differ in their understanding of the kinds of possible intermediary events. Humans postulate *unobservable* intermediate events or phenomena, whereas the chimpanzee does not. Suppose that one of our apes, Candy, sees an apple resting on a board that is just out of her reach. Next, suppose that she observes a caretaker use his hand to tip the board toward her, causing the apple to fall within reach. Unlike Tomasello and Call (1997), we would not be the least surprised if Candy, on her next encounter with this situation, picked up a stick and used it to tip the board. Notice the parallel between this example and the one cited above:

wind blows ⇒ limb shakes ⇒ fruit falls

hand touches board ⇒ board tips ⇒ apple falls

The reason for our intuitions about Candy's behavior is that we grant chimpanzees the ability to envision alternative means for bringing about particular events (e.g. limbs shaking, boards tipping). Unlike Tomasello and Call, we propose that the striking patterns that our chimpanzees exhibited derive not from their inability to envision alternative means for creating intermediary events, but from the fact that they do not map causal forces (or any unobservable phenomena) onto events or scenes in the first place. In this context, it may be instructive to return to Leslie's (1994) proposal, which we reviewed in Chapter 3. Recall that Leslie has argued that human infants possess a specialized system that takes information about the surface layout of the environment, and the objects within that environment (including the motion and relative positions of objects), and stamps them with a neural code that corresponds to energy distributions. In Chapter 3, we suggested that, regardless of whether this system is as modularized as Leslie proposes, or whether it is present at the exact age he suggests, it provides a starting point for thinking about the potential differences between humans' and chimpanzees' understanding of the physical world.

If some variant of this idea is correct, then chimpanzees will detect many of the same contingencies in the world, and under the right set of circumstances they will (contra Tomasello and Call) have insights about how novel means may be used to generate desired effects (e.g. Köhler 1927), thus allowing them to imagine the appropriate actions for generating the relevant intermediate events (e.g. the limb shaking or the board tipping). However, if we are correct that they do not possess a system for reinterpreting observable physical events in terms of unobservable causal phenomena, then the limits on their insight in such cases will be defined by their understanding of the contingencies involved. For instance, in their effort to recreate the event of the apple falling, a rope that is loosely draped over the board might initially elicit just as enthusiastic a pull as a rope that is firmly tied to the board. In summary, if our proposal is correct, then the characteristic patterns of performances exhibited by our chimpanzees do not derive from their failure to understand the 'web of possibilities' that connect the initial actions to the outcome, nor from the fact that they have not directly acted on the situation.[4] Rather, we propose that their performances derive from the fact that chimpanzees do not form concepts about entities or processes that are not within the province of perception.

Skeptical concerns and replies

We expect that many researchers will object to our portrait of the chimpanzee's folk physics. Indeed, our readers will note that we possess a healthy skepticism about our conclusions as well. In order to air out these objections, we now outline several concerns that we have struggled with over the past several years, followed by our speculative replies.

Are some apes smarter than others?

One immediate concern relates to possible individual differences that may exist among our animals: '*In your experiments, it often seemed as if one or more of your chimpanzees performed better than the others. Indeed, two of your apes, Jadine and Megan, consistently appeared to perform at levels exceeding their peers. Doesn't this suggest that at least some apes, some of the time, utilize concepts related to unobservable causes?*'

This is an intriguing idea, but it contains a hidden assumption which may be false. On the one hand, the idea is intriguing because it highlights a frequently overlooked aspect of working with chimpanzees. However, the idea is misleading as well, because it frequently lures one into imagining that 'smarter' apes are somehow more human-like—a conclusion we sincerely doubt.

---

4   To be clear, we have no doubt that chimpanzees are better at registering contingencies that they themselves have produced, as opposed to those that they have merely observed. However, as the results of our experiments make clear, even when chimpanzees produce a particular effect through their own action on the world in the context of tool use, they still do not appear to attend to unobservable causal phenomenon.

Researchers who have worked with the great apes (and chimpanzees, in particular) have long noted that not all of them are created equal in terms of their general intelligence. For example, Köhler's (1927) outstanding chimpanzee pupil was a particularly bright male named Sultan, and the German psychologist repeatedly contrasted his performance to those of his other, less gifted animals (in particular, a female named Rana). Many years after Köhler's work, Timothy Gill and Duane Rumbaugh (1974) even went as far as to propose a classification of 'bright' versus 'dull' apes based on differences in their ability to transfer knowledge across a particular set of tasks. Thus, it is only reasonable to ask if some of our apes displayed evidence that they possess a folk physics more similar to our own.

The difficulty here rests in determining the precise manner in which 'bright apes' stand out from their peers. In order to gain some perspective on the range of possibilities, let us consider the two most extreme alternatives. First, such apes may appear different from the others because they possess a more 'human-like' causal understanding of the problems that they face. At the other extreme, it is also possible that they are simply 'smarter chimpanzees'—exhibiting more of what chimpanzees naturally have to begin with. In other words, they might perform better on our problems not because they possess a more human-like psychology, but because they are simply better at thinking about the world in the manner that chimpanzees have evolved to think about the world.

How can we evaluate these alternatives? As a beginning, we can review the results of each of our experiments, isolate which ape (or apes) exhibited outstanding performances, and then assess which alternative best explains each result. The results of this review are presented in Table 12.1, and they reveal two things of direct interest. First, Megan and Jadine did consistently perform better than their peers (although several of the other apes occasionally exhibited outstanding performances as well). However, this analysis also reveals that in virtually every case, these 'outstanding performances' were the result of either (1) an animal learning a particular relation faster than the other apes or (2) an animal transferring a very specific set of knowledge from one experiment to the next. In virtually no case did an animal seem to exhibit an immediate solution to a problem in a way that suggested the application of causal concepts. The sole possible exception may have been Jadine in experiment 26, although even here there are reasons to suspect that she did not use explicit causal reasoning (see Chapter 11, General Discussion). Typically, follow-up experiments strongly favored the idea that the exceptional performances were generated by very specific and rigid procedural rules or, as in the case of Jadine's flawless performance in the flimsy-tool problem (experiment 9), the result of some very basic emotional reaction to the test stimuli.

Even if each outstanding performance could be shown to be the result of faster learning or the construction of rules unrelated to the causal structure of the problem at hand, one might still be tempted to argue that the sheer *consistency* of Jadine and Megan's above-average performances suggests that they possess a more human-like understanding than their peers. For example, we might suppose that Jadine and Megan were in the process of learning what human infants and children learn as they develop. On such a

Table 12.1 A summary of the outstanding individual performances across experiments 1–27

Experiment		Outstanding subject(s)	Remarks
1	Trap-tube I	Megan	Follow-up studies (1 (a)–(e) revealed that her performance was governed by rigid, flow-forward procedural rule.
2	Trap-tube II	Megan, Brandy, Candy	Transfer tests revealed that their performance was governed by rigid procedural rules.
3	Trap-table I	Megan	Performance was erratic; displayed no retention 1 year later in experiment 4.
4	Trap-table II	none	—
5	Inverted- and broken-rake	none	—
6–7	Inverted- and broken-rake	Megan	Displayed weak evidence of learning from experiment 5 which used same procedure.
8	Inverted- and broken rake II	none	—
9	Flimsy-tool	Jadine	Experiment 10 clearly established that she was not reasoning about the strength–mass interaction.
10	Flimsy-tool II	none	—
11	Tool-insertion I	none	—
12	Tool-insertion II	none	—

Table 12.1 (*continued*)

Experiment		Outstanding subject(s)	Remarks
13	Tool-insertion II	Jadine	Jadine appeared to learn proper tool orientation across experiment 11–13; indeed, she simply learned faster than two other apes (Megan, Apollo).
14	Rope-and-banana	none	—
15	Hook-retrieval I	none	—
16	Hook-retrieval II	Megan, Jadine	Megan and Jadine both exhibited very narrow transfer of correct option from experiment 15; Megan performed worse than the other animals in the easier of the conditions, and Jadine performed randomly on the most diagnostic trials.
17	Touching-stick I	none	—
18	Touching-stick II	none	—
19	Rake with unconnected base	Jadine, Brandy	Jadine showed no initial comprehension, but may have learned faster than other apes; Brandy showed evidence of initial comprehension but then was erratic.
20	Platform with unconnected post	none	—

Table 12.1 (*continued*)

Experiment		Outstanding subject(s)	Remarks
21	Cloth support I	Mindy, Megan	Follow-up studies (experiments 22 and 23) revealed that Mindy was using a very simple rule related to the visibility of the apple, or the degree of current or imminent contact; for Megan, see below.
22	Cloth support II	Megan	Megan performed well on the correct options from experiment 21, but was random on two of the three new conditions; in addition, experiment 23 revealed that Megan was not reasoning about support.
23	Cloth support III	none	—
24	Bendable-tool I	none	—
25	Bendable-tool II	none	—
26	Bendable-tool III	Jadine	Strong evidence that Jadine learned the necessity of unbending the tool to solve the tool-insertion problem.
27	Tool-construction	none	—

view, Jadine and Megan might never take the final step and develop a full-blown appreciation of unobservable causes, but they might be on the right track.

Setting aside for the moment the question of how children come to construct the understanding that they do, what about the possibility that Jadine and Megan may simply be smarter *chimpanzees*? After all, if we are right, and the chimpanzee's conceptual knowledge about the world is closely tied to entities that are directly accessible to the senses, then an individual with a very well-developed chimpanzee intelligence might be expected to exhibit exactly the kinds of performances that Jadine and Megan displayed. On their initial (and most diagnostic) test trials, they ought to look just like their peers; after all, on our view they possess the same kind of causal understanding as other apes. From that point forward, however, they ought to exhibit faster rates of learning as they home in on the relevant perceptual features of a problem. Furthermore, because of their accentuated reliance on perceptual features, these apes might appear even more rigid than their peers about what they have learned. In contrast, their peers may be quicker to shift strategies in the face of conflicting information, even though they also may rely on exclusively observable information (for evidence in favor of this interpretation, see especially experiments 1, 2, and 17).

In summary, there can be no doubt that there are individual differences in various aspects of the intelligence of our apes. But this does not make them more human. It is possible that they are simply smarter chimpanzees.

Are the tests too difficult?

Another objection to our conclusions concerns the difficulty of our tests: '*Even if you are correct, and reasoning about unobservable causal variables is not something that the chimpanzee brain evolved to do, doesn't this merely show that you have picked problems and tests that are beyond the ability of chimpanzees? Isn't it likely that your approach is like trying to test young children's understanding of calculus?*'

To some extent, we agree. However, this does not mean that we intentionally selected tasks on which we knew our chimpanzees would flounder. On the contrary, our tests were specifically designed to determine whether the things that chimpanzees naturally do with tools—probing, pulling, pushing—are mediated by abstract causal notions. In many of our experiments, we were surprised by the manner in which our chimpanzees initially responded to the problems we presented to them. Thus, it appears correct that our tests are probing at concepts that chimpanzees do not naturally construct. Furthermore, even in those cases where we scaffolded our apes' performances through repeated trials, explicit demonstration, and even overt shaping, we may simply have been pushing them to employ their chimpanzee way of thinking about the world in a manner or context in which they naturally would not. Rather than constructing human concepts for coping with these tasks, our chimpanzees may simply have deployed their existing conceptual structures in new and more extensive ways.

Are the tests 'anthropocentric'?

The previous discussion immediately raises a related concern: '*Look, you have focused on an ability—causal understanding—that is of concern to humans, not chimpanzees. Perhaps if you would simply get out of your anthropocentric way of thinking about the world, you could make better progress toward establishing a proper theory of the chimpanzee's way of thinking.*'

With respect to the first half of this concern, we are guilty as charged. Our research program *is* anthropocentric—at least in the sense that we are specifically interested in reconstructing the evolution of certain high-level cognitive abilities of humans (see Povinelli 1993, 1996; Povinelli and Eddy 1996*b*, Chapter 1). Indeed, this is the question that motivated us to begin with. We want to know which cognitive abilities that are present in humans were present in the common ancestor of the great apes and humans, and in contrast, which abilities uniquely arose during the course of human evolution. Unfortunately, this is an approach that has been consistently neglected in the past century (see Povinelli 1993; Povinelli and Preuss 1995; Povinelli and Prince 1998; Preuss 1993, 1995, in press). Thus, although our project has a strongly anthropocentric dimension, this is also one of its greatest strengths. To cast the issue more broadly, we contend that it is impossible to address the question of the evolution of human nature without being anthropocentric a fair amount of the time.

This does not mean that human specializations are the *only* interesting problems related to cognitive evolution; there are many others. Understanding how other species have evolved cognitive specializations for coping with the specific problems they face has been of increasing interest to many evolutionary biologists (e.g. Cosmides and Tooby 1995; Gaulin 1992; Kamil 1984; Pinker 1997). Indeed, our interest in determining how humans differ from chimpanzees will ultimately lay the foundation for even more creative studies of the unique flavor of chimpanzee cognition. As we explored above, our project has already led to several predictions about ways in which chimpanzees may be different from humans in how they reason about the physical world. Even more to the point, the *differences* between humans and chimpanzees reveal just as much about the fundamental nature of chimpanzee cognition as do the similarities.

Do chimpanzees have difficulty using the causal knowledge they possess?

Another objection to our conclusions is that chimpanzees may possess explicit causal knowledge, but may not be able to use it: '*Recent methodological advances in developmental psychology involving preferential looking and habituation–dishabituation techniques have led some researchers to argue that human infants possess much more knowledge about the physical world than was previously suspected. Maybe chimpanzees are in the same boat. Perhaps they understand specific causal concepts but, for one reason or another, simply can't use them? For instance, perhaps there is only a weak connection between their causal knowl-edge and their action systems, or they just get stuck in some previous way of responding?'*

This question presupposes that experimental measures of perceptual attention in infants (typically, the amount of time an infant spends looking at a display) tap into the kinds of physical phenomena that we have explored in this project. In Chapter 3, we briefly explored evidence derived from such techniques that human infants as young as six months of age may be sensitive to cause–effect relations (Leslie and Keeble 1987). These experiments also suggest that infants possess representations of numerous aspects of the physical world, including a recognition of support, containment, solidity, object constancy, etc. (e.g. Baillargéon *et al.* 1995; Spelke *et al.* 1995). One general inter-pretation of this research is that infants are born with more structured representations of the world than traditional behavioral tasks have revealed (e.g. Spelke 1988)—perhaps because traditional tasks have relied too heavily upon effortful behavioral responses. For example, one of the systematic errors made by young infants on Piaget's classic object permanence tasks (searching where they searched on the previous trial even though they just saw the object placed somewhere else), may be the result of persevera-tion errors (see Diamond 1988). On this view, the infant really knows where the object is, but cannot help but search where she searched the last time.

Do these results really show that human infants have conceptual abilities beyond those exhibited by our chimpanzees? Liz Spelke (1998) has recently argued that prefer-ential looking studies provide evidence for an early-developing sensitivity to three prin-ciples of the behavior of objects: (1) objects move as connected wholes, (2) objects move on connected, unobstructed paths, and (3) objects move on contact with one another. Clearly, our apes were sensitive to such principles. However, it remains an open ques-tion whether preferential looking experiments would reveal sensitivities to *unobservable* causal variables in human infants or chimpanzees.

Some preferential looking experiments suggest that human infants become sensitive to relations between objects such as support, containment, and occlusion (Baillargeon 1998). Does this reflect conceptual abilities beyond those exhibited by our chim-panzees? Not necessarily. After all, young infants may be constructing knowledge about the *behavior* of objects in the world, not concepts like force, gravity, or mass. Consistent with this possibility, infants develop their sensitivities in a piece-meal fashion (e.g., they are sensitive to the fact that a short screen will not completely cover a tall object long before they are sensitive to the fact that a short container will not have the same effect; Hespos and Baillargeon, in press). Human infants may gather information about specific kinds of perceptible events, not reason from general causal principles.

Thus, this 'objection' to our research really constitute two opportunities. First, we need to determine if chimpanzees display greater sensitivity on preferential looking tasks related to physical causality. If they did, we would need to determine the sources of this greater sensitivity. Second, it is now crucial to determine how human infants and apes perform in not-yet-designed preferential looking studies that require sensitivity to *unobservable* causal phenomena. The results of such twin studies would provide a better picture of the various levels at which the statistical regularities that exist in the world are represented and understood in both humans and chimpanzees.

Isn't it all just a matter of experience?

The preceding discussion directly leads to another, equally thorny concern: '*You have consistently portrayed the problem of comparing the psychological abilities of humans and chimpanzees as if it were a matter of identifying which cognitive developmental pathways are present and fixed in each species. But isn't it likely that the differences between chimpanzees and humans are in a large part due to their different experiences? In other words, with enough experience with particular objects and events, wouldn't chimpanzees develop the same concepts as human infants and children?'*

This concern strikes at the heart of a problem that philosophers have been struggling with for centuries, and more recently has become a central challenge for developmental psychologists. Namely, what role does experience play in the development of our mental structures? Obviously, how we answer this question for our own species will affect how we answer similar questions about other species.

One line of thinking is that our cognitive structures are innately specified, requiring only appropriate experiences in order to trigger their maturation (e.g. Fodor 1983). At the other extreme, some theorists maintain that our cognitive structures are literally constructed, bit by bit, through a complex feedback process between the organism and its environment (e.g. Piaget 1954). There is some middle ground between these two extremes, namely the idea that the infant arrives into the world with a set of innately endowed starting conditions, from which point later developments depart (e.g. Leslie 1994). As Alison Gopnik and Andy Meltzoff (1997) have pointed out, there are actually two camps that uncomfortably inhabit this middle ground. On the one hand, some theorists argue that infants arrive in the world with a set of core beliefs that are primitive building blocks for all later concepts. These initial beliefs are shielded from experience, and operate as fundamental, unalterable units of thought (e.g. Spelke *et al.* 1995). On the other hand, a less constrained view can be found in theorists who maintain that infants are equipped at birth with a set of biases in how incoming sensory information is represented (along with rules for operating on these representations) (e.g. Astington and Gopnik 1991). This latter view can be wedded to the idea that, in addition to a set of starting conditions, infants are born with a central cognitive system that serves as an engine for future discoveries about the world—including the discovery that some of the initial assumptions about the world are incorrect (e.g. Gopnik and Meltzoff 1997). This view of cognitive development has been branded the 'theory-theory', because it maintains that the central engine of cognitive development from infancy forward is a psychological system that operates very much like the way scientists construct, falsify, and revise theories about the world. More detailed statements of these views can be found elsewhere (Carey 1985; Fodor 1983; Gopnik and Meltzoff 1997; Leslie 1994; Pinker 1997; Spelke *et al.* 1995; Wellman 1990).

Although we cannot resolve the question of how cognitive structures mature and develop in humans, we can briefly explore how the possibilities outlined above affect our answer to the question of how experience influences the chimpanzee's understanding of causality. Let us start with the view of cognitive development that seems most amenable to the possibility that experience can indeed alter the chimpanzee's core beliefs about the world. As we have seen, the 'theory-theory' view of cognitive development argues that infants are born with a specific set of representations and cognitive rules, but that with experience the representations are modified, altered, and frequently rejected altogether. Thus, if one were looking for some theoretical support for the concern expressed above, one might turn to the theory-theory for assistance. A naive application of this theory to the problem of comparing chimpanzees and humans might lead one to argue that both species start out with common representations of the world, but, because of the different experiences that they receive, their representations begin to diverge as they develop. From this, it seems to follow that if chimpanzees received the same kind and amount of experiences that human infants have, they would arrive at the same set of beliefs.

At present, this possibility cannot be refuted. However, we can at least point out that there is nothing about the theory-theory which forces this conclusion. After all, the theory-theory was developed to explain *human* cognitive development. Its application to other species begins with the seemingly gentle assumption that at some level there are many similarities in the underlying mechanisms of cognitive development of human and chimpanzees. As we have seen, however, the existence of strong commonalities between the two species in no way implies that all outputs of the two systems will be identical. There is nothing about the theory-theory that precludes humans and chimpanzees from possessing a complex constellation of both similar and different starting structures and rules—rules and structures that ultimately lead them to both similar and different outputs.

A serious difficulty arises in attempting to sort out superficial similarities in behavior from deep similarities in the psychological processes which generate the behaviors, especially if the behavioral similarities are magnified by providing chimpanzees with experiences more like those received by our own children. The problem is all the more complicated because the cognitive specializations of our species may not have endowed us with behaviors that were impossible without them, but instead have made it much easier to generate, plan, and reorganize *existing* behaviors (see Chapter 2). Commonalities in the morphological, motivational, sensory, motor, and central cognitive systems of chimpanzees and humans are likely to be so extensive, and the problem space so limited, that similar performances are virtually guaranteed under the right set of circumstances. But this does not mean that the same psychological processes have produced them. Indeed, we have often been tempted to regard the improving performances our chimpanzees on a given task as a sort of marionette show, with experience serving as the invisible strings that orchestrate our apes' behavior. But there is one great difference between the performance of marionettes and our chimpanzees. Marionettes have no internal mental activity that ground them to the external world; chimpanzees do. Unlike wooden puppets, chimpanzees actively apply their principles of folk physics to the situations they encounter. But if our speculations are correct, when these principles fail (as in the cases where we design tasks that probe for an understanding of invisible causal mechanism), experience alone will not lead chimpanzees to construct concepts for which evolution did not adequately prepare them.

But what if we are wrong? What if experience does play a major role in the development of the psychological structures that are related to our species' ability to reason about causal concepts? In this century, there were two major attempts to immerse chimpanzees in our culture in an effort to determine if this would affect their cognitive development (Hayes 1951; Kellogg and Kellogg 1933). In addition, there have been other projects in which chimpanzees (and other great apes) have been heavily exposed to human culture in the context of attempting to teach them a linguistic system (Gardner and Gardner 1971; Miles 1994; Patterson and Linden 1981; Premack 1976; Rumbaugh 1977; Savage-Rumbaugh and Lewin 1994). Unfortunately, these projects typically relied on a single subject, and because of their focus on language acquisition the projects were not carried out in ways that can assist us in answering the questions we are addressing here (but see Premack 1976).

Tomasello (1995, 1996) has reviewed data from these projects, and has argued that apes who have been 'enculturated' with humans appear to develop cognitive structures not present in their un-enculturated cousins (see also Tomasello and Call 1997). Premack (1988) has also argued that learning certain aspects of human culture (in particular, specific linguistic abilities) fundamentally alters aspects of the chimpanzee's core cognitive structures. We are skeptical about such claims, mainly because the experimental evidence for them is currently abysmal (Povinelli 1996; Povinelli and Giambrone, in press). In our view, there has never been a serious, scientifically rigorous attempt to compare the psychological abilities of chimpanzees that have been reared exclusively with humans to chimpanzees that have been reared with each other. We recognize that such a project would be time-consuming and costly. But if it were conducted properly, it would stand as one of the most important achievements in the history of the cognitive sciences.

What about tool use in the wild?

It is fitting that the final concern that we explore is the one that may be the most difficult to resolve: '*Your tests involve captive chimpanzees. Now, of course your apes have had a rich set of experiences growing up with each other, and undoubtedly they have had a great deal of exposure to both humans and objects. Nonetheless, isn't it still possible that chimpanzees born and raised in the wild have a folk physics that is more similar to our own than the one possessed by your apes? After all, chimpanzees born in the wild spontaneously develop tool-using behaviors and interact with a much more complex physical environment on a daily basis.*'

Indeed, this is a concern, and it is one that could lead us to undertake a detailed comparison of the daily challenges faced by our chimpanzees versus those living in the wild (and, to be sure, they will turn out to be different!). Furthermore, unless we are careful, it could lead us into a (scientifically) unproductive debate about the ethics of keeping chimpanzees in captive settings, a debate that would lead us astray from a valid scientific concern. Thus, let us quickly get to the heart of the matter. Our chimpanzees had no trouble whatsoever learning to use the tools we presented to them. Furthermore, it is fair to say that we have seen our apes exhibit examples, or analogues, of nearly every kind of tool-using ability that has been reported for free-ranging chimpanzees (see McGrew 1992). We have also seen several kinds of tool use that have not been reported for free-ranging chimpanzees. For example, our chimpanzees are quite fond of taking plastic buckets, hats, and other toys, filling them with water, adding various foodstuffs, and making 'soups' (gumbos, perhaps) that they then slowly consume.

But does the commonality of tool use and manufacture in captive and free-ranging chimpanzees really speak to the concern addressed above? Perhaps the particular kind of interaction with physical objects and substrates experienced by free-ranging chimpanzees (like the limbs of trees while picking fruits) leads the wild ape to construct a fundamentally different way of interpreting the physical world. In other words, our indictment of the argument by analogy applies here as well! However, this possibility cuts both ways. Our captive chimpanzees may possess a more elaborated folk physics than their counterparts in the wild. After all, we have frequently pushed our apes to confront the conceptual 'joints' of tool using in ways that chimpanzees in the wild do not. Thus, although it is impossible to say what free-ranging chimpanzees understand without directly testing them, there is some reason to think they may develop less elaborated understandings of the physical world than do intensively tutored and trained captive chimpanzees. It is also possible that both of these positions are incorrect. The development of the core principles of chimpanzee folk physics may require experiences that are common to both groups of chimpanzees. If true, the differences between the two populations will reflect differences in acquired skills, not core psychological structures (see Köhler 1927; Yerkes 1943).

There are some field researchers who take a strong position against any information derived from captive settings, likening the similarity between wild and captive chimpanzees to the similarity between normal children and children that have been abandoned in the wild and raised by wolves (see McGrew 1992, p. 37). Still others will seize upon the most sophisticated instances of tool use exhibited by free-ranging chimpanzees, such as using smaller stones to stabilize a larger stone in the context of nutcracking, while simultaneously downplaying the fact that such instances have only been witnessed three times in the course of seven years of observation (see Matsuzawa 1996). We can say little to rebut such extreme positions except to note that, under far more controlled circumstances, we have regularly observed many an apparently brilliant instance of tool use, only to discover time and time again (through the use of proper control tests) that our common-sense interpretation of these behaviors were mistaken.

Perhaps the most fundamental lesson that we have learned from our research is that our naive interpretations are typically blind to psychological processes that differ substantially from our own.

Self-representation and the evolution of tool use

There is an important loose end in our account of chimpanzee folk physics and their manufacture and use of tools. In both captivity and in the wild, chimpanzees have a reputation for making and using tools more often and in more varied ways than other non-human primates—so much so that at least one researcher has even suggested that '*[t]he most parsimonious interpretation [of the data]…is that the chimpanzee is the only true tool-user…* All tool-use by other apes can then be written off as freak accidents or as somehow prompted by contact with human beings' (McGrew 1992, p. 59, italics in original). Although this may be regarded as a somewhat extreme statement, it does reflect a widely-held sentiment that chimpanzees may possess a more elaborate folk physics than other species.

Are chimpanzees special tool users?

Are chimpanzees somehow special (relative to other apes) in their manufacture and use of tools? Perhaps, but do not suggest this to the experienced zookeeper. Many years ago, we were told the following story which was attributed to a zookeeper who had worked with the great apes for many years: 'You can test the intelligence of the great apes—gorillas, chimpanzees, and orangutans—by tossing a screwdriver into each of their cages. The gorilla will approach the screwdriver, sniff it, and walk away. The chimpanzee will run up to the screwdriver, put it in its mouth, chew it up, and then spit it out. The orangutan, though, will calmly stroll up to the screwdriver, pick it up, and while you are not looking, put it under her arm; after you go home she will use it to dismantle her cage and escape.'

Although undoubtedly apocryphal, the story does capture something interesting about tool use in the anthropoid apes (chimpanzees, gorillas, orangutans, and gibbons). In the wild, chimpanzees clearly exhibit far more extensive use and manufacture of tools than do gorillas or orangutans, who exhibit far less (see McGrew 1992; but for evidence of habitual use of tools in one population of free-ranging orangutans, see van Schaik and Fox 1996). In captivity, however, orangutans exhibit a remarkable capacity for tool use—a capacity at least as great as that found in chimpanzees (e.g. Lethmate 1982). In contrast to chimpanzees and orangutans, gorillas and gibbons exhibit a much lower penchant for tool use and manufacture even in captivity (McGrew 1992). Thus, among the anthropoid apes, orangutans and chimpanzees appear quite different from gorillas and gibbons in the context of tool use and manufacture. But, as reflected in the zookeeper's story, perhaps the most interesting animal is the orangutan, displaying an extraordinary facility for making and using tools in captivity, but far less so in the wild. We shall return to this very important discrepancy shortly.

McGrew (1992) has attempted to account for the phyletic differences in tool use that appear to exist among the anthropoid apes. He examined the relationship between the degree of tool use in these species and numerous other factors, including brain size, diet, group size, locomotor styles, hand morphology, and cognition. Interestingly, McGrew discovered that the cognitive factor which best predicted the degree of tool use in the anthropoid apes was the ability of organisms to recognize themselves in mirrors. Chimpanzees and orangutans exhibit clear evidence of self-recognition, whereas gorillas and gibbons do not (see below). McGrew found this result puzzling, noting that, given that the ability to recognize oneself in a mirror does not involve object manipulation (as do the other cognitive tests he examined), 'the fit [between the capacity for self-recognition and tool use in a species] is even more striking' (p. 61).

We do not find this relation puzzling. But in order to understand why not, we first need to present our theory for why such a striking ability—self-recognition in mirrors—displays such a peculiar phylogenetic distribution.

Self-recognition in primates

The ability of chimpanzees to recognize themselves in mirrors was first demonstrated by Gordon Gallup (1970). His results revealed that chimpanzees can spontaneously learn to use mirrors to gain access to previously unavailable information about their physical appearance. When they first encounter their images in mirrors, chimpanzees respond as if they are seeing other chimpanzees. However, within minutes to hours of first seeing themselves in this manner, chimpanzees may display a shift from treating the image as another conspecific, to observing themselves as they make exaggerated facial contortions, and pick at their eyes, ears, teeth, and ano-genital region (Fig. 12.2; see Povinelli *et al.* 1993). In short, they learn to use the mirror to explore aspects of themselves that they have never seen before. Gallup (1970) also developed a more rigorous experimental demonstration of the self-recognition ability of chimpanzees. The animals were anesthetized, and a colorful red mark was placed on their upper eyebrow ridge and ear. Later, the chimpanzees made no attempts to touch these marks until a mirror was re-introduced. Upon seeing themselves, the subjects immediately reached up and touched the marks, occasionally followed by attempts to smell or inspect their fingers. Although some have challenged whether chimpanzees are really able to recognize themselves in mirrors (e.g. Heyes 1994), recent analyses provide clear support for the idea that chimpanzees are able to rapidly learn to use mirrored information about themselves in order to generate the behaviors described above (Povinelli *et al.* 1997a).

Shortly after Gallup's (1970) initial report was published, Lethmate and Dücker (1973) reported discovering the same ability in orangutans (see also Suarez and Gallup 1981). However, coincident with his original discovery of self-recognition in chimpanzees, Gallup also reported the failure to demonstrate the same ability in several species of monkeys. Indeed, despite numerous experiments that have involved weeks, months, and, in several cases, even a lifetime of exposure to mirrors, not a single

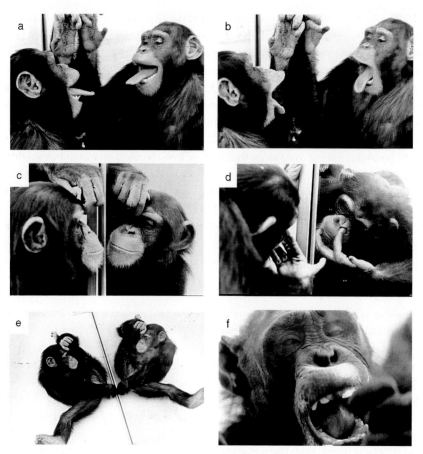

Figure 12.2 Examples of chimpanzees using mirrors to engage in exaggerated facial displays (a)–(b), and to explore otherwise unobservable body parts (c)–(f). Photos by Donna Bierschwale.

member of a species outside the great apes and humans has displayed the pattern of behaviors so characteristic of those chimpanzees and orangutans that display evidence of self-recognition (see Anderson 1983; Anderson and Roeder 1989; Bayart and Anderson 1985; Benhar *et al.* 1975; Fornasieri *et al.* 1991; Gallup 1970, 1977*b*; Gallup and Suarez 1991; Gallup *et al.* 1980; Itakura 1987*a,b*; Lethmate and Dücker 1973; Suarez and Gallup 1981). Equally intriguing is the fact that gorillas have also typically failed to exhibit evidence of this phenomenon (see Ledbetter and Basen 1982; Suarez and Gallup 1981). However, as we shall see, gorillas probably descended from an ancestor that possessed the ability, and thus still have a latent capacity for self-recognition (see Povinelli 1993, 1994). Attempts to demonstrate self-recognition in species outside the primate order, including elephants and dolphins, have also not been successful (Marino *et al.* 1994; Povinelli 1989).

In the 30 years that have elapsed since Gallup (1970) first published his failure to find self-recognition in monkeys, there have been several claims of self-recognition in one or more individual monkeys (and even dolphins) (e.g. Boccia 1994; Thompson and Boatright-Horowitz 1994). Perhaps the boldest claim of this type was made by Hauser, Kralik, Botto-Mahan, Garrett and Oser (1995), who reported evidence of self-recognition in a number of cotton-top tamarins. This report was widely heralded as finally establishing self-recognition in species outside the great apes and humans (e.g. Shettleworth 1998; Tomasello and Call 1997; de Veer and van den Bos 1999). However, after videotapes of the alleged instances of self-recognition were made available, and were publicly critiqued for not supporting the claims that had been published (see Anderson and Gallup 1997), Hauser and his colleagues then reported a failure to replicate their original findings (Hauser 1999*b* (unpublished manuscript)). As it stands, the capacity for self-recognition in mirrors appears restricted to humans, chimpanzees, and orangutans (Gallup 1994).

Claims about the presence and absence of self-recognition in various species has sparked an intense and often rancorous debate (see essays in Mitchell *et al.* 1997; Parker *et al.* 1994; see also Heyes 1994, 1995). We believe that the sources of the controversy have less to do with the question of potential phylogenetic discontinuities than with the psychological implications of such discontinuities. Gallup (1970), for example, interpreted his findings as evidence that chimpanzees possess an explicit self-concept, a capacity that may not extend 'below man and the great apes' (p. 87; see also Gallup 1977*a*). He has argued that in order for an organism to understand who it is seeing in a mirror, it must first have a concept of self. Later, Gallup (1982) elaborated this argument by speculating that the capacity for self-recognition indicates that chimpanzees and orangutans might possess some form of introspection. Furthermore, Gallup (1970, 1977*a*, 1982) has maintained that the absence of self-recognition in other species implies that they do not possess an explicit self-concept—a claim that (on intuitive grounds) has proven unpalatable to many comparative psychologists (as discussed in Povinelli 1993). On this interpretation of self-recognition in mirrors, it is easy to see why McGrew (1992) found the correlation between self-recognition and tool use so difficult to understand. First, the tests do not involve object manipulation, and second, other primate species which are known to use tools (such as capuchin monkeys), do not display evidence of self-recognition (see Anderson and Roeder 1989). Furthermore, the acquisition of tool use by any given monkey does not correctly predict that it will pass a test of self-recognition (see Bayart and Anderson 1985).

Self-recognition and the kinesthetic self-concept

Previously, we have offered an alternative to Gallup's explanation for the psychological factors which lead to self-recognition in mirrors (see Povinelli 1995, 1998)—one that may account for why chimpanzees and orangutans exhibit both self-recognition and elaborated patterns of tool use, whereas gorillas and gibbons exhibit neither. To begin, we agree with Gallup's (1970) original claim that the capacity for self-recognition in mirrors reveals the presence of an underlying self-concept—a type of self-concept that is not present in species which do not possess this capacity. However, our account argues that self-recognition in chimpanzees and orangutans, as well as human toddlers (e.g. Amsterdam 1972; Lewis and Brooks-Gunn 1979), is based on an explicit representation of on-line kinesthetic (or bodily) states. Briefly, we have argued that when toddlers, chimpanzees, and orangutans see themselves in mirrors they form an equivalence relation between the behaviors they observe in the mirror and what they experience themselves doing at that moment (for a detailed description of our model, see Povinelli 1995). Each time they move, the mirror image moves with them. From this, they conclude that everything that is true of the mirror image is also true of them, and vice versa. This allows these organisms to use their mirror images to explore themselves, as well as pass the mark test, because they know that whatever is true of the image is also true of them. Thus, although we agree with Gallup that an organism's capacity for self-recognition depends on the existence of an explicit self-concept, we believe that it is the organism's explicit representation of its own behavior that is relevant, not its representation of its *psychological* self. Furthermore, the chimpanzee or orangutan who succeeds in passing the mark test does not conclude, 'That's me!', but rather, 'That's the same as me!' Results of studies with young human children have revealed that entire aspects of self-recognition are strongly disrupted if the visual feedback about their behavior is even slightly delayed (see Povinelli 1995; Povinelli and Simon 1998; Povinelli *et al.* 1996a, 1999).

Several other investigators have proposed alternatives to, or elaborations of Gallup's ideas about the underlying causes of self-exploratory behaviors and passing the mark test (Epstein *et al.* 1981; Mitchell 1993; Parker 1991). Although they differ in a number of important ways, most of these models either explicitly state, or implicitly assume, that before an organism can display evidence of self-recognition, it must first learn more generally that mirrors reflect accurate images of things that are in front of them (Bertenthal and Fischer 1978; Mitchell 1993; see Shettleworth 1998 for a 'textbook' statement of this view). This line of thinking has led researchers to view the mark test as a problem in which the organism must search for the 'hidden' location of the red marks they see in the mirror (e.g. Bertenthal and Fischer 1978; Mitchell 1993). This reasoning appears to be incorrect. For example, in human infants there is no connection between the ability to pass the mark test and the understanding that mirrors reflect things that are in front of them (Loveland 1986; Robinson *et al.* 1990; Zazzo 1982). By contrast, our model holds that organisms 'recognize themselves' in mirrors because they detect an equivalence between what they see occurring in the mirror and their own internal kinesthetic representation of their body, and does not require them to understand the reflective properties of mirrors (see Povinelli 1995).

Thus, although our model agrees with Gallup's in postulating that passing the mark test reveals the presence of an explicit self-concept—a conceptual structure that is lacking or not well-developed in other species—we differ in our view of the nature and scope of the dimensions of the self that are being conceptualized. Gallup believes that chimpanzees possess an understanding of their own psychological states, whereas we believe that they possess an explicit mental representation of the position and movement of their own bodies—what could be called a kinesthetic self-concept. Ironically, this may be closer to what Gallup (1970) himself had in mind when he originally published his discovery of self-recognition in chimpanzees. He noted that self-recognition appears to require the ability to project 'kinesthetic feedback onto the reflected visual image so as to coordinate the appropriate visually guided movements via the mirror' (p. 87). Furthermore, we speculate that this kind of explicit, kinesthetic self-concept is not present in other species. Indeed, like Gallup, we see no reason why most organisms would need this kind of explicit self-representation, when other information processing systems would suffice.

On the evolutionary origins of the kinesthetic self-concept

Why, then, do humans, chimpanzees, and orangutans possess this explicit kinesthetic self-concept? One clue may lie in the large difference in body weight that exists between the great apes and other primates. Consider orangutans, who may represent the closest living approximation to the last common ancestor of the great apes and humans. Several years ago, John Cant and I spent a couple of field seasons observing the locomotor behavior of free-ranging orangutans in the rain forests of Northern Sumatra. On each occasion we spent several months documenting the orangutan's unique blend of slow, carefully-planned movements as they cross the formidable gaps between the high canopies of trees, and their cautious, breathtaking acrobatics. We concluded that the problems that these 40- to 80-kilogram (90- to 180-pound) animals face, as they move across the canopy from tree to tree in search of food, are qualitatively different than those faced by the much smaller-bodied monkeys and gibbons who inhabit the same environment (for examples of the remarkable techniques used by orangutans in these contexts, see Cant 1987, 1992a; Chevalier-Skolnikoff *et al.* 1982). The extreme body weight of these animals tends to deform the terminal ends of the limbs of trees, opening up gaps between trees. This problem is rarely encountered by monkeys and gibbons, whose much smaller body size results in minimal deformation, or who are easily able to leap across such gaps (see Cant 1988). Also unlike monkeys and gibbons, whose locomotor patterns are highly stereotyped and easily pigeon-holed (e.g. quadrupedal running or walking, leaping, etc.), the vast majority of orangutan locomotion involves a highly variable, difficult-to-describe behavior known as 'clambering'. Clambering is a form of locomotion in which the body's trunk is vertically oriented, with various combinations of the animal's appendages grasping supports in different directions, both above and below the animal (see Cant 1987; Povinelli and Cant 1995). Clambering appears to be directly linked to the extreme body weight of orangutans; other forms of locomotion are simply not possible given the effects of their body weight on the environment. Interestingly, orangutans frequently use the deformation caused by their body weight to help generate a solution to the problem that it created in the first place. They do so by generating back-and-forth motions until a tree begins to sway, ultimately allowing them to swing across gaps in the canopy (see Cant 1992*a*; Chevalier-Skolnikoff *et al.* 1982). For those who have not observed orangutans negotiating their way through the canopy, it is difficult to convey how the size and grace of these animals combine to form the impression that they are at once completely ill-suited and yet also perfectly adapted for their highly specialized arboreal lifestyle.

As we reflected on this odd mixture of extraordinary body size, highly arboreal lifestyle, and unusual form of locomotion (especially when crossing gaps between trees), an explanation for the initial evolution of an explicit, kinesthetic self-concept suddenly occurred to us. We hypothesized that as the ancestors of the great apes evolved—quadrupling in body size over a 10–20 million year period—natural selection favored an increasingly sophisticated self-representational system dedicated to planning movements in their arboreal environment (see Povinelli and Cant 1995). Unlike the much smaller-bodied species of primates that inhabit the same habitats, orangutans can hardly afford a fall from 30 meters up in the canopy. Our model posited that the ultimate consequence of this selection process was a representational system that permitted the common ancestor of humans and the great apes (a large-bodied, highly arboreal species) to 'see' itself in 'a three dimensional skein of highly variable fragility, compliance, and space, whose properties change in response to its movements' (p. 410). If true, we realized that this evolutionarily unprecedented increase in body size for a tree-dwelling mammal may have left its imprint on the common ancestor of the great apes and humans as an explicit kinesthetic self-concept. Indeed, if our theory is correct, it was this self-concept that Gallup (1970) inadvertently tapped millions of years later when he discovered the chimpanzee's capacity for self-recognition. Notably, our model only accounts for the evolution of an explicit motor, or kinesthetic, self-concept.

A crucial test case for our theory is the gorilla, the largest nonhuman primate. Although gorillas share a unique common ancestor with humans, chimpanzees, and orangutans, they have apparently readapted to spending the majority of their waking hours on the ground. The absence of self-recognition in this species, then, may reflect the fact that the ancestors of gorillas no longer needed to execute the complex motor planning procedures that were necessary to transport their enormous body weight across the gaps between trees. Indeed, their evolutionary history appears to have been centered around their readaptation to a terrestrial way of life, including a more rapid physical maturation rate than that found in chimpanzees and orangutans (Watts and Pusey 1993). There is some evidence that the selection for rapid physical development of gorillas may have occurred at the expense of later stages of sensorimotor development (Antinucci 1989; Potì and Spinozzi 1994). Given that self-recognition typically emerges at the end of the classic sensorimotor stages in both humans and chimpanzees (see Bertenthal and Fischer 1978; Povinelli *et al.* 1993), we have suggested that selection for rapid physical maturation interfered with the construction of a less-needed kinesthetic self-representational system (see Povinelli 1994). Human evolution, in contrast, appears to have favored *slower* growth rates, allowing more years for cognitive development (ultimately allowing for not just the preservation of the self-concept, but an extensive elaboration of it). A more complete discussion of the 'clambering hypothesis' and its implications can by found elsewhere (Bering 1999; Povinelli 1993, 1994; Povinelli and Cant 1995; Povinelli and Prince 1998; Shettleworth 1998).

Self-recognition and tool use: the kinesthetic connection

By this point, our reader may have anticipated the connection that we envision between self-recognition in mirrors and tool use. As we have seen, McGrew (1992) found the relation between the two puzzling, because self-recognition in mirrors does not involve object manipulation. However, if orangutans and chimpanzees possess an explicit kinesthetic self-concept, one which allows them to explicitly represent the distinction between their movements, the environment's response, and the connection between the two (see Povinelli and Cant 1995), then we can more easily see how tool use might become greatly elaborated in these species. Although many animals possess psychological systems which allow them to learn how to use tools, organisms with an explicit representation of their own actions and movements would be expected to develop even more elaborate patterns of tool use. This seems all the more likely given Povinelli and Cant's (1995) suggestion that the emergence of this kinesthetic self-concept may have been a by-product of selection for pre-planning the self's movements, as well as for anticipating the effects of those movements on the environment. Thus, extending the ideas of Povinelli and Cant, *we hypothesize that although many nonhuman primates may learn to use tools, chimpanzees and orangutans more explicitly represent the distinction between their actions, the tool, and the tool's actions on the environment.* Interestingly, in indicting the traditional Piagetian analysis of tool use, Tomasello and Call (1997) argue that 'when a subject manipulates a tool, it becomes an extension of the subject's own appendages; the subject controls the causal event in much the same way as if it had used its own hands' (p. 388). By contrast, we propose that chimpanzees and orangutans draw a clear distinction between their actions on a tool, and the tool's effect on the world, whereas other species do not. We are currently in the process of experimentally testing this prediction.

An evolutionary scenario

The preceding discussion suggests the following evolutionary scenario for the evolution of the explicit kinesthetic self-concept which we believe supports self-recognition in mirrors and the capacity for elaborated patterns of tool use in modern orangutans and chimpanzees. Based on fossil evidence, we assume that the ancestor of the great apes was a large-bodied arboreal animal (see Povinelli and Cant 1995). We suspect that it was committed to arboreality due to external constraints such as terrestrial predators.[5] As the body size of these ancestors increased through evolutionary time, this led to prob-

---

5   Based on the existing evidence, this would seem to be a plausible assumption. Modern orangutans, for example, are found only on the islands of Sumatra and Borneo. On Sumatra, terrestrial predators (large cats) are present and orangutans rarely or never come to the forest floor. In contrast, terrestrial predators have been extinct on Borneo for perhaps 10,000 years or more, and on this island, orangutans frequently descend to the ground if they are travelling considerable distances.

lems in crossing gaps between trees—an ability foundational to all other subsistence activities (Cant 1992*b*). Under these conditions, selection favored organisms with well-integrated systems for processing information about on-line bodily states, motor actions, and environmental responses. This ability was favored because it allowed these organisms to explicitly represent their own bodies as both the cause of, and solution to, problems created by their body weight.[6] We propose that this process led to the emergence of an explicit kinesthetic self-concept in the common ancestor of the great apes and human. From this point, each of the remaining lineages evolved in their own unique directions. Orangutans became even more specialized in an arboreal lifestyle, gorillas moved in the opposite direction, and chimpanzees (both *Pan troglodytes* and *Pan paniscus*) specialized in a niche somewhere between the two. Humans represent a special case altogether. At some point, our lineage became completely terrestrial, although the timing and reason for this event is hotly contested (see Conroy 1997; Foley 1987; Klein 1989). In any event, humans eventually specialized in a very unique way of life, presumably involving extreme selection for a specific type of altriciality.

Although this idea is only a scenario (or, more pejoratively, a 'just-so' story), it does offer a coherent interpretation of the otherwise puzzling aspects of tool use in the anthropoid apes. Because orangutans can be thought of as still utilizing their kinesthetic self-representation in the context in which it evolved, we might expect that they possess the most elaborate *capacity* for elaborated patterns of tool use. However, we also expect that this potential will only become apparent in captive, terrestrial settings where the opportunities for tool use are more abundant, and they are not preoccupied with arboreal travel. On the other hand, free-ranging chimpanzees travel on the ground to a great extent (*P. troglodytes* more so than *P. paniscus*), and we speculate that they found their kinesthetic self-representational system to be an excellent exaptation ('preadaptation') for tool using and tool making in the context of retrieving high-quality food resources. Gorillas, in contrast, followed a different evolutionary track. Although some gorillas may regularly climb trees to build nests or retrieve fruits, they do not typically cross gaps between them, and they spend the majority of their lives on the ground. We propose that this reduced the importance of an explicit kinesthetic self-representational system in this species. And, for whatever reason, as selection began to favor a larger

---

6   We use the term 'cause' here loosely, although it is intriguing to speculate that chimpanzees may have a better understanding of internal motor causes than of external causes of the type that we have been exploring here (see Povinelli and Prince 1998). In this vein, Povinelli and Cant (1995) argued that chimpanzees and orangutans may possess an Intention Monitor. As conceived by Frith and Done (1989), the Intention Monitor has three functions: (1) it determines if actions that are driven by a goal or plan (a willed intention) resulted in the desired outcome; (2) it monitors the environment to determine if actions that are elicited by external triggers achieved the appropriate outcome; and, perhaps most relevant to the clambering hypothesis, (3) it identifies the source of particular intentions and thus is able to discriminate between actions and effects that resulted from external versus internal causes.

body size in this species, several other ecological strategies were favored, including a lower-quality diet and a premium on rapid physical growth and development. We speculate that this created a cost–benefit tradeoff that ultimately resulted in truncating the developmental pathways responsible for the construction of their ancestral explicit kinesthetic self-concept (see Povinelli 1994 for details and biological precedents for this kind of phenomenon).

The zookeeper was right

If the idea we have outlined above is more or less correct, then it means the zookeeper was right: the orangutan should be one of the best tool users among the great apes. But if so, it is not because evolution specifically selected for elaborated patterns of tool use in that species. Indeed, if our account is correct, neither the capacity for elaborated tool use, nor the capacity for self-recognition was directly selected for in the ancestors of the great apes and humans. Rather, both capacities may be incidental by-products of a unique evolutionary convergence of a large body size, an arboreal lifestyle, and the anthropoid brain.

Reinterpretation reapplied: deflating the polemic of human uniqueness

Educating apes

For better or worse, the last three decades of research on the psychological abilities of the great apes have been driven by an attempt to undermine claims of human uniqueness (see Gardner and Gardner 1971; Premack 1976; Rumbaugh 1977; for more recent examples, see essays in Russon *et al.* 1996). For example, in the introductory chapter to a recent volume dedicated (*literally*) to the great apes, Anne Russon and Kim Bard (1996) attack the idea of human uniqueness, and assert that the minds of the great apes are 'very much like our own', that 'researchers are regularly finding heretofore unexpected realms and degrees of similarity', and these similarities are 'particularly useful for evolutionary reconstructions' (p. 14). They offer caveats, of course, but even these are cast in such a way that they are no threat to the idea of intellectual continuity between human and ape: 'Although great ape abilities fall well short of those achieved by humans, evidence that all the great apes can handle such tasks as rudimentary language, insightful or tool-assisted problem solving, and abstract learning is seriously challenging traditional views that their reach is bounded by symbolic level processing' (p. 8).

Some researchers see chimpanzees as 'the ultimate challenge to traditional definitions of human uniqueness', and see their own role as 'human tutors' (Boysen 1996, p. 177). Others are unembarrassed at describing their research as 'a process of negotiation within the transaction' between the human and the ape: 'Not only does Chantek [an orangutan] move closer to the target behavior,' explains Lyn Miles (1996, p. 295) in describing her studies of imitation, 'but the caregivers will sometimes adjust the target behavior toward Chantek's last action.' Determined to demonstrate similarity, many researchers train on, without ever seriously considering the possibility that the very extent of the efforts required to produce human-like behaviors in their animals undermines the very claims they wish to make in the first place. Nonetheless, the final results of such projects seem impressive—so impressive that the layperson may be excused for thinking that the only thing left to settle on is the degree of similarity between the minds of humans and apes. The visual rhetoric of *National Geographic* and *BBC* documentaries on chimpanzee social organization, tool use, and cooperative hunting has already paved the way, preparing the general public to be persuaded that the remarkable behavioral similarity between humans and apes is a sure guide to a comparable degree of psychological similarity.

But, as we have seen, this is the logic of the argument by analogy, a logic harkening to the days of Hume, Darwin, and Romanes. Even today, many researchers still find the core idea of the argument convincing. Unfortunately, as we have hopefully made clear, the argument by analogy is as logically flawed as it is intuitively persuasive.

Taking human specializations seriously

The reinterpretation hypothesis (see Chapter 2) offers a new and potentially more productive way of addressing the similarities and differences that exist between humans and apes. The reinterpretation hypothesis begins with the assumption that every species is unique—a veritable truism of modern biology. But in acknowledging the fact of this psychological diversity, our proposal does not shy away from the fact that humans are a particularly interesting and worthy case study. After all, it seems almost obvious that human evolution has been associated with the emergence of numerous cognitive specializations, including language itself.[7] Furthermore, our own research suggests that some of these specializations may have affected our understanding of the social and the physical world to equal degrees.

In considering the similarities and differences that appear to exist between humans and chimpanzees in their folk physics and folk psychology, we can see that there is at least one element common to both sets of comparisons. Unlike humans, the chimpanzee's reasoning about both physical objects and social beings appears restricted to concepts, ideas, and procedures that are linked to the world of tangible things. In both the social and the physical case, the chimpanzee learns about the observable properties of these entities, and the kinds of behaviors that these entities typically exhibit. The chimpanzee even takes the impressive leap of generalizing to new instances. But in

---

7   Recent neurobiological research is beginning to reveal underlying structural differences in the brains of humans and apes that may ultimately prove to be related to some of these differences. For example, Preuss, Qi, and Kaas (1999) have recently published the first well-documented difference between the cortical organization of humans and other apes—in the middle of the primary visual cortex! Additional human brain specializations are likely to be documented with increasing rapidity as neuroscientists begin to grasp the significance of exploring the diversity of brain organization that evolution has produced (Preuss *et al.* 1999).

neither case does the chimpanzee appear to generate additional concepts, related to perceptually non-obvious phenomena, concepts which could provide a unified account of why such regularities exist in the first place. No, this appears to be a specialization of the human species—a specialization that was woven into our brains right alongside a much older set of psychological systems, leaving us in the awkward position of being uncertain about which mechanisms are at work at any given moment in time.

Such a specialization may have left the human species in the position of constructing explanations for why we (and others) do what we do, and why the world operates the way it does—an ability not present in other species (see Gopnik and Meltzoff 1997; Karmiloff-Smith 1992; Povinelli and Prince 1998). We have argued that such a cognitive system may have been favored in human evolution because it allowed for a new degree of flexibility in both the social and physical realms (Povinelli and Prince 1998). In the physical domain, the ability to move beyond empirical generalizations, and to construct more fundamental accounts for why objects and events occur with the regularity that they do, would have provided humans with a cognitive tool with the power of unleashing a new level of technological productivity. And, from the standpoint of natural selection, individuals who understood *why* events occur the way they do were in a better position to both diagnose and develop technological or behavioral solutions to novel problems.

In the social domain, the ability to conceive of unobservable mental states may have generated a new dimension to social organization as well, but in a slightly different manner. As our species simultaneously evolved both a verbal language and a capacity to conceive of mental states as causes of behavior, we also evolved the ability to construct elaborate, culturally-specific narrative accounts of why social events take the shape that they do. In turn, this capacity for narrative formation (or 'explanation') may have created its own database, a storehouse of information not so very different from information accumulated through the primary senses. If true, then at some point in the course of human evolution our ancestors' decisions began to be influenced by not just what had happened, but why (from the perspective of a particular narrative) it happened. We believe that these social narratives (while not strictly 'accurate') provided human with a powerful adaptive device—a cognitive system which could function to rapidly alter existing behavioral patterns into novel cultural configurations. Indeed, the extraordinary diversity of humans' cultural beliefs and non-material cultural traditions may simply reflect the operation of a narrative-formation system—a cognitive device that allows for the rapid reconstruction of cultural practices in the face of new ecological challenges. If true, we may have isolated one of the critical 'triggers' that unleashed human populations into nearly every ecogeographic zone on the planet approximately 200,000 years ago, while the species of great apes remained restricted to the tropics and neotropics.

Thus, we question whether the great apes 'explain' or 'interpret' the world in any real sense whatsoever. But what would it be like to be a species that was exquisitely attuned to the social and physical dynamics of the world, and yet possessed no general frameworks for explaining those events? A comparison to young children may help. Imagine asking a 3-year-old the following riddle: 'Why did the little chicken cross the road?' Almost invariably, the child will launch into a fanciful story revolving around the wants, desires, and beliefs of the young chicken: 'Well, she was lonely and scared because her mother had already crossed the road, and she couldn't see her any more and so she wanted to go find her.' Now imagine asking a chimpanzee the same question. If we are right, the ape would simply reply, 'Yes.'

The most extreme reaction to this project will come from those researchers who find the possibility of profound cognitive differences between humans and the great apes as a threat to the latter's dignity. They will find it amazing that after nearly a century of breaking down the psychological barriers between human and ape, a project like the current one could surface—a project which seems to harken back to the days when we did not yet know that chimpanzees made and used tools in the wild, embraced each other after long absences, or stared off into the sunset with the same sense of awe and mystery that we do. Of course, we need not merely imagine such a reaction, for the heights of such sentiments may have already reached their peak. Penny Paterson, famed communicator with Koko the gorilla, proudly displays her gorilla's paintings (complete with Koko's digitally duplicated 'autograph') self-entitled, *Bird*, *Love*, and *Pink, Pink, Stink, Nice Drink*. Sue Savage-Rumbaugh, companion to Kanzi and several other pygmy chimpanzees, declares that she has met the mind of another species and has discovered that it is human: 'I found out that it was the same as ours,' she concludes. 'I found out that "it" was me!' (quoted in Dreifus 1999, p. 54). And so it is no wonder that the second strongest reaction to our work will come from the general public who have been fed a diet rich on anecdotes and edited images, and lean on the results of less glamorous (albeit controlled) scientific experimentation.

But the biologist and the philosopher will know better. The philosopher will detect the logical weaknesses in the polemics that have surrounded the debate over whether or not humans are unique. Furthermore, the philosopher will recognize the rhetorical attempts to persuade the public that there is no need for further empirical research in this area for exactly what they are. The biologist will know better as well, because the biologist lives in a world where both similarity and difference are the catch of the day, where the old and the new make comfortable bedfellows, and where the deep evolutionary connections between the wings of bats and the hooves of gazelles are not allowed to obscure the marvelous functional differences that keep the bats aloft and the gazelles dancing across the African Savannah.

REFERENCES

Alexander, R. (1974). The evolution of social behavior. *Annual Review of Ecology and Systematics*, **5**, 325–83.

Amsterdam, B. (1972). Mirror self-image reactions before age two. *Developmental Psychobiology*, **5**, 297–305.

Anderson, J. R. (1983). Responses to mirror image stimulation and assessment of self-recognition in mirror- and peer-reared stumptail macaques. *Quarterly Journal of Experimental Psychology*, **35B**, 201–12.

Anderson, J. R. and **Gallup, G. G., Jr.** (1997). Self-recognition in *Saguinus*? A critical essay. *Animal Behaviour*, **54**, 1563–7.

Anderson, J. R. and **Roeder, J. J.** (1989). Responses of capuchin monkeys (*Cebus apella*) to different conditions of mirror-image stimulation. *Primates*, **30**, 581–7.

Antinucci, F. (1989). *Cognitive structures and development in nonhuman primates*. Hillsdale, NJ: Lawrence Erlbaum.

Argyle, M. and **Cook, M.** (1976). *Gaze and mutual gaze*. Cambridge University Press.

Astington, J. W. and Gopnik, A. (1991). Developing understanding of desire and intention. In *Natural theories of mind: evolution, development and simulation of everyday mindreading*, (ed. A. Whiten), pp. 39–50. Basil Blackwell, Cambridge, MA.

Atran, S. (1990). *Cognitive foundations of natural history: towards an anthropology of science*. Cambridge University Press.

Atran, S. (1994). Core domains versus scientific theories: evidence from systematics and Itza-Maya folk biology. In *Mapping the mind: domain specificity in cognition and culture*, (ed. L. Hirschfeld and S. Gelman), pp. 316–40. Cambridge University Press.

Avis, J. and **Harris, P. L.** (1991). Belief–desire reasoning among Baka children: evidence for a universal conception of mind. *Child Development*, **62**, 460–7.

Baillargéon, R. (1986). Representing the existence and the location of hidden objects: object permanence in 6- and 8-month-old infants. *Cognition*, **23**, 21–41.

Baillargéon, R. (1987). Object permanence in 3.5- and 4.5-month-old infants. *Developmental Psychology*, **23**, 655–64.

Baillargéon, R. (1991). Reasoning about the height and location of a hidden object in 4.5- and 6.5-month-old infants. *Cognition*, **38**, 13–42.

Baillargéon, R. and **Hanko-Summers, S.** (1990). Is the object adequately supported by the bottom object? Young infants' understanding of support relations. *Child Development*, **5**, 29–54.

Baillargéon, R., Kotovsky, L., and **Needham, A.** (1995). The acquisition of physical knowledge in infancy. In *Causal cognition: a multidisciplinary debate*, (ed. D. Sperber, D. Premack, and A. Premack), pp. 79–116. Oxford University Press.

Baillargéon, R. (1999). Young infants' expectations about hidden objects: a reply to three challenges. *Developmental Science*, **2**, 115–32.

Balasch, J., Sabater Pi, J., and **Padrosa, T.** (1974). Perceptual learning ability in *Mandrillus sphinx* and *Cercopithecus nictitans*. *Revista Española de Fisiología*, **30**, 15–20.

Baldwin, D. A. (1991). Infants' contribution to the achievement of joint reference. *Child Development*, **63**, 875–90.

Baldwin, D. A. (1993). Early referential understanding: infants' ability to recognize referential acts for what they are. *Developmental Psychology*, **29**, 832–43.

Bard, K. A. (1990). 'Social tool use' by free-ranging orangutans: a Piagetian and developmental perspective of the manipulation of an animate object. In *'Language' and intelligence in monkeys and apes: comparative developmental perspectives*, (ed. S. T. Parker and K. R. Gibson), pp. 356–78. Cambridge University Press, New York.

Bard, K. A., Fragaszy, D., and **Visalberghi, E.** (1995). Acquisition and comprehension of tool-using behavior by young chimpanzees (*Pan troglodytes*): effects of age and modeling. *International Journal of Comparative Psychology*, **8**, 1–22.

Baron-Cohen, S. (1994). How to build a baby that can read minds: cognitive mechanisms in mindreading. *Current Psychology of Cognition*, **13**, 513–52.

Baron-Cohen, S. (1995). *Mindblindness: an essay on autism and theory of mind*. MIT Press, Cambridge, MA.

Baron-Cohen, S., Tager-Flusberg, H., and **Cohen, D. J.** (ed.) (1993). *Understanding other minds: perspectives from autism*, (1st edn). Oxford University Press.

Bates, E., Camaioni, L., and **Volterra, V.** (1975). The acquisition of preformatives prior to speech. *Merrill-Palmer Quarterly*, **21**, 205–26.

Bates, E., Carlson-Lunden, V., and **Bretherton, I.** (1980). Perceptual aspects of tool using in infancy. *Infant Behavior and Development*, **3**, 127–40.

Bayart, F. and **Anderson, J. R.** (1985). Mirror-image reactions in a tool-using, adult male *Macaca tonkeana*. *Behavior Processes*, **10**, 219–27.

Beck, B. (1967). A study of problem solving by gibbons. *Behaviour*, **28**, 95–109.

Beck, B. (1980). *Animal tool behavior: the use and manufacture of tools by animals*. Garland, New York.

Benhar, E. E., Carlton, P. L., and **Samuel, D.** (1975). A search for mirror-image reinforcement and self-recognition in the baboon. In *Contemporary primatology: proceedings of the Fifth International Congress of Primatology*, (ed. S. Kondo, M. Kawai, and S. Ehara), pp. 202–8. Karger, New York.

Bennett, J. (1978). Some remarks about concepts. *Behavioral and Brain Sciences*, **1**, 557–60.

Bering, J. (1999). Temporal segmentation and presyntactical planning in great apes: an exploratory investigation of the relation between arboreality and the emergence of self-representation. Unpublished Master's Thesis. University of Louisiana at Lafayette.

Bertenthal, B. I. and **Fischer, K. W.** (1978). Development of self-recognition in the infant. *Developmental Psychology*, **14**, 44–50.

Birch, H. G. (1945). The relation of previous experience to insightful problem-solving. *Journal of Comparative Psychology*, **38**, 367–83.

Blest, A. D. (1957). The function of eyespot patterns in the *Lepidoptera. Behaviour*, **11**, 209–55.

Boccia, M. L. (1994). Mirror behavior in macaques. In *Self-awareness in animals and humans*, (ed. S. T. Parker, R. W. Mitchell, and M. L. Boccia), pp. 350–60. Cambridge University Press, New York.

Boesch, C. (1994). Hunting strategies of Gombe and Taï chimpanzees. In *Chimpanzee cultures*, (ed. R. W. Wrangham, W. C. McGrew, F. B. M. deWaal, and P. G. Heltne), pp. 77–91. Harvard University Press.

Boesch, C. and **Tomasello, M.** (1998). Chimpanzee and human cultures. *Current Anthropology*, **39**, 591–614.

Bolles, R. C. (1971). Species-specific defense reactions. In *Aversive conditioning and learning*, (ed. R. R. Brush), pp. 183–233. Academic Press, New York.

Bond, A. H. (1996). A computational architecture for social agents. *Proceedings of Intelligent Systems: A Semiotic Perspective, An International Multidisciplinary Conference*. National Institute of Standards and Technology, Gaithersburg, MD.

Bond, A. H. Describing behavioral states using a system model of the primate brain. *American Journal of Primatology*. (In press *a*.)

Bond, A. H. A system model of the primate neocortex. *Neurocomputing Journal*. (In press *b*.)

Boysen, S. T. (1996). 'More is less': the elicitation of rule-governed resource distribution in chimpanzees. In *Reaching into thought: the minds of the great apes*, (ed. A. E. Russon, K. A. Bard, and S. T. Parker), pp. 177–89. Cambridge University Press.

Brésard, B. (1993). Some one- and two-handed functions and processes in tool use by pongids. In *The use of tools by human and non-human primates*, (ed. A. Berthelet and J. Chavaillon), pp. 78–94. Clarendon Press, Oxford.

Brown, A. L. (1990). Domain-specific principles affect learning and transfer in children. *Cognitive Science*, **14**, 107–33.

Brownell, C. A. and **Carriger, M. S.** (1990). Changes in cooperation and self–other distinction during the second year. *Child Development*, **61**, 1164–74.

Bullock, M. and **Gelman, R.** (1979). Preschool children's assumptions about cause and effect: temporal ordering. *Child Development*, **50**, 89–96.

Bullock, M., Gelman, R., and **Baillargéon, R.** (1982). The development of causal reasoning. In *The development psychology of time*, (ed. W. Friedman), pp. 209–54. Academic Press, New York.

Bunge, M. (1979). *Causality and modern science*, (3rd revised edn). Dover Publications, New York.

Burger, J., Gochfeld, M., and **Murray, B. G., Jr.** (1991). Role of a predator's eye size in risk perception by basking black iguana, *Ctenosaura similis. Animal Behaviour,* **42**, 471–6.

Burghardt, G. M. and **Greene, H. W.** (1988). Predator simulation and duration of death feigning in neonate hognose snakes. *Animal Behaviour,* **36**, 1842–4.

Butterworth, G. and **Cochran, E.** (1980). Towards a mechanism of joint visual attention in human infancy. *International Journal of Behavioral Development,* **3**, 253–72.

Butterworth, G. and **Jarrett, N.** (1991). What minds have in common is space: spatial mechanisms serving joint visual attention in infancy. *British Journal of Developmental Psychology,* **9**, 55–72.

Bygott, J. D. (1979). Agonistic behavior, dominance, and social structure in wild chimpanzees of the Gombe National Park. In *The great apes*, (ed. D. A. Hamburg and E. R. McCown), pp. 405–28. Benjamin/Cummings, Menlo Park, CA.

Byrne, R. W. (1995). *The thinking ape.* Oxford University Press.

Byrne, R. W. and **Whiten, A.** (1988). *Machiavellian intelligence. Social expertise and the evolution of intellect in monkeys, apes, and humans.* Oxford University Press, New York.

Byrne, R. W. and **Whiten, A.** (1991). Computation and mindreading in primate tactical deception. In *Natural theories of mind*, (ed. A. Whiten), pp. 127–41. Basil Blackwell Press, Oxford.

Call, J. and **Tomasello, M.** (1994). The production and comprehension of referential pointing by orangutans (*Pongo pygmaeus*). *Journal of Comparative Psychology,* **108**, 307–17.

Call, J. and **Tomasello, M.** (1998). Distinguishing intentional from accidental actions in orangutans (*Pongo pygmaeus*), chimpanzees (*Pan troglodytes*), and human children (*Homo Sapiens*). *Journal of Comparative Psychology,* **112**, 192–206.

Call, J. and **Tomasello, M.** (1999). A nonverbal false belief task: the performances of children and great apes. *Child Development,* **70**, 381–95.

Cant, J. G. H. (1987). Positional behavior of female Bornean orangutans (*Pongo pygmaeus*). *American Journal of Primatology,* **12**, 71–90.

Cant, J. G. H. (1988). Positional behavior of long-tailed macaques in northern Sumatra. *American Journal of Physical Anthropology,* **76**, 29–37.

Cant, J. G. H. (1992*a*). Positional behavior and body size of arboreal primates: a theoretical framework for field studies and an illustration of its application. *American Journal of Physical Anthropology,* **88**, 273–83.

Cant, J. G. H. (1992*b*). Positional behavior of arboreal primates and habitat compliance. In *Current primatology, Vol 1. Ecology and evolution*, (ed. B. Thierry, J. R. Anderson,

J. J. Roeder, and N. Herrenschmidt), pp. 187–93. Université Louis Pasteur, Strasbourg.

Carey, S. (1985). *Conceptual change in childhood.* Cambridge University Press.

Cha, J. and **King, J. E.** (1969). The learning of patterned string problems by squirrel monkeys. *Animal Behaviour*, **17**, 64–7.

Chance, M. R. A. (1967). Attention structure as the basis of primate rank orders. *Man*, **2**, 503–18.

Cheney, D. L. and **Seyfarth, R. M.** (1990). *How monkeys see the world: inside the mind of another species.* University of Chicago Press, Chicago.

Chevalier-Skolnikoff, S. (1989). Spontaneous tool use and sensorimotor intelligence in *Cebus* compared with other monkeys and apes. *Behavioral and Brain Sciences*, **12**, 561–627.

Chevalier-Skolnikoff, S., Galdikas, B. M. F., and **Skolnikoff, A. Z.** (1982). The adaptive significance of higher intelligence in orangutans: a preliminary report. *Journal of Human Evolution*, **11**, 639–52.

Conroy, G. (1997). *Reconstructing human origins: a modern synthesis.* W. W. Norton, New York.

Corkum, V. and Moore, C. (1994). Development of joint visual attention in infants. In *Joint attention: its origins and role in development*, (ed. C. Moore and P. Dunham), pp. 61–83. Erlbaum, Hillsdale, NJ.

Corkum, V. and **Moore, C.** (1998). The origins of joint visual attention in infants. *Developmental Psychology*, **34**, 28–38.

Cosmides, L. and **Tooby, J.** (1995). From function to structure: the role of evolutionary biology and computational theories in cognitive neuroscience. In *The cognitive neurosciences*, (ed. M. S. Gazzaniga), pp. 1199–210. MIT Press, Cambridge, MA.

Crawford, M. P. (1937). The coöperative solving of problems by young chimpanzees. *Comparative Psychology Monographs*, **14** (Serial No. 68).

Crawford, M. P. (1941). The cooperative solving by chimpanzees of problems requiring serial responses to color cues. *Journal of Social Psychology*, **13**, 259–80.

Darwin, C. (1859). *The origin of species.* John Murray, London. (Sixth Edition reprinted, Modern Library, New York, 1982.)

Darwin, C. (1871). *The descent of man.* (Reprinted, Modern Library, New York, 1982.)

Davenport, R. K. and **Rogers, C. M.** (1970). Intermodal equivalence of stimuli in apes. *Science*, **168**, 279–80.

Dennett, D. C. (1978). *Brainstorms.* Bradford Books, Montgomery, VT.

Desrochers, S., Morisette, P., and **Ricard, M.** (1995). Two perspectives on pointing in infancy. In *Joint attention: its origins and role in development*, (ed. C. Moore and P. J. Dunham), pp. 85–101. Erlbaum, Hillsdale, NJ.

Diamond, A. (1988). Differences between adult and infant cognition: is the crucial variable presence or absence of language? In *Thought without language*, (ed. L. Weiskrantz), pp. 335–70. Oxford Science Publications, Oxford.

Dickinson, A. and **Shanks, D.** (1995). Instrumental action and causal representation. In *Causal cognition: a multidisciplinary debate*, (ed. D. Sperber, D. Premack, and A. J. Premack), pp. 5–25. Clarendon Press, Oxford.

Domjan, M. (1983). Biological constraints on instrumental and classical conditioning: implications for general process theory. *Psychology of Learning and Motivation*, **17**, 215–77.

Domjan, M. and **Galef, B. G., Jr.** (1983). Biological constraints on instrumental and classical conditioning: retrospect and prospect. *Animal Learning and Behavior*, **11**, 151–61.

Dreifus, C. (1999, September). *Going ape*. Ms., pp. 48–54.

Emery, N. J., Lorincz, E. N., Perret, D. I., Oram, M. W., and **Baker, C. I.** (1997). Gaze following and joint attention in rhesus monkeys (*Macaca Mulatta*). *Journal of Comparative Psychology*, **111**, 286–93.

Epstein, R., Lanza, R. P., and **Skinner, B. F.** (1981). 'Self-awareness' in the pigeon. *Science*, **212**, 695–6.

Farrer, D. N. (1967). Picture memory in the chimpanzee. *Perceptual and Motor Skills*, **25**, 305–15.

Finch, G. (1941). The solution of patterned string problems by chimpanzees. *Journal of Comparative Psychology*, **32**, 83–90.

Fischer, G. J. and **Kitchener, S. L.** (1965). Comparative learning in young gorillas and orang-utans. *Journal of Genetic Psychology*, **107**, 337–48.

Fisher, R. A. (1930). *The genetical theory of natural selection*. Clarendon Press, Oxford.

Flavell, J. H., Shipstead, S. G., and **Croft, K.** (1978). What young children think you see when their eyes are closed. *Cognition*, **8**, 369–87.

Flavell, J. H., Flavell, E. R., Green, F. L., and **Wilcox, S.** A. (1980). Young children's knowledge about visual perception: effect of observer's distance from target on perceptual clarity of target. *Developmental Psychology*, **16**, 10–12.

Flavell, J. H., Everett, B. A., Croft, K., and **Flavell, E. R.** (1981). Young children's knowledge about visual perception: further evidence for the level 1–level 2 distinction. *Developmental Psychology*, **17**, 99–103.

Fodor, J. (1983). *Modularity of the mind*. MIT Press, Cambridge, MA.

Foley, R. (1987). *Another unique species*. Longman Scientific and Technical, Harlow, UK.

Fornasieri, I., Roeder, J. J., and **Anderson, J. A.** (1991). Les reactions au miroir chez trois especes de lemuriens (*Lemur fulvus, L. macaco, L. catta*), [Responses to mirror-image stimulation in three species of lemurs (*Lemur fulvus, L. macaco, L. catta*)]. *C. R. Acad. Sci. Paris*, **312**, 349–54.

Fragaszy, D. M. (1989). Tool use, imitation, and insight: apples, oranges, and conceptual pea soup. *Behavioral and Brain Sciences*, **12**, 596–602.

Franco, F. The development of meaning in infancy: early communication and social understanding. In *The development of social cognition*, (ed. S. Hala). UCL Press, London. (In press.)

Frith, C. and **Done, J.** (1989). Experiences of alien control in schizophrenia reflect a disorder in the central monitoring of action. *Psychological Medicine*, **19**, 359–63.

Frith, U. (1989). *Autism: explaining the enigma*. Oxford: Blackwell Science.

Galef, B. G., Jr. (1988). Imitation in animals: history, definition and interpretation of data from the psychological laboratory. In *Social learning: psychological and biological perspectives*, (ed. T. R. Zentall and B. G. Galef, Jr.), pp. 1–28. Erlbaum, Hillsdale, NJ.

Galilei, G. (1939). *Two new sciences*. New York: The Macmillan Company.

Gallup, G. G., Jr. (1970). Chimpanzees: self-recognition. *Science*, **167**, 86–7.

Gallup, G. G., Jr. (1977*a*). Absence of self-recognition in a monkey (*Macaca fascicularis*) following prolonged exposure to a mirror. *Developmental Psychobiology*, **10**, 281–4.

Gallup, G. G., Jr. (1977*b*). Self-recognition in primates: a comparative approach to the bi-directional properties of consciousness. *American Psychologist*, **32**, 329–38.

Gallup, G. G., Jr. (1982). Self-awareness and the emergence of mind in primates. *American Journal of Primatology*, **2**, 237–48.

Gallup, G. G., Jr. (1994). Self-recognition: research strategies and experimental design. In *Self-awareness in animals and humans*, (ed. S. Parker, R. Mitchell, and M. Boccia), pp. 35–50. Cambridge University Press.

Gallup, G. G., Jr. and **Suarez, S. D.** (1991). Social responding to mirrors in rhesus monkeys (*Macaca mulatta*): effects of temporary mirror removal. *Journal of Comparative Psychology*, **105**, 376–9.

Gallup, G. G., Jr., Nash, R. F., and **Ellison, A. L., Jr.** (1971). Tonic immobility as a reaction to predation: artificial eyes as a fear stimulus for chickens. *Psychonomic Science*, **23**, 79–80.

Gallup, G. G., Jr., Wallnau, L. B., and **Suarez, S. D.** (1980). Failure to find self-recognition in mother–infant and infant–infant rhesus monkey pairs. *Folia Primatologica*, **33**, 210–9.

Garcia, J. and **Koelling, R. A.** (1966). Relation of cue to consequence in avoidance learning. *Psychonomic Science*, **4**, 123–4.

Garcia, J., Ervin, F. R., and **Koelling, R. A.** (1966). Learning with prolonged delay of reinforcement. *Psychonomic Science*, **5**, 121–2.

Gardner, B. T. and **Gardner, R. A.** (1971). Two-way communication with an infant chimpanzee. In *Behavior in nonhuman primates*, (ed. A. Schrier and F. Stollnitz). Academic Press, New York.

Gaulin, S. J. C. (1992). Evolution of sex differences in spatial ability. *Yearbook of Physical Anthropology*, **35**, 125–51.

Gelman, S. A. and **Kremer, K. E.** (1991). Understanding natural cause: children's explanations of how objects and their properties originate. *Child Development*, **62**, 396–414.

Gelman, S. A. and **Medin, D. L.** (1993). What's so essential about essentialism? A different perspective on the interaction of perception, language, and conceptual knowledge. *Cognitive Development*, **8**, 157–67.

Gelman, S. A. and **Wellman, H. M.** (1991). Insides and essences: early understandings of the non-obvious. *Cognition*, **38**, 213–44.

Gelman, S. A., Coley, J. D., and **Gottfried, G. M.** (1994). Essentialist beliefs in children: the acquisition of concepts and theories. In *Mapping the mind: domain specificity in cognition and culture*, (ed. L. Hirschfeld and S. Gelman), pp. 341–65. Cambridge University Press.

Gill, T. V. and **Rumbaugh, D. M.** (1974). Learning processes of bright and dull apes. *American Journal of Mental Deficiency*, **78**, 683–7.

Goldenberg, G. and **Hagmann, S.** (1998). Tool use and mechanical problem solving in apraxia. *Neuropsychologia*, **36**, 581–9.

Gómez, J. C. (1990). The emergence of intentional communication as a problem-solving strategy in the gorilla. In *'Language' and intelligence in monkeys and apes: comparative developmental perspectives*, (ed. S. T. Parker and K. R. Gibson), pp. 333–55. Cambridge University Press.

Gómez, J. C. (1991). Visual behavior as a window for reading the minds of others in primates. In *Natural theories of mind: evolution, development and simulation of everyday mindreading*, (ed. A. Whiten), pp. 330–43. Blackwell, Oxford.

Gómez, J. C. (1994). Shared attention in ontogeny and phylogeny: SAM, TOM, and the great apes. *Current Psychology of Cognition*, **13**, 590–8.

Gómez, J. C. (1996*a*). Non-human primate theories of (non-human primate) minds: some issues concerning the origins of mind-reading. In *Theories of theories of mind*, (ed. P. Carruthers and P. K. Smith), pp. 330–43. Cambridge University Press, New York.

Gómez, J. C. (1996*b*). Ostensive behavior in great apes: the role of eye contact. In *Reaching into thought: the minds of the great apes*, (ed. A. E. Russon, K. A. Bard, and S. T. Parker), pp. 131–51. Cambridge University Press, New York.

Goodall, J. (1968*a*). Expressive movements and communication in free-ranging chimpanzees: a preliminary report. In *Primates: studies in adaptation and variation*, (ed. P. Jay), pp. 313–74. Holt, Rinehart and Winston, New York.

Goodall, J. (1968*b*). The behavior of free-ranging chimpanzees in the Gombe Stream Reserve. *Animal Behavior Monographs*, **1**, 161–311.

Goodall, J. (1971). *In the shadow of man*. Houghton Mifflin, Boston, MA.

Goodall, J. (1986). *The chimpanzees of Gombe: patterns of behavior.* Belknap, Harvard University Press, Cambridge, MA.

Gopnik, A. (1993). How we know our minds: the illusion of first-person knowledge of intentionality. *Behavioral and Brain Sciences,* **16**, 1–14.

Gopnik, A. and **Graf, P.** (1988). Knowing how you know: young children's ability to identify and remember the sources of their beliefs. *Child Development,* **59**, 1366–71.

Gopnik, A. and **Meltzoff, A. N.** (1997). *Words, thoughts, and theories.* MIT Press, Cambridge, MA.

Gopnik, A. and **Sobel, D.** Detecting Blickets: how young children use information about novel causal powers in categorization and induction. *Child Development.* (In press.)

Gopnik, A., Meltzoff, A. N., and **Esterly, J.** (1995). *Young children's understanding of visual perspective-taking.* Poster presented at the first annual Theory of Mind Conference, Eugene, Oregon.

Grant, D. (1946). New statistical criteria for learning and problem solution in experiments involving repeated trials. *Psychological Bulletin,* **43**, 272–82.

Greenfield, P. M. (1991). Language, tools and brain: the ontogeny and phylogeny of hierarchically organized sequential behavior. *Behavioral and Brain Sciences,* **14**, 531–95.

Guillaume, P. and **Meyerson, I.** (1930). Recherches sur l'usage de l'instrument chez les singes. I. Le Probleme du detour. *Journal de Psychologie Normale et Pathologique,* **27**, 177–236.

Haggerty, M. E. (1913). Plumbing the minds of apes. *McClure's Magazine,* **41**, 151–4.

Haith, M. M. (1998). Who put the cog in infant cognition? Is rich interpretation too costly? *Infant Behavior and Development,* **21**, 167–79.

Haith, M. M., Hazan, C., and **Goodman, G. S.** (1988). Expectation and anticipation of dynamic visual events by 3.5-month-old babies. *Child Development,* **59**, 467–79.

Haldane, J. B. S. (1932). *The causes of evolution.* Longmans Green, New York.

Happé, F. (1996). Studying weak central coherence at low levels: children with autism do not succumb to visual illusions: a research note. *Journal of Child Psychology and Psychiatry,* **37**, 873–7.

Happé, F. (1999). Autism: cognitive deficit or cognitive style? *Trends in Cognitive Science,* **3**, 216–22.

Harlow, H. F. and **Settlage, P. H.** (1934). Comparative behavior of primates. VII. Capacity of monkeys to solve patterned string tests. *Journal of Comparative Psychology,* **18**, 423–35.

Harman, G. (1978). Studying the chimpanzee's theory of mind. *Behavioral and Brain Sciences,* **4**, 576–7.

Harre, R. and **Madden, E. H.** (1975). *Causal powers: a theory of natural necessity.* Blackwell, Oxford.

Hauser, M. D., Kralik, J., Botto-Mahan, C., Garrett, M., and Oser, J. (1995). Self-recognition in primates: phylogeny and the salience of species-typical features. *Proceedings of the National Academy of Sciences*, **92**, 10811–4.

Hauser, M. D., Kralik, J., and Botto-Mahan, C. (1999*a*). Problem solving and functional design features: experiments on cotton-top tamarins, *Saguinus oedipus oedipus*. *Animal Behaviour*, **57**, 565–82.

Hauser, M. D., Miller, C. T., Liu, K., and Gupta, R. (1999*b*). Cotton top tamarins (*Saguinus oedipus*) fail to recognize their mirror-image: different procedures, different results? Unpublished manuscript.

Hayes, C. (1951). *The ape in our house*. Harper and Brothers, New York.

Heaton, P., Hermelin, B., and Pring, L. (1998). Autism and pitch processing: a precursor for savant musical ability. *Music Perception*, **15**, 291–305.

Hespos, S. J. and Baillargéon, R. (2000). Infants' knowledge about occlusion and containment events: a surprising discrepancy. Manuscript under review.

Heyes, C. M. (1994). Reflections on self-recognition in primates. *Animal Behaviour*, **47**, 909–19.

Heyes, C. M. (1995). Self-recognition in mirrors: further reflections create a hall of mirrors. *Animal Behaviour*, **50**, 1533–42.

Hughes, L. (1993). *ChimpWorld: a wind-tunnel for the social sciences*. Ph.D. Thesis. Yale University, New Haven, CT.

Hume, D. (1739–40/1911). *A treatise of human nature*, (Vols 1–2), (ed. A. D. Lindsay). Dent, London.

Humphrey, N. K. (1976). The social function of intellect. In *Growing points in ethology*, (ed. P. P. G. Bateson and R. A. Hinde), pp. 303–17. Cambridge University Press.

Humphrey, N. K. (1980). Nature's psychologists. In *Consciousness and the physical world*, (ed. B. D. Josephson and V. S. Ramachandran), pp. 57–75. Pergamon Press, New York.

Humphrey, N. (1998, October). *Necessity as the mother of invention: how cognitive deficit may have advanced the human mind*. Paper presented at the Human Cognitive Specializations conference, University of Louisiana, New Iberia, Louisiana.

Hunt, G. R. (1996). Manufacture and use of hook-tools by New Caledonian crows. *Nature*, **379**, 249–51.

Itakura, S. (1987*a*). Mirror guided behavior in Japanese monkeys (*Macaca fuscata fuscata*). *Primates*, **28**, 149–61.

Itakura, S. (1987*b*). Use of a mirror to direct their responses in Japanese monkeys (*Macaca fuscata fuscata*). *Primates*, **28**, 343–52.

Jolliffe, T. and Baron-Cohen, S. (1997). Are people with autism and Asperger syndrome faster than normal on the Embedded Figures Test? *Journal of Child Psychology and Psychiatry*, **38**, 527–34.

Jolly, A. (1966). Lemur social intelligence and primate intelligence. *Science*, **153**, 501–9.

Jouffroy, F. K. (1993). Primate hands and the human hand: the tool of tools. In *The use of tools by human and non-human primates*, (ed. A. Berthelet and J. Chavaillon), pp. 6–35. Clarendon Press, Oxford.

Kafka, F. (1936/1952). *Selected short stories of Franz Kafka*, (trans. W. and E. Muir). The Modern Library, New York.

Kamil, A. C. (1984). Adaptation and cognition: knowing what comes naturally. In *Animal Cognition*, (ed. H. L. Roitblat, T. G. Bever, and H. S. Terrace), pp. 533–44. Erlbaum, Hillsdale, NJ.

Kanner, L. (1943). Autistic disturbances of affective contact. *The Nervous Child*, **2**, 217–50.

Kant, I. (1781/1933). *A critique of pure reason*, (2nd edn), (trans. N. K. Smith). Macmillan, London.

Karmiloff-Smith, A. (1992). *Beyond modularity: a developmental perspective on cognitive science*. MIT Press, Cambridge, MA.

Kaye, K. (1982). *The mental and social life of babies*. University of Chicago Press, Chicago.

Keil, F. (1979). The development of the young child's ability to anticipate the outcomes of simple causal events. *Child Development*, **50**, 455–62.

Kellogg, W. N. and **Kellogg, L. A.** (1933). *The ape and the child: a study of environmental influence on early behavior*. McGraw-Hill, New York.

Klein, R. (1989). *The human career*. University of Chicago Press, Chicago.

Klüver, H. (1933). *Behavior mechanisms in monkeys*. University of Chicago Press, Chicago.

Köhler, W. (1927). *The mentality of apes*, (2nd edn). Vintage Books, New York.

Kohts, N. (1935). *Infant ape and human child. Instincts, emotions, play, habits*. Scientific Memoirs of the Museum Darwinianum in Moscow. [In Russian with English Summary.]

Kosslyn, S. M. (1994). *Image and brain: the resolution of the imagery debate*. MIT Press, Cambridge, MA.

Krause, M. A. and **Fouts, R. S.** (1997). Chimpanzee (*Pan troglodytes*) pointing: hand shapes, accuracy, and the role of eye gaze. *Journal of Comparative Psychology*, **111**, 330–6.

Kuhl, P. K. (1991). Human adults and human infants show a 'perceptual magnet effect' for the prototypes of speech categories, monkeys do not. *Perception and Psychophysics*, **50**, 93–107.

Kummer, H. (1995). Causal knowledge in animals. In *Causal cognition: a multidisciplinary debate*, (ed. D. Sperber, D. Premack, and A. J. Premack), pp. 26–39. Clarendon Press, Oxford.

Kun, A. (1978). Evidence for preschoolers' understanding of causal direction in extended causal sequences. *Child Development*, **49**, 218–22.

Leavens, D. A., Hopkins, W. D., and **Bard, K. A.** (1996). Indexical and referential pointing in chimpanzees (*Pan troglodytes*). *Journal of Comparative Psychology*, **110**, 346–53.

Ledbetter, D. H. and **Basen, J. D.** (1982). Failure to demonstrate self-recognition in gorillas. *American Journal of Primatology*, **2**, 307–10.

Lempers, J. D., Flavell, E. R., and **Flavell, J. H.** (1977). The development in very young children of tacit knowledge concerning visual perception. *Genetic Psychology Monographs*, **95**, 3–53.

Leslie, A. M. (1982). The perception of causality in infants. *Perception*, **11**, 173–86.

Leslie, A. M. (1994). ToMM, ToBy, and Agency: core architecture and domain specificity. In *Mapping the mind: domain specificity in cognition and culture*, (ed. L. Hirschfeld and S. Gelman), pp. 119–48. Cambridge University Press.

Leslie, A. M. and **Keeble, S.** (1987). Do six-month-old infants perceive causality? *Cognition*, **25**, 265–88.

Lesser, H. (1977). The growth of perceived causality in children. *Journal of Genetic Psychology*, **130**, 145–52.

Lethmate, J. (1977). Werkzeugherstellung eines jungen Orang-utans. *Behaviour*, **62**, 174–89. [With English Summary.]

Lethmate, J. (1982). Tool-using skills of orang-utans. *Journal of Human Evolution*, **11**, 49–64.

Lethmate, J. and **Dücker, G.** (1973). Untersuchungen zum selbsterkennen im spiegel bei orang-utans einigen anderen affenarten, [Self-recognition by orangutans and some other primates]. *Zietschrift für Tierpsychologie*, **33**, 248–69.

Leung, E. and **Rheingold, H.** (1981). Development of pointing as a social gesture. *Developmental Psychology*, **17**, 215–20.

Lewis, M. and **Brooks-Gunn, J.** (1979). *Social cognition and the acquisition of self.* Plenum Press, New York.

Lillard, A. (1998). Ethnopsychologies: cultural variations in theories of mind. *Psychological Bulletin*, **123**, 3–33.

Limongelli, L., Boysen, S. T., and **Visalberghi, E.** (1995). Comprehension of cause–effect relations in a tool-using task by chimpanzees (*Pan troglodytes*). *Journal of Comparative Psychology*, **109**, 18–26.

Loveland, K. A. (1986). Discovering the afffordances of a reflecting surface. *Developmental Review*, **6**, 1–24.

Luria, A. R. (1968). *The mind of a mnemonist*, (trans. L. Solotaroff). Basic Books, New York.

McCloskey, M. T. (1983). Intuitive physics. *Scientific American*, **248**(4), 122–30.

McCloskey, M., Caramazza, A., and Green, B. (1980). Curvilinear motion in the absence of external forces: naive beliefs about the motion of objects. *Science*, **210**, 1139–41.

McCloskey, M. and Kohl, D. (1983). Naive physics: the curvilinear impetus principle and its role in interreactions with moving objects. *Journal of Experimental Psychology: Learning, Memory & Cognition*, **9**, 146–56.

McGrew, W. C. (1992). *Chimpanzee material culture: implications for human evolution.* Cambridge University Press.

MacPhail, E. M. (1987). The comparative psychology of intelligence. *Behavioral and Brain Sciences*, **10**, 645–56.

Maida, A. S. (1992). Knowledge representation requirements for description-based communication. In *Principles of knowledge representation and reasoning: proceedings of the Third International Conference, October 25–29 1992*, (ed. B. Nebel, C. Rich, and W. Swartout). Cambridge, MA.

Maida, A. S. and Tang, S. (1996). Referent misidentification and recovery among communicating agents. In *Proceedings of the second International Conference on Multiagent Systems, December 1996.* Kyota.

Maida, A. S., Wainer, J., and Cho, S. (1991). A syntactic approach to introspection and reasoning about the beliefs of other agents. *Fundamenta Informaticae*, **15**, 333–56.

Marino, L., Reiss, D., and Gallup, G. G., Jr. (1994). Mirror-self-recognition in bottle-nosed dolphins: implications for comparative investigations of highly dissimilar species. In *Self-awareness in animals and humans*, (ed. S. Parker, R. Mitchell, and M. Boccia), pp. 380–91. Cambridge University Press.

Masangkay, Z. S., McKluskey, K. A., McIntyre, C. W., Sims-Knight, J., Vaughn, B. E., and Flavell, J. H. (1974). The early development of inferences about the visual percepts of others. *Child Development*, **45**, 357–66.

Mathieu, M. and Bergeron, G. (1981). Piagetian assessment on cognitive development in chimpanzees (*Pan troglodytes*). In *Primate behavior and sociobiology*, (ed. A. B. Chiarelli and R. S. Corruccini), pp. 142–7. Springer-Verlag, Berlin.

Mathieu, M., Daudelin, N., Dagenais, Y., and Decarie, C. (1980). Piagetian causality in two house-reared chimpanzees (*Pan troglodytes*). *Canadian Journal of Psychology*, **34**, 179–86.

Matsuzawa, T. (1994). Field experiments on use of stone tools by chimpanzees in the wild. In *Chimpanzee cultures*, (ed. R. Wrangham, W. McGrew, F. deWaal, and P. Heltne), pp. 351–70. Harvard University Press.

Matsuzawa, T. (1996). Chimpanzee intelligence in nature and in captivity: isomorphism of symbol use and tool use. In *Great ape societies*, (ed. W. McGrew, L. Marchant, and T. Nishida), pp. 196–209. Cambridge University Press.

Medin, D. L. (1989). Concepts and conceptual structures. *American Psychologist*, **44**, 1469–81.

Mendelson, R. and **Shultz, T. R.** (1976). Covariation and temporal contiguity as principles of causal inference in young children. *Journal of Experimental Child Psychology*, **22**, 408–12.

Menzel, E. W., Jr. (1974). A group of young chimpanzees in a one-acre field. In *Behavior of non-human primates: modern research trends*, (ed. A. Schrier and F. Stollnitz), pp. 83–153. Academic Press, New York.

Michotte, A. (1963). *The perception of causality.* Basic Books, New York.

Miles, H. L. W. (1994). ME CHANTEK: the development of self-awareness in a signing orangutan. In *Self-awareness in animals and humans*, (ed. S. T. Parker, R. W. Mitchell, and M. L. Boccia), pp. 254–72. Cambridge University Press.

Miles, H. L. W. (1996). Simon says: the development of imitation in an enculturated orangutan. In *Reaching into thought: the minds of the great apes*, (ed. A. E. Russon, K. A. Bard, and S. T. Parker), pp. 278–99. Cambridge University Press, New York.

Mitchell, R. B. (1993). Mental models of mirror-self-recognition: two theories. *New Ideas in Psychology*, **11**, 295–325.

Mitchell, R. W., Thompson, N. S., and **Miles, H. L.** (ed.) (1997). *Anthropomorphism, anecdotes, and animals.* State University of New York Press, Albany, NY.

Moore, C. P. (1994). Intentionality and self–other equivalence in early mindreading: the eyes do not have it. *Current Psychology of Cognition*, **13**, 661–8.

Moore, C., Angelopoulos, M., and **Bennett, P.** (1997). The role of movement and the development of joint visual attention. *Infant Behavior and Development*, **20**, 83–92.

Moses, L., Baldwin, D., and **Povinelli, D. J.** (1994). [Chimpanzees' ability to use attentional cues to infer the location of dangerous and desirable objects.] Unpublished raw data.

Natale, F. (1989). Causality II. The stick problem. In *Cognitive structure and development in nonhuman primates*, (ed. F. Antinucci), pp. 121–33. Erlbaum, Hillsdale, NJ.

Nishida, T. (1970). Social behavior and relationships among wild chimpanzees of the Mahale Mountains. *Journal of Human Evolution*, **2**, 357–70.

Oakes, L. M. and **Cohen, L. B.** (1990). Infant perception of a causal event. *Cognitive Development*, **5**, 193–207.

O'Neill, D. K. and **Gopnik, A.** (1991). Young children's ability to identify the sources of their beliefs. *Developmental Psychology*, **27**, 390–7.

O'Neill, D. K., Astington, J. W., and **Flavell, J. H.** (1992). Young children's understanding of the role that sensory experiences play in knowledge acquisition. *Child Development*, **63**, 474–90.

Parker, S. T. (1991). A developmental approach to the origins of self-recognition in great apes. *Human Evolution*, **2**, 435–49.

Parker, S. T. and **Gibson, K. R.** (1977). Object manipulation, tool use and sensorimotor intelligence as feeding adaptations in cebus monkeys and great apes. *Journal of Human Evolution*, **6**, 623–41.

Parker, S. T. and **Gibson, K. R.** (1979). A developmental model for the evolution of language and intelligence in early hominids. *Behavioral and Brain Sciences*, **2**, 367–408.

Parker, S. T. and **Potí, P.** (1990). The role of innate motor patterns in ontogenetic and experiential development of intelligent use of sticks in cebus monkeys. In '*Language' and intelligence in monkeys and apes: comparative developmental perspectives*, (ed. S. T. Parker and K. R. Gibson), pp. 219–43. Cambridge University Press.

Parker, S. T. and **Russon, A. E.** (1996). On the wild side of culture and cognition in the great apes. In *Reaching into thought: the minds of the great apes*, (ed. A. E. Russon, K. A. Bard, and S. T. Parker), pp. 430–50. Cambridge University Press.

Parker, S. T., Mitchell, R. W., and **Boccia, M. L.** (ed.) (1994). *Self-awareness in animals and humans*. Cambridge University Press.

Patterson, F. and **Linden, E.** (1981). *The Education of Koko*. Holt, Rinehart, and Winston, New York.

Pavlov, I. P. (1927). *Conditioned reflexes*, (trans. G. V. Anrep). Oxford Univeristy Press: New York.

Pearce, J. M., Colwill, R. M., and **Hall, G.** (1978). Instrumental conditioning of scratching in the laboratory rat. *Learning and Motivation*, **9**, 255–71.

Perner, J. and **Ogden, J.** (1988). Knowledge for hunger: children's problems with representation in imputing mental states. *Cognition*, **29**, 47–61.

Perrett, D., Harries, M., Mistlin, A., Hietanen, J., Benson, P., Bevan, R., Thomas, S., Oram, M., Ortega, J., and **Brierly, K.** (1990). Social signals analyzed at the single cell level: someone is looking at me, something touched me, something moved! *International Journal of Comparative Psychology*, **4**, 25–55.

Piaget, J. (1930). *The child's conception of physical causality*, (trans. M. Worden). Kegan Paul, London. [Original work published in 1927.]

Piaget, J. (1952). *The origins of intelligence in children*, (trans. M. Cook). International Universities Press, New York.

Piaget, J. (1954). *The construction of reality in the child*. Ballantine Books, New York. [Original work published 1937.]

Piaget, J. (1962). *Play, dreams, and imitation in childhood*. Norton, New York.

Piaget, J. (1972). *The principles of genetic epistemology*, (trans. W. Mays). Basic Books, New York. [Original work published 1970.]

Piaget, J. (1974). *Understanding causality*, (trans. D. Miles and M. Miles). Norton, New York. [Oringinal work published 1971.]

Pinker, S. (1997). *How the mind works*. Norton, New York.

Plooij, F. X. (1978). Some basic traits of language in wild chimpanzees? In *Action, gesture and symbol*, (ed. A. Lock), pp. 111–31. Academic Press, London.

Potì, P. and **Spinozi, G.** (1994). Early sensorimotor development in chimpanzees (*Pan troglodytes*). *Journal of Comparative Psychology*, **108**, 93–103.

Povinelli, D. J. (1989). Failure to find self-recognition in Asian elephants (*Elephas maximus*) in contrast to their use of mirror cues to discover hidden food. *Journal of Comparative Psychology*, **102**, 122–31.

Povinelli, D. J. (1993). Reconstructing the evolution of mind. *American Psycholgist*, **48**, 493–509.

Povinelli, D. J. (1994). How to create self-recognizing gorillas (but don't try it on macaques). In *Self-awareness in animals and humans*, (ed. S. Parker, R. Mitchell, and M. Boccia), pp. 291–4. Cambridge University Press.

Povinelli, D. J. (1995). The unduplicated self. In *The self in early infancy*, (ed. P. Rochat), pp. 161–92. North-Holland-Elsevier, Amsterdam.

Povinelli, D. J. (1996). Growing up ape. Reply in D. J. Povinelli and T. J. Eddy *Monographs of the Society for Research in Child Development*, **61**(**3**), (Serial No. 247), 174–89.

Povinelli, D. J. (1998). Can animals empathize? *Scientific American Presents: Exploring Intelligence*, **9**(**4**), 67, 72–5.

Povinelli, D. J. and Cant, J. G. H. (1995). Arboreal clambering and the evolution of self-conception. *Quarterly Review of Biology*, **70**, 393–421.

Povinelli, D. J. and deBlois, S. (1992*a*). Young children's (*Homo sapiens*) understanding of knowledge formation in themselves and others. *Journal of Comparative Psychology*, **106**, 228–38.

Povinelli, D. J. and deBlois, S. (1992*b*). On (not) attributing mental states to monkeys: first, know thyself. *Behavioral and Brain Sciences*, **15**, 164–6.

Povinelli, D. J. and Eddy, T. J. (1994). The eyes as a window: what young chimpanzees see on the other side. *Current Psychology of Cognition*, **13**, 695–705.

Povinelli, D. J. and Eddy, T. J. (1996*a*). What young chimpanzees know about seeing. *Monographs of the Society for Research in Child Development*, **61**(**3**), (Serial No. 247).

Povinelli, D. J. and Eddy, T. J. (1996*b*). Chimpanzees: joint visual attention. *Psychological Science*, **7**, 129–35.

Povinelli, D. J. and Eddy, T. J. (1996*c*). Factors influencing young chimpanzees' (*Pan troglodytes*) recognition of attention. *Journal of Comparative Psychology*, **110**, 336–45.

Povinelli, D. J. and Eddy, T. J. (1997). Specificity of gaze-following in young chimpanzees. *British Journal of Developmental Psychology*, **15**, 213–22.

Povinelli, D. J. and Giambrone, S. Inferring other minds: failure of the argument by analogy. *Philosophical Topics.* (In press.)

Povinelli, D. J. and Godfrey, L. R. (1993). The chimpanzee's mind: how noble in reason? How absent of ethics? In *Evolutionary ethics*, (ed. M. Nitecki and D. Nitecki), pp. 227–324. SUNY Press, Albany, NY.

Povinelli, D. J. and Hughes, L. (1993). *Why chimpanzees attribute mental states.* Unpublished manuscript.

Povinelli, D. J. and **O'Neill, D. K.** (2000). Do chimpanzees use gestures to instruct each other during cooperative situations? In *Understanding other minds: perspectives from autism*, (ed. S. Baron-Cohen, H. Tager-Flusberg, and D. J. Cohen), (2nd edn), pp. 459–87. Oxford University Press.

Povinelli, D. J. and **Preuss, T. M.** (1995). Theory of mind: evolutionary history of a cognitive specialization. *Trends in Neuroscience*, **18**, 418–24.

Povinelli, D. J. and **Prince, C. G.** (1998). When self met other. In *Self-awareness: its nature and development*, (ed. M. Ferrari and R. J. Sternberg), pp. 37–107. Guilford Press, New York.

Povinelli, D. J. and **Simon, B. B.** (1998). Young children's reactions to briefly versus extremely delayed visual images of the self: emergence of the autobiographical stance. *Developmental Psychology*, **43**, 118–94.

Povinelli, D. J., Nelson, K. E., and **Boysen, S. T.** (1990). Inferences about guessing and knowing by chimpanzees (*Pan troglodytes*). *Journal of Comparative Psychology*, **104**, 203–10.

Povinelli, D. J., Nelson, K. E., and **Boysen, S. T.** (1992). Comprehension of social role reversal by chimpanzees: evidence of empathy? *Animal Behaviour*, **43**, 633–40.

Povinelli, D. J., Rulf, A. B., Landau, K. R., and **Bierschwale, D. T.** (1993). Self-recognition in chimpanzees (*Pan troglodytes*): distribution, ontogeny, and patterns of emergence. *Journal of Comparative Psychology*, **107**, 347–72.

Povinelli, D. J., Rulf, A. B., and **Bierschwale, D.** (1994). Absence of knowledge attribution and self-recognition in young chimpanzees (*Pan troglodytes*). *Journal of Comparative Psychology*, **180**, 74–80.

Povinelli, D. J., Landau, K. R., and **Perilloux, H. K.** (1996*a*). Self-recognition in young children using delayed versus live feedback: evidence of a developmental asynchrony. *Child Development*, **67**, 1540–54.

Povinelli, D. J., Zebouni, M. C., and **Prince, C. G.** (1996*b*). Ontogeny, evolution and folk psychology. *Behavioral and Brain Sciences*, **19**, 137–8.

Povinelli, D. J., Gallup, G. G., Jr., Eddy, T. J., Bierschwale, D. T., Engstrom, M. C., Perilloux, H. K., and **Toxopeus, I. B.** (1997*a*). Chimpanzees recognize themselves in mirrors. *Animal Behaviour*, **53**, 1083–8.

Povinelli, D. J., Reaux, J. E., Bierschwale, D. T., Allain, A. D., and **Simon, B. B.** (1997*b*). Exploitation of pointing as a referential gesture in young children, but not adolescent chimpanzees. *Cognitive Development*, **12**, 423–61.

Povinelli, D. J., Perilloux, H. K., Reaux, J. E., and **Bierschwale, D. T.** (1998). Young and juvenile chimpanzees' (*Pan troglodytes*) reactions to intentional versus accidental and inadvertent actions. *Behavioral Processes*, **42**, 205–18.

Povinelli, D. J., Bierschwale, D. T., and **Čech, C. G.** (1999). Comprehension of seeing as a referential act in young children, but not juvenile chimpanzees. *British Journal of Developmental Psychology*, **17**, 37–60.

Povinelli, D. J., Bering, J., and **Giambrone, S.** 'Pointing' in chimpanzees: another error of the argument by analogy. In *Pointing: where language culture and cognition meet,* (ed. S. Kita). Cambridge University Press. (In press *a.*)

Povinelli, D. J., Landry, A. M., Theall, L. A., Clark, B. R., and **Castille, C. M.** (1999). Development of young children's understanding that the recent past is causally bound to the present. *Developmental Psychology,* **35,** 1426–39.

Premack, D. (1976). *Intelligence in ape and man.* Erlbaum, Hillsdale, New Jersey.

Premack, D. (1984). Pedagogy and aesthetics as sources of culture. In *Handbook of cognitive neuroscience,* (ed. M. S. Gazzaniga), pp. 15–35. Plenum Press, New York.

Premack, D. (1988). Minds with and without language. In *Thought without language,* (ed. L. Weiskrantz), pp. 46–65. Clarendon Press, Oxford.

Premack, D. and **Premack, A. J.** (1983). *The mind of an ape.* Norton, New York.

Premack, D. and **Premack, A. J.** (1994). Levels of causal understanding in chimpanzees and children. *Cognition,* **50,** 347–62.

Premack, D. and **Woodruff, G.** (1978). Does the chimpanzee have a theory of mind? *Behavioral and Brain Sciences,* **1,** 515–26.

Preuss, T. M. (1993). The role of the neurosciences in primate evolutionary biology: historical commentary and prospectus. In *Primates and their relatives in phylogenetic perspective,* (ed. R. D. E. MacPhee), pp. 333–62. Plenum Press, New York.

Preuss, T. M. (1995). The argument from animals to humans in cognitive neuroscience. In *The cognitive neurosciences,* (ed. M. S. Gazzaniga), pp. 1227–41. MIT Press, Cambridge, MA.

Preuss, T. M. What's human about the human brain? In *The New Cognitive Neurosciences,* (ed. M. S. Gazzaniga). (In press.)

Preuss, T. M. and **Kaas, J. H.** (1999). Human brain evolution. In *Fundamental neuroscience,* (senior editors F. E. Bloom, S. C. Landis, J. L. Robert, L. R. Squire, and M. J. Zigmond). Academic Press, San Diego, CA.

Preuss, T. M., Qi, H. S., and **Kaas, J. H.** (1999). Distinctive compartmental organization of human primary visual cortex. *Proceedings of the National Academy of Sciences, USA,* **96,** 11601–11606.

Reaux, J. E., Theall, L. A., and **Povinelli, D. J.** (1999). A longitudinal investigation of chimpanzees' understanding of visual perception. *Child Development,* **70,** 275–90.

Redican, W. K. (1975). Facial expressions in nonhuman primates. In *Primate behavior,* Vol. 4, (ed. L. A. Rosenblum), pp. 103–94. Academic Press, New York.

Ricardson, H. M. (1932). The growth of adaptive behavior in infants: an experimental study of seven age levels. *Genetic Psychology Monographs,* **12,** 195–359.

Ristau, C. A. (1991). Before mindreading: attention, purposes and deception in birds? In *Natural theories of mind: evolution, development and simulation of everyday mindreading,* (ed. A. Whiten), pp. 209–22. Basil Blackwell, Cambridge.

Robinson, J. A., Connell, S., McKenzie, B. E., and **Day, R. H.** (1990). Do children use their own images to locate objects reflected in a mirror? *Child Development*, **16**, 1558–68.

Romanes, G. J. (1882). *Animal intelligence.* Keagan Paul, London.

Romanes, G. J. (1883). *Mental evolution in animals.* Appleton, New York.

Rosengren, K. S. Gelman, S. A. Kalish, C. W. and **McCormick, M.** (1991). As time goes by: children's early understanding of growth in animals. *Child Development*, **62**, 1302–20.

Ruffman, T. K. and **Olson, D. R.** (1989). Children's ascriptions of knowledge to others. *Developmental Psychology*, **25**, 601–6.

Rumbaugh, D. M. (1977). Language learning by a chimpanzee: the Lana project. Academic Press, New York.

Russell, B. (1948). *Human knowledge: its scope and limits.* Unwin Hyman, London.

Russell, J. (1998). *Autism as an executive disorder.* Oxford University Press.

Russon, A. E. and **Bard, K. A.** (1996). Exploring the minds of the great apes: issues and controversies. In *Reaching into thought: the minds of the great apes*, (ed. A. E. Russon, K. A. Bard, and S. T. Parker), pp. 1–20. Cambridge University Press.

Russon, A. E., Bard, K. A., and **Parker, S. T.** (ed.) (1996). *Reaching into thought: the minds of the great apes.* Cambridge University Press.

Sackett, G. P. (1966). Monkeys reared in isolation with pictures as visual input: evidence for an innate releasing mechanism. *Science*, **154**, 1468–73.

Savage-Rumbaugh, E. S. (1986). *Ape language: from conditioned response to symbol.* Columbia University Press, New York.

Savage-Rumbaugh, E. S. and **Lewin, R.** (1994). *Kanzi, the ape at the brink of the human mind.* John Wiley and Sons, New York.

Scaife, M. and **Bruner, J.** (1975). The capacity for joint visual attention in the infant. *Nature*, **253**, 265–6.

van Schaik, C. P. and **Fox E. A.** (1996). Manufacture and use of tools in wild Sumatran Orangutans. *Naturwissenschaften*, **83**, 186–8.

van Schaik, C. P., van Noordwijk, M. A., Warsono, B., and **Sutriono, E.** (1983). Party size and early detection of predators in Sumatran forest primates. *Primates*, **24**, 211–21.

Schaller, G. B. (1963). *The mountain gorilla: ecology and behavior.* University of Chicago Press, Chicago.

Schiller, P. H. (1957). Innate motor action as a basis of learning. In *Instinctive behavior*, (ed. C. H. Schiller), pp. 264–87. International Universities Press, New York.

Selk, E. S. (1998). Nativism, empriricism, and the origins of knowledge. *Infant Behaviour and Development*, **21**, 181–200.

Settlage, P. H. (1939). The effect of occipital lesions on visually guided behavior in the monkey. *Journal of Comparative Psychology*, **27**, 93–131.

Shah, A. and **Frith, U.** (1983). An islet of ability in autistic children: a research note. *Journal of Child Psychology and Psychiatry*, **24**, 613–20.

Shah, A. and **Frith, U.** (1993). Why do autistic individuals show superior performance on the Block Design Task? *Journal of Child Psychology and Psychiatry*, **34**, 1351–64.

Shettleworth, S. J. (1975). Reinforcement and the organization of behavior in golden hamsters: hunger, environment, and food reinforcement. *Journal of Experimental Psychology: Animal Behavior Processes*, **1**, 56–87.

Shettleworth, S. J. (1998). *Cognition, evolution, and behavior*. Oxford University Press, New York.

Shultz, T. R. (1982*a*). Rules of causal attribution. *Monographs of the Society for Research in Child Development*, **47**(**1**), (Serial No. 194).

Shultz, T. R. (1982*b*). Causal reasoning in the social and nonsocial realms. *Canadian Journal of Behavioural Science*, **14**, 307–22.

Shultz, T. R. and **Coddington, M.** (1981). Development of the concepts of energy conservation and entropy. *Journal of Experimental Child Psychology*, **31**, 131–53.

Shultz, T. R. and **Kestenbaum, N. R.** (1985). Causal reasoning in children. *Annals of Child Development*, **2**, 195–249.

Shultz, T. R. and **Mendelson, R.** (1975). The use of covariation as a principle of causal analysis. *Child Development*, **46**, 394–9.

Shultz, T. R. and **Ravinsky, F.** (1977). Similarity as a principle of causal inference. *Child Development*, **48**, 1552–8.

Shultz, T. R., Wells, D., and **Sarda, M.** (1980). Development of the ability to distinguish intended actions from mistakes, reflexes, and passive movements. *British Journal of Social and Clinical Psychology*, **19**, 301–10.

Shultz, T. R., Pardo, S., and **Altmann, E.** (1982). Young children's use of transitive inference in causal chains. *British Journal of Psychology*, **73**, 235–41.

Shultz, T. R., Altmann, E., and **Asselin, J.** (1986*a*). Judging causal priority. *British Journal of Developmental Psychology*, **4**, 67–74.

Shultz, T. R., Fisher, G. W., Pratt, C. C., and **Rulf, S.** (1986*b*). Selection of causal rules. *Child Development*, **57**, 143–52.

Siegler, R. S. (1975). Defining the locus of developmental differences in children's causal reasoning. *Journal of Experimental Child Psychology*, **20**, 512–25.

Siegler, R. S. (1976). The effects of simple necessity and sufficiency relationships on children's causal inferences. *Child Development*, **47**, 1058–63.

Siegler, R. S. and **Liebert, R. M.** (1974). Effects of contiguity, regularity, and age on children's inferences. *Developmental Psychology*, **10**, 574–9.

Sober, E. (1998). Black box inference—when should an intervening variable be postulated? *British Journal for the Philosophy of Science*, **49**, 469–98.

Sokolov, Y. N. (1963). *Perception and the conditioned reflex.* Pergamon, New York.

Spelke, E. S. (1985). Preferential looking methods as tools for the study of cognition in infancy. In *Measurement of audition and vision in the first year of postnatal life*, (ed. G. Gottlieb and N. Krasnegor). Ablex, Norwood, NJ.

Spelke, E. S. (1988). Where perceiving ends and thinking begins: the apprehension of objects in infancy. In *Perceptual development in infancy. Minnesota Symposium on Child Psychology*, Vol. 20, (ed. A. Yonas), pp. 191–234. Erlbaum, Hillsdale, NJ.

Spelke, E. S. (1990). Principles of object perception. *Cognitive Science*, **14**, 29–56.

Spelke, E. S. (1991). Physical knowledge in infancy: reflections on Piaget's theory. In *The epigenesis of mind: essays on biology and cognition*, (ed. S. Carey and R. Gelman). Erlbaum, Hillsdale, NJ.

Spelke, E. S., Phillips, A., and **Woodward, A. L.** (1995). Infants' knowledge of object motion and human action. In *Causal cognition: a multidisciplinary debate*, (ed. D. Sperber, D. Premack, and A. J. Premack), pp. 44–78. Clarendon Press, Oxford.

Spinozzi, G. and **Potí, P.** (1989). Causality I: the support problem. In *Cognitive structure and development of nonhuman primates*, (ed. F. Antinucci). Erlbaum, Hillsdale, NJ.

Spinozzi, G. and **Potí, P.** (1993). Piagetian stage 5 in two infant chimpanzees (*Pan troglodytes*): the development of permanence of objects and the spatialization of causality. *International Journal of Primatology*, **14**, 905–17.

Suarez, S. D. and **Gallup, G. G., Jr.** (1981). Self-recognition in chimpanzees and orang-utans, but not gorillas. *Journal of Human Evolution*, **10**, 175–88.

Sugiyama, Y. (1997). Social tradition and the use of tool-composites by wild chimpanzees. *Evolutionary Anthropology*, **6(1)**, 23–7.

Sugiyama, Y. and **Koman, J.** (1979). Tool-using and -making behavior in wild chimpanzees at Bossou, Guinea. *Primates*, **20**, 513–24.

Teleki, G. (1973). *The predatory behavior of wild chimpanzees.* Bucknell University Press, E. Brunswick, NJ.

Theall, L. A. and **Povinelli, D. J.** (**1999**) Do chimpanzees (*Pan troglodytes*) tailor their gestural signals to fit the attentional states of others? *Animal Cognition*, **2**, 207–14.

Thompson, R. L. and **Boatright-Horowitz, S. L.** (1994). The question of mirror-mediated self-recognition in apes and monkeys: some new results and reservations. In *Self-awareness in animals and humans*, (ed. S. T. Parker, R. W. Mitchell, and M. L. Boccia), pp. 330–49. Cambridge University Press, New York.

Tomasello, M. (1995). Joint attention as social cognition. In *Joint attention: its origins and role in development*, (ed. C. Moore and P. Dunham), pp. 103–30. Erlbaum, Hillsdale, NJ.

Tomasello, M. (1996). Chimpanzee social cognition. *Monographs of the Society for Research in Child Development*, **61(3)**, (Serial No. 247), 161–73.

Tomasello, M. and **Call, J.** (1997). *Primate cognition.* Oxford University Press.

Tomasello, M., Kruger, A. C., and Ratner, H. H. (1993). Cultural learning. *Behavioral and Brain Sciences*, **16**, 495–552.

Tomasello, M., Call, J., Nagell, K., Olguin, R., and Carpenter, M. (1994). The learning and use of gestural signals by young chimpanzees: a trans-generational study. *Primates*, **35**, 137–54.

Tomasello, M., Call, J., and Hare, B. (1998). Five primate species follow the visual gaze of conspecifics. *Animal Behavior*, **55**, 1063–9.

Uzgiris, I. C. and Hunt, J. M. (1975). *Assessment in infancy: ordinal scales of psychological development.* University of Illinois Press.

de Veer, M. W. and Van den Bos, R. (1999). A critical review of methodology and interpretation of mirror self-recognition research in nonhuman primates. *Animal Behaviour*, **58**, 459–68.

Vinden, P. G. (1996). Junín Quechua children's understanding of the mind. *Child Development*, **67**, 1707–16.

Vinden, P. G. and Astington, J. W. (2000). Culture and understanding other minds. In *Understanding other minds: perspectives from autism and cognitive neuroscience*, (ed. S. Baron-Cohen, H. Tager-Flusberg, and D. Cohen). Oxford University Press.

Visalberghi, E. (1993). Capuchin monkeys: a window into tool use activities by apes and humans. In *Tools, language, and cognition in human evolution*, (ed. K. Gibson and T. Ingold), pp. 138–50. Cambridge University Press.

Visalberghi, E. and Limongelli, L. (1994). Lack of comprehension of cause–effect relations in tool-using capuchin monkeys (*Cebus apella*). *Journal of Comparative Psychology*, **108**, 15–22.

Visalberghi, E. and Limongelli, L. (1996). Acting and understanding: tool use revisited through the minds of capuchin monkeys. In *Reaching into thought: the minds of the great apes*, (ed. A. Russon, K. Bard, and S. Parker), pp. 57–79. Cambridge University Press.

Visalberghi, E. and Trinca, L. (1989). Tool use in capuchin monkeys: distinguishing between performing and understanding. *Primates*, **30**, 511–21.

Visalberghi, E., Fragaszy, D. M., and Savage-Rumbaugh, S. (1995). Performance in a tool-using task by common chimpanzees (*Pan troglodytes*), bonobos (*Pan paniscus*), an orangutan (*Pongo pygmaeus*), and capuchin monkeys (*Cebus apella*). *Journal of Comparative Psychology*, **109**, 52–60.

Vygotsky, L. (1962). *Thought and language.* MIT Press, Cambridge, MA.

de Waal, F. B. M. (1982). *Chimpanzee politics: power and sex among apes.* Harper and Row, New York.

de Waal, F. B. M. (1986). Deception in the natural communication of chimpanzees. In *Deception: perspectives on human and nonhuman deceit*, (ed. R. W. Mitchell and N. S. Thompson), pp. 221–44. SUNY Press, Albany, NY.

de Waal, F. B. M. (1989). *Peacemaking among primates*. Harvard University Press, Cambridge, MA.

de Waal, F. B. M. (1992). Intentional deception in primates. *Evolutionary anthropology*, **1**, 86–92.

de Waal, F. B. M. (1996). *Good natured*. Harvard University Press, Cambridge, MA.

Warden, C. J. and **Jackson, T. A.** (1935). Imitative behavior in the rhesus monkey. *Pedagogical Seminary and Journal of Genetic Psychology*, **46**, 103–25.

Watts, D. P. and **Pusey, A. E.** (1993). Behavior of juvenile and adolescent great apes. In M. E. Pereira and L. Fairbanks (Eds.), *Socioecology of juvenile primates*, pp. 148–67. Oxford: Oxford University Press.

Wellman, H. M. (1990). *The child's theory of mind*. MIT Press, Cambridge, MA.

White, P. A. (1988). Causal processing: origins and development. *Psychological Bulletin*, **104**, 36–52.

Whiten, A. (1996). When does smart behaviour-reading become mind-reading? In *Theories of theories of mind*, (ed. P. Carruthers and P. Smith), pp. 277–92. Cambridge University Press.

Whiten, A. (1998). Evolutionary and developmental origins of the mindreading system. In *Piaget, evolution, and development*, (ed. J. Langer and M. Killen), pp. 73–99. Erlbaum, Mahwah, NJ.

Whiten, A. (1999). Parental encouragement in *Gorilla* in comparative perspective: implications for social cognition and the evolution of teaching. In *The mentalities of gorillas and orangutans in comparative perspective*, (ed. S. T. Parker, R. W. Mitchell, and H. L. Miles), pp. 342–66. Cambridge University Press.

Whiten, A. and **Bryne, R. W.** (1988). Tactical deception in primates. *Behavioral and Brain Sciences*, **11**, 233–44.

Whiten, A. and **Ham, R.** (1992). On the nature and evolution of imitation in the animal kingdom: reappraisal of a century of research. *Advances in the Study of Behavior*, **21**, 239–83.

Willats, P. (1984). The stage-IV infant's solution of problems requiring the use of supports. *Infant Behavior and Development*, **7**, 125–34.

Wimmer, H. and **Perner, J.** (1983). Beliefs about beliefs: representation and constraining function of wrong beliefs in young children's understanding of deception. *Cognition*, **13**, 103–28.

Wimmer, H., Hogrefe, G. J., and **Perner, J.** (1988). Children's understanding of informational access as a source of knowledge. *Child Development*, **59**, 386–96.

Witmer, L. (1909). A monkey with a mind. *The Psychological Clinic*, **3**, 179–205.

Woodruff, G. and **Premack, D.** (1979). Intentional communication in the chimpanzee: the development of deception. *Cognition*, **7**, 333–62.

Wright, S. (1931). Evolution in Mendelian populations. *Genetics*, **16**, 97–159.

Wright, S. (1932). The roles of mutation, inbreeding, crossbreeding, and selection in evolution. *Proceedings of the XI International Congress of Genetics*, **1**, 356–66.

Yerkes, R. M. (1916). The mental life of monkeys and apes: a study of ideational behavior. *Behavior Monographs*, **3**, 1–145.

Yerkes, R. M. (1927*a*). The mind of a gorilla. *Genetic Psychology Monographs*, **2**, 1–190.

Yerkes, R. M. (1927*b*). The mind of a gorilla: part II. Mental development. *Genetic Psychology Monographs*, **2**, 1–193.

Yerkes, R. M. (1928–9). The mind of a gorilla: part III. Memory. *Comparative Psychology Monographs*. John Hopkins Press: Baltimore.

Yerkes, R. M. (1943). *Chimpanzees: a laboratory colony.* Yale University Press.

Yerkes, R. M. and **Learned, B. W.** (1925). *Chimpanzee intelligence and its vocal expressions.* Williams and Wilkins, Baltimore.

Yuill, N. (1984). Young children's coordination of motive and outcome in judgements of satisfaction and morality. *British Journal of Developmental Psychology*, **2**, 73–81.

Zazzo, R. (1982). The person: objective approaches. In *Review of child development research*, Vol. 6, (ed. W. W. Hartup), pp. 247–90. University of Chicago Press, Chicago.

TIMELINE FOR EXPERIMENTAL RESEARCH (1994–99)

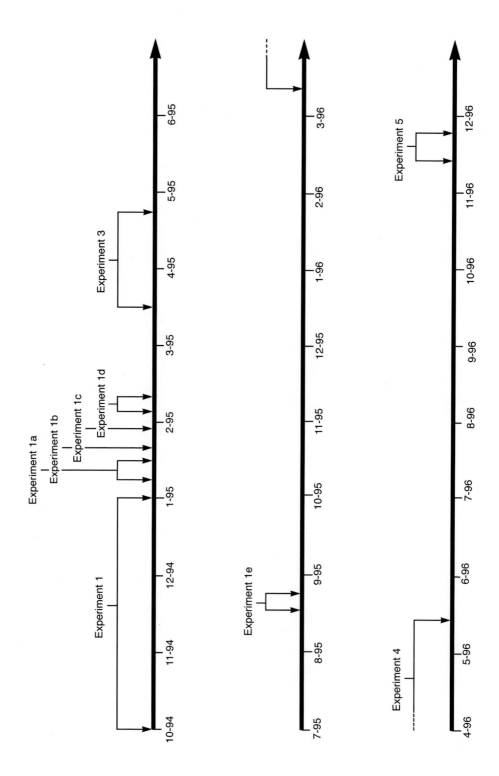

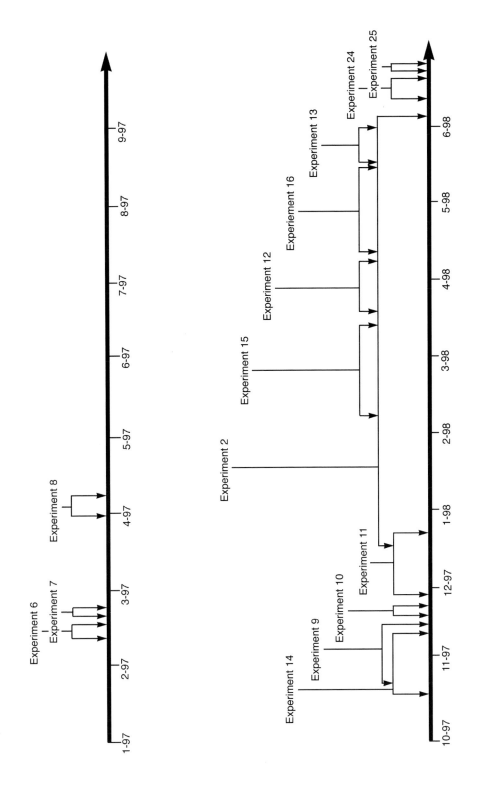

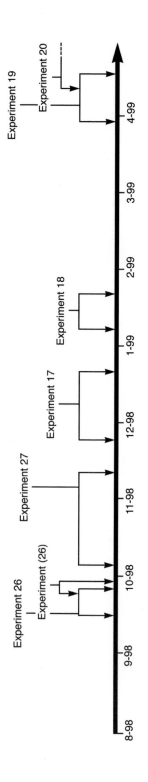

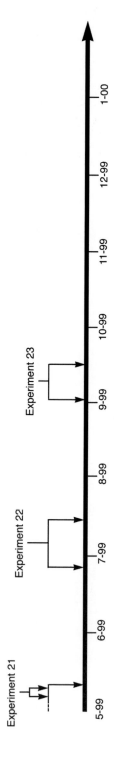

TRIAL-BY-TRIAL DATA FOR EXPERIMENT 13 (FURTHER TESTS OF THE GRASPING-AFFORDANCE MODEL, CHAPTER 8)

Orientation sequence for ⊥ }C = Correct end

⊐ }I = Incorrect end

Subject	Trial	Sequence
APO	1	I ⇨ C+
	2	I ⇨ C+
	3	C+
	4	I ⇨ C+
KAR	1	I
	2	I
	3	I
	4	C
CAN	1	NR
	2	I
	3	NR
	4	NR
JAD	1	C ⇨ I ⇨ C+
	2	I ⇨ C+
	3	C+
	4	C+
BRA	1	C+
	2	C+
	3	C+
	4	C+
MEG	1	I ⇨ C ⇨ I ⇨ C ⇨ I ⇨ C+
	2	I ⇨ C+
	3	C+
	4	C+
MIN	1	I
	2	C ⇨ I
	3	I ⇨ C ⇨ I ⇨ C ⇨ I
	4	I ⇨ C ⇨ I ⇨ C

Note. Each bout (see text) is separated by an arrow (⇨); '+' indicates success in dislodging the apple; 'NR' = no response.

Orientation sequence for   }C = Correct end
                            }I = Incorrect end

Subject	Trial	Sequence
APO	1	I
	2	I ⇨ C+
	3	C ⇨ I ⇨ C ⇨ I ⇨ C ⇨ I ⇨ C+
	4	C ⇨ I ⇨ C+
KAR	1	I
	2	I
	3	I
	4	I
CAN	1	I
	2	I
	3	NR
	4	NR
JAD	1	C+
	2	C+
	3	C+
	4	C+
BRA	1	I
	2	C+
	3	C+
	4	C+
MEG	1	C ⇨ I
	2	C ⇨ I ⇨ C ⇨ I ⇨ C ⇨ I
	3	I ⇨ C+
	4	C+
MIN	1	C+
	2	C ⇨ I ⇨ C+
	3	C ⇨ I ⇨ C+
	4	C+

Note. Each bout (see text) is separated by an arrow (⇨); '+' indicates success in dislodging the apple; 'NR' = no response.

Orientation sequence for

}I = Incorrect end

}C = Correct end

Subject	Trial	Sequence
APO	1	I ⇨ C+
	2	I ⇨ C+
	3	I ⇨ C+
	4	I ⇨ C+
KAR	1	I
	2	I
	3	I
	4	I
CAN	1	I
	2	I
	3	NR
	4	NR
JAD	1	I ⇨ C+
	2	I ⇨ C+
	3	C+
	4	C+
BRA	1	I
	2	I
	3	I
	4	I
MEG	1	I ⇨ C+
	2	I ⇨ C+
	3	I ⇨ C+
	4	I ⇨ C+
MIN	1	I ⇨ C ⇨ I ⇨ C ⇨ I ⇨ C ⇨ I
	2	I ⇨ C ⇨ I
	3	I
	4	I ⇨ C ⇨ I ⇨ C ⇨ I

Note. Each bout (see text) is separated by an arrow (⇨); '+' indicates success in dislodging the apple; 'NR' = no response.

Orientation sequence for ⊓
}I = Incorrect end

}C = Correct end

Subject	Trial	Sequence
APO	1	I
	2	I ⇨ C+
	3	C+
	4	C+
KAR	1	I
	2	I
	3	I
	4	I
CAN	1	I
	2	I
	3	NR
	4	NR
JAD	1	I ⇨ C+
	2	I ⇨ C+
	3	C+
	4	C+
BRA	1	I
	2	I
	3	I
	4	I
MEG	1	I
	2	I ⇨ C ⇨ I ⇨ C+
	3	I ⇨ C+
	4	C+
MIN	1	I ⇨ C
	2	I ⇨ C ⇨ I ⇨ C ⇨ I
	3	I
	4	I ⇨ C ⇨ I ⇨ C ⇨ I ⇨ C ⇨ I

Note. Each bout (see text) is separated by an arrow (⇨); '+' indicates success in dislodging the apple; 'NR' = no response.

TRIAL-BY-TRIAL DATA FOR EXPERIMENT 27 (THE TOOL-CONSTRUCTION PROBLEM, CHAPTER 11)

Hook-retrieval task

Subject	Tool form	Trial	First four bouts of tool manipulation			
			1	2	3	4
APO	[straight tool ‖]	1	no modification → attempt with incorrect end	assemble → attempt with incorrect end	disassemble (accidental) → attempt with incorrect end	no modification → attempt with incorrect end
		2	no modification → attempt with incorrect end	no modification → attempt with incorrect end	no modification → attempt with incorrect end	no modification → attempt with correct end → success
	[hook tool ⊢⊢]	1	no modification → attempt with correct end	no modification → attempt with correct end	no modification → attempt with correct end	
		2	disassemble (deliberate)→ no attempt	disassemble (deliberate) → no attempt		
KAR	[hook tool ⊢⊢]	1	assemble → no attempt	disassemble (deliberate) → no attempt	assemble → attempt with correct end → success	
		2	no modification → attempt with incorrect end	assemble → attempt with incorrect end	no modification → attempt with correct end	disassemble (accidental) → attempt with incorrect end → success
	[straight tool ‖]	1	no modification → attempt with correct end → success			
		2	disassemble (deliberate) → no attempt	disassemble (deliberate) → no attempt	assemble → no attempt	disassemble (deliberate) → no attempt

Hook-retrieval task (*continued*)

Subject	Tool form	Trial	First four bouts of tool manipulation			
			1	2	3	4
CAN	[straight tool]	1	no modification → attempt with incorrect end → success			
		2	no modification → attempt with incorrect end	no modification → attempt with incorrect end	no modification → attempt with incorrect end	no modification → attempt with incorrect end
	[hooked tool]	1	no modification → attempt with correct end → success			
		2	no modification → attempt with correct end	disassemble (accidental) → attempt with incorrect end	no modification → attempt with correct end → success	
JAD	[straight tool]	1	no modification → attempt with incorrect end	no modification → attempt with incorrect end	no modification → attempt with incorrect end	no modification → attempt with incorrect end
		2	no modification → attempt with incorrect end			
	[hooked tool]	1	no modification → attempt with correct end → success			
		2	no manipulation			

Hook-retrieval task (continued)

Subject	Tool form	Trial	First four bouts of tool manipulation			
			1	2	3	4
BRA	[tool diagram]	1	no modification → attempt with incorrect end	assemble → no attempt	disassemble (deliberate) → no attempt	assemble → no attempt
		2	no modification → attempt with incorrect end	no modification → attempt with incorrect end	no modification → attempt with incorrect end	no modification → attempt with incorrect end
	[tool diagram]	1	no modification → attempt with correct end → success			
		2	no modification → attempt with correct end	no modification → attempt with correct end	no modification → attempt with correct end	no modification → attempt with correct end
MEG	[tool diagram]	1	no modification → attempt with incorrect end	assemble → no attempt	disassemble (accidental) → no attempt	assemble → attempt with incorrect end → success
		2	no modification → attempt with incorrect end	assemble → no attempt	disassemble (accidental) → no attempt	assemble → no attempt
	[tool diagram]	1	no modification → attempt with correct end → success			
		2	no modification → attempt with correct end → success			

Hook-retrieval task (*continued*)

Subject	Tool form	Trial	First four bouts of tool manipulation			
			1	2	3	4
MIN	││‖	1	no modification → attempt with incorrect end	assemble → no attempt	disassemble (accidental) → no attempt	assemble → no attempt
		2	no modification → attempt with incorrect end	no modification → attempt with incorrect end	assemble → no attempt	disassemble (accidental) → no attempt
	┼┤	1	disassemble deliberate) → no attempt	disassemble deliberate) → no attempt	assemble → no attempt	disassemble (deliberate) → no attempt
		2	disassemble (deliberate) → no attempt	assemble → no attempt	disassemble (deliberate) → no attempt	disassemble (deliberate) → no attempt

Tool-insertion task

Subject	Tool form	Trial	First four bouts of tool manipulation			
			1	2	3	4
APO	(symbol)	1	no modification → attempt with correct end → success			
		2	no modification → attempt with correct end → success			
	(symbol)	1	disassemble (deliberate) → no attempt	assemble → attempt with incorrect end	disassemble (deliberate) → attempt with incorrect end	assemble → no attempt
		2	disassemble (deliberate) → attempt with incorrect end	no modification → attempt with correct end → success		
KAR	(symbol)	1	no modification → attempt with correct end → success			
		2	no modification → attempt with correct end → success			
	(symbol)	1	no modification → attempt with incorrect end	disassemble (deliberate) → attempt with incorrect end	disassemble (deliberate) → attempt with correct end → success	
		2	disassemble (deliberate) → no attempt	disassemble (deliberate) → attempt with correct end → success		

Tool-insertion task (*continued*)

Subject	Tool form	Trial	First four bouts of tool manipulation			
			1	2	3	4
CAN	‖|	1	no modification → attempt with correct end → success			
		2	no modification → attempt with correct end → success			
	⊥|	1	no modification → attempt with incorrect end	disassemble (deliberate) → no attempt	assemble → no attempt	disassemble (deliberate) → no attempt
		2	no modification → attempt with incorrect end	no modification → attempt with incorrect end	disassemble (deliberate) → attempt with incorrect end	no modification → attempt with correct end → success
JAD	‖|	1	no modification → attempt with correct end	no modification → attempt with correct end → success	no modification → attempt with correct end → success	
		2	no modification → attempt with correct end → success			
	⊥|	1	disassemble (deliberate) → no attempt	disassemble (deliberate) → attempt with correct end → success		
		2	no modification → attempt with incorrect end	disassemble (deliberate) → no attempt	disassemble (deliberate) → attempt with correct end → success	

Tool-insertion task (*continued*)

Subject	Tool form	Trial	First four bouts of tool manipulation			
			1	2	3	4
BRA	|||	1	assemble → no attempt	disassemble (deliberate) → no attempt	assemble no attempt	disassemble (deliberate) → attempt with correct end → success
		2	no modification → attempt with correct end → success			
	⊢	1	disassemble (deliberate) → attempt with incorrect end	no modification → attempt with correct end → success		
		2	disassemble (deliberate) attempt with correct end → success			
MEG	|||	1	no modification → attempt with correct end → success			
		2	no modification → attempt with correct end → success			
	⊢	1	no modification → attempt with incorrect end	no modification → attempt with correct end →	no modification → attempt with incorrect end	no modification → attempt with incorrect end
		2	disassemble (accidental) → attempt with correct end	assemble → attempt with incorrect end →	disassemble (accidental) → attempt with incorrect end	no modification → attempt with correct end

Tool-insertion task (*continued*)

Subject	Tool form	Trial	First four bouts of tool manipulation			
			1	2	3	4
MIN	⫴	1	no modification → attempt with correct end → success			
		2	no modification → attempt with correct end	no modification → attempt with correct end → success		
	⊥	1	disassemble (deliberate) → no attempt	disassemble (deliberate) → no attempt	assemble → no attempt	disassemble (accidental) → no attempt
		2	no modification → attempt with incorrect end	disassemble (deliberate) → no attempt	disassemble (deliberate) → no attempt	no attempt

INDEX

Location references suffixed with 'fn' indicate information in footnotes. References to appendices are indicated in **bold** type.